D0152684

FAMILY LAW
REIMAGINED

FAMILY LAW
REIMAGINED

Jill Elaine Hasday

Harvard University Press

Cambridge, Massachusetts
London, England
2014

Copyright © 2014 by Jill Elaine Hasday
All rights reserved
Printed in the United States of America

Library of Congress Cataloging-in-Publication Data

Hasday, Jill Elaine, author.
Family law reimagined / Jill Elaine Hasday.
pages cm
Includes bibliographical references and index.
ISBN 978-0-674-28128-8
1. Domestic relations—United States.   2. Parent and child (Law)—United States.
3. Common law marriage—United States.   4. Domestic relations (Canon law)   I. Title.
KF505.H39 2014
346.7301'5—dc23   2013040290

For my family through the generations:

My grandparents, Rose and Irving, and Dora and Isaac
My parents, Carol and Robert
My siblings, Michael and Lisa
My husband, Allan
My children, Sarah, Daniel, and David

CONTENTS

FAMILY LAW
REIMAGINED

INTRODUCTION

The Family Law Canon

The law shapes all of our lives, even when we do not realize it is there. It decides who has rights to what, who can make enforceable claims on whom, who is entitled and who is not. Family life is sometimes presumed to be a realm so private and intimate as to be beyond the law's power. Indeed, the United States Supreme Court itself has contributed to that notion, repeatedly declaring that there is a "private realm of family life which the state cannot enter."[1]

But in fact, one of the law's most important and far-reaching roles is to govern family life and family members. Family law regulates the creation and dissolution of legally recognized family relationships and establishes the legal rights and responsibilities that are tied to family status. This means that family law decides who counts as kin in the eyes of the law and who does not, how family relationships are legally formed and severed, and what turns on legal recognition as a family member—what it means legally to be a spouse, parent, child, sibling, or other relative as one interacts with the government and with other people inside and outside of one's family.

Family law is extraordinarily consequential, whether measured in terms of impact on people's lives, volume of litigation, or monetary, psychological, and cultural goods at stake. Family law shapes social organization, economic status, intergenerational relationships, intimacy, childhood, maturity, and everyday experience. It reflects and influences how Americans think about gender, race, class, sexual orientation, and other divides and helps determine how those categories will impact people's opportunities, choices, rights, and constraints. Family law helps

1

structure both the details of daily existence and the overarching features of society.

Family law pervades state and federal law, in part because many sources of law that are now identified exclusively with other legal fields are also forms of family law. Family law extends far beyond statutes, judicial opinions, and regulations that are explicitly and officially classified as family law to run through tort law, contract law, property law, constitutional law, criminal law, tax law, employment law, labor law, immigration law, citizenship law, international relations law, military law, welfare law, social benefits law, public health law, education law, housing law, bankruptcy law, intellectual property law, agricultural law, Native American law, evidence law, personal jurisdiction law, and more.

Family law questions are perennial subjects of popular fascination, political contestation, and legal dispute. Countless judges, legislators, regulators, lawyers, advocates, and individuals face family law issues every day, family law cases fill a substantial proportion of court dockets,[2] and law schools offer family law courses every semester. Yet despite its significance, family law remains remarkably undertheorized and poorly understood.

Family Law Reimagined is the first book to explore family law's canon. By "canon," I mean the dominant narratives, stories, examples, and ideas that judges, lawmakers, and (to a less crucial extent) commentators repeatedly invoke to describe and explain family law and its governing principles.

The existing scholarship on canons, which has long centered on the literary canon and recently turned to the constitutional law canon,[3] has most commonly understood a canon to be a set of foundational texts that exemplify, guide, and constitute a discipline. In some respects, the family law canon tracks this traditional focus on the inclusion and exclusion of texts, such as statutes and judicial opinions. Family law's canon treats some regulation of families as falling within family law and ignores or overlooks other regulation of families. But canons are not necessarily limited to texts, and the family law canon does not take the form of a short and definitive reading list.

Instead, family law's canon centers on a series of overriding stories that purport to make sense of how the law governs family members and family life. When judges decide cases, legislators debate bills, administrators draft regulations, or scholars write casebooks or academic articles, they frequently draw on these stories to convey family law's nature and overriding tenets. The stories are so embedded in the field, and they have been reiterated, reinforced, and relied on so many times, that they are routinely assumed to be matters of common sense—so taken for granted as to supposedly require no explanation or defense.

These canonical narratives shape how authorities and advocates understand family law's current operation, how they envision the dilemmas and decisions that family law faces, and how they structure and reason about specific family law policies. Family law's canon helps guide family law's response to the many forces pushing and pulling against it, including economic pressures, broader cultural trends, political developments, and religious convictions. The canon helps explain the answers that are considered established wisdom in family law, the questions about the field that go unasked, and the choices that decisionmakers endorse. The canon helps structure and constrain family law's imaginative universe.

This book reveals how the family law canon misdescribes the reality of family law, misdirects attention away from the actual problems that family law confronts, and misshapes the policies that courts, legislatures, and advocates pursue. Much of the "common sense" that legal decisionmakers expound and repeat about family law actually makes little sense. *Family Law Reimagined* uncovers, explores, and critiques the family law canon and outlines a path to reform. The book challenges the answers that the canon assumes and asks questions that the canon never considers.

The family law canon is enormously appealing to many decisionmakers and commentators, who produce, perpetuate, and promulgate it through countless acts of legislation, regulation, judgment, litigation, teaching, scholarship, and discussion. Family law's canonical narratives often present the field as a haven from changes swirling outside family law at dizzying speed. The canon envisions family law as an oasis of stable and certain local control in an ever-shifting and increasingly centralized legal order. The canon describes family law as a sphere shielded from the expanding reach of the market and its self-interested bargaining.

At the same time, family law's canonical narratives report that family law has kept pace with progressive reform. The canon promises that family law's evolution over time has been in the direction of consistent and overwhelming improvement, aligning family law with the many historical narratives within and outside the law that recount change over time as a story of enormous progress.[4] The canon overlooks unfair, inequitable, unjust, or unfortunate aspects of family law, or contends that such problems have been left safely behind.

Lawmakers and judges have the most influence over the family law canon because they shape family law most directly. Their statutes, regulations, and judicial opinions have inherent and independent legal force, whether or not legal scholars, practicing lawyers, litigants, or individual citizens agree with them. This book focuses most of its attention on what judges, legislators, and regulators say, write, and do because legal authorities exercise disproportionate control over family law's canon. Canonical narratives contending that family law is exclusively local, that family law repudiates market principles, that family law has eradicated the imprint of common law doctrines that subordinated married women, or that family law consistently prioritizes children's interests over parents' rights are most prominent and most powerful in the work of courts and lawmakers, rather than scholars. The canon's structure bends toward the views of decisionmakers who wield more power over the law.

Academics have less immediate legal influence, but they also help shape family law's canon through their writing and perhaps especially their teaching. How family law is taught helps determine how the next generation of lawyers, including some future legislators, regulators, judges, and their aides and clerks, will understand family law and its guiding principles. Even some scholars steeped in family law and accustomed to critiquing specific family law policies rely on and reinforce canonical narratives in describing the field and its guiding precepts. These narratives, too often taken to be matters of common sense, are used and repeated by some people who might (on more reflection) actually disagree with how the narratives portray family law.

Of course, some judges, lawmakers, lawyers, scholars, and family members already reject some or all parts of the family law canon. These dissenting voices can be natural allies in this book's project to recast the canon, even if they have not thought about themselves or their work in those terms before.

But family law's canonical narratives persist as dominant and resilient ways of thinking about the field even though some lawmakers, judges, and commentators disagree with some or all of them. The canon provides widely, although not universally, accepted frameworks, points of reference, and stock stories that legal actors routinely revisit and deploy in considering family law, in making decisions about its future, and in instructing new generations about how to understand the subject.

The problem is that family law's canonical narratives about itself are frequently inaccurate, unhelpful, and misleading. They distort the judgments that courts and lawmakers reach and the arguments that commentators make.

The canon insists that family law is inherently local, facilitating persistent arguments that any federal intervention in the family is unprecedented and inappropriate, no matter the appeal of its substantive goals. Many judges, lawmakers, advocates, and scholars rely on family law's supposed inherent localism as a powerful reason to oppose specific federal statutes or proposals. Yet federal family law is actually well established, wide-ranging, and voluminous.

The canon contends that family law rejects market principles that otherwise suffuse the law, when family law actually enforces myriad economic exchanges and forbids only a select few transactions—mostly involving payments to women and poorer people. The canonical narrative declaring family law's separation from the market obscures how family law's actual regulation of economic exchange can place disproportionate burdens on less powerful people and helps legal authorities avoid explaining why the imposition of such unequal burdens is appropriate. This story makes it appear natural and ordinary for family law to dramatically restrict or deny compensation to housewives, or to people who sacrificed their own economic opportunities in order to support their spouses through school, when such limitations on economic exchange are actually highly unusual in family law.

The canon reports that family law prioritizes sex equality and children's interests and has freed itself from its historic entanglements in subordination and injustice. This narrative has helped some decision-makers assert that the field no longer needs to be concerned about its treatment of women or children and has helped more legal authorities avoid considering how family law's roots continue to influence the field and impact family members. But common law doctrines and presumptions that favored husbands over wives, and parents over children, still shape family law in important respects.

The canon focuses on marriage, parenthood, and (sometimes) their functional equivalents, while overlooking and offering little protection to other family ties, such as the relationships among siblings, grandparents, grandchildren, aunts, uncles, nieces, nephews, and cousins. The canon ignores how welfare law can also be family law, helping decision-makers avoid acknowledging, much less explaining, why laws regulating rights and responsibilities in poor families turn on norms of suspicion and interference that are diametrically opposed to the generally more respectful principles that family law applies to families not considered poor.

Family Law Reimagined exposes and analyzes family law's canon and seeks to guide the field's reconception for lawmakers, judges, lawyers, scholars, and family members. The thirst for stories that purport to explain how the law regulates family relationships and family members is powerful, and the existence of such stories is probably all but inevitable. This book does not propose eliminating family law's canon, but recasting it. My goal is to reveal how family law's canonical narratives currently misrepresent the field, distract from the pressing questions that family law confronts, and distort the policy choices that legal authorities make. Recasting family law's canon to more accurately describe family law and its guiding principles frees judges, legislators, and regulators, as well as scholars, lawyers, and family members, to assess family law as it is and to consider and debate the actual choices facing the field.

Family law is extraordinarily important and influential. It impacts all of us and touches virtually every aspect of society. Yet while there are some wonderful scholars and far-thinking courts and legislatures working in family law, the field has attracted much less critical scrutiny than it merits.

The Book's Organization

The book is organized into three parts. The first part—"Family Law Exceptionalism"—focuses on the canonical understanding of family law's differences from other legal fields. The second part—"The Family Law Canon's Progress Narratives"—examines the canonical understanding of family law's relationship to its past. The third part—"What's Missing from the Family Law Canon?"—considers what the family law canon excludes and ignores.

Part One, encompassing Chapters 1 and 2, explores the canonical depiction of family law as a field sharply set off from the rest of the law, where standard rules governing legal interactions are inapplicable or even reversed. The family law canon portrays family law as local in an age when the reach of the national government is steadily expanding and stresses family law's separation from market principles that increasingly pervade many areas of the law.

The premise that family law rejects what the law otherwise embraces, and embraces what the law otherwise rejects, may help explain why legal decisionmakers and academics have devoted less sustained attention to family law than to other areas of legal regulation. Moreover, the presumption of family law's exceptionalism may help account for the lack of scholarly focus on family law's canon. Academic theorists have frequently written about legal canons as if they emanate only from prestigious, powerful, centralized, and federal institutions like the United States Supreme Court. These theorists may have ignored the family law canon because they incorrectly assumed—ironically, because of the power of canonical narratives about family law's exceptionalism—that an institution like the Supreme Court has played little role in the development of family law.

In fact, family law's operative principles much more closely resemble those governing the rest of the law than canonical narratives of family law exceptionalism acknowledge. The premise of family law's exceptionalism distorts how legal authorities understand family law, diverts their attention from considering the real policy choices the field faces, and hampers their decisionmaking. Exceptionalist assumptions about family law encourage legal decisionmakers to rely on misguided and categorical aphorisms about family law's supposed uniqueness, rather than individualized analysis of specific policy options.

Chapter 1—"Federalism and the Family"—considers the canonical narrative maintaining that family law is a rare outpost of localism in an era when the federal government regulates virtually every other aspect of life. This narrative has permitted many legislators, judges, and commentators to oppose specific federal laws regulating families on the ground that any federal family law is unprecedented and inappropriate by definition. For instance, few challenged the substantive aims of the 1994 Violence Against Women Act (VAWA), which gave victims of gender-motivated violence the right to sue their attackers in federal court for civil rights violations. But many lawmakers, judges, and critics (dubiously) identified VAWA's civil rights remedy as federal family law and relied on the canonical premise that family law is local to secure the remedy's limitation in Congress and invalidation in the Supreme Court.

The canonical assumption of family law localism also shaped debates over the 1996 Defense of Marriage Act (DOMA), which defined marriage for purposes of federal law to exclude same-sex couples. Some legislators, litigants, advocates, and scholars contended that this definition of marriage for federal purposes needed to be condemned whatever one's views on the substantive merits of DOMA's policy objectives because the definition constituted federal family law. Moreover, some courts relied on arguments grounded in family law's supposed localism in finding this part of DOMA unconstitutional. Indeed, the Supreme Court itself invoked and celebrated the canonical narrative about family law localism in its 2013 opinion striking down DOMA's federal definition of marriage.

If the localism narrative were consistently deployed and consistently successful, then its description of family law as a field that the federal government does not and should not enter would be much more accurate. Instead, however, legal authorities and commentators use the localism narrative selectively to counter specific federal initiatives. Proponents of this narrative assume and insist in some contexts that family law's localism is a matter of common sense and many legal authorities take arguments asserting family law's localism to have real persuasive power, yet the premise of family law localism is also frequently disregarded.

Federal family law is well established and extensive. While the weight and persistence of state family law are undeniable, federal statutes, regulations, and judicial decisions routinely structure the creation and dissolution of legally recognized family relationships and determine the rights and responsibilities of family members. Family law runs through federal law on employment, labor, retirement, Social Security, immigration, citizenship, international relations, taxes, bankruptcy, housing, crime, the military, veterans, intellectual property, Native Americans, evidence, personal jurisdiction, child support, adoption, foster care, family violence, and more. Indeed, federal family law is sometimes unavoidable given the requirements of the federal Constitution and the extent of exclusive federal jurisdiction.

A present or proposed policy cannot be convincingly dismissed just by identifying it as federal family law. For example, no one should have rejected DOMA out of hand simply because it was a form of federal family law. There was a problem with DOMA, but it was a problem grounded in civil rights concerns, rather than federalism objections. This specific example of federal family law discriminated against gay people.

The narrative about family law localism takes time away from addressing the pressing choices that decisionmakers face. The live questions in family law are not about whether the federal government can or should be involved at all. Federal involvement is already pervasive. The real questions in family law are about whether any particular family law policy is substantively desirable on its own merits and about which level of government is best situated (or which levels of government working together are best situated) to effectuate that specific policy.

Chapter 2—"Family Law and Economic Exchange"—examines the canonical narrative contending that family law is removed from the market and committed to prohibiting economic exchanges that the law allows elsewhere. This narrative assumes family law's hostility to market principles and directs attention toward debating whether that hostility is well-founded. Yet family law already permits and enforces a wide variety of economic exchanges within the family. Spouses are free to enter into legally valid agreements specifying with great variety, creativity, and detail how they will distribute property, earnings, and other economic assets between themselves during and after their relationship. Courts allow and uphold even more economic transactions between other family members.

The most pressing questions for family law are not about whether to permit and enforce economic exchange, but about when to permit and enforce such exchange, in what forms, for what purposes, and to what ends. For instance, current legal regulation of economic exchange within the family often operates in ways that perpetuate and exacerbate distributive inequality. The law enforces many intrafamilial contracts and employment relationships, but prohibits or refuses to enforce some of the exchanges that would particularly help women and poorer people. For instance, no state will enforce contracts providing that one spouse will pay the other for housework. Some states regulate the flow of funds to birth mothers so strictly that adoptive parents may not pay for a birth mother's living expenses while she is pregnant, her lost wages, her maternity clothes, or even her Lamaze classes and prenatal care. Uncovering how family law's regulation of economic relations actually operates reveals the disproportionate burden that this regulation can impose on already burdened people, an inequality that is difficult to justify. The canonical story of family law's separation from the market misdescribes the field and misdirects focus away from pressing issues that family law confronts, such as how best to regulate the economics of marital labor, adoption, and surrogacy.

Part Two, which includes Chapters 3 and 4, examines another over-arching theme in the family law canon, the prevalence of progress narratives recounting family law's break from history. These canon-ical progress narratives are in some unacknowledged tension with the canonical stories about family law's exceptionalism. Where exception-alist accounts of family law often stress the field's resistance to trends shaping the rest of the law and depict family law as an oasis of stability, family law's progress narratives emphasize that the field has changed dramatically over time and promise that family law has kept pace with contemporary norms.

However, these progress narratives significantly overstate the extent and nature of family law's historical transformations, while underem-phasizing and obscuring continuity in family law rules, practices, and presumptions. Family law has changed over time in ways that have fre-quently promoted the interests of less powerful family members. But family law's canonical progress narratives too often tend to envision reform more as an achieved goal within family law than as an ongoing project.

The narratives can divert decisionmakers from considering whether, how, and to what extent current family law policies still operate to pro-mote and perpetuate subordination and injustice. Indeed, legal authori-ties sometimes explicitly use family law's canonical progress narratives as arguments for directing attention away from persistent disparities, on the ground that family law has already left its support for normatively illegitimate or problematic policies securely in the past.

Chapter 3—"Progress Narratives for Adults"—focuses on canonical narratives about historical transformations in family law's treatment of adults. It first explores the canonical story of common law coverture's demise, which contends that family law has eradicated the common law doctrines that once legally subordinated wives to husbands. This story takes its strength from the undeniable ways in which the legal regime of coverture that existed in early nineteenth-century America has under-gone profound transformations. But the narrative presents the changes that have occurred as more complete, absolute, and unwavering than they have actually been. Coverture principles continue to shape signifi-cant aspects of modern family law in ways that operate to women's systematic detriment. For example, family law's roots in coverture are still visible in laws and doctrines that prohibit important forms of inter-spousal litigation, keep some interspousal lawsuits out of federal courts, or treat the infliction of injury less seriously when it occurs between spouses. In fact, at least twenty-three states still treat marital rape more leniently than rape outside marriage. Modern family law reflects the sustained imprint of coverture doctrines and reasoning, and one cannot understand family law's present contours without reference to the field's origins in coverture. The persistent manifestations of coverture's influ-ence on family law continue to disadvantage women, adding to the other forces within and outside family law that help maintain sex inequality. The canonical story of coverture's demise masks the perpetuation of rules and policies from the common law regime, directs attention away from examining how these rules and policies undermine women's equality, and obscures the case for further progress by suggesting that the legacy of coverture has already been eradicated.

Chapter 3 also considers the canonical status to contract story, which exists in unacknowledged tension with the canonical narrative main-taining that family law rejects market principles. The status to contract story reports that family law was once dominated by status rules with terms that the state decreed and no individual could adjust, but is now controlled by contract rules whose terms are individually negotiable. Like the story of coverture's demise, the canonical status to contract story is a progress narrative. It presumes that contract rules are prefer-able to status rules. Yet the canon's status to contract story is descrip-tively oversold and normatively underdefended. Status rules determining who may marry and establishing unalterable features of familial rela-tionships remain central to family law. The descriptive assertion that contract rules dominate family law diverts attention from examining these persistent status rules. At the same time, contract rules can have disadvantages, especially for parties with less bargaining power. The normative presumption that contract rules are more desirable takes focus away from evaluating the costs and benefits of implementing any particular family law policy in status or contract form, as those costs and benefits vary by context.

Chapter 4—"A Progress Narrative for Children"—focuses on a canon-ical narrative about historical transformations in family law's treatment of children. This chapter explores the canonical story contending that family law once gave parents almost property-like control over their children, but now prioritizes children's best interests. The evolution of the legal regulation of parenthood has actually been more continuous and less transformative than this story suggests. Family law still grants parents tremendous power over their children's custody, education, employment, punishment, and safety, even when such authority may be inconsistent with children's best interests. Indeed, courts have taken parents' common law prerogatives to be so foundational to American law and society that they have enshrined many of these prerogatives into constitutional law. This chapter does not argue that family law should necessarily prioritize children's interests in every context. Where the canonical narrative appears to presume the desirability of privileging children's interests, I do not make that normative assumption. Instead, this chapter explores how celebrating the supposed triumph of children's best interests obscures the current state of the law, in which family law frequently places parents' rights over children's interests where the two conflict. Simply as a descriptive matter, family law does not always put children's interests first. Moreover, the canonical narrative takes attention away from the normative question that family law still faces: whether, when, why, where, and to what extent the continued prioritization of parental rights is appropriate or in need of reform.

The third and final part of the book, which includes Chapters 5 and 6, considers some of what is missing from the family law canon. The canon's power to shape how lawmakers, judges, and commentators understand family law and make decisions about the field stems not just from what the canon includes and describes, but from what the canon excludes and overlooks. The family law canon pays scant attention to many family relationships and ignores important sources of family law. The canon's narrow focus is so ingrained that it operates at the level of common sense, routinely assumed but rarely, if ever, discussed or explained.

Chapter 5—"Sibling Ties and Other Noncanonical Family Relationships"—examines family law's tight focus on marriage, parenthood, and (sometimes) their functional equivalents, such as cohabitation between unmarried sexual partners or de facto parenthood. Legal decisionmakers regularly take this aspect of family law to be so commonsensical as to require no explicit acknowledgment or defense. Yet siblings, grandparents, grandchildren, aunts, uncles, nieces, nephews, cousins, and other noncanonical relatives can also be central to family life and to the flourishing of family members. Family law's reflexive orientation around marriage, parenthood, and their functional equivalents diverts attention and scrutiny from considering how the law should regulate and protect other family relationships. For instance, the sibling relationship is a crucial, yet noncanonical, family tie. Family law views children almost exclusively through the lens of children's relationships with their parents, rather than the lens of children's relationships with their siblings. The law offers siblings only modest and sporadic protection, too often permitting adoption or parental divorce or death to separate siblings and sometimes leave them with no right to contact each other or even learn of each other's existence. But siblings can be vital sources of support, love, nurturing, and stability for children, and family law could do more to safeguard sibling bonds when they are threatened. This chapter uses the example of sibling ties, which have received remarkably little legal attention, to examine the law's treatment of noncanonical family relationships and to consider some of the reform possibilities that emerge for legislators, regulators, judges, advocates, scholars, and family members to explore and debate when we free ourselves from the assumption that family law should revolve around marriage and parenthood.

Chapter 6—"Family Law for the Poor"—explores the poor's absence from canonical narratives about family law. The family law canon omits virtually any examination of the legal regulation of poor families. Yet much of welfare law is family law as well, determining crucial rights and responsibilities tied to family status. The exclusion of welfare law from the family law canon has helped judges and lawmakers avoid acknowledging and discussing why the legal regulation of poor families is so different from the legal regulation of other families. The family law governing the poor is premised on inspection and interference, where the family law governing other families stresses the government's interests in protecting privacy and reducing intrusion—even when distributing financial benefits. For example, Temporary Assistance for Needy Families, the most prominent federal-state welfare program, systematically scrutinizes families and freely employs punitive measures in an attempt to reshape family life. In contrast, redistributive family law programs directed at families who are not considered poor, such as the Social Security system's program of benefits for children, parents, and spouses, are structured to minimize their examination of families and interference with family relations. Recognizing welfare law as family law brings the bifurcation in family law into clear view. It reveals the starkly divergent treatment of poor families as a practice that courts and lawmakers have to explain and justify, or eliminate.

The book concludes by reflecting on the path to reforming the family law canon. Changing the family law canon is difficult by definition. The very concept of a canonical idea is that it is an entrenched, widely shared, oft-repeated way of thinking about a subject. Legislators, regulators, judges, lawyers, scholars, and family members transmit canons intergenerationally, teaching new generations to think along the lines their predecessors do. Moreover, judges, legislators, and regulators have the most control over the canon, and their power to wield the force of law makes it easier for them to resist outside scrutiny and critique. But recognizing how the family law canon misdescribes the field, misdirects the attention of lawmakers, courts, and commentators, and misguides their decisions, is the first step to recasting the canon.

I

FAMILY LAW EXCEPTIONALISM

One of the guiding concepts that judges, legislators, and commentators often invoke to describe and explain family law is the idea of family law's exceptionalism. Many narratives about family law describe the field as distinctly set off from other areas of the law, so that legal rules and presumptions in force elsewhere do not apply or are actually reversed within family law. For instance, one scholar has explained that "[s]ociety has devised special laws to apply to the family" and observed that "'family law' can be thought of as a system of exemptions from the everyday rules that would apply to interactions among people in a non-family context, complemented by the imposition of a set of special family obligations."[1] Another scholar has recounted that "[l]egal, social, and popular discourse all agreed that the principles of family operation were not part of, and were necessarily different from, those found in other legal and social enterprises."[2] Two more scholars "start with the observation that family and family law are often treated as occupying a unique and autonomous domain—as exceptional."[3]

Where family law's canonical progress narratives insist on the field's profound transformations over time, canonical stories grounded on the premise of family law's exceptionalism frequently picture family law as a haven of stability in a nation otherwise undergoing significant, sometimes disorienting change. On these exceptionalist accounts, family law helps to safeguard principles of legal regulation that are elsewhere on the decline. That notion appeals to many judges and lawmakers, as well as some advocates and scholars, particularly if they are somewhat uneasy about the pace or direction of change outside family law.

But family law actually resembles other legal arenas much more closely than the premise of family law exceptionalism suggests. Canonical narratives grounded on the assumption of family law's exceptionalism significantly overstate family law's separation from ordinarily applicable legal principles, divert the attention of lawmakers and jurists, and misshape the decisions they make. The narratives encourage reliance on categorical generalizations about family law's supposed differentness, rather than focused analysis of specific policy choices.

This part considers two examples of the canonical insistence on family law's exceptionalism. Chapter 1 examines the canonical idea that family law is a respite of localism in an age when the reach of federal power is steadily expanding and the federal government regulates almost every other legal arena. Chapter 2 explores the canonical idea that family law rejects and repudiates market principles that increasingly saturate other areas of law and life.

1

FEDERALISM AND THE FAMILY

The whole subject of the domestic relations of husband and wife, parent and child, belongs to the laws of the States and not to the laws of the United States.

—*United States v. Windsor* (United States Supreme Court 2013)[1]

A canonical story in family law describes the field as a rare respite of localism in an era when the federal government regulates virtually every other legal arena. Many judges, legislators, and other lawmakers, as well as scholars, litigants, and advocates, repeatedly tell this story about family law. The localist narrative is premised on family law's exceptionalism. It portrays family law as clearly beyond the federal government's boundaries when the limits on federal power are otherwise murky. It presents family law as an almost pastoral oasis of jurisdictional stability and certainty when the federal government has otherwise dramatically expanded its reach over time.

Localist arguments about family law are sometimes descriptive, sometimes normative, and often both. They purport to describe family law's present character, and they simultaneously contend that family law should preserve its supposed localism into the future.

If localist arguments about family law were consistently deployed and consistently successful, their description of the field would be much more accurate. The arguments would have succeeded in preventing most, albeit not all, federal family law. (As we will see, some federal family law is unavoidable given federal constitutional requirements and areas of exclusive federal jurisdiction.)

Instead, however, the localist narrative about family law is employed selectively against specific federal initiatives and not others. Decisionmakers and the people who seek to influence them frequently make arguments grounded in family law localism, insisting that federal family law is unprecedented and categorically inappropriate, no matter how desirable its substantive policy goals might otherwise be. Many legal authorities take such arguments to have real persuasive power. Yet the premise of family law localism is also frequently disregarded. While the weight of state family law remains enormous, federal family law is extensive, wide-ranging, and well established.

Claims that family law is local cannot be evaluated without a working definition of family law. Yet remarkably little attention has focused on the meaning of the term "family law." The assumed and asserted boundaries of the field oscillate widely between contexts without acknowledgment, explanation, clarity, or specificity. Indeed, some of the most vigorous advocates of the notion that family law is local offer only vague, underspecified, shifting, and inconsistent accounts of what they mean by family law.

My working definition is that family law regulates the creation and dissolution of legally recognized family relationships and determines legal rights and responsibilities that turn on family status. This means that family law decides who counts as a legal family member and who does not, how legalized family relationships are begun and ended, and what turns on being a family member—what it means legally to be a spouse, parent, child, sibling, or other relative as one interacts with the government and with other people inside and outside of one's family. This is not the only possible definition of family law, but it is a reasonable and functional one that provides a starting point for analysis.[2] It helps us to escape the intellectual silos that often isolate family law from other bodies of law and to see family law's reach into numerous legal arenas where family law's presence and significance have routinely been overlooked. Many federal statutes, regulations, and judicial decisions fall squarely within this definition, although they frequently are not recognized as family law.

Moreover, federal law covers all aspects of this definition of family law. Some federal law regulates the creation and dissolution of legal family relationships, determining who counts as kin for federal purposes. This federal law often tracks state law, so that family members and family relationships recognized under state law are recognized under federal law as well. But federal law also sometimes diverges from state law on those issues. In addition, there is an enormous body of federal law establishing legal rights and responsibilities that turn on family status. This proportion between the various functions of federal family law mirrors state family law, which similarly has an enormous body of law setting out rights and responsibilities tied to family status under state law.

The canonical assumption of family law's localism has distorted how legal authorities understand the field, diverted their attention from the real questions that family law faces, and misshaped the judgments they reach. The urgent questions for family law are not about whether the federal government can or should be involved at all. They are about whether any particular family law policy is substantively desirable on its own merits and about which level of government is best situated (or which levels of government working together are best situated) to effectuate that specific policy.

This chapter explores the power of the canonical narrative about family law localism, reviews some of the federal family law that the narrative has helped obscure, and then illustrates how legal analysis can proceed when freed from canonical assertions that family law is only local.

Proclamations of family law's localism appear across a range of legal materials, including judicial opinions; statements from judicial organizations and judges; legislative debates, reports, and testimony; legal briefs; scholarly and professional books and articles; and family law casebooks and treatises. For instance, the Supreme Court has frequently announced that "the laws of marriage and domestic relations are concerns traditionally reserved to the states,"[3] that "[t]he regulation of domestic relations is traditionally the domain of state law,"[4] that "domestic relations [is] an area that has long been regarded as a virtually exclusive province of the States,"[5] that "there is no federal law of domestic relations,"[6] that—even more emphatically—"'[t]he whole subject of the domestic relations of husband and wife, parent and child, belongs to the laws of the States and not to the laws of the United States.'"[7]

The tone of these pronouncements often implies that their correctness is self-evident. Indeed, Chief Justice William Rehnquist went so far as to suggest that courts should not rely on "'logic'" in concluding that family law is for the states alone. He wrote that "[i]f ever there were an area in which federal courts should heed the admonition of Justice Holmes that 'a page of history is worth a volume of logic,' it is in the area of domestic relations. This area has been left to the States from time immemorial, and not without good reason." Rehnquist did not identify that "good reason."[8]

Some (although happily not all) scholarly books and law review articles also present localist accounts of family law. They maintain that "[f]amily law is considered one of the last sacred refuges of states' rights,"[9] report that "[s]tates enjoy exclusive authority over family law,"[10] advise that "[l]egislative jurisdiction over matters of domestic relations and family law are among the powers reserved to the States,"[11] note that "[f]amily law has traditionally been an area of state prerogative,"[12] observe that "[i]n the United States, family law has traditionally remained in the domain of the states,"[13] explain that "the entire field of child custody and private adoption has always been regarded by Congress and the Supreme Court as each individual state's concern, with virtually no federal interest at stake,"[14] contend that "[s]tate court judges, unlike federal judges, have the unique opportunity to hear issues of family law,"[15] and declare that "we consider . . . domestic relations to be the province of the states."[16] Some (although again not all) family law treatises and casebooks describing the present contours of the law similarly announce that "the institution of marriage is regulated by the states,"[17] proclaim "that family law is inherently local,"[18] recount that "state legislatures have traditionally defined the family and enacted the laws that regulate marriage, parentage, divorce, family support obligations, and family property rights,"[19] and repeat that "[t]he whole subject of the domestic relations of husband and wife, parent and child, belongs to the laws of the states and not to the laws of United States."[20]

More than just declarations, the narrative about family law localism has powerfully shaped family law. As we will see, the narrative has not prevented the development of abundant federal family law. But the Supreme Court has relied on the premise that family law belongs to the states to structure decisionmaking about both family law and many other subjects, reasoning from the starting point of family law localism in areas as disparate as the Court's federalism jurisprudence, its domestic relations exception to federal diversity jurisdiction, and its judgments on civil rights law. Many courts, judges, and legislators, along with advocates and scholars, have similarly drawn on family law's canonical localism narrative to oppose congressional bills and statutes, such as the 1994 Violence Against Women Act[21] and the 1996 Defense of Marriage Act,[22] on the ground that they constituted federal family law and were inappropriate for that reason. Let's start with the Supreme Court's jurisprudence.

The Presumption of Family Law Localism
in the Supreme Court's Federalism Jurisprudence

The presumption of family law's localism is central to the Supreme Court's recent federalism jurisprudence, even in cases where family law is not directly at issue. The Court's new direction in federalism first emerged in *United States v. Lopez* (1995),[23] a case about a criminal gun control law. For over a half century before *Lopez,* the Court had consistently upheld a wide array of federal statutes as falling within Congress's constitutional authority to regulate interstate commerce.[24] The Court routinely permitted federal laws that appeared at first to be far removed from interstate commerce, such as a law that authorized the federal government to regulate a farm's production of wheat for the farm's own consumption. The only requirement the Court imposed on Congress, which was not much of a hurdle in practice, was that the regulated activity have a substantial aggregate impact on the national economy.[25] However, a five-Justice majority in *Lopez* concluded that Congress had exceeded its commerce power in enacting the Gun-Free School Zones Act, which made it a federal crime to knowingly possess a firearm near a school.[26] The United States argued that the act fell within congressional authority to regulate interstate commerce because the presence of firearms threatened the learning environment in schools, which would lead to a less productive population and accordingly have a substantial aggregate impact on the national economy.[27] The Court rejected this argument, insisting that the government's interpretation of Congress's commerce power could not be correct because that interpretation would also mean that Congress has the constitutional authority to regulate family law.

Lopez did not explain why congressional regulation of family law would be inappropriate. The Court took that as a baseline proposition and matter of common sense, stating that "under the Government's 'national productivity' reasoning, Congress could regulate any activity that it found was related to the economic productivity of individual citizens: family law (including marriage, divorce, and child custody), for example."[28] On this account, family law's localism was a manifest certainty in a world in which the boundaries of federal authority were otherwise contested and difficult to identify. The *Lopez* majority returned three more times to the idea that family law is inherently local, repeatedly stressing that no interpretation of Congress's commerce power could be plausible if the interpretation would allow Congress to regulate "family law" and "child rearing." *Lopez* argued that "the dissent's expansive analysis" would not permit "limitations on Congress' commerce power, such as family law."[29] It contended that the dissent's argument for upholding the Gun-Free School Zones Act "would be equally applicable, if not more so, to subjects such as family law."[30] And *Lopez* charged that "[u]nder the dissent's rationale, Congress could just as easily look at child rearing as 'fall[ing] on the commercial side of the line.'"[31] Perhaps the Court found this last proposition particularly disturbing given the canonical premise (which Chapter 2 will discuss) that family law rejects market principles. But *Lopez* saw no need to elaborate. The Court accepted as given that family law is inherently local.

A concurring opinion in *Lopez* added that Congress's commerce authority "can by no means encompass authority over mere gun possession, any more than it empowers the Federal Government to regulate marriage." "Any interpretation of the Commerce Clause that even suggests that Congress could regulate such matters is in need of reexamination."[32]

In fact, all the Justices on the *Lopez* Court seemingly agreed that family law is local. The four *Lopez* dissenters rejected virtually every other aspect of the majority opinion. But they did not challenge the premise that Congress could not and should not regulate family law. Instead, the dissenters focused on explaining why even a broad reading of Congress's interstate commerce power would still keep family law under local control. "To hold this statute constitutional is not to 'obliterate' the 'distinction between what is national and what is local,'" the *Lopez* dissenters insisted, "nor is it to hold that the Commerce Clause permits the Federal Government . . . to regulate 'marriage, divorce, and child custody.'"[33]

The Presumption of Family Law Localism in the Supreme Court's Diversity Jurisdiction Jurisprudence

The canonical story about family law localism also helps explain the persistence of the Supreme Court's domestic relations exception to federal diversity jurisdiction. Federal diversity jurisdiction permits federal courts to adjudicate a lawsuit that would otherwise have to be brought in state court, when the parties to the case have "diversity" of citizenship—meaning that the plaintiff(s) and defendant(s) live in different states. The Founders believed that federal diversity jurisdiction was needed to protect out-of-state litigants from the potential parochial biases of another state's courts.[34]

The constitutional provision creating diversity jurisdiction and the federal law regulating it do not distinguish based on the subject matter of lawsuits.[35] Indeed, Congress has provided that federal "district courts shall have original jurisdiction of *all* civil actions where the matter in controversy exceeds the sum or value of $75,000, exclusive of interest and costs, and is between . . . citizens of different States."[36] There is also no apparent reason to suppose that in-state favoritism is limited to only certain subjects.

However, the Supreme Court has created a "domestic relations exception" to federal diversity jurisdiction that "divests the federal courts of power to issue divorce, alimony, and child custody decrees."[37] As the Court has explained, "the domestic relations exception encompasses only cases involving the issuance of a divorce, alimony, or child custody decree" and does not extend beyond these specific decrees to cover the rest of family law.[38]

While the domestic relations exception is limited in scope, the Court has repeatedly relied on its cases upholding the exception to support broad declarations of family law localism that leave the meaning of "family law" ambiguously defined but expansive in reach. *Lopez* asserted that Congress's commerce power necessarily stopped short of "family law (including marriage, divorce, and child custody)."[39] The individual family law subjects that the *Lopez* Court listed to illustrate the supposed absurdity of federal family law seemed designed to build on the foundation of the domestic relations exception. Yet *Lopez* left the exact definition of family law indeterminate, while signaling that it is broader than the simple issuance of decrees at stake with the domestic relations exception. Similarly, the Supreme Court's 1979 decision in *Hisquierdo v. Hisquierdo* concerned whether federal retirement benefits for railroad workers may count as community property.[40] But *Hisquierdo* relied on a Supreme Court opinion from 1890 that first included child custody decrees within the domestic relations exception, quoting *In re Burrus* for the absolutist proposition that "'[t]he whole subject of the domestic relations of husband and wife, parent and child, belongs to the laws of the States and not to the laws of the United States.'"[41] The Supreme Court's 1987 opinion in *Rose v. Rose* quoted the same passage to explain "the constitutional standard" that the Court had applied in order to determine that federal laws governing veterans' disability benefits did not preempt a state child support statute.[42]

The canonical premise of family law localism, in turn, has helped keep the domestic relations exception in place. The Court's initial reasons for creating the exception now appear patently discriminatory and unconvincing. The Court first announced the exception in *Barber v. Barber*,[43] an 1859 decision tightly entangled in the common law doctrine of coverture. This doctrine, which Chapter 3 will consider at more length, provided that a wife's civil identity merged into her husband's at marriage and essentially disappeared. Some states began to modify some aspects of their own coverture doctrines beginning in the 1830s. But in the United States Supreme Court, both *Barber*'s majority and its dissent endorsed coverture without qualm in 1859.

All the *Barber* Justices began with the presumption that diversity of citizenship between a husband and wife was ordinarily impossible by definition because coverture principles disabled a married woman from establishing a separate legal residence from her husband, no matter where she actually lived.[44] The only disagreement in *Barber* focused on whether coverture permitted a special exemption for a wife living apart from her husband under a judicial order of separation. The *Barber* majority found such an exemption and allowed Huldah Barber to invoke diversity jurisdiction in order to enforce a state alimony award against her husband.[45]

However, in a flourish unnecessary for the resolution of the *Barber* case, the Court advanced what was apparently its earliest expression of localist discourse in family law, declaring that it "disclaim[ed] altogether any jurisdiction in the courts of the United States upon the subject of divorce, or for the allowance of alimony."[46] The outraged dissent charged nonetheless that the majority's decision threatened coverture's foundations, by treating a husband and wife as "beings wholly disconnected, and each *sui juris*."[47]

Barber, which reasoned inextricably within common law coverture, marked the beginning of the strange career of the domestic relations exception in the Court's case law. Throughout the nineteenth and early twentieth centuries, the Court repeated *Barber*'s localist declaration and barred federal litigation seeking divorce, alimony, or (after 1890)[48] child custody decrees that was brought outside federal territorial courts.[49] *Barber* became the seminal decision excepting "domestic relations" claims from diversity jurisdiction. Indeed, *Barber*, as reinterpreted to emphasize its gratuitous localist pronouncement, became the essential foundation for the entire jurisprudence. Neither *Barber* nor the decisions following offer any explanation or authority for the proposition that some family law cases are not for the federal courts other than to entwine the notion with coverture principles. The Supreme Court itself in *Ankenbrandt v. Richards* (1992) noted that *Barber* "cited no authority" for its holding.[50]

Without question, the reasoning behind the Supreme Court's creation of the domestic relations exception to diversity jurisdiction is no longer persuasive, if it ever was. The *Barber* opinion rested on the general proposition that a wife under coverture could not maintain a legal domicile separate from her husband. *Barber*'s proclamation of an exception to diversity jurisdiction for divorce or alimony suits between husbands and wives was nothing other than the expression of this domicile rule in jurisdictional form. *Barber* makes no sense outside the context of coverture. Its logic no longer counts as such.

The Court could eliminate the domestic relations exception at any time because the exception has always been a judicial creation without constitutional basis or statutory codification.[51] Although the Court has "presume[d]" that Congress has implicitly accepted the exception, no statute has ever established that there is a domestic relations exception to federal diversity jurisdiction.[52] Nonetheless, the Court confirmed the exception's continued existence in *Ankenbrandt* (while holding that the exception did not reach the *Ankenbrandt* plaintiff's federal suit against her ex-husband and his girlfriend for their alleged abuse of the plaintiff's children).[53]

Unsurprisingly, *Ankenbrandt* swiftly passed over the exception's origins in coverture doctrine and did not consider whether the Court's decision to uphold the exception would functionally perpetuate coverture's legacy.[54] *Ankenbrandt* also did not explain why the concerns about in-state favoritism that motivated the Founders to create federal diversity jurisdiction are not also present in divorce, alimony, and child custody cases. Instead, *Ankenbrandt* relied on the canonical idea of family law's long-standing localism, drawing on the same narrative that the Court has used the domestic relations exception to support. The *Ankenbrandt* Court, "unwilling to cast aside an understood rule that has been recognized for nearly a century and a half,"[55] asserted that federal courts should not issue divorce, alimony, and child custody decrees because "state courts are more eminently suited to work of this type than are federal courts."[56] The Court reaffirmed the continued existence of the domestic relations exception in 2004[57] and 2006.[58]

The Presumption of Family Law Localism and the Violence Against Women Act

The reach of the canonical narrative about family law's localism extends from the opinions of the Supreme Court to the arguments of many lawmakers and commentators across the political spectrum. Consider the struggles over the 1994 Violence Against Women Act (VAWA)[59] and the 1996 Defense of Marriage Act (DOMA).[60] Very different groups of decisionmakers and critics opposed these federal statutes, but opponents of each statute repeatedly relied on stories about family law localism. They contended that federal family law is unprecedented and categorically inappropriate, so it should be condemned regardless of the substantive merits of the particular law at issue.

Let's start with VAWA's civil rights remedy, which was vigorously opposed for years before its enactment, substantially limited in Congress before becoming law, and then struck down by the Supreme Court in 2000.[61] This remedy recognized a federal civil right to be protected from "crimes of violence motivated by gender"[62] and entitled the victims of such violence to sue their assailants in federal court for money damages.[63]

VAWA's civil rights remedy rested on the premise that protection from gender-motivated violence was central to women's equal citizenship[64] and a necessary precondition to women's ability to exercise other civil rights, such as the rights to work and to travel.[65] For instance, the congressional record supporting the remedy contained myriad examples of how gender-motivated violence limited women's ability to participate in the national economy by affecting women's decisions about which jobs to take, which to leave, and whether to work in the market at all.[66]

VAWA's civil rights remedy was designed to compensate for state responses to gender-motivated violence that Congress found were riddled with "discrimination"[67] and "prejudice,"[68] failed to "adequately provide victims the opportunity to vindicate their interests," and insufficiently addressed "the bias element of gender crimes, which separates these crimes from acts of random violence."[69] The remedy's provisions drew directly from older federal civil rights laws targeting racial discrimination, statutes now thought to be at the core of national jurisdiction.[70] In enacting the remedy, Congress relied on its constitutional authority to regulate interstate commerce and its constitutional right and responsibility to enforce the equal protection guarantees of the Fourteenth Amendment.[71]

While VAWA's civil rights remedy was designed to fit within civil rights law, there were good reasons to conclude that the civil rights remedy was not a form of family law at all. The remedy did not regulate the creation or dissolution of legally recognized family ties, and it did not give people legal rights and responsibilities that turned on family status or relationships. The remedy was available to victims of gender-motivated violence without regard to whether there was a familial connection between perpetrator and victim. In fact, only a little more than a quarter (27.5%) of the fifty-one reported cases under VAWA's civil rights remedy as of November 1999 involved claims against current or former spouses or boyfriends. Almost half (45.1%) of the fifty-one cases involved workplaces, other commercial settings, or educational settings.[72] *United States v. Morrison,*[73] the Supreme Court decision in 2000 that found VAWA's civil rights remedy unconstitutional,[74] was representative in this respect. The case involved gender-motivated violence with no connection to family relationships or family life. Christy Brzonkala had sued Antonio Morrison and James Crawford for violating her civil rights under VAWA after the men, two of Brzonkala's classmates at Virginia Polytechnic Institute, allegedly raped her repeatedly within thirty minutes of meeting her.[75]

However, legal decisionmakers have often paired their arguments asserting family law's localism with expansive, imprecise, and unexplained applications of the family law label. During the years of debate over VAWA in Congress, few disputed the proposition that gender-motivated violence was an important problem deserving remedy. But discussions of gender-motivated violence immediately led many legislators, judges, and critics to focus on how VAWA's civil rights remedy would give wives the right to sue their husbands in federal court for damages stemming from marital violence. This possibility may have attracted so much attention because the civil rights remedy, in treating marital violence no differently than violence between legal strangers, sought to counter a long legal tradition of more lenient responses to violence between family members.[76] One of the congressional findings included in the earliest version of the VAWA bill and still present in the final conference report made clear that the remedy would target gender-motivated violence both within the family and outside it, by expanding upon existing federal law that "provide[d] a civil rights remedy for gender crimes committed in the workplace, but not on the street or in the home."[77] The enacted remedy explicitly established that victims of gender-motivated violence could bring suit under VAWA's civil rights remedy regardless of whether the violence at issue would be treated more leniently under state law because of the relationship between victim and perpetrator.[78]

With the possibility of interspousal litigation in mind, the remedy's opponents classified the remedy as federal family law and condemned the remedy as misguided for that reason alone. The Conference of Chief Justices, the Judicial Conference of the United States, and Chief Justice Rehnquist never challenged VAWA's substantive goal of combating violence against women. The Conference of Chief Justices, the organization for state chief justices, told Congress that "[o]bviously, there is a need to protect women."[79] It declared that "the Conference of Chief Justices commends Congress for addressing the critical problems of sexual and spousal violence and supports the intended objectives of [VAWA]."[80] The Judicial Conference of the United States, the organization for federal judges, endorsed on its own and through Chief Justice Rehnquist "the underlying objective of [VAWA]—to deter violence against women."[81]

Nonetheless, the Conference of Chief Justices voted on January 31, 1991, to oppose VAWA's civil rights remedy on the ground that the remedy was a form of federal family law and family law "is not federal in nature."[82] The Judicial Conference of the United States did the same in September 1991,[83] after the Judicial Conference's Ad Hoc Committee on Gender-Based Violence warned that VAWA's civil rights remedy would involve the federal courts in "domestic relations disputes" "that have traditionally been within the province of the state courts."[84] Chief Justice Rehnquist, acting in his capacity as chief administrator of the federal courts, similarly opposed VAWA's civil rights remedy because it "could involve the federal courts in a whole host of domestic relations disputes," an area of "law that ha[s] traditionally been reserved to state courts."[85]

Some scholars have contended that federal judges seek "to confirm their prestige" by limiting their docket to nationally important issues and do not understand "[w]omen and the families they sometimes inhabit" to be important.[86] This may be an accurate assessment of the federal judiciary's perceived self-interest. For my purposes, however, I am less interested in how the campaign that judges and judicial organizations waged against VAWA's civil rights remedy reflected attempted self-promotion and more interested in how the strength of the canonical story about family law localism meant that it would count as a convincing argument against the civil rights remedy to assert that the remedy was unprecedented and inappropriate because the remedy was supposedly a form of federal family law. When judges and judicial organizations advanced this argument—whether from self-interest, sincere belief, or most likely a combination of the two—the claim resonated with both Congress and the courts.

The attack on VAWA's civil rights remedy as federal family law proved extraordinarily powerful, sparking concrete results in addition to rhetorical pronouncements. Although the argument that the remedy constituted family law was doubtful from the start, criticism drawing on the canonical idea of family law localism helped push Congress to limit the remedy significantly before enacting it in modified form in 1994. Most notably, the initial versions of the remedy covered all violent crimes "committed because of gender or on the basis of gender"[87] and presumed that every rape fell into this category.[88] However, in 1993 the Senate Judiciary Committee restricted the civil rights remedy to those crimes that would constitute a felony involving the risk of physical injury[89] and that were "committed because of gender or on the basis of gender; *and* due, at least in part, to an animus based on the victim's gender."[90]

The revised bill did not define its new "animus" requirement, but the requirement was clearly meant to limit the remedy's scope. The sole discussion of animus in the Senate Judiciary Committee's report stated that "[t]his new language elucidates the committee's intent that a victim alleging a violation under this section must have been targeted on the basis of his or her gender. The defendant must have had a specific intent or purpose, based on the victim's gender, to injure the victim."[91] The report indicated that the committee no longer presumed that the civil rights remedy would cover all rapes. Indeed, the report trumpeted in its own italics that the revised version of VAWA's civil rights remedy *"does not create a general Federal law for all assaults or rapes against women."*[92]

Senator Orrin Hatch, who was pivotal in drafting the committee's revisions to VAWA,[93] suggested that requiring gender-based animus would keep VAWA away from family relationships by preventing women from using the civil rights remedy to sue their husbands or other intimate partners for damages stemming from gender-motivated violence.

In language charged with emotion, Hatch described the revised remedy as focused on violent strangers without any familial feelings for their targets:

> We're not opening the federal doors to all gender-motivated crimes. Say you have a man who believes a woman is attractive. He feels encouraged by her and he's so motivated by that encouragement that he rips her clothes off and has sex with her against her will. Now let's say you have another man who grabs a woman off some lonely road and in the process of raping her says words like, "You're wearing a skirt! You're a woman! I hate women! I'm going to show you, you woman!" *Now, the first one's terrible. But the other's much worse. If a man rapes a woman while telling her he loves her, that's a far cry from saying he hates her. A lust factor does not spring from animus.*[94]

Hatch did not explicitly state that VAWA's civil rights remedy would not reach violence within marriage, and he never said that violence within the family is less serious than violence outside it. But marital rape might be the paradigmatic case of "'a man rap[ing] a woman while telling her he loves her,'" a less "'terrible'" offense that Hatch wanted to keep the federal government away from remediating.

VAWA's revised version also responded to the charge that the civil rights remedy constituted federal family law by including a seemingly superfluous reference to the domestic relations exception. It stated that the civil rights remedy did not "confer on the courts of the United States jurisdiction over any State law claim seeking the establishment of a divorce, alimony, equitable distribution of marital property, or child custody decree."[95] In addition, VAWA's revised version explicitly established concurrent jurisdiction in federal and state courts over all civil rights claims brought under the act, meaning that plaintiffs could choose whether to sue in federal or state court.[96]

Even these limitations, however, did not quell the argument that VAWA's civil rights remedy was a form of federal family law and unprecedented and improper for that reason. After the modified bill became law in September 1994,[97] defendants soon challenged the remedy's constitutionality with arguments drawing on the canonical assumption of family law localism.[98] The challenges enjoyed significant success in the lower courts.[99] For instance, the Fourth Circuit held that VAWA's civil rights remedy was unconstitutional in an en banc opinion that identified the remedy as a form of family law[100] and insisted at least seven times that the federal government could not and had never intervened in family law.[101]

The Supreme Court also relied on the canonical premise of family law's localism in striking down VAWA's civil rights remedy in *United States v. Morrison*. Indeed, this was perhaps unsurprising as Chief Justice Rehnquist wrote the Court's opinion holding the civil rights remedy unconstitutional. Rehnquist opted not to recuse himself from judging the remedy, although he had lobbied against the remedy before its enactment.[102]

The government argued in *Morrison* that VAWA's civil rights remedy fell within Congress's constitutional authority to regulate interstate commerce because gender-motivated violence has a substantial aggregate impact on interstate commerce.[103] Rehnquist's majority opinion in *Morrison* assumed and insisted upon family law's localism in rejecting this argument. *Morrison* never directly identified VAWA's civil rights remedy as a form of federal family law, presumably because of the difficulties involved in such an identification. But much like *Lopez*, which *Morrison* quoted at length,[104] the *Morrison* Court presumed that federal family law was unprecedented and categorically inappropriate and used that presumption to place limits on Congress's authority that operated far beyond family law.

Morrison contended that the government's interpretation of Congress's commerce power had to be incorrect because this interpretation would permit federal regulation of the family. The government's reasoning, *Morrison* explained, "will not limit Congress to regulating violence but may, as we suggested in *Lopez*, be applied equally as well to family law and other areas of traditional state regulation since the aggregate effect of marriage, divorce, and childrearing on the national economy is undoubtedly significant."[105] The *Morrison* Court emphasized that family law is self-evidently and categorically local, contending that "[t]he Constitution requires a distinction between what is truly national and what is truly local."[106]

The Presumption of Family Law Localism and the Defense of Marriage Act

The canonical narrative about family law localism also shaped debates over the 1996 Defense of Marriage Act (DOMA). DOMA's third section, which the Supreme Court struck down in 2013, defined "'marriage'" for purposes "of any Act of Congress, or of any ruling, regulation, or interpretation of the various administrative bureaus and agencies of the United States" as "a legal union between one man and one woman as husband and wife." It defined "'spouse'" as "a person of the opposite sex who is a husband or a wife."[107] Unlike VAWA's civil rights remedy, DOMA's third section clearly was an example of federal family law, regulating who would be recognized as married for purposes of federal law. Congress enacted DOMA's prohibition on federal recognition of same-sex marriages preemptively, before same-sex marriage was legal in any state. The Massachusetts Supreme Judicial Court held in 2003 that prohibiting same-sex marriage violated the Massachusetts constitution,[108] and in 2004 Massachusetts became the first state to allow same-sex couples to marry under state law.[109] As of this writing, same-sex couples may marry in seventeen states and the District of Columbia.[110]

DOMA's third section had practical import because many other federal laws and regulations are also forms of family law, creating significant federal rights and responsibilities that turn on whether a person is recognized as married in the eyes of the federal government. DOMA's supporters in Congress repeatedly noted (with some slight variations in the exact figures given) that the word "marriage" appeared over 800 times and the word "spouse" appeared over 3,100 times in federal statutes and regulations.[111] They cited federal regulation of marriage through Social Security, Medicare, immigration law, tax law, veterans' benefits, and insurance and pension benefits for federal employees.[112] DOMA supporters stressed the ubiquity of federal family law to contend, in Senator Dirk Kempthorne's words, that "[t]here is nothing shocking" in "establish[ing] the Federal definition of the terms 'marriage' and 'spouse'" as "[c]ombined, these terms appear in nearly 4,000 places in Federal statutes and regulations."[113] DOMA supporters also highlighted the volume of federal family law to emphasize how much was materially at stake in the DOMA debate. As Senator Don Nickles declared, "[w]e are talking about a lot of benefits."[114]

Whatever their political purposes, however, DOMA supporters were right to recognize the pervasiveness and significance of federal family law. Indeed, the nonpartisan United States General Accounting Office identified 1,049 federal laws that turned on marital status at the time of DOMA's enactment.[115] (The General Accounting Office found 1,138 federal laws turning on marital status when the office conducted the same survey as of December 31, 2003.)[116] These laws establish the multitude of benefits and burdens that are tied to marital status under federal law and in this way determine what it means to be married in the eyes of the federal government.

Nevertheless, a major argument that dissenting legislators and critics advanced against DOMA's third section while DOMA was being debated in Congress insisted on family law's inherent localism and condemned section three on the ground that the section constituted federal family law. Members of Congress declared that "marriage is very clearly an area which has been left to the States,"[117] that "the Federal Government does not have marriage laws,"[118] that "marriage and divorce has always been a State matter, never to be tampered with by Congress or by the Federal Government,"[119] that "the laws governing marriage are traditionally and constitutionally under the authority of the States,"[120] that "[o]ur country has just gone through 220 years without Federal law on marriages,"[121] that "[h]istorically, family law matters, including marriage, divorce, and child custody laws, have always been within the jurisdiction of State governments, not the Federal Government."[122] Congressional witnesses added that "[t]he definition and administration [of marriage] has in all previous times in our history been left to the States of this Nation"[123] and insisted that "[f]rom the very beginning, the courts of this country, the framers were clear: issues of marriage were issues for the States, the States to decide."[124]

DOMA's opponents took their descriptive account maintaining that federal family law was supposedly unprecedented as sufficient to establish their normative claim asserting that federal family law was inherently inappropriate. Here, as with VAWA, the thrust of the localism argument was that members of Congress should oppose DOMA's third section *whatever their views on the substantive merits of the section's policy objectives.* Senator Dianne Feinstein nicely encapsulated the argument: "*Whether one accepts the idea of same-sex marriages or not is not the central issue here.* The legislation before us will not prevent States from recognizing same-sex marriages. The issue before us is whether we want to inject the Federal Government into an area that has, for 200 years, been the exclusive purview of the States."[125] Senator J. Robert Kerrey similarly contended that DOMA "proposes to have the Federal Government intervene in matters previously reserved to the States. Conservative advocates of States rights should not brush aside this interference merely because they find a purpose which holds special appeal to them. And with this law the Federal Government will have taken the first—and if history is a good guide, probably not the last—step into the States' business of marriage and family law."[126]

After DOMA's enactment, the statute's opponents continued to attack section three on localist grounds. Some advocates, scholars, and litigants took this line of criticism to have significant force. More importantly, several courts—including ultimately the Supreme Court—invoked the canonical idea of family law localism in opinions finding DOMA's third section unconstitutional.

Localist arguments against DOMA's third section appeared in law reviews. A leading gay rights lawyer condemned section three on the ground that the section was an "unprecedented federal intrusion into the law of marriage" because, "[w]ithout exception, domestic relations law has been a matter of state, not federal, concern and control since the founding of the Republic."[127] Along with a coauthor, he contended that "because DOMA effectively nationalizes domestic relations law, shattering historical precedent, it is unconstitutional."[128] Law professors, in turn, explained "that our federalist system entrusts domestic relations, including marriage, to the states rather than to the federal government,"[129] reported that DOMA's third section was "where the federal government defined marriage for the first time in U.S. history,"[130] and insisted that section three represented "the first time in our history that Congress has interfered in an area where any regulation is quintessentially a matter of state, not federal, concern—namely, family law and domestic relations."[131]

Litigants also used localist arguments to challenge the constitutionality of DOMA's third section. For example, In re Kandu,[132] a 2004 case in United States Bankruptcy Court, considered the claims of Lee Kandu, an American woman who had married another American woman in Canada and sought to be recognized as married for purposes of filing a federal bankruptcy petition in the United States.[133] Kandu insisted that the power to regulate marriage "has traditionally been reserved to the States."[134] She contended that DOMA's third section violated the Tenth Amendment to the United States Constitution, which provides that "[t]he powers not delegated to the United States by the Constitution, nor prohibited by it to the States, are reserved to the States respectively, or to the people."[135] Kandu's theory was that DOMA "regulates domestic relations, specifically marriage [and] that is a power not granted to Congress in Article I of the U.S. Constitution and, therefore, reserved to the States by the Tenth Amendment."[136] The bankruptcy court rejected this argument, concluding that "[t]he Tenth Amendment is not implicated because the definition of marriage in DOMA is not binding on states and, therefore, there is no federal infringement on state sovereignty. States retain the power to decide for themselves the proper definition of the term marriage."[137]

However, several federal courts drew on arguments grounded in family law's supposed localism in striking down DOMA's third section. Localist arguments were not the only ones that these courts deployed in finding section three unconstitutional. But localist claims about family law were remarkably prevalent—because courts remained convinced by this canonical narrative, because courts sought to harness the narrative's power to convince others, or both.

For instance, the United States District Court for the District of Massachusetts struck down DOMA's third section in two cases that the court decided simultaneously in 2010.[138] The district court insisted in one opinion, *Gill v. Office of Personnel Management*, that "[t]here can be no dispute that the subject of domestic relations is the exclusive province of the states" and concluded that Congress had no "interest in a uniform definition of marriage for purposes of determining federal rights, benefits, and privileges."[139] The district court's other opinion, *Massachusetts v. United States Department of Health and Human Services,* quoted the Supreme Court's *Morrison* decision for the proposition that "'[t]he Constitution requires a distinction between what is truly national and what is truly local'"[140] and announced that family law "is often held out as the archetypal area of local concern."[141] *Massachusetts* presented family law's localism as a self-evident and essential part of federalism, concluding "that the authority to regulate marital status is a sovereign attribute of statehood."[142]

The United States District Court for the Northern District of California similarly called upon the localist narrative about family law in finding DOMA's third section unconstitutional.[143] *Golinski v. United States Office of Personnel Management* (2012) approvingly quoted the Supreme Court for the extreme claims that "'[t]he whole subject of the domestic relations . . . belongs to the laws of the States and not to the laws of the United States,'"[144] "that 'domestic relations' have 'long been regarded as a virtually exclusive province of the States,'"[145] and that "'[t]he State . . . has absolute right' to regulate marriage."[146]

That same year, the United States District Court for the District of Connecticut summoned up the idea of family law localism in striking down section three.[147] *Pedersen v. Office of Personnel Management* "[r]ecogniz[ed] that the subject of domestic relations is the exclusive province of the states, including the powers to establish eligibility requirements for marriage, as well as to issue determinations of marital status, which lie at the very core of such domestic relations law."[148] *Pedersen* also quoted the Supreme Court for the oft-heard proclamation that "'the whole subject of the domestic relations of husband and wife, parent and child, belongs to the laws of the States and not to the laws of the United States.'"[149]

The Supreme Court found DOMA's third section unconstitutional in *United States v. Windsor* (2013).[150] Edith Windsor, the plaintiff in that case, became engaged to Thea Spyer in 1967, decades before any state would recognize same-sex marriages.[151] In 2007, with Spyer's health worsening, the couple traveled from their home in New York to Ontario, Canada, to marry. Windsor and Spyer then returned to New York, and the state recognized their marriage as legally valid. Spyer died in 2009, leaving Windsor her entire estate. Federal law provides that a deceased spouse's estate can pass to the surviving spouse without the surviving spouse owing any federal estate taxes. However, DOMA's third section meant that Windsor and Spyer were not married for purposes of federal law. Windsor had to pay $363,053 in federal estate taxes. She sued, challenging section three's constitutionality.[152]

The Supreme Court's opinion striking down section three included a lengthy localist account of family law. For example, *Windsor* announced that "[b]y history and tradition the definition and regulation of marriage . . . has been treated as being within the authority and realm of the separate States."[153] It contended that "[s]tate laws defining and regulating marriage, of course, must respect the constitutional rights of persons; but, subject to those guarantees, regulation of domestic relations is an area that has long been regarded as a virtually exclusive province of the States."[154] *Windsor* highlighted the domestic relations exception to federal diversity jurisdiction, declaring that "[f]ederal courts will not hear divorce and custody cases even if they arise in diversity because of the virtually exclusive primacy of the States in the regulation of domestic relations."[155] And *Windsor* repeated the Court's declaration from *In re Burrus* that "'[t]he whole subject of the domestic relations of husband and wife, parent and child, belongs to the laws of the States and not to the laws of the United States.'"[156]

Indeed, much of the *Windsor* opinion discussed DOMA as a source of injury to states that recognize same-sex marriage, rather than simply focusing on how DOMA harmed individuals who wanted the federal government to recognize their same-sex marriages. The Court criticized the Congress that enacted DOMA for striving "to put a thumb on the scales and influence a state's decision as to how to shape its own marriage laws."[157] It described DOMA as "directed to a class of persons that the laws of New York, and of 11 other States, have sought to protect"[158] and—more sharply—as "seek[ing] to injure the very class New York seeks to protect."[159] *Windsor* declared that New York "State's decision to give this class of persons the right to marry conferred upon them a dignity and status of immense import. When the State used its historic and essential authority to define the marital relation in this way, its role and its power in making the decision enhanced the recognition, dignity, and protection of the class in their own community. DOMA, because of its reach and extent, departs from this history and tradition of reliance on state law to define marriage."[160]

Windsor highlights the persistent strength of localist claims in family law. The Court used the narrative about family law localism to help frame its opinion, even in a case involving a statutory provision that had such an enormous practical impact because more than a thousand federal laws establish legal rights and responsibilities that turn on a person's marital status in the eyes of the federal government.

Ultimately, the *Windsor* Court contended that it was "unnecessary to decide whether [DOMA's] federal intrusion on state power is a violation of the Constitution because it disrupts the federal balance."[161] Instead, *Windsor* found DOMA's third section unconstitutional under the Fifth Amendment, concluding that section three "violates basic due process and equal protection principles applicable to the Federal Government."[162] The Court explained that "DOMA instructs all federal officials, and indeed all persons with whom same-sex couples interact, including their own children, that their marriage is less worthy than the marriages of others. The federal statute is invalid, for no legitimate purpose overcomes the purpose and effect to disparage and to injure those whom the State, by its marriage laws, sought to protect in personhood and dignity. By seeking to displace this protection and treating those persons as living in marriages less respected than others, the federal statute is in violation of the Fifth Amendment."[163]

Presumably, one reason that the Court did not find section three unconstitutional on federalism grounds is that striking down section three on the theory that regulating marriage is for the states alone would seem to call into question the constitutionality of the thousand-plus examples of federal family law that DOMA impacted in providing federal definitions of the terms marriage and spouse.[164] Despite all the Court's invocations of family law localism, *Windsor* took it to be "established that Congress, in enacting discrete statutes, can make determinations that bear on marital rights and privileges."[165] Indeed, the *Windsor* Court itself cited many examples of federal family law running through tax law, immigration law, Social Security law, housing law, criminal law, copyright law, veterans' benefits law, healthcare law, bankruptcy law, student financial aid law, ethics law, and more.[166] *Windsor* also observed that DOMA was not the only federal statute that created a situation in which a couple could be married for state law purposes and not for federal purposes or vice versa, reporting that "these discrete examples establish the constitutionality of limited federal laws that regulate the meaning of marriage in order to further federal policy."[167]

In sum, *Windsor* recounted and celebrated the canonical narrative about family law localism, while simultaneously protecting an extensive body of federal family law. This tension within *Windsor* nicely illustrates how legal authorities can apply the family law localism narrative inconsistently. If the Court unfailingly adhered to the localist account of family law, striking down any example of federal family law that it could, then the description of family law as local would be significantly more accurate. But *Windsor* expressed no interest in destabilizing the vast body of federal family law that DOMA's third section touched, never suggesting that all the federal statutes, regulations, and decisions that establish who counts as married in the eyes of the federal government or that determine the federal rights and responsibilities tied to marriage are troubling from the perspective of either constitutional law or public policy. Nonetheless, the *Windsor* Court repeatedly returned to the family law localism narrative. The Court suggested that the localist account of family law was a key guide to understanding the field, even in a case where the reach, importance, and extent of federal family law were essentially undeniable.

Federal Family Law in the Courts and Congress

As we have seen, many courts, judges, legislators, litigants, advocates, and scholars who agree on little else continue to invoke the contention that family law is and should be local, relying on that canonical idea to describe family law's guiding principles and to make arguments and judgments about family law's future course. They frequently assert that federal family law is unprecedented and inappropriate, regardless of the specific substantive merits of the particular law at issue.

Yet despite such declarations, state family law coexists with extensive and far-reaching federal family law. Federal legislators and judges who announce family law's inherent localism have simultaneously created a robust body of federal family law. Of course, it is hardly unusual for lawmakers and jurists to say and even believe one thing, while doing another. The steady and confident repetition of the idea that family law is local may help decisionmakers overlook or not perceive the tensions between their words and their deeds. Moreover, legal authorities committed to the premise that family law belongs to the states may assume without further analysis that what the federal government is doing simply cannot be family law.

Nonetheless, myriad federal statutes, regulations, and judicial decisions govern the creation and dissolution of legally recognized family relationships and/or determine the legal rights and responsibilities that are tied to family status. These statutes, regulations, and decisions are forms of family law, whatever other legal categories they fall into as well. Just as state family law decides for purposes of state law who counts as a legal family member, how legalized family relationships are begun and ended, and what turns on legal recognition as a family member, federal family law decides these issues for purposes of federal law.

I make these observations for positive and descriptive reasons, rather than for normative or prescriptive ones. I am not arguing that federal family law is necessarily more, or less, desirable than state family law— that the federal government should aggressively intervene to preempt state law or that the federal government should defer to state law to the extent possible. Indeed, I do not believe that the desirability of federal family law can be judged categorically, rather than case by case.

My point instead is that federal family law is already far-reaching and well established. In addition, federal family law is sometimes unavoidable given the demands of the federal Constitution and the existence of exclusive federal jurisdiction. To be sure, family law, like many legal arenas, has never been under predominantly federal control. The weight and persistence of certain forms of state regulation are undeniable. However, the localist story about family law simply misdescribes the field, masking the scope and even the existence of federal family law.

Federal family law is much too voluminous to describe fully in one chapter. But we can review some of the most interesting and important examples to begin mapping what the localist narrative about family law obscures.

Most of this survey will focus on congressional statutes and federal regulations implementing those statutes. Lawmakers exercise more control over the subject matter of their work than courts do. Elected legislators also enjoy more of a democratic mandate than appointed judges. However, we can briefly review some of the federal family law that the United States Supreme Court has produced before we consider some of the family law within federal legislation and regulation.

The Supreme Court's Federal Family Law

While the Supreme Court has frequently trumpeted its commitment to remaining uninvolved in family law, the Court regularly creates and administers family law—sometimes in the very same opinions declaring family law's inherent localism and "the Court's duty to refrain from interfering with state answers to domestic relations questions."[168]

Constitutional Law. As an initial matter, family law is a pervasive and significant part of the Court's constitutional jurisprudence interpreting due process, equal protection, and other constitutional principles. Of course, the existence of family law within federal constitutional law should be unsurprising. Although canonical stories premised on family law's exceptionalism describe family law as distinctly set off from other legal fields, the federal Constitution applies to family law just as it applies to any other site of government activity. This is one reason why federal family law is not just extensive, it is unavoidable.

It is worth noting, however, some of the Supreme Court's constitutional decisions that create both constitutional law and family law at the same time. The Court's constitutional jurisprudence has established uniform family law rules for the nation with striking frequency. Indeed, the Court's constitutional case law has transformed family law.

Consider some of the Supreme Court's constitutional decisions regulating the legal creation and dissolution of marriage. The Court has recognized a fundamental right to marry that precludes many restrictions on marriage formation. For instance, *Loving v. Virginia* (1967) outlawed prohibitions on interracial marriage at a time when sixteen states still had such prohibitions.[169] *Zablocki v. Redhail* (1978) prohibited states from requiring people subject to child support orders to obtain judicial approval before marrying.[170] *Turner v. Safley* (1987) struck down a state prison regulation that prevented many prisoners from marrying.[171]

The Court has also reshaped divorce law. *Boddie v. Connecticut* (1971) provided that states cannot deny people access to divorce "solely because of inability to pay" court fees and costs.[172] Supreme Court decisions on alimony and child support awards at divorce have sparked tremendous change. *Orr v. Orr* (1979) established that laws regulating the provision of alimony must apply equally to husbands and wives.[173] *Stanton v. Stanton* (1975) held that laws governing the provision of child support cannot set different ages of majority for male and female children.[174] These decisions pushed states to rewrite virtually all their family law in language that is facially sex-neutral, so that family law codes that once spoke ubiquitously of husbands and wives, fathers and mothers, and sons and daughters, now govern "spouses," "parents," and "children."

In addition to regulating marriage formation and dissolution, the Court's constitutional decisions determine some of the rights that are, and are not, associated with marriage. For example, the Court has held that a husband has no right to notice of his wife's decision to have an abortion, much less the right to override that decision.[175] The Court has decided that a married couple has the right to use contraception without being subject to criminal prosecution.[176]

The Court's constitutional judgments similarly regulate how legally recognized relationships between parents and children are created and dissolved. The Court's case law provides that an illegitimate child must have more than one year in which to establish a legal relationship with her biological father.[177] The Court has held that a biological father has no constitutional right to create a legally recognized relationship with his child if the child is born to another man's wife.[178] The Court has determined that parental rights may be involuntarily terminated only if the parent is proven unfit by at least clear and convincing evidence[179] and that indigent parents in termination proceedings do not always have a right to appointed legal counsel.[180]

The Court's constitutional decisions also regulate the rights and responsibilities that parents and children have when their relationship is legally recognized. As Chapter 4 will discuss in more detail, these decisions constitutionalize a robust and far-reaching vision of parental prerogatives that grants parents enormous power "to direct the upbringing and education of children under their control."[181] For instance, the Court's decisions establish that a parent may place his child in private rather than public school[182] or remove his child from school entirely in some circumstances.[183] The Court's case law gives parents substantial control over the access that third parties, including grandparents, have to a child.[184] The Court has held that a parent's right to the custody of his child is not diminished by the parent's interracial marriage.[185] The Court's jurisprudence regulates a parent's authority to participate in his daughter's decision to have an abortion, determining that parental consent may be required as long as the daughter has the option of seeking judicial authorization instead.[186] At the same time, the Court has held that a child may be subjected to child labor restrictions against his parent's wishes.[187]

Along the same lines, the Court has regulated rights tied to family relationships beyond marriage and parenthood. It held that a housing ordinance may not deny an extended family the right to live together.[188]

Family law similarly runs through the Court's constitutional jurisprudence on personal jurisdiction, which determines rights that family members have and governs how family members may exercise those rights. The Supreme Court's "divisible divorce" doctrine separates judicial control over marital status from judicial control over the legal incidents of divorce, such as property division, alimony, child support, and child custody. The doctrine provides that a spouse who would like to be granted a divorce that will be entitled to full faith and credit in other states must seek the divorce in a state where at least one spouse is domiciled, meaning that the spouse is physically present in the state and intends to remain there. The state court dissolving the marriage need not have personal jurisdiction over the defendant spouse.[189]

This means that it is more difficult for a state to effectively restrict the grounds for divorce. A married person living in a state with laws limiting the availability of divorce may move by herself to a state that does not attempt to constrain the grounds for divorce and dissolve her marriage there in a way that will be recognized throughout the United States. However, a spouse who would like a court judgment that is entitled to full faith and credit in other states on the legal incidents of divorce must litigate in a court with personal jurisdiction over both spouses.[190]

Moreover, the Court's constitutional decisions shape the strategies that a current or former spouse may employ in maneuvering to give her preferred state court personal jurisdiction over both spouses. *Burnham v. Superior Court* (1990) held that a wife living in California, who was married to a man living in New Jersey and had sued him for divorce in California state court, could ensure that California courts would have personal jurisdiction over both spouses by serving her husband with process while he was temporarily visiting California.[191] (This is colloquially known as "tag jurisdiction" because the wife's process server successfully "tagged" the husband while he was in the wife's state.)

In *Kulko v. Superior Court* (1978), a divorced wife and mother who lived with her two children in California had gone to California state court to seek increased child support payments from her former husband, a New York resident who had never visited his children in California.[192] Rather than pay, the former husband challenged the California court's jurisdiction to adjudicate the claim for increased support and litigated the issue to the United States Supreme Court.[193] The Supreme Court sided with the father, holding that California courts did not have personal jurisdiction over him. In reaching this judgment about jurisdiction, the Court insisted that the children's father lacked "'minimum contacts'" with California, although his children lived there,[194] and concluded that requiring the father to bear "the substantial financial burden and personal strain of litigating a child-support suit in a forum 3,000 miles away" would contravene "basic considerations of fairness."[195] Deciding that the father in New York should not have to travel to California in order to resist paying more child support meant that the mother in California would have to litigate across the country in the New York courts in order to seek more support for her children. The Supreme Court's ruling made it more difficult for custodial parents to have courts adjudicate child support obligations involving noncustodial parents living in other states.

Federal Common Law. The Supreme Court has also created significant family law as a matter of federal common law. Here, the Court has reached beyond its basic responsibilities to interpret the Constitution and federal statutes. The Court's jurisprudence on federal common law holds that the Court itself should create federal rules when no federal constitutional provision, statute, or treaty directly decides a case, if federal rules are needed to protect federal interests against conflicting state interests.[196] The Court has repeatedly created federal common law to govern family rights and responsibilities, recognizing and safeguarding federal interests in family law.

Some of the Court's federal common law decisions create family law governing current or former servicemembers and their relatives. For instance, the Court has held that federal law preempts state community property law on the distribution of proceeds from an army insurance policy,[197] that federal law precludes state courts from dividing military nondisability retirement pay pursuant to state community property laws,[198] and that federal law permitting a servicemember to change the beneficiary of his life insurance policy trumps a state divorce decree requiring the servicemember to name the children from his first marriage as beneficiaries.[199]

Some of the Court's federal common law decisions create family law governing people with no connection to military service. For example, the Court has held that federal law preempts state community property law on survivorship rights to federal bonds purchased with community property,[200] that federal law governs whether a federal bondholder has defrauded his wife under state property law,[201] and that federal law precludes a state court from treating as community property a spouse's expectancy interest in receiving benefits under the Railroad Retirement Act.[202]

Federal Evidentiary Privileges. In addition, the Supreme Court's jurisprudence on federal evidentiary privileges is replete with family law, establishing which legal privileges are and are not associated with marriage. Congress has authorized the federal courts to interpret, enforce, and alter common law evidentiary privileges,[203] and the Supreme Court has emphasized its family law goals in carrying out this responsibility. For example, the Court's case law grants a privilege against adverse spousal testimony to people whose spouses are defendants in federal criminal prosecutions. This means that a witness spouse may choose to testify in federal court on behalf of,[204] or against her defendant spouse, but federal courts cannot compel a witness spouse to testify against her defendant spouse if the witness spouse does not want to do so.[205] The Court explained its decision to structure the adverse spousal testimonial privilege this way by contending that leaving the decision about whether to testify to the witness spouse "furthers the important public interest in marital harmony without unduly burdening legitimate law enforcement needs."[206]

The "confidential marital communications" privilege in federal criminal prosecutions, which is meant to safeguard the sanctity of marital relationships, is another site where the Court has configured federal evidence law to establish legal rights and obligations tied to marriage that promote the Court's family law policy goals. This privilege means that even if a witness spouse would like to testify against her defendant spouse, the witness spouse may only testify about "evidence of criminal acts and of communications made in the presence of third persons" and may not testify about "information privately disclosed between husband and wife in the confidence of the marital relationship."[207]

Federal Family Law in Statutes and Regulations

If the Supreme Court is enmeshed in federal family law, congressional and administrative involvement is even more extensive. Federal legislators and regulators have promulgated a wide range of family law governing the creation and dissolution of legally recognized family relationships and/or determining legal rights and responsibilities associated with family status. These lawmakers have produced a far-reaching body of federal family law.

Family Law Within Areas of Special or Exclusive Federal Control

First, federal legislators and regulators have created considerable family law in contexts where the federal government governs exclusively or has special regulatory authority, such as military law, immigration law, citizenship law, international relations law, Native American law, bankruptcy law, intellectual property law, and benefits law for federal employees and veterans. To some degree, federal family law is simply unavoidable in these contexts, suggesting again the implausibility of claims about family law's inherent localism. But federal legislators and regulators have gone far beyond any necessary minimum of regulation, producing federal family law that often diverges from state law to express and enforce the federal government's own family law policies.

Military Law. Consider a few examples from the federal family law governing the military, which regulates servicemembers and their families in ways that frequently differ from state law. Military law criminalizes adultery,[208] and military courts actively and "routinely" enforce that prohibition.[209] This federal criminalization of adultery constitutes an important legal burden tied to marital status. Remarkably, it persists in an era when states have all but ceased to prosecute adultery.[210] Indeed, state adultery prosecutions faded into obscurity decades before the Supreme Court's decision in *Lawrence v. Texas* (2003),[211] which struck down a state law criminalizing same-sex sodomy.[212] *Lawrence* cast at least some doubt on the constitutionality of civilian criminalization of adultery by recognizing "an emerging awareness that liberty gives substantial protection to adult persons in deciding how to conduct their private lives in matters pertaining to sex."[213]

Military law also regulates legal rights tied to parenthood. For instance, military regulations grant servicewomen who are the mothers of newborns the right to avoid deployment for at least four months after their child's birth, while giving servicemen who are new biological fathers no right to avoid deployment.[214] The explicit sex-specificity of these military regulations contrasts starkly with the overwhelming trend in state family law toward policies written in sex-neutral language.

Immigration Law. Federal immigration law is replete with family law and family law policy choices. This body of law prioritizes family unification, especially for spouses, parents, and children. Sometimes this privileging of family ties takes the form of special exceptions that depend on family status. For example, immigration law permits illegal immigrants who have been in the United States for at least ten continuous years, have maintained a "good moral character," and have not been convicted of specified crimes to avoid deportation and become lawfully admitted for permanent residence if deportation "would result in exceptional and extremely unusual hardship to the alien's spouse, parent, or child, who is a citizen of the United States or an alien lawfully admitted for permanent residence."[215]

More systematically, federal immigration law makes it much easier for the " 'immediate relatives' " of United States citizens to legally immigrate and exempts these relatives from numerical limitations on immigration.[216] In 2011, 42.7% of the people (453,158 out of 1,062,040) who obtained legal permanent resident status were citizens' immediate relatives.[217]

Classification as an immediate relative is accordingly an enormously important legal benefit, and federal law defines that family law category in ways that build on, but differ from, state law. For instance, the term immediate relatives generally includes the children, spouses, and parents of citizens, but immigration law does not count parents as immediate relatives of a citizen child until the child turns twenty-one.[218] In other words, federal immigration law chooses to ease the immigration of children who would like to live in the United States with their citizen parents and opts not to ease the immigration of parents who would like to live in the United States with their citizen children, until the citizen children are already adults themselves. Courts explain that "[a] minor child who is fortuitously born here due to his parents' decision to reside in this country, has not exercised a deliberate decision to make this country his home, and Congress did not give such a child the ability to confer immigration benefits on his parents."[219]

Immigration law also does not recognize so-called sham marriages, meaning marriages "entered into for the purpose of evading the immigration laws."[220] These can be marriages in which both parties agreed to wed only for immigration purposes or marriages in which one party deceived the other into matrimony in order to obtain immigration benefits. Either way, the marriages are legal unions under state law, with binding effect until the parties divorce or have their marriage annulled.[221] But the marriages are invalid within federal immigration law and subject to federal immigration and criminal penalties. A noncitizen who entered or attempted to enter a sham marriage will never be able to legally immigrate to the United States[222] and is deportable if in the United States.[223] Any person, citizen or noncitizen, who knowingly enters a sham marriage is subject to up to five years in prison, up to a $250,000 fine, or both.[224]

The rights tied to marriage under federal immigration law and the penalties for sham marriages require federal regulators and judges to determine what constitutes a bona fide marriage. Federal regulations listing evidence that can establish whether a couple married for the purpose of evading immigration laws do not focus simply on direct evidence of the parties' intent. Instead, these regulations make judgments about which marital choices suggest the legitimacy of a marital relationship, stating that immigration officials will consider among other factors whether the couple owns property jointly, leases a home together, commingles financial resources, and/or has children together.[225] This policy functions to privilege immigration claims from married couples who have organized their relationships in ways that federal regulators anticipate and perhaps implicitly approve, while disadvantaging couples who have chosen for cultural, economic, ideological, personal, or other reasons to structure their relationships differently—even if those couples married for reasons unrelated to immigration law.

The *Adjudicator's Field Manual* for United States Citizenship and Immigration Services similarly reflects federal administrative assumptions that marriages between certain types of people are suspicious. The manual's list of "[s]ome indications that a marriage may have been contracted solely for immigration benefits" includes among other factors: "Large disparity of age"; "Vast difference in cultural and ethnic background"; and "Beneficiary is a friend of the family." As the manual notes, "[w]hether an alleged marriage is valid for purposes of immigration is a question of Federal law, not of State law."[226]

Judgments about appropriate marital behavior also shape federal criminal regulation of immigration. A person is less likely to be prosecuted for, and convicted of, marriage fraud if his marriage conformed to the expectations of federal prosecutors and judges. Federal courts adjudicating whether a person committed marriage fraud consider such factors as whether the spouses consummated their marriage,[227] whether they were sexually faithful,[228] whether they had a long courtship before marrying,[229] whether they were "'in love'" when they married,[230] whether they performed unpaid domestic labor for each other,[231] whether they issued wedding invitations, whether they had a formal wedding reception, whether they went on a honeymoon, and whether the man gave the woman an engagement ring.[232] Many married couples do conform to these expectations, but there are reasons besides immigration fraud why a couple might not. For instance, a couple might be unable to afford an engagement ring, wedding reception, or honeymoon trip; might want to resist the materialism of the wedding industry (which I call the matrimonial-industrial complex); might think a long courtship is unnecessary or unexciting; and might believe that shared marital love is less important than other compatibilities. Nonetheless, this case law reflects and enforces what federal judges and prosecutors take to be reliable indicia of bona fide marital relationships.

In addition to evaluating the legitimacy of existing marriages, federal immigration law simultaneously structures the creation of marital relationships, facilitating some marriages and making others harder to enter. Immigration law provides that a citizen may sponsor a noncitizen for a so-called "fiancé visa," which permits the noncitizen to stay in the United States for up to ninety days in order to marry the citizen.[233] Fiancé visas are available only where the couple has met in person within two years of the visa application and has "a bona fide intention to marry,"[234] which federal consular officials must assess. Federal law requires citizens to disclose criminal convictions on their fiancé visa applications,[235] limits the frequency with which a citizen may apply for a fiancé visa, and restricts the total number of fiancé visa applications that one citizen may submit.[236]

Citizenship Law. Federal citizenship law determines legal rights and responsibilities tied to the parent-child relationship. This body of law establishes which children born outside the United States will be granted American citizenship because of their status as the children of citizens. Congress is unwilling to extend that privilege to all children of citizens and sometimes prefers children with citizen mothers over children with citizen fathers.

Consider the citizenship law regulating children born abroad to one citizen parent, which favors children with an unmarried citizen mother, then children with a married citizen parent, and then children with an unmarried citizen father. The child of an unmarried citizen mother is a citizen at birth so long as the child's mother has previously spent one continuous year in the United States or its possessions.[237] The child of a married citizen parent is a citizen at birth so long as the citizen parent previously spent a total of at least five years in the United States or its possessions, at least two years of which were after the citizen parent turned fourteen.[238]

Congress has made it much more difficult for children born abroad to unmarried citizen fathers to establish their American citizenship. A child in this situation must establish her biological relationship with her father "by clear and convincing evidence," prove that her father agreed in writing to support her financially until the age of eighteen, and demonstrate that her legal relationship with her father was established before she reached age eighteen, either because she was legally legitimated, her father acknowledged paternity in writing under oath, or a competent court adjudicated paternity. The unmarried citizen father must also have spent a total of at least five years in the United States or its possessions before the child's birth, at least two years of which were after the citizen father turned fourteen.[239] These federal requirements mean that many children born abroad to unmarried citizen fathers are denied United States citizenship, even though it is clear that they are the biological children of citizens.

Critics of citizenship law's sex-based distinctions between the children of unmarried citizen mothers and the children of unmarried citizen fathers have powerfully argued that the distinctions reflect Congress's assumption that unmarried mothers of children born abroad will raise and care for their children, while unmarried fathers of children born abroad will be much less involved in their children's lives or even entirely absent.[240] Certainly, current citizenship law makes it less likely that unmarried citizen fathers will have close relationships with their children born abroad, by making it harder for these children to become citizens and live in the United States.

Nevertheless, the Supreme Court in *Nguyen v. Immigration and Naturalization Service* (2001) held that Congress could constitutionally apply legitimation requirements to the children of unmarried citizen fathers that do not apply to the children of unmarried citizen mothers.[241] A more recent Court case, *Flores-Villar v. United States* (2011), considered the constitutionality of placing more onerous parental residency requirements on the children of unmarried citizen fathers compared to the children of unmarried citizen mothers. The Court divided evenly on the question and issued no opinion, automatically affirming the lower court decision that had upheld this sex-based differential.[242]

International Relations Law. Family law runs through federal international relations law as well. For instance, Congress has implemented international conventions focusing on family law. The Intercountry Adoption Act (IAA), which implements the Convention on Protection of Children and Co-operation in Respect of Intercountry Adoption, governs international adoptions involving United States residents and other countries that are parties to the convention.[243] The IAA empowers the Secretary of State to regulate these international adoptions,[244] requires federal accreditation or approval before an agency or person in the United States may offer or provide international adoption services,[245] and preempts all inconsistent state law.[246] The International Child Abduction Remedies Act (ICARA), which implements the Convention on the Civil Aspects of International Child Abduction, is designed to stop people from obtaining custody of children by wrongfully removing the children to another country or wrongfully retaining the children in another country.[247] The ICARA establishes procedures for returning a child who "has been wrongfully removed or retained" back to the child's country of "habitual residence."[248]

Native American Law. Family law is also an important part of federal Native American law. The Indian Child Welfare Act[249] creates a unique set of rules to govern the termination of parental rights over Native

American children and the adoption of Native American children, which prioritize keeping Native American children with Native American parents. For instance, the act provides that a parent voluntarily terminating his rights to a Native American child must consent to the termination in writing and before a judge who certifies that the parent understands the consequences of his consent.[250] The parent may withdraw his consent to the termination within two years if the consent was obtained through fraud or duress.[251] More strikingly, the act provides that "[i]n any adoptive placement of an Indian child under State law, a preference shall be given, in the absence of good cause to the contrary, to a placement with (1) a member of the child's extended family; (2) other members of the Indian child's tribe; or (3) other Indian families."[252] These federal requirements override state family law, and state courts must comply with them. As the Supreme Court has observed, the Indian Child Welfare Act "establishes federal standards that govern state-court child custody proceedings involving Indian children."[253]

Bankruptcy Law. Family law appears in federal bankruptcy law. The bankruptcy code privileges spouses, former spouses, and children as creditors based on their family status and enforces special responsibilities on debtors that turn on marriage and parenthood. Bankruptcy law provides that a bankrupt debtor cannot discharge "a domestic support obligation,"[254] a category that federal law defines to include alimony, maintenance, or support to a spouse, former spouse, child, or child's parent.[255] The bankruptcy code also prevents debtors from discharging any other debt "to a spouse, former spouse, or child of the debtor . . . that is incurred by the debtor in the course of a divorce or separation or in connection with a separation agreement, divorce decree or other order of a court of record, or a determination made in accordance with State or territorial law by a governmental unit."[256] Moreover, bankruptcy law provides that all of the debtor's property is available to satisfy nondischargeable domestic support obligations, including property that bankruptcy law otherwise exempts from the reach of creditors.[257]

Intellectual Property Law. Family law is also evident in federal intellectual property law. Federal copyright law defines who falls within the terms " 'children,' " " 'widow,' " and " 'widower' " for purposes of copyright law[258] and establishes legal rights over a copyright that an author's widow or widower, surviving children, and surviving grandchildren have upon the author's death. These federally created rights for surviving spouses, children, and grandchildren can be extremely valuable, and they take precedence over the deceased author's will and state law governing inheritance.[259]

Benefits for Federal Employees. Federal law governing benefits for federal employees similarly creates important rights tied to family status. The Federal Employees Health Benefits program provides health insurance[260] and the Federal Employees Group Life Insurance program provides life insurance[261] to the spouses and some unmarried dependent children of federal employees. The Federal Employees Compensation Act makes surviving spouses, parents, minor or dependent unmarried siblings, minor or dependent unmarried children, and minor or dependent grandchildren eligible for compensation when a federal employee is killed while performing his job.[262] The Foreign Service Act provides that a former spouse of a foreign service employee is entitled to a pro rata share, up to half, of the employee's foreign service retirement benefits if the couple was married for at least ten years during the employee's creditable service and the employee's former spouse did not remarry before age sixty.[263]

Veterans' Benefits. Veterans' benefits are also enmeshed in family law. Veterans' benefits law both establishes significant rights that depend on family status and determines who counts as a family member in ways that sometimes diverge from state law. A veteran's surviving spouse, child, or parent is entitled to monthly dependency and indemnity compensation payments if the veteran's death was service-connected,[264] and a veteran's surviving spouse or child is entitled to pension payments if the veteran's death was not service-connected.[265] Some people are surviving spouses for purposes of veterans' benefits law, even though they are not surviving spouses for purposes of state law. If a person married a veteran unaware that there was a legal impediment that made the marriage invalid under state law and then lived with the veteran for at least a year immediately before the veteran's death or lived with the veteran for any period of time if the couple had a child together, that person counts as a surviving spouse under federal veterans' benefits law, so long as there is not another surviving spouse seeking and entitled to benefits who is the veteran's legal widow or widower under state law.[266]

Family Law Within the Federal Administrative and Regulatory State

In addition to the federal family law within areas of special or exclusive federal control, federal family law pervades the federal administrative and regulatory state. Family law is entwined into federal regulation of tax, Social Security, employment, labor, housing, and criminal law. Here again, federal legislators and regulators have produced a plethora of federal family law that expresses and enforces the federal government's own family law policies.

Tax Law. Let's begin with the family law that runs through the federal tax system. Federal tax law regulates the creation and dissolution of legally recognized family relationships in ways that build on, but differ from, state law in order to further Congress's own goals and concerns. For instance, a person widowed during the year is no longer married for purposes of state law, but is still married for the rest of the taxable year for purposes of federal tax law.[267] A person married to a nonresident alien is married for purposes of state law, but not married for purposes of federal tax law.[268] A person who divorces at the end of one year to reduce his tax liability and then promptly remarries the same spouse in the new year may be briefly single for purposes of state law, but continuously married for purposes of federal tax law.[269]

Moreover, the federal tax code creates a tremendous number of legal advantages and disadvantages that turn on family status. For example, parents are entitled to federal tax deductions for their dependent children,[270] and federal tax law provides up to $10,000 in tax credit to an adopting parent with an adjusted gross income of $150,000 or less.[271]

Federal tax provisions that depend on marital status are even more common. A 1996 study from the United States General Accounting Office found fifty-nine federal income tax provisions in which tax liability varied according to the taxpayer's marital status, including provisions on the income tax rate, earned income tax credit, standard deduction, home mortgage interest tax deduction, taxation of Social Security benefits, and limitations on capital losses.[272]

Judges, legislators, and commentators often discuss the myriad benefits and burdens that the federal tax code ties to marriage by using the terms "marriage penalties" and "marriage bonuses." A marriage penalty exists when a married couple pays more in taxes than the couple would pay if unmarried. A marriage bonus exists when a married couple pays less in taxes than the couple would pay if unmarried.

The federal income tax code makes marriage penalties and bonuses pervasive and distributes these burdens and rewards in ways that systematically favor particular marital arrangements. In general, a married couple is more likely to pay a federal marriage penalty the more equal the spouses' incomes and is more likely to receive a federal marriage bonus the more disparate the spouses' incomes.[273] The Congressional Budget Office concluded that approximately 42% of married couples paid federal marriage penalties in 1996, while approximately 51% of married couples received federal marriage bonuses.[274] The Urban Institute reported that 50.7% of unmarried cohabitants would have owed more in 2003 federal income taxes if they married and 42.0% would have owed less.[275]

Studies have found that federal income tax law impacts the rate[276] and timing[277] of marriage and the rate of divorce.[278] An especially tax-sensitive couple, Joan and James Druker, unsuccessfully challenged the constitutionality of federal marriage penalties in 1982 and confirmed to the court that they had divorced to avoid such penalties in their federal taxes.[279] Other constitutional challenges to marriage penalties in the federal income tax code have been similarly unavailing.[280]

A perhaps more enterprising couple, Angela and David Boyter, attempted to evade federal marriage penalties by divorcing at the end of 1975 and remarrying at the start of 1976 and then divorcing again at the end of 1976 and remarrying at the start of 1977. After the Internal Revenue Service refused to accept the two short-lived divorces as valid for purposes of federal tax law, the Boyters divorced for a third time in 1977 and lived together without remarrying to avoid marriage penalties in their federal taxes.[281] The Boyters—whose flurry of tax-motivated divorces attracted widespread notice on television, radio, and "in every newspaper from the Wall Street Journal to the National Enquirer"[282]— even published "a fact sheet," aptly titled "'Divorce for Fun and Profit.'"[283] Angela Boyter testified before Congress in 1980 that she and her former husband had already saved almost $15,000 in taxes by divorcing and would have paid a lifetime marriage penalty of over $130,000 if they had stayed married. She concluded that "such a price is too high to pay for legal marital bliss."[284]

Sharon Mallory, whose plight attracted less attention than the Boyters' escapades, testified before Congress in 1998 that she and her boyfriend,

Darryl Pierce, wanted to marry, but had not done so because of federal marriage penalties. Mallory reported that if the couple married their annual federal income tax liability would increase by $3,700. She explained that "[t]o us, this is real money. It's food on our table and clothes on our backs. For Darryl and me, the marriage penalty was large enough that we were forced to put off our marriage."[285]

Social Security Law. The federal Social Security program abounds with family law. This program is best known for providing old-age insurance benefits to qualified workers based on their histories of paid employment.[286] But Social Security also provides child's insurance benefits to the dependent minor children of qualified workers[287] and spousal insurance benefits to the current, divorced, and surviving spouses of qualified workers.[288]

Child's and spousal benefits turn solely on the recipient's family relationship with the "primary" beneficiary and are calculated based on the payments that the primary beneficiary is entitled to collect. A child with a living qualifying parent can receive a child's insurance benefit that is 50% as large as the payment the qualifying parent receives, and a child with a deceased qualifying parent can receive a child's insurance benefit that is 75% as large as the payment that the qualifying parent would have received.[289] A current or divorced spouse can receive a spousal benefit that is up to 50% as large as the payment the primary beneficiary receives,[290] and a surviving spouse can receive a spousal benefit that is up to 100% as large as the payment that the primary beneficiary would have received.[291] Current, divorced, and surviving spouses eligible to receive Social Security benefits based on their past employment must forgo such payments in order to collect spousal benefits based on their marital relationship.[292]

These family-based benefits are central to the Social Security program. Indeed, only 47.5% of the women aged sixty-two or older who received Social Security in 2011 collected benefits based on their own histories of paid employment. Most (52.5%) collected as a wife, widow, or mother, either because their own working histories did not entitle them to Social Security at all (25.2%) or because they were entitled to more Social Security benefits as a family member than they would have been able to claim based on their working histories (27.3%).[293]

In addition to creating important legal benefits attached to family status, the Social Security system regulates the creation and dissolution of legally recognized family relationships in ways that differ in important respects from state law. Some people are family members for purposes of state law, but not for purposes of federal Social Security law. For instance, the Social Security program recognizes the spouse of a qualified worker only if (with a few exceptions) the spouse has been married to the qualified worker for at least one year under state law or has a child with the qualified worker.[294] The Social Security program recognizes a divorced spouse only if she was married to the qualified worker for at least ten years under state law[295] and (with a few exceptions) has not remarried.[296] The Social Security program recognizes a surviving spouse only if (with a few exceptions) she was married to the qualified worker for at least nine months under state law or had a child with the qualified worker[297] and she has not remarried before the age of sixty.[298] The Social Security program recognizes the relationship between a qualified worker and his dependent minor child only if the child is unmarried.[299]

Conversely, some people are family members under Social Security law, but not under state law. For example, the Social Security system treats an applicant as the spouse or surviving spouse of a qualified worker if the applicant went through a marriage ceremony with the worker in good faith, without knowing about a legal impediment that made the marriage invalid under state law, and continued to live with the qualified worker until the worker's death or until the applicant filed to collect Social Security benefits.[300]

The Supreme Court has also indicated in an analogous case on federal railroad retirement benefits that the Social Security program deviates from state divorce law in providing that Social Security benefits are not community property subject to division at divorce.[301]

Employment Law. Family law is similarly evident in federal regulation of employment, which creates still more legal benefits that turn on family status. The Family and Medical Leave Act (FMLA) entitles eligible employees to take up to twelve weeks of unpaid leave a year because of the birth or adoption of a child, or to care for a spouse, child, or parent with a serious health condition.[302] The FMLA entitles eligible employees to take up to twenty-six weeks of unpaid leave a year to care for a spouse, child, parent, or next of kin who is a servicemember.[303]

The Employee Retirement Income Security Act (ERISA), which regulates private employee benefit plans with a combined worth of trillions of dollars,[304] is full of family law and family law policy choices. For instance, ERISA requires employees to name their spouses as the beneficiaries of their employee benefit plans unless the spouse waives that right, and ERISA imposes strict rules on such waivers.[305] ERISA also regulates how divorce impacts a spouse's right to collect as the beneficiary of an employee benefit plan. Some states have "revocation by divorce" statutes providing that if a married person names his spouse as the beneficiary of a pension plan or life insurance policy, that designation is automatically revoked if the couple divorces. Such laws operate on the reasonable assumption that a person's desire to leave money to his spouse often diminishes radically upon divorce. However, ERISA preempts state revocation by divorce laws and keeps the ex-spouse as the beneficiary of any plan or policy that ERISA regulates unless and until the employee names a new beneficiary.[306] Indeed, the Supreme Court has "not hesitated to find state family law pre-empted when it conflicts with ERISA or relates to ERISA plans."[307]

Labor Law. Family law runs through federal labor law as well, creating legal rights and disadvantages tied to family status. This body of law frequently excludes people who work for immediate family members from many of the legal protections accorded to other workers. Congress may believe that this approach helps express the idea that family and market are separate realms (a notion that Chapter 2 will consider at more length). But exempting family members from important labor law protections can actually create additional incentives for employers to hire their relatives and may mean that these family members are subject to particularly harsh working conditions. The National Labor Relations Act (NLRA) provides that a person working for his parent or spouse is not a covered employee under the NLRA[308] and accordingly does not have the rights that covered employees have to organize, join unions, and bargain collectively.[309] The Fair Labor Standards Act (FLSA), which sets minimum wage and maximum hours rules,[310] does not regulate a business if its only regular employees are the business's owner or the parent, spouse, child, or other immediate family member of the owner.[311] In addition, the FLSA excludes from its protections agricultural workers who are employed by their parent, child, spouse, or other immediate family member.[312]

Housing Law. Family law appears within federal housing law. Federal law prohibits housing discrimination based on "familial status,"[313] while defining familial status in ways that protect families with minor children and exclude other families. For purposes of federal housing law, " '[f]amilial status' means one or more individuals (who have not attained the age of 18 years) being domiciled with—(1) a parent or another person having legal custody of such individual or individuals; or (2) the designee of such parent or other person having such custody, with the written permission of such parent or other person." Federal protections against housing discrimination based on familial status also "apply to any person who is pregnant or is in the process of securing legal custody of any individual who has not attained the age of 18 years."[314]

Criminal Law. Family law regulating rights and responsibilities tied to family status appears within federal criminal law. For example, the International Parental Kidnapping Crime Act makes it a federal crime to remove a child from the United States with the intent to obstruct the lawful exercise of parental rights.[315] The Child Protection and Obscenity Enforcement Act makes it a federal crime for a parent to sell his child in interstate or international commerce with knowledge that the child will be used in the production of pornography.[316] The Safe Homes for Women Act makes it a federal crime to commit or attempt to commit violence against a spouse in the course of, or as a result of, interstate or international travel undertaken with the intent to kill, injure, harass, or intimidate a spouse.[317] The Child Support Recovery Act,[318] amended by the Deadbeat Parents Punishment Act,[319] makes it a federal crime to willfully fail to pay child support for a child living in another state or to travel out of state or internationally with the intent to evade a child support obligation, if the child support obligation has remained unpaid for more than a year or is for more than $5,000. Federal civil law supplements this criminal statute by providing that the federal government will not issue a passport to a United States citizen who owes more than $2,500 in child support "and may revoke, restrict, or limit a passport" previously issued to a citizen who now owes more than $2,500 in child support.[320]

More Federal Family Law

Finally, there are federal statutes that are perhaps even more manifest examples of family law. Consider the statutes that Congress has enacted to regulate the termination of parental rights and the adoption of children.[321] We have already reviewed the Indian Child Welfare Act, which regulates termination and adoption proceedings involving Native American children in ways designed to keep Native American children with Native American parents. A provision of the Small Business Job Protection Act, which applies to adoptions that the Indian Child Welfare Act does not cover,[322] takes a markedly different approach, prohibiting states and organizations that receive federal funding from denying or delaying an adoption or foster care placement based on the race, color, or national origin of the child or prospective parent.[323]

Other federal statutes use federal funding to require states to promulgate specific rules for determining when existing parent-child relationships should be protected, when parental termination proceedings should be initiated, and when adoption should be pursued.[324] For instance, the Adoption and Safe Families Act requires states receiving federal funds to seek the termination of parental rights when a child has been in non-kinship foster care for fifteen of the past twenty-two months or when a parent has committed specified acts of violence against the child or the child's sibling, unless the state has documented a compelling reason why termination would not be in the child's best interests or the state has failed during the time the child was in foster care to provide reasonable reunification services to a parent who has not committed the specified acts of violence.[325]

Similarly, many federal civil statutes (in addition to federal criminal laws) regulate and strengthen a child's right to parental support.[326] For instance, these statutes use financial and other incentives to require states to petition for the inclusion of medical care in child support orders.[327] They specify detailed procedures that states must adopt to facilitate the determination of paternity.[328]

Still more federal civil statutes supplement federal criminal law in structuring the rights that a family member has to be protected from violence or other abuse by another family member.[329] For example, the Victims of Child Abuse Act requires various professionals to report suspected child abuse,[330] while indicating that "discipline administered by a parent or legal guardian to his or her child" does not constitute child abuse so long as "it is reasonable in manner and moderate in degree and otherwise does not constitute cruelty."[331] The Keeping Children and Families Safe Act specifies that states receiving federal funds must require healthcare providers to notify child protective authorities when an infant is born showing signs of prenatal exposure to illegal drugs.[332]

Evaluating Federal Law Without the
Canonical Premise of Family Law Localism

In sum, the canonical premise of family law localism misdescribes and obscures the field. Federal family law is wide-ranging, abundant, indeed sometimes unavoidable. Federal law routinely regulates the creation and dissolution of legally recognized family relationships and determines legal rights and responsibilities tied to family status, in ways that frequently deviate from state law.

Family law's canonical localism narrative has distorted how many courts, judges, and legislators understand family law, distracted their attention, and misshaped their judgments and policy decisions. Canonical stories to the contrary, American family law is not exclusively or inherently local. The question of whether the federal government can or should be involved in family law has long been settled as a matter of actual practice. Legal decisionmakers relying on the canonical localism premise have opposed federal initiatives they identified as family law on the ground that any instance of federal family law is unprecedented and inappropriate per se, no matter how otherwise attractive its policy goals. But the existence and extent of federal family law make clear that a federal law cannot be logically undermined simply by classifying it as a form of family law. Claims based on family law's supposed localism do not provide coherent grounds for decisionmaking.

Instead, lawmakers and judges need to evaluate each existing or proposed family law policy on its individual substantive merits and to consider which level (or levels) of government is best situated to carry out that particular policy. These are the real questions confronting family law, and they are the same questions that policymakers should ask in any legal arena where both federal and state action are possible. There is no good reason to think that family law is a special exception—a rare holdout of localism in an age of extensive nationalization. In family law, as elsewhere, federal involvement is neither categorically inappropriate nor always well-advised. The advantages and disadvantages of any example of federal family law, and the wisdom of establishing a national policy or facilitating state control in any specific instance, must be assessed in each case. For example, sometimes federal family law is a wiser choice because the rights or protections at stake are so important that they should be available throughout the nation, or the federal government has superior or more abundant resources to address a problem, or permitting states to enforce different answers to the same legal question will impose undue burdens. In contrast, sometimes the wisest course is to leave a family law issue to the states, so that each state government can implement its own policy choices and the variations between the laws of different states can help produce useful information about the comparative effectiveness and consequences of different family law policies, which states can then use in adjusting their policies over time. Sometimes the federal government and the states can best address a family law issue by coordinating their efforts and working together.

With this in mind, let's return to the debates over VAWA and DOMA. VAWA's civil rights remedy recognized a federal civil right to be protected from gender-motivated violence and gave victims of gender-motivated violence the right to sue their attackers in federal court for money damages.[333] Few participants in the debate over VAWA's civil rights remedy disputed the substantive desirability of countering gender-motivated violence, either because the participants recognized the harm of gender-motivated violence or because they understood that arguments directly questioning the importance of empowering victims of gender-motivated violence were unlikely to persuade. The debate over the civil rights remedy focused on objections to federal involvement in family law. But even if VAWA's civil rights remedy constituted family law—which is doubtful—federal family law cannot be categorically rejected as unprecedented and improper. Once we recognize that federal family law cannot be dismissed out of hand, we can consider the specific merits of federal involvement in this particular instance.

In my view, the case for a federal civil rights remedy against gender-motivated violence is substantial. Enforcing equal protection guarantees and regulating interstate commerce are core federal responsibilities. As one Senate report noted, "[t]his country has been using Federal civil rights laws to fight discriminatory violence for 120 years."[334] The Congress that enacted VAWA had compiled overwhelming evidence that gender-motivated violence impairs women's ability to live as equal citizens, jeopardizing women's physical safety and their freedom to work and travel. Congress had also amassed compelling evidence that state laws against domestic violence, rape, and other gender-motivated violent crimes were inadequate, underenforced, and/or enforced in ways that were discriminatory according to the findings of the states' own gender bias task forces. As another Senate report observed, "[s]tudy after study commissioned by the highest courts of the States—from Florida to New York, California to New Jersey, Nevada to Minnesota—has concluded that crimes disproportionately affecting women are often treated less seriously than comparable crimes against men. Collectively these reports provide overwhelming evidence that gender bias permeates the court system and that women are most often its victims."[335]

VAWA's civil rights remedy pursued a classic federal response to the civil rights problem Congress had identified, one familiar from the older federal civil rights laws about race discrimination on which VAWA was modeled. The civil rights remedy did not stop states from enacting and enforcing criminal and civil penalties against gender-motivated violence. Instead, the remedy addressed the documented inadequacies in state law enforcement by empowering victims of gender-motivated violence to bring their own federal lawsuits, without needing to rely on the cooperation of state prosecutors, juries, or judges.

Limiting and then eliminating VAWA's civil rights remedy did nothing to keep family law local. Federal family law was already extensive, and there are good reasons to conclude that VAWA's civil rights remedy was not a form of family law at all. But restricting and then striking down this remedy did help keep the law's response to gender-motivated violence more closely confined to state institutions that virtually all agreed were frequently inadequate and biased. The defeat of VAWA's civil rights remedy functionally helped shield from intervention an important site of women's inequality—a result that few, if any, would defend on those terms.

We can apply a similarly individualized analysis to evaluating DOMA's third section, which defined "'marriage'" for purposes of federal law as "a legal union between one man and one woman as husband and wife."[336] Some legislators, litigants, advocates, and scholars criticized DOMA's third section as inappropriate because it was federal family law. Moreover, the Supreme Court's opinion striking down section three offered an extensive localist account of family law, and several lower courts also drew on localist claims in concluding that section three was unconstitutional.

Many localist arguments against DOMA's third section suggested that the section should have been rejected simply because it was federal family law, whatever one's views on the substantive merits of the section's policy objectives. But DOMA *needed* to be considered and debated on its merits.

Federal family law was ubiquitous and entrenched well before DOMA's enactment. Many long-established federal statutes, regulations, and judicial decisions determine who counts as married for federal purposes and/or establish the federal rights and responsibilities of spouses. Indeed, one function of DOMA's third section was to impose a rule for interpreting the plethora of federal marriage law that already existed. The section had such powerful effects precisely because there are so many federal benefits, burdens, rights, and responsibilities that turn on marital status under federal law. Rather than enacting DOMA's third section, Congress could have amended each of these individual statutory and regulatory provisions to specify that same-sex couples would not count as married under each provision.

In my view, there was a problem with DOMA's third section. But the problem was grounded in civil rights concerns, rather than federalism ones. It turned on the specific substantive merits of this particular piece of family law. DOMA's third section needed to be repealed or struck down because it discriminated against gay people. It treated marriages differently based solely on whether the marriages were between people of the same sex.

If a person lives in a state that recognizes that person as married, Congress is usually willing to extend federal recognition to the marriage as well. As we have seen, this is not always the case. For instance, federal immigration law, Social Security law, tax law, and veterans' benefits law create situations in which state officials treat a person as married while federal officials treat the same person as unmarried, or vice versa. But Congress generally extends federal recognition to marriages that states recognize, and this tendency holds even where the state in question permits first cousins to marry when other states do not, or recognizes common law marriages when other states require official wedding ceremonies, or allows people to marry at a younger age than other states would accept. Yet Congress refused to extend federal legal recognition to any same-sex marriage that a state recognized. This suggests that Congress's interest in enacting DOMA's third section was not uniformity so much as a specific aversion to same-sex marriages. As the *Windsor* Court noted in striking down section three, "DOMA's unusual deviation from the usual tradition of recognizing and accepting state definitions of marriage here operates to deprive same-sex couples of the benefits and responsibilities that come with the federal recognition of their marriages. This is strong evidence of a law having the purpose and effect of disapproval of that class."[337]

Denying federal recognition to same-sex marriages could leave the people in such marriages enormously disadvantaged in the most basic material terms. Many of the benefits that federal law ties to marriage are extremely valuable and unobtainable through either state law or private agreement. For instance, DOMA's third section meant that a noncitizen could not count as his same-sex spouse's "immediate relative" for purposes of legally immigrating to the United States, that a same-sex spouse could not collect spousal benefits from the Social Security program, and that a same-sex spouse married to a federal employee or veteran was excluded from federal health insurance, life insurance, and retirement benefits available to other spouses.

Reporters at the *New York Times,* with the help of outside experts, attempted in 2009 to calculate the added costs that gay couples faced compared to similarly situated heterosexual couples. The study found that a gay couple with two children and $140,000 in annual income would incur between $41,196 and $467,562 in additional lifetime expenses. Nearly all of the added expense that a same-sex married couple would encounter stemmed from the federal government's refusal to recognize same-sex marriages, which meant that same-sex spouses were treated as unmarried for purposes of federal income taxes, federal estate taxes, federal Social Security benefits, federal Individual Retirement Accounts, and more.[338]

Beyond the immediate practical consequences for people in same-sex marriages, moreover, DOMA's third section functioned ideologically to reaffirm, reinforce, and perpetuate a long legal, political, and cultural tradition privileging heterosexuality and penalizing homosexuality. Section three excluded people in same-sex marriages from full membership in the national community of equal citizens.

Indeed, it is not clear what purpose section three served *other* than to express disapproval of homosexuality and to disadvantage gay people. In striking down section three, the Supreme Court concluded that the provision impinged upon constitutional principles of liberty and equality, by relegating same-sex couples to "second-class marriages."[339] *Windsor's* lengthy invocation of localist claims about family law served only to distract from the well-founded reasons to condemn DOMA.

Moreover, the localist theme in *Windsor* may complicate future cases and make the path forward more arduous. *Windsor* used localist arguments as grounds to criticize section three. The localist account of family law does not provide a coherent basis for decisionmaking, but at least in *Windsor* localist claims pointed the Court in the direction of striking down a statute that violated constitutional rights to equality and liberty.

In some future case, however, the Court will have to judge the constitutionality of a state prohibition on same-sex marriage—an issue that *Windsor* explicitly did not decide.[340] When this suit ultimately arrives at the Court, opponents of same-sex marriage will surely cite localist accounts of family law and *Windsor*'s invocation of localism as grounds for upholding state bans on same-sex marriage, placing these localist claims at odds with equality and liberty concerns.

In fact, the three dissenting opinions in *Windsor* made this argument. Chief Justice John Roberts insisted in his dissent that the localism within the *Windsor* majority opinion cuts in favor of finding that "the States, in the exercise of their 'historic and essential authority to define the marital relation,' may continue to utilize the traditional definition of marriage."[341] Roberts contended that "while '[t]he State's power in defining the marital relation is of central relevance' to the majority's decision to strike down DOMA here, that power will come into play on the other side of the board in future cases about the constitutionality of state marriage definitions. So too will the concerns for state diversity and sovereignty that weigh against DOMA's constitutionality in this case."[342] Justice Antonin Scalia's dissent noted his agreement with Roberts's view "that lower federal courts and state courts can distinguish today's case when the issue before them is state denial of marital status to same-sex couples," adding that "[s]tate and lower federal courts should take the Court at its word and distinguish away."[343] Justice Samuel Alito's dissent declared that "[t]o the extent that the Court takes the position that the question of same-sex marriage should be resolved primarily at the state level, I wholeheartedly agree. I hope that the Court will ultimately permit the people of each State to decide this question for themselves."[344]

In my view, the parts of *Windsor* that recognize section three's violation of constitutional principles of equality and liberty provide ample support for a future Court decision finding state prohibitions on same-sex marriage unconstitutional. But as the *Windsor* dissenters aptly noted, the localist theme in *Windsor* mars the clarity of the Court's message and could be read to suggest that the case for striking down state bans on same-sex marriage is less compelling. The persistent incantation of the idea that family law is inherently local may create a needless hurdle to a future Court judgment requiring states to recognize same-sex marriage.

The contention that family law is and should be local is a story that many courts, judges, and legislators, as well as some advocates and scholars, repeatedly tell about family law, relying on its canonical familiarity to convince. The contention fits with the idea of family law's exceptionalism, a canonical premise and theme in family law. Decisionmakers frequently insist that family law is sharply set off from other legal fields and governed by different, even oppositional, rules and presumptions. But in the federalism context, as elsewhere, family law actually resembles other areas of the law much more closely than canonical narratives about family law suggest. Assumptions and assertions about family law's localism misdescribe the substance of family law, misdirect policy debates away from the real questions that family law faces, and misshape the choices that decisionmakers pursue.

2

FAMILY LAW AND ECONOMIC EXCHANGE

> [E]ven if few things are left that cannot command a price,
> marital support remains one of them.
>
> —*Borelli v. Brusseau* (California Court of Appeal 1993)[1]

Family law is routinely described in ways that stress the separation
between family and market. This theme manifests itself in legal scholarship and appears with even more frequency and significantly more
immediate practical impact in the work of courts. But the canonical
narrative about family law's separation from market principles obscures
the state of the field more than it illuminates. Family law and family
relationships are already suffused with legally permissible and enforceable economic exchange that the narrative overlooks or underempha-
sizes. The faulty premise that family law does not countenance economic
exchange to any notable extent misdirects debate and discussion in
family law. The pressing questions for family law are not about whether
to permit and enforce economic exchange, but about how to permit and
enforce such exchange, when, why, in what forms, and to what ends.

Writing about family law often presumes the field's separation from the
market. As one critic observed, "[t]he dichotomization of market and
family pervades our thinking, our language, and our culture."[2] Scholars
state that "[b]oth social custom and the law have treated ['the market and
the family'] as entirely separate."[3] They remark that "one way to look at
the family is as a discourse explicitly opposed to its market counterpart"
and report "that we generally have viewed families as entities that ought
to be insulated from market forces to a considerable degree."[4]

Indeed, the assumption that family law is committed to rejecting and
reversing market principles that apply in other areas of the law unites

some scholars who agree on little else. Family law's canonical narrative about separation from the market has led scholars across the ideological spectrum to accept that a central question confronting family law is whether the law should allow and uphold economic exchanges between family members.

These "pro-market" and "anti-commodification" scholars agree that family law maintains a strict boundary between family life and economic exchange, although they disagree about whether to condemn or applaud that boundary. Pro-market scholars criticize family law for keeping economic exchange out of family relationships and argue for change. They report "the existing law's refusal or, at best, reluctance, to enforce" economic agreements between intimates,[5] and they explain "that women's key problem" in the family "has been too little commodification."[6] Anti-commodification scholars, in turn, celebrate family law for keeping "the principles of commercial contract law" out of family relationships and argue for constancy.[7] Michael Walzer identifies marital and parental rights as spheres in which "monetary exchanges are blocked, banned, resented, conventionally deplored."[8] Elizabeth Anderson warns of a newfound threat to the "parental norms" now governing "the ways we allocate and understand parental rights and responsibilities over children": "the encroachment of the market into the sphere of reproductive labor."[9]

Courts have embraced the canonical story about family law's separation from the market still more wholeheartedly and with more direct consequences for the law. It is not that courts consistently refuse to permit or enforce economic exchanges between family members. If courts did, the assertion that family law rejects market principles would be much more accurate. Instead, courts recounting the canonical story about family law's market separation repeatedly invoke and rely upon a few examples where family law loudly rejects market principles. But these examples actually illustrate exceptions within family law more than rules.

Moreover, family law doctrines that deviate from standard market principles often have normatively undesirable consequences, inflicting disproportionate harm on women and poorer people. Relying on the canonical premise of family law's market separation has helped courts sustain and enforce these doctrines with arguments that are disengaged from the real contours of family law. Courts use their select examples to support the canonical narrative about family law's separation from the market and then (circularly) invoke the idea that family law is intrinsically hostile to market principles to explain why the market-rejecting doctrines they discuss should be preserved.

Consider two examples that courts cite to illustrate the canonical market separation story: the prohibition on interspousal contracts for domestic services and the refusal to recognize human capital as divisible marital or community property at divorce.

The Prohibition on Interspousal Contracts for Domestic Services

Spouses cannot make enforceable agreements providing that one spouse will pay the other for domestic services, such as housework, childcare, or nursing.[10] This prohibition on enforceable contracts for domestic labor applies only to spouses.[11] Courts are ordinarily willing to enforce contracts specifying that one party will pay the other for cleaning a house, preparing meals, caring for a child, or nursing an elderly or ill person, including when the contract for domestic labor is between two people in a nonmarital sexual relationship (whether heterosexual or homosexual).[12]

Within marriage, however, courts assume that domestic labor is performed for free, no matter how demanding or time-intensive the work. Moreover, courts enforce that assumption even where it clearly contradicts the understanding that a particular married couple reached. Spouses can agree between themselves with great detail and explicitness that one will compensate the other for domestic services. But if one spouse refuses to pay after the labor is performed, the other spouse cannot enforce their agreement in court.

The judiciary's consistent refusal to enforce interspousal contracts for domestic services means that few litigants bring such contracts to court. This doctrine demonstrates its power by discouraging lawsuits rather than producing them. When a spouse does sue, judges frequently justify their refusal to enforce interspousal contracts for household labor by asserting that family law rejects the market principles that govern other areas of law.

Consider *Borelli v. Brusseau*,[13] which the California Court of Appeal decided in 1993. According to Hildegard Borelli, her husband, Michael, did not want to enter a nursing home after his stroke, although he required round-the-clock nursing care. Michael asked Hildegard to nurse him herself, in exchange for some real estate, cash, and other assets that he would leave her in his will. Hildegard agreed to this oral contract and performed her part of the bargain. After Michael died, however, Hildegard discovered that Michael had not changed his will to provide her with the assets he had promised to transfer. Hildegard sued to enforce the contract.[14]

The California court held that agreements between spouses for domestic labor are categorically unenforceable.[15] One of the arguments that *Borelli* advanced in support of this judgment rested on the premise that family law rejects market norms and economic exchange. The court stressed that enforcing the Borellis' contract would allow market principles to enter the family and asserted that family law was committed to its separation from the market. Spouses, *Borelli* proclaimed, cannot "be treated just like any other parties haggling at arm's length." "[E]ven if few things are left that cannot command a price, marital support remains one of them."[16] This was an important argument for the *Borelli* court, as its other main line of reasoning (discussed more in Chapter 3) emerged from and was entangled with principles of common law coverture, a set of doctrines designed to legally subordinate wives to their husbands and give husbands ownership of their wives' labor.

Other courts explaining why interspousal contracts for domestic services are unenforceable have similarly invoked the idea that family law is committed to repudiating market principles and to separating marriage from economic exchange. The New Mexico Supreme Court announced that "[i]t is the policy of this state to foster and protect the marriage institution. It is not the policy of the state to encourage spouses to marry for money."[17] The Virginia Supreme Court worried about "'plac[ing] the marriage relation on too much of a commercial basis'" and "'treat[ing] the marital relation as any other business association, whereby each expects to obtain material advantage from the marriage. This is not,'" the court stressed, "'the true concept of the relation.'"[18]

The Refusal to Recognize Human Capital as Divisible Marital or Community Property at Divorce

Courts also rely on the premise that family law is removed from the market in refusing to treat human capital as marital or community property subject to valuation and distribution at divorce. These decisions can be better understood if first placed in the wider context of divorce law.

When a couple with no prenuptial or postnuptial agreement divorces, each spouse is usually entitled to keep what the divorce court identifies as that spouse's separate property. Separate property typically consists of assets that a spouse acquired before marriage, or gifts or bequests made to one spouse alone. In contrast, marital or community property typically consists of assets that either or both spouses acquired during marriage through the efforts of one or both spouses. When a couple has not signed a prenuptial or postnuptial agreement, divorce courts divide the couple's marital or community property either "equitably" or equally.[19]

The issue of whether human capital acquired during marriage should count as marital or community property is typically litigated in divorce cases where one spouse has worked to put the other spouse through professional school,[20] sometimes at the cost of delaying or foregoing her own educational advancement. The supporting spouse looked forward to sharing in the degreed spouse's higher income after graduation, but the couple never entered into any formalized agreement about how to treat the value of the professional degree in the event of divorce.

If a couple stays married for many years after the degreed spouse receives his diploma, then the supporting spouse may receive much of what she anticipated—even if the couple eventually divorces. Any income the degreed spouse earns during marriage with the help of his professional degree will constitute marital or community property, and courts will routinely divide such income between the spouses at divorce (unless the couple signed a prenuptial or postnuptial agreement providing otherwise).

However, if a couple divorces soon after the degreed spouse graduates, the graduate often has not earned much money yet. Rather than cash, the most significant asset that either spouse possesses may be the enhanced earning capacity associated with the professional degree.[21] Indeed, economists recognize human capital—skills, knowledge, talents, and experience that increase a person's productivity and earning capacity—as the largest source of wealth in modern society.[22]

Nonetheless, the overwhelming majority of courts insist that human capital is not a form of marital or community property divisible at divorce.[23] This means that in the vast majority of states (New York is the most prominent exception)[24] a person who worked to put her spouse through school cannot claim part of the economic value of the professional degree or other human capital.

That doctrine applies whether the spouse who earned the degree is male or female. But the available case law is overwhelmingly sex-specific, featuring divorcing women seeking compensation for work they did to help their husbands acquire human capital. Indeed, these cases are sometimes called—even by judges themselves—" 'Ph.T.' " cases, referring to wives who devoted themselves to "putting hubby through school."[25]

Courts holding that human capital is not marital or community property sometimes use the language of economics to explain their decisions, contending that human capital is too difficult to appraise, too speculative in value, and too ephemeral in nature.[26] Such arguments have a serious weakness, however. Courts routinely value human capital in personal injury or wrongful death suits for lost future income or lost earning capacity.[27] Perhaps with this in mind, courts rejecting claims on human capital at divorce frequently turn to arguments grounded in family law's purported separation from the market.

Courts often explain that recognizing human capital as marital or community property would inappropriately insert market principles into the family, reducing marriage to an economic relation and an economic bargain. The Arizona Court of Appeals' opinion in *Pyeatte v. Pyeatte* is representative. Margrethe Pyeatte had postponed entering a master's degree program and worked as a teacher so that she could support her husband, Charles, while he attended law school. Charles graduated from law school and informed Margrethe soon thereafter that he wanted a divorce. Although the law degree was essentially the only valuable asset that either spouse possessed,[28] the Arizona court quickly dismissed the idea that the value of the degree should count as community property subject to some form of division at divorce.[29]

The court's opinion stressed the need to enforce and maintain the dichotomy between market and family: "[W]e reject the view that the economic element necessarily inherent in the marital institution (and particularly apparent in its dissolution) requires us to treat marriage as a strictly financial undertaking upon the dissolution of which each party will be fully compensated for the investment of his various contributions. When the parties have been married for a number of years, the courts cannot and will not strike a balance regarding the contributions of each to the marriage and then translate that into a monetary award. To do so would diminish the individual personalities of the husband and wife to economic entities and reduce the institution of marriage to that of a closely held corporation."[30]

This account suggested that the court's unwillingness to tally what each spouse had contributed economically to their marriage left both husband and wife better off, rather than "diminish[ed]." Perhaps the court believed that spouses are more likely to give freely and abundantly to each other when there is no precise accounting of contributions. Yet even if that is true in some cases, what about marriages where one spouse made many economic sacrifices, while the other did not? The *Pyeatte* court's decision to exclude the law degree from community property certainly benefited Charles. But it is harder to argue that the court left Margrethe better off, and she did not appear to think so.

Other courts have also seized on decisions excluding human capital from marital or community property as prime occasions to proclaim that the law governing marriage rejects the market principles that dominate other legal arenas. In *Martinez v. Martinez,* for instance, Karen Martinez contended that the value of her husband's medical degree should count as marital property subject to some form of distribution at divorce.[31] The Utah Supreme Court rejected the claim, emphasizing that "[a]lthough marriage is a partnership in some respects, a marriage is certainly not comparable to a commercial partnership."[32]

Janice DeWitt was similarly unsuccessful in claiming a property interest in the value of her husband John's law degree. Janice and John married after Janice had completed one year of college and John had finished one semester. The couple's son was born that same year, and Janice was presumably pregnant at the wedding. After marrying, John remained a full-time student, graduating from college and then law school. Meanwhile, Janice left school, worked full-time, cared for their son, and did most of the domestic labor.[33] John filed for divorce within two years of his law school graduation.[34]

In *DeWitt v. DeWitt,* Janice "testified that at the time of the marriage she and [John] agreed that it would be financially preferable for [John] to attend school and complete his law degree first, and that she would then complete her college education."[35] In other words, Janice testified that she and her husband had a basic deal: She would work so he could obtain his law degree, both spouses would benefit from his higher income as a lawyer, and then Janice would earn her college degree.

The Wisconsin Court of Appeals emphasized the separation between market and family in holding that the value of John's law degree could not count as a marital asset.[36] The court announced that divorce courts cannot treat spouses "as though they were strictly business partners, one of whom has made a calculated investment in the commodity of the other's professional training, expecting a dollar for dollar return. We do not think that most marital planning is so coldly undertaken."[37] The court's account of married life purported to be simply descriptive, but it also suggested how the court hoped married couples would behave. Note that the court's pronouncement about how "marital planning" proceeds appeared in a case where, on the wife's account, the couple actually *had* made an economic bargain (even if not an explicit contract), expecting that the arrangement would benefit both of them financially. The court did not suggest that Janice was wrong to delay her education in order to help her husband complete his schooling. The court's objection appeared to be that Janice was too market-minded in expecting more legal protection when her husband failed to uphold his end of their understanding.

The Connecticut Supreme Court in *Simmons v. Simmons* similarly stressed its rejection of market principles for family law. Aura Simmons worked to support her husband, Duncan, while he attended medical school, and he filed for divorce soon after graduating.[38] The *Simmons* court refused to treat the value of the medical degree as a form of marital property, emphasizing that "while we have acknowledged that the marital union is *akin* to a partnership, we have never held that it is an actual economic partnership."[39]

Unlike the Wisconsin court in *DeWitt,* the Connecticut court's account of how married couples actually conducted themselves was unclear about whether spouses themselves were inclined to view their marriages in economic terms. *Simmons* first contended that "[t]he parties to a marriage do not enter into the relationship with a set of ledgers and make yearly adjustments to their capital accounts." But immediately thereafter, the Connecticut court quoted a suggestion from the West Virginia Supreme Court that spouses might be more economically oriented: "'Marriage is not a business arrangement, and this Court would be loathe to promote any more tallying of respective debits and credits *than already occurs in the average household.*'"[40]

Whatever the individual inclinations of spouses, however, the Connecticut court declared that it was family law's mission to keep marriage separate from what the court envisioned as the crassness of the market. Like *Pyeatte, Simmons* made the (highly debatable) assertion that refusing to treat the value of Duncan's medical degree as marital property left Aura as well as Duncan better off: "Reducing the relationship, even when it has broken down, to such base terms serves only to degrade and undermine that relationship and the parties."[41] The implication was that Aura had misjudged her own interests in concluding that the desirability of concrete material rewards outweighed the loftier, if more ephemeral, benefits associated with rejecting market principles.

Legalized Economic Exchange Within the Family

The prohibition on interspousal contracts for domestic services and the refusal to recognize human capital as divisible marital or community property at divorce are practically important doctrines with significant material consequences. They also function as symbols that courts conspicuously invoke to mark family law's separation from the market. Judges repeatedly proclaim family law's rejection of market norms, presenting this theme as a guide to their decisionmaking.

But in fact, legally permissible and enforceable economic exchanges run through family law and family relationships. Legal authorities routinely allow, uphold, even sometimes compel economic exchanges between family members in many arenas. Indeed, perhaps the most remarkable aspect of the canonical narrative about family law's repudiation of market principles is that this narrative survives despite so much evidence that contradicts its depiction of the field.

Interspousal Economic Agreements

Family law permits and enforces a wide variety of economic exchanges between spouses. Spouses, like nonmarital sexual partners (whether heterosexual or homosexual),[42] may enter into agreements governing how they will distribute property, earnings, and other assets between themselves during and after their relationship. Before the 1970s, courts often refused to enforce agreements that determined in advance how spouses would divide assets and pay support at divorce.[43] Judicial opinions declared that such agreements were contrary to public policy and void on the theory that the agreements anticipated and facilitated divorce.[44] Courts were concerned that contracts governing the economic consequences of divorce would encourage husbands to mistreat their wives, either because the husbands would be financially better off if their wives filed for divorce or because divorce would be so inexpensive for husbands that the men would have too little incentive to behave well during marriage.[45] At the same time, courts worried that wives who had signed unfavorable agreements governing their economic rights at divorce would be forced to stay with husbands whom they had good grounds to leave.[46]

Starting in the 1970s and 1980s, however, more and more courts began enforcing agreements governing the distribution of property and cash between spouses, whether the agreements were signed before or during marriage.[47] Courts upholding prenuptial or postnuptial agreements argued that such contracts did not promote divorce, but instead encouraged marriage among people who were reluctant or unwilling to subject their assets to family law's default rules.[48] Courts also posited that permitting people to plan the financial aspects of their marriages and then safeguarding spouses' financial expectations could strengthen and stabilize marital relationships.[49]

Prenuptial and postnuptial agreements have become widely enforced. As a practical matter, these contracts are most accessible to wealthier people, who have the money for lawyers and the economic assets to make paying legal fees to protect those assets worthwhile. Indeed, discussions of prenuptial or postnuptial agreements often focus on extremely wealthy and famous individuals. Their well-compensated attorneys are likely to be particularly creative (or, depending on your perspective, particularly conniving) in taking advantage of the full range of legal possibilities. Moreover, the media's focus on celebrities means that their prenuptial or postnuptial agreements are sometimes publicized even without litigation, whereas many other agreements never come to public attention because they succeed in avoiding litigation at divorce.

Whether the parties are celebrated or little-known, however, courts routinely uphold prenuptial or postnuptial agreements enforcing a wide variety of economic transactions between spouses. States vary in how much they scrutinize these agreements for substantive and procedural fairness, with some jurisdictions making it very difficult to invalidate contracts and others proving more willing to invalidate or modify contracts on fairness grounds.[50] But under either approach, spouses may now structure their prenuptial or postnuptial agreements to facilitate myriad economic arrangements. In fact, spouses may use prenuptial or postnuptial contracts to directly or indirectly circumvent judicial doctrines about human capital and domestic labor that purport to keep marriage separate from market principles.

For instance, spouses may design their agreements so that one spouse will be entitled to more assets or a future income stream upon the other spouse's completion of an educational degree, allowing spouses who expressly negotiate and plan in advance to circumvent judicial refusals to recognize human capital as marital or community property. For example, Gloria and Dallen Ashby allegedly agreed after marrying in 1997 that Gloria would support Dallen "while he attended medical school in exchange for Dallen's promise to support 'her at a certain level with the income he would earn as the holder of a medical degree.' "[51] The couple separated in 2005, about a year after Dallen graduated from medical school, and Gloria filed for divorce and breach of contract.[52] The Utah Supreme Court held that "student support contracts" between spouses are enforceable at divorce so long as "they satisfy the normal conditions imposed on postnuptial contracts" in Utah,[53] meaning that they must be "negotiated in good faith or . . . not unreasonably constrain the district court in the performance of its equitable and statutory duties."[54]

In addition, spouses may design their agreements so that one spouse will be entitled to more money or assets upon the birth of a child. To take a stark example, actors Tom Cruise and Katie Holmes, who married in 2006,[55] reportedly signed a prenuptial agreement providing that she would receive a monetary award ($25 million, according to one account)[56] for each biological child she had with him.[57] Two family lawyers reported in 2004 that "a homebuilder agreed to pay his wife $100,000 for every child she carried. Why? Because his wife felt that the wear and tear on her physically and emotionally during pregnancy and delivery deserved some compensation! (He paid her twice.)"[58] In a more quotidian case, the Connecticut Superior Court in 1997 enforced an oral agreement between Diane Ehlert, a certified public accountant, and Charles Ehlert, the owner of a home improvement and construction business, that their prenuptial contract would simply become void once the couple had a child together.[59] A Maine statute attempts to achieve a similar result through default rules. It provides that premarital agreements signed before October 1, 1993, become "void 18 months after the parties to the agreement become biological or adoptive parents or guardians of a minor," unless "within the 18-month period, the parties sign a written amendment to the agreement either stating that the agreement remains in effect or altering the agreement."[60]

These arrangements do not turn on how much or how little work a spouse does to raise a child. From this perspective, they do not provide direct compensation for domestic labor (unless one counts pregnancy and childbirth themselves as domestic labor). But these agreements are enforceable contracts in which the onset of greater domestic responsibilities triggers greater financial rewards, and accordingly the agreements can function to indirectly circumvent the unenforceability of interspousal contracts for household work.

Courts refusing to enforce interspousal contracts for domestic labor contend that such work must be shielded from market principles. Having a child would seem to have more potential to be special and sacred than performing ordinary housework. Having a child also typically leads to enormous amounts of housework, particularly by women. Yet courts apparently perceive no problem with enforcing prenuptial contracts under which wives receive more money from their husbands because they gave birth.

Spouses may also expressly structure their prenuptial or postnuptial agreements so that one spouse will receive more money or assets from the other spouse at death or divorce depending on the length of marriage. These agreements effectively establish rates of payment for marital time served. They have attracted public attention in America for decades, revealing terms that are sometimes quite generous and sometimes remarkably stingy. Brooke Astor married Vincent Astor in 1953,[61] when Vincent was one of the richest men in America with a fortune estimated to be between $100 million and $200 million.[62] Their prenuptial agreement reportedly gave her $1 million if the marriage (the third for each spouse)[63] lasted less than a year and $5 million if the marriage lasted more than a year.[64] The prenuptial agreement that actor Michael Douglas and his second wife, actress Catherine Zeta-Jones, signed before marrying in 2000 reportedly provides that if the couple divorces she will receive $2.8 million for each year of the marriage, plus an additional $5 million if he commits adultery while they are married.[65]

Less notoriously, the D.C. Court of Appeals in 1980 upheld a prenuptial agreement between Samuel Burtoff, a doctor with over $1 million in assets, and Wilma Burtoff, a nurse who had $10,000 in assets and earned less than $8000 the year before their marriage. The agreement provided that Samuel would give Wilma a total of $10,000 at divorce if the marriage lasted less than a year, $25,000 at divorce if the marriage lasted one to three years, $35,000 at divorce if the marriage lasted more than three years, and $50,000 if Samuel died while the couple was still married.[66]

The Georgia Supreme Court in 2011 upheld a prenuptial agreement between Richard Sides, a telecommunications company owner worth approximately $4.2 million when he married, and Barbara Sides, a flight attendant pregnant with Richard's child when she married.[67] The agreement provided that if the couple divorced just before their twentieth anniversary, Barbara would receive the car she was driving and $25,000 a year for ten years.[68] She would receive "substantially more" at divorce if the marriage lasted more than twenty years.[69]

Payments under prenuptial or postnuptial agreements sometimes escalate so sharply over time that while purportedly rewarding marital longevity, they functionally create tremendous economic incentives for the wealthier spouse to seek divorce sooner rather than later. Real estate developer Donald Trump and his second wife, actress Marla Maples, reportedly signed a prenuptial agreement in 1993 that limited her to $1 to $5 million at divorce unless the couple remained married for more than a set time period, after which time she would be entitled to a significantly larger payment calculated as a percentage of Trump's net worth. Trump and Maples announced their separation within eleven months of the contractual deadline, with an anonymous source "familiar with [Trump's] portfolio and marital situation" explaining to the *New York Times* that Trump "'has been forced economically to act.'"[70] Trump filed for divorce three months later.[71]

Billionaire Ron Perelman and his fourth wife, actress Ellen Barkin, married in 2000 and reportedly signed a prenuptial agreement that limited her to $20 million at divorce unless the marriage lasted until a predetermined date, at which point she would be entitled to a much bigger payment. Perelman also announced his intent to divorce shortly before his contractual deadline.[72] An anonymous "Barkin friend" told the *New York Daily News* that Perelman "'can't get that deal thing out of his mind. The finances are a huge part of it.'"[73]

Pop star Britney Spears and backup dancer Kevin Federline married in 2004 and reportedly signed a prenuptial agreement providing that the alimony payments Federline would receive at divorce would increase on a sliding scale depending on the length of the marriage. Spears announced her intent to divorce on the last day before the prenuptial agreement would have treated the couple as beginning their third marital year. "A close Spears associate who requested anonymity" explained to the *Chicago Sun-Times* that "a third year of marriage—even the beginning of that third year—potentially would have cost the singer another $5 million."[74]

Even Dr. Samuel Burtoff—whose prenuptial agreement the D.C. Court of Appeals upheld in 1980—separated from his wife Wilma eight days before their first anniversary, ensuring that she would receive $10,000 rather than $25,000 at divorce.[75] Richard Sides—whose prenuptial agreement the Georgia Supreme Court enforced in 2011—finalized his divorce from his wife Barbara sixty-two days before the couple's twentieth anniversary, so that Barbara would not receive the substantially larger payments triggered by reaching that milestone.[76]

There is a plausible argument that courts should refuse to enforce prenuptial or postnuptial agreements with steep escalation clauses, on the ground that such contracts violate public policy by creating unreasonable incentives for the wealthier spouse to pursue early divorce. To date, however, courts have not embraced this theory. Consider, for instance, the Connecticut Appellate Court's decision in *Peterson v. Sykes-Peterson* (2012).[77]

Robert Peterson and Laurie Sykes-Peterson signed a prenuptial agreement three days before their July 14, 2000, wedding that included what the court called "a sunset provision," which provided that the agreement would become void on the couple's seventh wedding anniversary.[78] In other words, if the couple divorced while the prenuptial agreement was in effect, Laurie would be limited to whatever the agreement provided for her. If the couple divorced after their prenuptial agreement became void, a court would equitably divide their marital property and Laurie would receive more.[79] Robert filed for divorce on March 1, 2007, a few months before the couple's seventh anniversary. He argued that the prenuptial agreement governed the terms of the couple's divorce.[80]

The case turned on what the "sunset provision" meant and on whether the provision was enforceable. Robert lost on both issues. First, the court held that the prenuptial agreement was written so that it became void if Robert and Laurie were still married on their seventh wedding anniversary, even if they were already in the process of divorcing by then.[81] Second, and more interesting for our purposes, the court rejected Robert's argument that the sunset "provision acted as an incentive to divorce and therefore violated public policy."[82] Robert "suggest[ed]" to the court "that because he clearly stood to benefit more financially from the enforcement of the prenuptial agreement than from an equitable distribution of the marital assets, the existence of the sunset provision actually encouraged him to seek a divorce before the sunset provision took effect."[83] Robert's statement about his own motivations was certainly plausible, and the timing of his divorce filing supported the contention that he had taken into account the economic incentives the prenuptial agreement created—albeit without realizing that he needed to finalize his divorce by his seventh anniversary, rather than simply initiate divorce proceedings by then. Nonetheless, the court was "not persuaded that the sunset provision in the present case provided such an incentive to divorce so as to warrant the conclusion that it violated public policy."[84] Prenuptial and postnuptial agreements flourish, even when they provide for payments at divorce that escalate dramatically depending on the length of the marriage.

Separated spouses, in turn, may make enforceable contracts in many states in which one spouse agrees to pay the other for returning to the marriage.[85] For instance, the Kansas Court of Appeals enforced an oral agreement in which a wife who was homebound with Parkinson's disease agreed to bequeath $25,000 to her husband if he did not file for divorce and returned to care for her. When the wife's will failed to provide for her husband as promised, the court ordered the $25,000 transferred to the husband from the wife's estate.[86] The court explained that "[i]t is well-established law that a contract between spouses made when they are separated for just cause, whereby one agrees to pay the other if marital relations are resumed, rests upon valuable consideration and is enforceable. The agreement to abandon the divorce and renew cohabitation accords with the public policy favoring resolution of marital discord and preservation of the family unit."[87] In another case, the New York Supreme Court enforced an agreement in which a husband promised to transfer stock to his wife if she resumed living with him after he had left her and then returned seeking reconciliation.[88]

Judges enforcing agreements to pay for reconciliation often stress society's interest in preserving marriages. But courts also uphold these agreements where there is good reason to think that the public interest might have been better served if the specific couple at issue had terminated their relationship rather than reuniting. For example, the North Carolina Court of Appeals enforced a contract that a husband had made with his wife in which he agreed to transfer land to their joint ownership if she returned to him after separating because of his physical abuse.[89]

California courts have also upheld agreements to pay for reconciliation,[90] explaining that such contracts " 'further and fortify the marriage relationship.' "[91] In other words, if Hildegard Borelli had left her husband Michael after his stroke and then agreed to return to him in exchange for real estate, property, and other assets, the court would have enforced that agreement—presumably without a word about the supposed separation between family law and economic exchange.[92]

In short, economic exchange pervades the legal regulation of marriage. Family law routinely allows and enforces interspousal contracts about property, earnings, and other assets, even when those contracts attach monetary rewards to the fact that one's spouse has acquired human capital, or to the birth of a child, or to the simple ability to remain married for a set time period. Indeed, separated spouses may pay each other to return to the marriage. Spouses are also free to hire and pay each other as employees or business partners. Courts will enforce such agreements so long as the work at issue does not consist of household domestic labor.[93]

Economic Agreements Between Family Members Other than Spouses

Courts permit and enforce an even wider range of economic transactions between other family members, such as parents and children, or siblings. When nonspousal family members are adults, they may contract for the exchange of property and cash and hire each other as employees. For instance, a court will express no qualms in adjudicating an economic dispute between " 'two brothers, the employer and the employee.' "[94]

Nonspousal family members may also enter into enforceable agreements providing that one family member will pay the other for domestic labor. Consider *Brown v. Brown* (1987),[95] which involved siblings who had allegedly entered into a contract much like the one at issue in *Borelli*. Sarah Key needed full-time nursing care after a lengthy hospital stay, and her doctors advised her to move into a nursing home. But Sarah returned to her own home instead, and her brother, Johnnie Brown, moved in to take care of her.[96]

According to Johnnie, the siblings had entered into an oral contract in which he agreed to provide the full-time nursing Sarah required in exchange for Sarah's agreement to pay him " 'well' " for his work. Johnnie "testified that, except for doing necessary errands, he had remained at his sister's home continuously, meaning 24 hours a day, until she died three and a half months later. [Johnnie] claimed he had paid his sister's bills, including funeral expenses, cooked her meals, cleaned the house, done the laundry, changed her bedpan, and had provided other practical nursing care." After Sarah died, however, Johnnie discovered that she had not abided by their agreement and had left him nothing in her will. Johnnie sued, seeking "$10,000 for personal services" as well as $1118 to reimburse him for money he had spent on Sarah's behalf.[97]

The District of Columbia Court of Appeals held that express or implied contracts between siblings for domestic services are enforceable. An express contract is grounded in an explicit agreement between the parties, while an implied contract is "proven by facts and circumstances which show that both parties, at the time the services were performed, contemplated or intended pecuniary recompense."[98] Johnnie would have to prove on remand by a preponderance of the evidence that a contract actually existed—that the siblings had "either an express or implied agreement" under which Johnnie "expected to be paid" and Sarah "intended to make payment."[99] But if Johnnie did prove the existence of such an agreement, the court would enforce the siblings' contract for domestic work.

Compelled Economic Exchange Within the Family

It is also worth noting that the law often intervenes to order economic exchanges between family members when the family members have not made their own economic arrangements. Here, courts are compelling economic transfers, rather than enforcing economic contracts.

For instance, divorce courts may impose continuing support obligations when a married couple has not contracted about support. Alimony laws vary by state, but commonly provide that a divorcing spouse may collect alimony if she can demonstrate need (often defined in terms of maintaining the marital standard of living rather than basic subsistence), an inability to support herself, and that the wealthier spouse can afford to pay the alimony after meeting his own needs.[100] Some state alimony statutes explicitly provide that courts deciding whether to award alimony must consider the value of the domestic labor a divorcing spouse performed during marriage and her contributions, if any, to her spouse's education, training, career, or earning capacity.[101] In practice, judges rarely award alimony.[102] But these alimony statutes do attempt to monetize and reimburse domestic labor in marriage and contributions to a spouse's human capital that courts loudly declare elsewhere to be beyond market logic.

If a married couple has not contracted about property distribution, states with equitable distribution regimes at divorce frequently consider each spouse's economic contribution to the marriage in determining how to divide marital property.[103] For instance, some courts that refuse to recognize human capital as marital property hold that a person who supported her spouse through school made a greater economic contribution to the marriage and is accordingly entitled at divorce to a larger share of the assets that do count as marital property.[104] Some state statutes explicitly instruct courts dividing marital property to consider whether one spouse contributed to the other spouse's human capital development.[105] Once again, these rulings and statutes hardly help the supporting spouse in cases where the couple has little but the educational degree. Moreover, focusing on the costs associated with acquiring an educational degree does not capture the actual economic value of a degree once obtained. But the rulings and statutes do immerse the law of marriage in market principles. Courts adjudicating the equitable distribution of marital property at divorce routinely calculate each spouse's marital contribution in economic terms. Indeed, some judicial decisions and statutes count the economic value of domestic labor in determining each spouse's economic contribution to the marriage.[106] The judicial decisions refusing to recognize human capital as marital property do not separate family law and family life from the market. They simply disregard one asset in their otherwise pervasive economic calculations.

If a married couple has not contracted about inheritance, the law frequently intervenes at death to mandate economic transfers between spouses. Most states provide that a person who dies while married has a legal obligation to leave his surviving spouse at least a specified percentage of his estate, unless the spouses contracted otherwise in a prenuptial or postnuptial agreement. If the deceased spouse's will does not comply with this legal obligation, the surviving spouse has the legal option to take the specified percentage of the estate (known as the "elective" or "forced" share) rather than abide by the will.[107] States vary in the percentage established for the elective share and the precise assets included in the share.[108] However, the percentage set for the elective share is never more than fifty percent of the deceased spouse's estate and sometimes significantly less than that, meaning that surviving spouses in unharmonious marriages can sometimes be left much worse off economically than divorcing spouses in unharmonious marriages. Some states provide that a surviving spouse is entitled to one-third of the deceased spouse's estate.[109] Other states specify that a surviving spouse is entitled to less of the estate if the deceased spouse left a certain number of descendants and more of the estate if the deceased spouse left fewer or no descendants.[110] Some states provide that a surviving spouse is entitled to an escalating share of the deceased spouse's estate (up to half in some states, less in other states) depending on the length of the marriage,[111] an interesting parallel to prenuptial or postnuptial contracts that similarly provide for escalating payments.

The law also compels or facilitates economic transfers between parents and children. Parents have a legal obligation to support their children financially until the age of majority, and courts may strip a person of his legal status as a parent if the parent fails without cause to provide financial support to his child.[112] Parents may recoup some of their financial investment in their minor children by employing them, and parent-employers are exempt from many federal and state laws limiting and regulating child labor. Many state statutes also grant parents legal control over their minor children's earnings.[113] In addition, a majority of states have enacted (although dramatically underenforced) "filial responsibility" statutes requiring adult children to support their parents financially if the parents are needy and unable to support themselves and the children are able to provide support.[114]

Some judges and commentators have argued in recent years that the law should order economic exchanges between some intimates who are not connected by marriage or parenthood. The Washington Supreme Court held in 1995 that when an unmarried couple ends "a stable, marital-like relationship where both parties cohabit with knowledge that a lawful marriage between them does not exist,"[115] "[t]he property that would have been characterized as community property had the couple been married is before the trial court for a just and equitable distribution."[116] Under this approach, "[t]here is a rebuttable presumption that property acquired during the relationship is owned by both of the parties and is therefore before the court for a fair division."[117] The American Law Institute's *Principles of the Law of Family Dissolution* (2002) proposes a similar legal regime for regulating the dissolution of relationships between "domestic partners," which the ALI defines as "two persons of the same or opposite sex, not married to one another, who for a significant period of time share a primary residence and a life together as a couple."[118] On the ALI's proposal, most "property is domestic-partnership property if it would be marital property . . . had the domestic partners been married to one another during the domestic-partnership period,"[119] and "[d]omestic-partnership property should be divided according to the principles set forth for the division of marital property."[120]

How to Regulate Economic Exchange Within the Family

In sum, the canonical story about family law's separation from the market takes attention away from the actual choices that family law confronts. The question of whether the law should permit and enforce economic exchanges within the family is largely moot, as a practical matter. Family law already allows such exchanges and sometimes requires them. It authorizes married couples to bargain over everything from the rate of return for helping a spouse earn a degree, to financial compensation for having a child, to the yearly price of staying married. It authorizes other family members to bargain over even more. Indeed, legalized economic exchange within the family is all but unavoidable, given the pervasive economic transfers and negotiations within and across generations.

The pressing issue for family law is *how* to regulate economic exchange within the family, in what forms, for what purposes, and to what ends. Family law's present regulation of economic exchange is not fully consistent or coherent, but it does contain recurring patterns. When courts and legislatures decide to trumpet family law's supposed separation from the market by loudly refusing to enforce particular economic exchanges, they are more likely to target certain groups. Much legal regulation of economic exchange within the family has harmful distributional consequences for women and poorer people, imposing its greatest costs on groups that are already disproportionately burdened. The canonical narrative about family law's separation from market principles obscures this disparate distribution of injury. Exploring how family law actually regulates economic exchange helps make more visible the unequal burdens that family law currently inflicts.

Let's return to the prohibition on interspousal contracts for domestic services and also examine the legal regulation of surrogacy and adoption. Courts celebrate the law's refusal to enforce interspousal contracts for domestic services as evidence of family law's separation from the market. But this refusal imposes its most direct costs on wives. Women are the parties to marriage most likely to be performing domestic labor and seeking economic compensation for that work.[121] The doctrine means that husbands can choose to compensate their wives for domestic labor as a matter of individual beneficence or customary practice. Yet wives cannot create an enforceable right to be paid directly for their household work—a right to be compensated that would not vanish if a husband changed his mind before paying, a right independent of a husband's continued goodwill.

Refusing to enforce interspousal contracts for domestic services, especially when combined with other family law doctrines that Chapter 3 will discuss, leaves many wives who follow conventionally feminine life courses economically vulnerable during marriage and economically devastated at divorce. Household labor consumes disproportionate amounts of married women's time and energy. It frequently diminishes the time and energy that wives have to perform paid work outside the home or to undertake the most highly demanding and well-compensated forms of market work. Phrased differently, spending significant time on domestic labor often means that married women earn less, or sometimes no, money in the market and have substantially diminished long-term earning potential there. Meanwhile, husbands routinely benefit from their wives' domestic work. They receive the benefit of the services themselves as well as the advantage of being able to spend more of their own time and energy on leisure or on paid work in an economy that offers disproportionate rewards to workers who have freed themselves from competing time commitments. In sum, wives' domestic labor can generate enormous value for their husbands and performing it can cost women dearly.

The disproportionate burden that women bear for this symbol of family law's rejection of market principles comes into focus even more sharply when we recognize that courts do enforce agreements between spouses about the transfer and distribution of property and cash. If anything, husbands are probably more likely than wives to have property and cash that they would like to protect through marital contract.

The *Borelli* case vividly illustrates the disparate impact that the refusal to enforce interspousal contracts for domestic work can have on women's economic welfare. Hildegard and Michael Borelli entered into two major economic agreements over the course of their relationship. Their first agreement was a prenuptial contract apparently providing that many or all of Michael's assets would remain his separate property and be excluded from Hildegard's elective share. The Borellis made their second agreement about Hildegard's nursing care against the background of this prenuptial agreement. In return for Hildegard's round-the-clock nursing, Michael agreed to transfer to Hildegard some of the real estate, cash, and other assets that he had kept as his separate property in the prenuptial agreement.[122] Without the prenuptial contract in place, Hildegard would have stood to inherit much more at Michael's death and might have seen no need to receive economic compensation for her nursing services. The California Court of Appeal assumed the validity of the Borellis' first agreement, which was designed to protect Michael's real estate and other economic assets from Hildegard's claims. But the court refused to enforce the Borellis' second agreement, which was designed to protect Hildegard's right to be paid for the domestic labor she provided to Michael. The court cited the principle of family law's separation from the market in refusing to enforce the Borellis' second contract.[123] Yet *Borelli* itself reveals how family law routinely enforces economic exchanges between spouses, even in circumstances where spouses are likely to have unequal bargaining power. Current judicial doctrines do not separate family law from the market. However, the judicial refusal to recognize interspousal contracts for domestic work does function to impose a disproportionate burden on women that invocations of the myth of family law's separation from the market do nothing to justify.

Laws governing surrogacy and adoption also illustrate how the symbolic expression of family law's rejection of the market can come at the price of disproportionate harm to women and poorer people.

Some states have a relatively uncomplicated approach to surrogacy agreements. Either they reject surrogacy agreements and provide that such agreements are always unenforceable,[124] or they embrace these agreements and permit parents to compensate surrogates.[125]

However, other states seek to express the idea that surrogacy is separate from the market by dramatically restricting permissible payments to surrogate mothers. Some of these states provide that surrogacy contracts are unenforceable if the surrogate receives compensation.[126] Another set of states specifies that a surrogate may be reimbursed for her medical and living expenses, but may not be paid for serving as a surrogate and surrendering her rights to the child.[127] These rules somewhat resemble judicial refusals to enforce interspousal contracts for domestic labor, in that they permit the work of surrogacy, while displaying much more hostility toward payment for that work. Indeed, gestating a child and undertaking the labor of childbirth can be understood as quintessential forms of domestic work, although their risks, rewards, agonies, and joys can be much larger and more vivid than those associated with ordinary daily housework.

Adoption regulation focuses even more intently on scrutinizing and restricting economic transfers to birth mothers. While lawyers, doctors, and agencies are routinely and legally paid for their services in adoptions,[128] states signify that adoption is not a market transaction by strictly distinguishing between permissible and prohibited forms of payment to birth mothers. Some states specify that adoptive parents may pay for only adoption expenses and services and for the birth mother's living and medical expenses.[129] Some states limit the flow of money to birth mothers more tightly. Courts have held that adoptive parents may not pay for a birth mother's living expenses while she is pregnant,[130] her lost wages,[131] or her maternity clothes.[132]

Indeed, the Pennsylvania Supreme Court held that adoptive parents could not pay for a birth mother's "Lamaze classes, pre-natal care and sonograms" on the remarkable ground that "these expenses are not directly connected with the birth, and, thus, are outside the parameters of the traditional allowable expenses in adoption."[133] This court was so intent on signifying that adoption law rejects market principles that its reasoning veered toward absurdity. Lamaze classes, prenatal care, and sonograms *are* all demonstrably and directly connected with childbirth. Prenatal care and sonograms are designed to monitor and safeguard a fetus's health. One of the many reasons to do this is so that doctors can be appropriately prepared for childbirth and can take steps beforehand to mitigate or avoid complications during childbirth.[134] Lamaze classes seek to improve women's experiences with labor and delivery, but they also seek to promote deliveries that will be safer and healthier for babies.[135]

Presumably the Pennsylvania Supreme Court sought to bar adoptive parents from paying for a birth mother's Lamaze classes, prenatal care, and sonograms on the theory that those services would help the birth mother rather than (or as well as) her child. The court's opinion later explained that adoptive parents may not pay for services "which directly benefit the natural mother," even if "the child may enjoy an indirect benefit from these services."[136] But this impulse is a striking illustration of the tremendous and disproportionate costs that some courts are willing to impose on less powerful people in order to express family law's supposed rejection of market principles. The Pennsylvania Supreme Court thought it appropriate to deny birth mothers reimbursement for Lamaze classes, prenatal care, and sonograms that the women might be unable to afford on their own, even if that meant that birth mothers would have to experience pregnancy, labor, and delivery in ways that were more risky, more complicated, more painful, and/or more medicated.

States have good reason for wanting to distinguish surrogacy and adoption from baby selling, and one way to do that is to limit and channel the flow of funds. But the financial burden of signifying family law's rejection of economic principles frequently falls on poorer women. The available evidence suggests that surrogate mothers typically occupy a relatively low socioeconomic status[137] and that women placing their children for adoption tend to be disadvantaged compared to the rest of the population.[138] Legal prohibitions or restrictions on payments to surrogates or birth mothers deny or reduce compensation to the poorest parties in surrogacy or adoption arrangements, while often allowing high-status professionals such as doctors and lawyers to collect their fees. In both contexts, more vulnerable people frequently shoulder the weight of family law's desire to declare its separation from the market.

Sharply restricting permissible payments to surrogates or birth mothers means that the women are likely to remain relatively poor and to be in no better position to support themselves after surrogacy or adoption than before. Indeed, a woman may be less able to support herself than she was before becoming pregnant if her pregnancy causes her to leave work for any significant period. Reimbursement for lost wages during pregnancy, assuming a surrogate or birth mother even receives such reimbursement, may not fully compensate her for the reduced long-term earning potential that is often associated with disruptions in workforce participation.[139]

It is also worth remembering in this context that courts are willing to allow women to receive economic rewards for giving birth if they contract for those rewards through prenuptial or postnuptial agreements. To be sure, such agreements differ from surrogacy or adoption contracts in that prenuptial or postnuptial agreements ordinarily contemplate that the woman giving birth will raise the child in question, whereas surrogacy or adoption agreements presuppose that the surrogate or birth mother will not raise the child. At the same time, it bears mentioning that prenuptial or postnuptial agreements typically involve couples in which at least one party has significant economic assets. By upholding prenuptial or postnuptial agreements providing that one spouse will receive more money or assets upon the birth of a child, states permit wealthier couples to attach financial rewards to childbirth—rewards that may be far larger than any money directed to a surrogate or birth mother.

Canonical narratives insisting that family law rejects market principles obscure the disproportionate burden that family law's present regulation of economic exchange can inflict on women and poorer people, maintaining and worsening distributive inequality. Examining the legally enforceable economic exchange that actually runs through family law reveals these uneven distributive consequences and allows us to redirect our energies. Rather than dwell on lengthy disputes about whether to allow economic exchange, we can direct our attention to the live question for family law—how best to regulate such exchange. This is the arena where discussion, debate, and deliberation should focus, and where courts and legislatures, along with scholars, advocates, and individuals, should concentrate on articulating and defending their views about how family law should proceed.

This book aims to promote such debate, rather than preempt it. In the interest of encouraging further discussion, I will conclude this chapter with some of my own thoughts about how family law could better regulate economic exchange. These comments are meant to spark further dialogue. One need not accept my specific suggestions for reform to agree that a key question for family law centers on how to regulate economic exchange, rather than on whether to permit such exchange at all.

In my view, states should remove some of their current limitations on economic exchange within the family. For instance, there are good reasons to enforce interspousal contracts for domestic services. As we have seen, courts routinely uphold interspousal contracts about property, earnings, cash, and nondomestic labor. People can plausibly debate whether courts or legislatures should adjust this regime at the margins. For instance, the law might take more account of stark differences in bargaining power or do more to guard against the possibility that steep escalation clauses in prenuptial or postnuptial agreements will create powerful incentives to divorce. Similarly, people can plausibly debate whether courts or legislatures should require interspousal contracts to be in writing or enforce oral contracts as well. That said, the basic legal commitment to enforcing interspousal contracts about property, earnings, cash, and nondomestic labor is unlikely to change in the foreseeable future.

Refusing to enforce interspousal contracts for household labor does not separate marriage from the market, even if we were to presuppose that such a separation would be normatively desirable. Denying enforcement to interspousal contracts for domestic work instead ensures that more wives receive some or all of their economic assets in the form of provided support rather than legally negotiated compensation and accordingly helps perpetuate married women's dependence on their husbands. The doctrine assumes and helps entrench a marital structure in which wives, including wives who work only in the home, can be denied a right to compensation for their domestic labor because they are supposed to be supported rather than earn their own support. Refusing to recognize interspousal contracts for domestic labor enforces female dependence and mandates female altruism, in circumstances where women have attempted to secure compensation for their labor.

States should adjust some of family law's other restrictions on economic exchange without removing them entirely. For example, there are practical and compelling reasons to retain prohibitions on buying and selling children. Child selling would exploit, without systematically redressing, vast disparities in wealth. If children could be legally exchanged for enormous sums, a poor parent might feel tremendous pressure to sell a child—if only to secure sufficient resources to care for the parent's other children. Allowing the sale of children would be likely to endanger children's welfare, undermine the parent-child relationship, traumatize siblings, disrupt extended family relationships, and lessen the societal value placed on human life. A child is not a commodity and should not be subject to the same rules of economic exchange applied to commodities.[140]

Nonetheless, a state concerned about the distributive consequences of its current restrictions on economic exchange within adoption and surrogacy should consider allowing more resources to flow to birth mothers and surrogates in ways that would help the women improve their life chances and their ability to support themselves. For instance, states might permit adoptive or intended parents to pay for a birth mother's or surrogate's educational expenses or job training, something that some state adoption statutes now explicitly prohibit.[141] This regulatory change would still enable states to distinguish adoption and surrogacy from child selling, by continuing to limit and channel the exchange of money.

But at the same time, the proposed reform would make it less likely that a state's desire to condemn child selling will leave those parties to adoption and surrogacy with the fewest assets and the least bargaining power resourceless and impoverished.

States should also consider how they might do more to regulate the economic activities of actors in the adoption and surrogacy process other than birth mothers and surrogates. These regulations could be designed so that the law better respects and protects the dignity and autonomy of birth mothers and surrogates, while simultaneously pushing wealthier and more powerful people to bear more of the burdens associated with distinguishing adoption and surrogacy from ordinary commercial transactions.

For example, states might prohibit agencies, lawyers, and doctors from collecting fees related to adoptions and surrogacies unless the agencies, lawyers, and doctors take specified steps to ensure that the consent of the birth mother or surrogate is informed. This might mean that agencies, lawyers, and doctors must fully inform a birth mother or surrogate about the potential dangers, risks, and challenges associated with adoption or surrogacy. It might mean that agencies, lawyers, and doctors must provide a birth mother or surrogate with any information that a diligent fiduciary would discover that casts doubt on the ability of the adoptive or intended parents to raise a child. It might mean that adoptive or intended parents, or adoption or surrogacy agencies, must pay for independent legal counsel for the birth mother or surrogate, or otherwise ensure that she is fully informed of her legal rights. For instance, California requires adoptive parents to pay for a birth mother's separate legal counsel if the birth mother so requests,[142] and California law provides that before "executing [a] written assisted reproduction agreement for gestational carriers, a surrogate and the intended parent or intended parents shall be represented by separate independent licensed attorneys of their choosing."[143] States might also require adoptive or intended parents, or adoption or surrogacy agencies, to cover the expenses associated with having a state official verify in person at the time of an adoption or surrogacy agreement that agencies, lawyers, doctors, and adoptive or intended parents have complied with all legal requirements.

The narrative about family law's separation from the market continues a canonical theme in family law, which stresses the field's exceptionalism and differences from other areas of law. But here, as with the story about family law's supposed localism, the canonical insistence on family law's exceptionalism paints a distorted picture of the field that directs the attention of legal authorities away from the real questions that family law faces. The pressing issues for family law are not about whether to permit and enforce economic exchange, but about how and when to permit and enforce economic exchange, for what purposes, and with what consequences. At present, family law's regulation of economic exchange frequently operates to impose its greatest burdens on women and poorer people, perpetuating and exacerbating distributive inequality. The contention that family law simply rejects market principles that govern other legal arenas has obscured this disproportionate infliction of injury. Recognizing the pervasive economic exchange within family law allows us to examine how family law's regulation of economic exchange actually operates and to explore how this regulation should be reformed.

II

THE FAMILY LAW CANON'S
PROGRESS NARRATIVES

A second canonical theme in family law focuses on family law's relationship to its past. Canonical stories about family law prominently feature progress narratives recounting family law's evolution over time. The narratives stress sharp breaks from history, dramatic transformations in family law rules and policies, and the abandonment of historical practices grounded in subordination and injustice.

These progress narratives are in unacknowledged tension with canonical accounts of family law's exceptionalism. Stories describing family law as exceptional tend to depict family law as a haven of unusual stability while other legal fields undergo rapid and turbulent change. In contrast, family law's canonical progress narratives contend that family law has dramatically transformed itself over time and evolved to keep pace with progressive reform. Moreover, where exceptionalist stories insist on family law's differences from other legal arenas, the prevalence of progress narratives within family law constitutes yet another way in which the field resembles other areas of the law. Many stories in the American tradition present legal history as a tale of steady and striking improvement.[1]

Without question, family law has changed over time in ways that have often improved the position of disadvantaged family members. Indeed, progress narratives about family law would not be even facially plausible without the ability to point to some positive evolution over time.

Family law's progress narratives can also sometimes be used in ways that advance the field. These stories are sometimes deployed for aspirational purposes, with family law's past successes invoked in the interest of bolstering arguments for further reform.

But family law's canonical progress narratives significantly overstate the extent and nature of family law's historical transformations, while underemphasizing and obscuring continuity in family law doctrines, practices, and presumptions. The stories too frequently tend to envision reform more as a fulfilled goal within family law than as an ongoing project. They are inclined to focus on celebration rather than scrutiny, criticism of the past rather than examination of the present.

These progress narratives can divert legal decisionmakers from considering whether, when, why, and to what extent family law might still operate to perpetuate injustice and subordination. In fact, judges and legislators sometimes explicitly draw on these narratives as arguments for directing attention away from persistent disparities, on the ground that family law has already left its support for normatively illegitimate or problematic policies safely in the past.

This part explores family law's canonical progress narratives. Chapter 3 examines canonical stories describing historical transformations in family law's regulation of adults. Chapter 4 examines a canonical story describing historical transformations in family law's regulation of children.

3

PROGRESS NARRATIVES FOR ADULTS

When our divorce law was originally drawn, woman's role in society was almost totally that of mother and homemaker. She could not even vote. Today, increasing numbers of married women are employed, even in the professions. In addition, they have long been accorded full civil rights. Their approaching equality with the male should be reflected in the law governing marriage dissolution and in the decisions of courts with respect to matters incident to dissolution.

—California Assembly Judiciary Committee (1969)[1]

[T]he movement of the progressive societies has hitherto been a movement *from Status to Contract.*

—Henry Sumner Maine (1861)[2]

Descriptions of change over time in family law's regulation of adults prominently feature two canonical stories. The first story contends that modern family law has renounced and repudiated the common law regime of coverture that legally subordinated married women to their husbands and denied wives most aspects of a separate legal identity. The second story reports that family law was once controlled by status rules whose terms were set by the state and unchangeable by the parties involved, but is now dominated by contract rules subject to individual negotiation and alteration.

Both canonical stories are progress narratives. One declares that family law has disentangled itself from a legal system that enforced the legal supremacy of husbands over wives. The other celebrates the rise of contract rules on the presumption that they are preferable to status rules.

Both narratives can rightly point to some important historical change. The story of coverture's demise takes its power from the undeniable ways in which the legal regime of coverture that existed in early nineteenth-century America has been profoundly transformed in the years since then. The status to contract narrative relies on some central examples in which family law has become more contractualized than it once was.

But both narratives tend to exaggerate change over time, while understating and overlooking continuity in family law. The strict emphasis in both stories on breaks from past practices and progress achieved can divert attention from considering which aspects of modern family law might still require reform.

The story of coverture's demise presents the dismantling of coverture as more complete, absolute, and unwavering than it has actually been. This narrative overlooks the ways in which rules, policies, and principles founded in coverture still shape significant features of modern family law. Coverture's imprint remains visible in today's family law, and one cannot understand the contours of contemporary family law without recognizing the field's origins in coverture.

The persistent manifestations of coverture doctrines and principles continue to operate to women's systematic detriment, adding to the other factors within and outside family law that help perpetuate women's unequal status. The canonical narrative about coverture's demise obscures the perpetuation of rules and policies from the common law regime and directs attention away from examining how these rules and policies disproportionately harm women. This narrative can make additional progress toward sex equality more difficult by envisioning coverture's eradication as a project already accomplished. Indeed, some legal authorities have used this narrative as an argument against focusing on persistent disparities between the status of women and men, on the ground that family law has already erased the evidence of its roots in coverture.

The status to contract story is descriptively overstated and normatively underdefended. Important status rules remain in force and contract rules can have disadvantages, especially for parties with less bargaining power. Descriptively, the status to contract story obscures the continued significance of status rules within family law, diverting focus from examining laws and doctrines that establish unalterable legal features of familial relationships. Some of these status rules reflect the persistent imprint of coverture doctrines, while others extend beyond the boundaries of coverture's legacy. Normatively, the tendency to presume that contract rules are superior to status rules takes attention away from assessing the costs and benefits of implementing any specific family law policy in status or contract form, as those costs and benefits vary by context.

The Story of Coverture's Demise

Let's begin with the story of coverture's demise. The common law organized married women's legal status around principles of coverture that placed wives under their husbands' wide-ranging control. Coverture doctrine, also known as the doctrine of marital unity, held that "the husband and wife are one person in law: that is, the very being or legal existence of the woman is suspended during the marriage, or at least is incorporated and consolidated into that of the husband: under whose wing, protection, and *cover,* she performs every thing."[3] Common law treatises explained that a married woman was "not, in legal contemplation, a distinct person," that the law "places her almost absolutely within her husband's keeping, so far as her civil rights are concerned."[4] A wife at common law had little, or no, right to sue, be sued, contract, keep her earnings, make a will, buy or sell property, or claim legal custody of her children. A husband had legal dominion over his wife's labor and his wife's person.[5]

Judges, legislators, and commentators have repeatedly declared that family law has cast off its common law roots in married women's legalized subordination. Indeed, the canonical story of coverture's demise is both remarkably old and persistently vibrant.

Announcements that coverture has been eradicated are not always clear or consistent in dating coverture's endpoint. Some courts and commentators reported in the early twentieth century that coverture had already been vanquished. They cited or alluded to legal reforms that occurred before or during the era of the first organized woman's rights movement in the United States. That movement ran from approximately 1848, when woman's rights advocates coalesced at a convention in Seneca Falls, New York,[6] to 1920, when the movement won the ratification of the Nineteenth Amendment securing women's right to vote.[7] However, judges and legislators who announced in the late twentieth century that coverture had ended sometimes suggested that coverture's demise was a relatively recent phenomenon, linked to the rise of the second women's movement in the 1970s and 1980s. These courts and lawmakers implicitly shifted the purported end date of coverture forward in time, even as they asserted that coverture had been removed from the law by the time they were writing. In any event, legal authorities routinely agree that, whenever coverture was last in place, it is now firmly in the past.

Law journals and treatises began proclaiming coverture's end as early as the turn of the last century. An article in the *Harvard Law Review* declared in 1908 that "in Massachusetts within fifty years the common law unity of husband and wife, and all the rules resulting from that unity, have been swept away by statute, almost completely."[8] A leading family law treatise announced in 1921 that "[t]he old common-law theory of marriage, that of unity of person and property in the husband, is so repugnant to modern ideas that it has been almost entirely swept away."[9] The treatise formally applauded this purported legal change, even as it simultaneously expressed enthusiasm for how family life was organized under coverture and satisfaction that the social and economic roles of men and women had not changed. "There was," the treatise elaborated, "during the latter part of the nineteenth century, a remarkable movement for giving the wife equal rights in all respects with the husband, which has been so far successful that it can almost be said now that the modern wife has a legal right which, fortunately for all of us, she does not exercise, to leave home in the morning and go to work, collect and keep her own wages and leave her husband to do the housework and take care of the babies."[10]

The Supreme Court announced the end of coverture well before the Court began applying rigorous equal protection principles to the legal treatment of women. The Court did not strike down a single law on the ground that it violated a woman's constitutional right to equal protection until 1971.[11] But the Court began declaring coverture's demise in the early twentieth century, in decisions that we will turn to shortly. By 1960, the Court noted "the vast changes in the status of woman—the extension of her rights and correlative duties—whereby a wife's legal submission to her husband has been wholly wiped out, not only in the English-speaking world generally but emphatically so in this country."[12] The Court in 1966 described "[t]he institution of coverture" as "peculiar and obsolete,"[13] "quaint," and "now, with some exceptions, relegated to history's legal museum."[14]

State courts likewise proclaimed the end of coverture long before the creation of modern sex discrimination jurisprudence. The Kansas

Supreme Court announced in 1913 that "[t]he common-law doctrine of coverture, with all its incidents, has been relegated to the past by modern legislation and decisions."[15] The Tennessee Supreme Court stated in 1919 "that married women are no longer under the disability of coverture, and are completely emancipated."[16] The South Carolina Supreme Court reported in 1938 "that the law of servitude in marriage is repealed in this State."[17] The Florida Supreme Court declared in 1942 that "[i]n the marital state, husband and wife are partners and equals."[18] The California District Court of Appeal explained in 1954 that "[t]he legal status of a wife has changed. Her legal personality is no longer merged in that of her husband."[19]

Declarations of coverture's end have become still more common in recent years. Since the advent of the Supreme Court's modern sex discrimination jurisprudence, the Court has proclaimed that "[n]owhere in the common-law world—indeed in any modern society—is a woman regarded as chattel or demeaned by denial of a separate legal identity and the dignity associated with recognition as a whole human being."[20] The Court has announced that "the marital couple is not an independent entity with a mind and heart of its own, but an association of two individuals each with a separate intellectual and emotional makeup."[21] The Court has stated that "a view of marriage consonant with the common-law status of married women" is "repugnant to our present understanding of marriage and of the nature of the rights secured by the Constitution. Women do not lose their constitutionally protected liberty when they marry."[22]

Many lower courts in recent decades have similarly announced the end of coverture. They explain that "[t]he old common law doctrine that a husband and wife are to be regarded as one entity has long since been discarded in modern jurisprudence,"[23] that "[t]he old fiction of the unity of person of the husband and wife has been completely abrogated,"[24] that "curtesy and all the other burdens of coverture are gone,"[25] that "the notions that a woman should be regarded as her husband's chattel and deprived of her dignity and recognition as a whole human being through the denial of a separate legal identity have been thoroughly rejected,"[26] that "[w]e do not believe that the common law disability of coverture has any sanction in our jurisprudence or any relevance in our society,"[27] that "the theory of legal identity of husband and wife" "cannot be seriously defended today,"[28] that "[a]s states moved to recognize the equality of the sexes, they eliminated laws and practices like coverture that had made gender a proxy for a spouse's role within a marriage. Marriage was thus transformed from a male-dominated institution into an institution recognizing men and women as equals."[29]

The canonical narrative about coverture's demise seems to celebrate family law's commitment to sex equality. The narrative might be used, and sometimes is deployed, as a rallying point in seeking additional progress. For instance, some courts considering constitutional challenges to state prohibitions on same-sex marriage have cited the story of coverture's demise as evidence that marriage law can be reformed to better promote equality.[30] But too frequently, judges and legislators invoke the story of coverture's end as an argument against focusing on persistent disparities between the status of women and men, on the ground that family law has already disentangled itself from its roots in women's legalized subordination.

Many of the Supreme Court's first opinions declaring that family law had renounced coverture actually upheld rules denying women equal rights. The Court used the story that family law had repudiated its origins in coverture as a means of indicating some normative commitment to sex equality, while simultaneously dismissing the possibility that such a commitment might require any material change in legal arrangements. Consider *Muller v. Oregon*,[31] *Goesaert v. Cleary*,[32] and *Hoyt v. Florida*.[33]

Muller (1908) upheld an Oregon law limiting women's working hours,[34] at a time when the Court was convinced that such restrictions on working hours unconstitutionally violated freedom of contract if applied to men who were not employed in especially hazardous occupations.[35] The *Muller* decision endorsed a legal regime that assumed and perpetuated women's marginalization from market labor, but the Court began its opinion in *Muller* by declaring coverture's demise. The Court asserted that under Oregon law "women, whether married or single, have equal contractual and personal rights with men"[36] and contended that "putting to one side the elective franchise, in the matter of personal and contractual rights [women] stand on the same plane as the other sex."[37] The *Muller* Court then proceeded to argue that this legal transformation was perfectly compatible with continued male supremacy and sex-based restrictions on women's market work. *Muller* concluded that: "Even though all restrictions on political, personal, and contractual rights were taken away, and she stood, so far as statutes are concerned, upon an absolutely equal plane with him, it would still be true that she is so constituted that she will rest upon and look to him for protection; that her physical structure and a proper discharge of her maternal functions—having in view not merely her own health, but the well-being of the race—justify legislation to protect her from the greed as well as the passion of man."[38]

Goesaert v. Cleary (1948) upheld a Michigan law that prohibited women from working as bartenders in large cities, unless the woman was the wife or daughter of the bar's male owner.[39] The *Goesaert* Court stressed "the vast changes in the social and legal position of women,"[40] but insisted that "despite" these changes "Michigan could, beyond question, forbid all women from working behind a bar."[41] On this account, the supposed transformation in women's legal status was completely consistent with a statute that tracked common law coverture in denying women access to market employment unless they labored under the control and "protecting oversight" of a husband or father.[42] As the Court explained, "[t]he fact that women may now have achieved the virtues that men have long claimed as their prerogatives and now indulge in vices that men have long practiced, does not preclude the States from drawing a sharp line between the sexes, certainly, in such matters as the regulation of the liquor traffic."[43]

Hoyt v. Florida (1961), in turn, upheld a Florida law that automatically included men on jury rolls, but excluded women unless they registered for inclusion.[44] Here, too, the Court began by declaring "the enlightened emancipation of women from the restrictions and protections of bygone years, and their entry into many parts of community life formerly considered to be reserved to men."[45] Describing women's emancipation as "enlightened" signaled judicial approval, but the *Hoyt* Court stressed that this "enlightened emancipation" had done little to alter women's fundamental position in law and society. The Court insisted that "woman is still regarded as the center of home and family life" and explained that "[w]e cannot say that it is constitutionally impermissible for a State, acting in pursuit of the general welfare, to conclude that a woman should be relieved from the civic duty of jury service unless she herself determines that such service is consistent with her own special responsibilities."[46]

More recently, state legislators enacting divorce laws and state courts adjudicating such laws have relied on the canonical story of coverture's demise in contending that the legal system no longer needs to be much concerned about women's economic welfare after divorce. Consider

California's 1969 Family Law Act,[47] which sparked a wave of legislative revisions to divorce statutes across the nation that marked the beginning of the modern law of divorce.[48] California law prior to the Family Law Act permitted divorce only upon proof of marital fault and favored the legally faultless spouse, who was usually the wife, in dividing community property at divorce.[49] The Family Law Act established that none of the grounds for securing a divorce in California would turn on marital fault.[50] The act also instructed divorce courts to divide community property equally in most cases, regardless of each spouse's fault or future earning capacity,[51] and to consider in deciding whether to award alimony "the ability of the supported spouse to engage in gainful employment without interfering with the interests of the children of the parties in the custody of such spouse."[52]

Before the Family Law Act became law, the California Assembly's Judiciary Committee issued a report explaining the committee's intent.[53] The report suggested that coverture's end meant that divorce law should assume women's legal and economic equality, rather than work to protect it. The committee contended:

> When our divorce law was originally drawn, woman's role in society was almost totally that of mother and homemaker. She could not even vote. Today, increasing numbers of married women are employed, even in the professions. In addition, they have long been accorded full civil rights. Their approaching equality with the male should be reflected in the law governing marriage dissolution and in the decisions of courts with respect to matters incident to dissolution.[54]

James A. Hayes, who wrote this report as the Judiciary Committee's Chair and helped shepherd the Family Law Act through the California legislature,[55] worked to disseminate his argument to the legal profession. He wrote a 1970 article about the Family Law Act for the *American Bar Association Journal* that paraphrased his language from the Judiciary Committee report, under a heading that read "Women's Rights Observed by California Legislature."[56]

Indeed, James Hayes soon cited his own language from the Judiciary Committee report in a brief arguing that he should no longer have to pay alimony to his ex-wife. James and his wife, Janne, divorced in 1969 before the Family Law Act went into effect in 1970.[57] James agreed to pay $650 a month in alimony to Janne,[58] who had been raising the couple's four children and had not worked outside the home since the first year of their marriage in 1941.[59] As early as 1972, however, James began quoting his own official declarations about coverture's demise in an effort to end his alimony payments.[60] He convinced the California Superior Court in 1973 to reduce his alimony payments to $300 a month and then persuaded the Superior Court in 1975 to further shrink his monthly alimony payments to $200.[61]

Janne, who was fifty-three in 1975, ill, and without market work experience, applied for federal food stamps and county welfare benefits.[62] James by then earned $40,322 a year as the Chairman of the Los Angeles County Board of Supervisors, but he told reporters that his ex-wife's welfare application "'doesn't embarrass me at all.'"[63] The California Court of Appeal ultimately restored Janne's $650 alimony payments later in 1975 on the ground that courts lacked the authority to modify the binding agreement the divorcing couple reached in 1969.[64] Nonetheless, James continued to litigate in an attempt to end his alimony obligations,[65] albeit unsuccessfully because the Court of Appeal had already decided the issue.[66] Janne was still eligible for and receiving food stamps as of 1976.[67] Meanwhile, the mode of argument that James Hayes utilized has continued to thrive.

Since the 1970s, state courts deciding whether to award divorcing women alimony have repeatedly relied on the contention that family law has eradicated its roots in coverture. The New York Court of Appeals justified its greater reluctance to award alimony on the ground that "the times have changed, owing not alone to the coequal status which a married woman today shares with her husband but also to the increase in the number of married women working in gainful occupations."[68] The Illinois Appellate Court took "judicial notice of the recent emancipation of women socially and economically, and particularly in the area of employment opportunity."[69] The Florida District Court of Appeal explained that divorce law no longer needed to treat women "with compassion, tenderness and mercy" because "[t]he law [now] properly protects them in their right to independently acquire, encumber, accumulate, and alienate property at will. They now occupy a position of equal partners in the family relationship resulting from marriage, and more often than not contribute a full measure to the economic well-being of the family unit."[70] The Florida court felt no need to consider empirical evidence on the actual opportunities or disadvantages that married or divorced women encountered in the workplace. But the court used the canonical story about the end of coverture to assert nonetheless that "[w]hether the marriage continues to exist or is severed through the device of judicial decree, the woman continues to be as fully equipped as the man to earn a living and provide for her essential needs."[71]

Courts upholding prenuptial agreements that deny or limit alimony have also invoked the story of coverture's demise. The Connecticut Superior Court argued "that the former complete protective role of the court regarding alimony is no longer necessary" as "[t]he law formerly attaching the aforementioned subjection to the legal status of a married woman has been abolished either by legislation or by the continuous pressure of judicial interpretation."[72] The Kentucky Supreme Court explained that restrictions on prenuptial agreements developed at a time when "the Nineteenth Amendment to the Constitution of the United States had not yet been ratified, married women's property acts were not yet in existence or were in their infancy, and in general the status of women in this society was decidedly second class." The court declared that "[s]ubsequent changes in society and seventy-five years of experience have rendered such restrictions inappropriate."[73] The Illinois Appellate Court reported that "[w]hen the rules regarding the husband's duty of support were first enunciated, the roles of a husband and wife were more rigid and defined," but now "[w]here a woman is trained, healthy, and employable, and where a woman's efforts have not contributed to her husband's wealth or earning potential, the necessity for an alimony award upon breakup of the marriage is not great."[74]

In *Simeone v. Simeone* (1990),[75] the Pennsylvania Supreme Court used the story of coverture's demise to argue more broadly that courts should no longer focus on reviewing the substantive and procedural fairness of prenuptial agreements. When the Simeones married in 1975, Catherine was a twenty-three-year-old unemployed nurse and Frederick was a thirty-nine-year-old neurosurgeon with an annual income of approximately $90,000 and assets worth approximately $300,000. On the eve of the wedding, Frederick's lawyer presented Catherine with a prenuptial agreement that limited Catherine at separation or divorce to alimony payments of $200 a week, with a maximum total payment of $25,000. Catherine signed the agreement without consulting a lawyer or being advised about the legal rights she was surrendering. The couple separated in 1982 and began divorce proceedings in 1984. Catherine challenged the prenuptial agreement's validity, relying on precedent that subjected such agreements to relatively exacting review.[76]

States vary in how much they scrutinize the substantive and procedural fairness of prenuptial agreements.[77] In *Simeone,* the Pennsylvania Supreme Court attached itself to a far end of the spectrum. The court held that it would enforce the Simeones' agreement without considering whether the agreement's provisions for Catherine were substantively reasonable or whether Catherine had an informed understanding of the legal rights she was giving up in the agreement.[78]

Simeone justified its decision by arguing that family law had renounced its historical role in women's legalized subordination. The court reported that its past scrutiny of prenuptial agreements "rested upon a belief that spouses are of unequal status," with women "regarded as the 'weaker' party in marriage, [and] in society generally."[79] *Simeone* contended that such scrutiny was "now insupportable" in light of women's transformed legal status and the inclusion of an Equal Rights Amendment in the Pennsylvania Constitution.[80] Pennsylvania's ERA (adopted in 1971) provides that "[e]quality of rights under the law shall not be denied or abridged in the Commonwealth of Pennsylvania because of the sex of the individual."[81] One might suppose that this constitutional provision would give the Pennsylvania Supreme Court more cause to evaluate its decisions from the standpoint of sex equality. But the *Simeone* court used the Pennsylvania ERA as evidence that "the law" had already "advanced to recognize the equal status of men and women in our society" and as a reason why courts no longer needed to consider whether their judgments in divorce cases would inflict economic harm on women that was unreasonable, inequitable, or unfair. In a case involving a woman who had married without a job or apparent assets, the court blithely observed that "women nowadays quite often have substantial education, financial awareness, income, and assets."[82]

Coverture's Persistent Imprint on Family Law

The narrative about coverture's demise is canonical in family law. It is a stock story that judges and legislators repeatedly deploy to explain family law and their decisions about its course. But the tale significantly misdescribes the current state of the law. Coverture principles continue to shape important aspects of family law in ways that systematically disadvantage women, adding to the other forces within and outside family law that help maintain women's unequal status. The story of coverture's end overlooks the persistent imprint of coverture, directs attention away from examining how the enduring manifestations of coverture's influence work against women's equality, and obscures the case for further progress by suggesting that coverture's legacy has already been eradicated.

We can focus on three contexts in exploring how family law's roots in coverture continue to shape the field: laws and doctrines that prohibit important forms of interspousal litigation, keep some interspousal lawsuits out of federal courts, or treat the infliction of injury more leniently when it occurs between spouses. Courts and legislatures almost always describe modern family law in the sex-neutral language that I have employed here. But the substantive law in all three of these contexts emerged out of the sex-specific regime of married women's common law coverture. Courts creating this jurisprudence reasoned within the boundaries of a legal universe that explicitly and enthusiastically subordinated married women to their husbands.

Doctrines with their roots in coverture still routinely and foreseeably operate to women's detriment. Women's historical experiences under coverture helped foster many disadvantages that women continue to confront more frequently than men, such as a lesser likelihood of earning high wages in the market and a greater likelihood of having a violent spouse. Still operative legal doctrines that emerged out of coverture continue to worsen and make more severe the consequences of the disadvantages that women disproportionately encounter. These doctrines erect legal barriers to contracts that women are more likely to want to make, close off judicial forums that women may disproportionately need to avoid or mitigate bias elsewhere, or treat marital violence that women are more likely to experience as a less serious offense than violence committed outside marriage.

Legal Prohibitions on Interspousal Litigation

Let's begin with legal prohibitions on interspousal litigation. Common law courts were systematically opposed to hearing suits between spouses. At first, the common law prohibited interspousal litigation as part of a more general prohibition on suits by or against married women. Starting in the 1830s, however, a wave of states enacted married women's property acts providing that married women now had the rights to sue and be sued, make contracts, own separate property, and keep their wages.[83]

Some modern judicial opinions recounting the story of coverture's demise take the enactment of these nineteenth-century statutes as their central piece of proof. They explain that the married women's property acts were "[t]he beginning of the end of coverture,"[84] that "the common law unity concept. . . . was largely dissipated by the widespread enactment of 'Married Women's Acts' in the mid-nineteenth century,"[85] that the married women's property acts "fully and effectively eradicated the common law disability of coverture."[86]

The married women's property acts were significantly less transformative than such accounts indicate. Wives quickly brought a variety of suits against their husbands after the statutes became law. But nineteenth- and twentieth-century courts concluded that the prospect of a wife suing her husband was fundamentally inconsistent with coverture principles and interpreted the married women's property acts to permit virtually no interspousal litigation, except suits for torts to property and suits for divorce.[87]

When wives sued their husbands for damages stemming from wife beating, courts in the second half of the nineteenth century and the beginning of the twentieth century created the common law doctrine of interspousal tort immunity and read the married women's property acts to leave interspousal tort immunity undisturbed. This doctrine held that a person injured by her spouse, whether intentionally[88] or negligently,[89] could not sue her spouse for damages.

Courts devising the doctrine often contended that interspousal tort immunity benefited both husbands and wives, on the theory that providing tort remedies for marital violence would jeopardize marital privacy and harmony. But judges created the doctrine of interspousal tort immunity in cases where wives had gone to court seeking civil remedies against their husbands. The doctrine predictably operated to shield men's marital violence from outside scrutiny and legal redress and to preserve and uphold men's power over their wives.

For instance, the United States Supreme Court in *Thompson v. Thompson* (1910)[90] held that the married women's property act for Washington, D.C., did not permit a wife who had suffered her husband's assault and battery to sue her husband for damages.[91] The statute authorized married women "'to sue separately . . . for torts committed against them, as fully and freely as if they were unmarried.'"[92] But the Court explained that this statutory provision could not be interpreted to allow wives to sue their husbands because such an interpretation would "open the doors of the courts to accusations of all sorts of one spouse against the other, and bring into public notice complaints for assault, slander and libel, and alleged injuries to property of the one or the other, by husband against wife or wife against husband."[93]

State courts interpreted married women's property acts similarly, reasoning that permitting assaulted wives to sue their husbands for damages would be "contrary to the policy of the law, and destructive of that conjugal union and tranquility, which it has always been the object of the law to guard and protect,"[94] would "mak[e] public scandal of family discord, to the hurt of the reputation of husband and wife, their families and connections,"[95] and "would strongly tend to separations and divorces, which probably would not otherwise occur, and would thereby tend to impair the institution of marriage, which is the chief support of the social edifice the world over, and without which the structure would fall."[96] One judge declared that he was "unwilling . . . to obliterate the primary obligations growing out of the marriage relation, to revolutionize the whole law relating to husband and wife, and open the courts to the public discussion of domestic differences, which, when of sufficient consequence, may be settled by the chancellor in suits for divorce, or by prosecution for violation of the criminal laws of the state."[97]

When wives sued their husbands to enforce contracts for domestic services, courts held that contracts between spouses for household labor were categorically unenforceable.[98] As Chapter 2 explored, modern courts refusing to enforce such contracts invoke the canonical, if faulty, premise that family law rejects market transactions. This theme appeared in some earlier cases,[99] but earlier judicial refusals to enforce interspousal contracts for household labor relied heavily on a very different argument that still appears as a supplemental contention in some modern opinions (including the *Borelli v. Brusseau* decision that Chapter 2 considered).[100]

Courts in the nineteenth and early to mid-twentieth centuries reasoned that a husband owned his wife's domestic services under coverture. Courts interpreted the married women's property acts to leave this male prerogative intact, even where the acts granted married women the rights to both contract and keep their own "earnings." On the courts' theory, a husband contracting to pay for his wife's household work had agreed to pay for labor that already "belong[ed] absolutely" to him.[101] This meant that interspousal contracts for domestic labor represented nothing more than a husband's promise to give his wife a gift, and standard contract law provides that gift promises are not legally enforceable contracts.[102]

When wives sued their husbands for failing to support them, courts responded with the doctrine of necessaries. Courts enforcing this doctrine recognized that a husband had a legal obligation to support his wife because he owned his wife's domestic labor and services. Yet courts overwhelmingly concluded that permitting a wife to sue her husband directly for support would be inconsistent with coverture's idea of marital union.[103] Instead, the doctrine of necessaries established that a wife whose husband failed to provide her with necessities through no fault of her own could purchase necessary items from a third party, such as a merchant or doctor.[104] If her husband refused to pay the bill, the third party could sue the husband for payment and collect if the court agreed that the wife was faultless and had purchased a necessity rather than a luxury.[105] The exact judicial definition of a necessity fluctuated, with courts more likely to agree that an item was a necessity the higher the perceived class status of the married couple at issue.[106] There were a few extreme decisions in which courts were willing to accept that even a fur coat[107] or an expensive sofa[108] might constitute a necessity for a wealthy man's wife. But these sometimes amusing decisions aside, the serious import of the doctrine of necessaries was that wives had no right to cash from their husbands and to the autonomy, anonymity, and possibilities of escape associated with cash. Instead, married women were dependent on the cooperation of third parties to secure necessities if their husbands refused to provide them. Wives might be clever, cunning, or even deceptive in enlisting the aid of third parties to acquire necessities. Yet ultimately third parties had little incentive to cooperate if they suspected that collecting payment would require resort to often unpredictable litigation in which the third parties bore the burden of proof.[109]

All of these prohibitions on suits between spouses originated out of coverture principles and reasoning, yet all persist in some form today. As Chapter 2 discussed, no court will enforce interspousal contracts for domestic services. At least thirty-three states retain some form of the doctrine of necessaries,[110] and four of those states have sex-specific doctrines.[111] However, courts overwhelmingly refuse to permit one spouse in a legally intact marriage to sue the other spouse directly for increased support.[112] Virginia explicitly provides by statute that its "doctrine of necessaries . . . shall in no event create any liability between such spouses as to each other."[113]

In *Wright v. Wright*, a 1990 case before the Delaware Family Court, Emma Wright unsuccessfully sought additional support from Roy, her husband of forty-eight years.[114] The Wrights' marriage was legally intact, although unharmonious. The couple shared the same home, and neither spouse intended to seek a divorce. But Emma and Roy had "occupied separate bedrooms for at least four years," and the court reported that there was "some evidence that the parties [did] not get along very well and that they essentially live[d] separate lives while living under the same roof."[115]

Emma had apparently been managing the couple's finances. She sued because Roy ended this arrangement, insisted on keeping his finances separate,[116] and refused to pay for Emma's "food, medical, clothing, life insurance and gasoline expenses."[117] Emma sought an order giving her "one-half of the aggregate net family income," contending that she had "insufficient funds of her own to meet her essential needs."[118]

Emma's only income consisted of a $299 monthly Social Security check, while her husband received $1,404.06 per month. Roy's larger monthly income suggested a history of sustained market work, a typically masculine life pattern. Roy collected a $601.06 monthly pension from the Chrysler Corporation and received $803 per month from the Social Security system.[119] In contrast, Emma's finances suggested a more conventionally feminine life course, in which she either had not worked in the market at all or had worked in significantly less remunerative occupations. Emma collected no pension, and her smaller Social Security check was likely a spousal benefit based on Roy's status as a primary beneficiary. Recall from Chapter 1 that Social Security law provides that a spousal benefit can only be up to half as large as the payment that the primary beneficiary receives.

The *Wright* court found that Emma needed to "be extremely frugal in her expenditure of money" in order to pay for food, healthcare, clothing, life insurance, and gasoline on $299 a month and that Emma might "sometimes not have enough money for gasoline or other 'extras.'"[120] The court was also "convinced" that Roy, who was illiterate and apparently in mental decline, was "totally incompetent to manage money in any way, shape or form."[121]

Nonetheless, *Wright* held that Emma was not "entitled to receive support from [her] husband."[122] The court invoked the language of privacy and nonintervention to justify its decision. It explained that "the Court simply does not believe that it should become involved in the internal financial arrangements of married persons who choose to stay together. It is not the function of this Court to attempt to budget or allocate funds between spouses living under the same roof every time some disagreement arises between them anymore than the Court should be involved in deciding when and where they should eat, sleep or engage in sexual relations. This Court, although its jurisdiction over family matters is extremely broad, should not invade private households except in cases of extreme emergency or where one spouse subjects the other to physical or emotional harm. Regulation and supervision of family finances should normally be left to the spouses themselves unless and until they decide to separate."[123]

The first point to note about this line of argument is that the *Wright* court was articulating its concern about privacy in a situation where neither spouse had sought privacy. Emma chose to bring her case to court because she wanted half of the aggregate net family income, and Roy chose to litigate in response rather than settle the matter privately because he wanted to keep all the assets in his name under his control. Both spouses preferred to discuss their conflict in a public forum in order to win a favorable judicial resolution. Both asked the court to adjudicate their dispute.

It is also important to recognize that the Delaware court, despite its rhetoric about nonintervention, did not actually stay out of the Wrights' dispute over support. Instead, the court decided that dispute, and it did so using essentially the same doctrine that a court would have relied on more than a century earlier. *Wright* held that during marriage Roy could keep the assets in his name to himself. Indeed, Roy's financial control during marriage extended to his pension, even though that asset would probably count as marital property subject to division if the couple were to divorce. Emma, like a wife living in the early nineteenth century, had no means of directly enforcing her right to support while she remained in an ongoing marriage. She might seek to cajole (or berate) her husband into giving her more, but any negotiations she pursued with her husband would take place against the background of that legal doctrine.

Unlike some nineteenth-century courts, *Wright* was careful to use facially sex-neutral language about leaving "[r]egulation and supervision of family finances . . . to the spouses themselves." But of course, the

Wright decision systematically favored the spouse with greater assets in his name. The facts of *Wright* itself suggest why such a legal advantage has predictably gendered consequences, benefiting men more often than women.

The *Wright* court cited as support for its holding a 1953 decision from the Nebraska Supreme Court.[124] In *McGuire v. McGuire*,[125] Lydia McGuire sought "suitable maintenance and support money" from Charles, her husband of almost thirty-four years.[126] Charles had over $117,000 in cash and bonds, an annual income of $8,000 or $9,000, and 398 acres of farmland worth $83,960.[127] However, he also "had a reputation for more than ordinary frugality."[128] Indeed, Charles refused to install a kitchen sink, bathtub, shower, or indoor toilet in their home, to replace the house's malfunctioning furnace (in Nebraska), or to repair the car's inadequate heater.[129]

Lydia did the housework (without indoor plumbing!) and also worked on Charles's farm, but Charles had no legal obligation to pay Lydia for her domestic labor and he did not. In fact, he had not provided Lydia with any money for the past three or four years.[130] Lydia had previously been able to earn some money for herself by raising chickens and selling eggs and poultry. But at age sixty-six and after "three abdominal operations," she apparently no longer had the physical stamina to continue this additional work.[131]

Lydia lost her suit. The Nebraska Supreme Court explained that "[t]he living standards of a family are a matter of concern to the household, and not for the courts to determine, even though the husband's attitude toward his wife, according to his wealth and circumstances, leaves little to be said in his behalf. As long as the home is maintained and the parties are living as husband and wife it may be said that the husband is legally supporting his wife and the purpose of the marriage relation is being carried out. Public policy requires such a holding."[132] Foreshadowing *Wright,* the *McGuire* court suggested that it was leaving decisions about marital living standards "to the household." But in reality, the court's holding empowered Charles McGuire to make those decisions alone. Lydia spent her time working hard in Charles's house and on his farm, and Charles responded with miserliness so extreme that the court took care to detail it. Nonetheless, Lydia had no legal ability to directly enforce her right to support so long as she stayed in the marriage.

There has been more change over time in the doctrine of interspousal tort immunity, but at least seven states retain some form of this immunity.[133] Moreover, even where states permit interspousal suits to seek damages for injuries stemming from marital violence, this type of litigation remains infrequent and marginalized in the law. One study of "approximately 2600 reported state cases of battery, assault, or both, from 1981 through 1990" found that "only fifty-three involved adult parties in domestic relationships. Similarly, during the same time frame, only four reported federal cases involved a claim or counterclaim between adult parties in a domestic relationship."[134] As Chapter 1 elaborated, the prospect that the Violence Against Women Act's civil rights remedy would treat wife beating like any other form of gender-motivated violence and allow wives subject to marital violence to sue their husbands in federal court for damages was so striking that it pushed many legislators, judges, courts, and advocates to categorize the civil rights remedy as a form of family law. The multiyear effort to enact the Violence Against Women Act also uncovered abundant evidence that bias and inadequacy in state judicial responses to marital violence discourage lawsuits and make legal victories more difficult for plaintiffs to achieve. Several state courts have further discouraged interspousal tort litigation by upholding "family member exclusion" clauses in insurance policies that deny insurance coverage for interspousal torts.[135]

Judges and legislators now almost always state the prohibitions on suits between spouses in sex-neutral language. They sometimes expressly attempt to reconcile the prohibitions with the canonical story of coverture's demise. For instance, the California Court of Appeal in *Borelli v. Brusseau* (1993) made an argument along those lines in response to a dissenting opinion. Justice Marcel Poché, the lone dissenter in *Borelli,* cited two cases from the late nineteenth and mid-twentieth centuries that reasoned in explicitly sex-specific terms in refusing to enforce interspousal contracts for domestic services. Poché's dissent observed that "[s]tatements . . . to the effect that a husband has an entitlement to his wife's 'services' smack of the common law doctrine of coverture which treated a wife as scarcely more than an appendage to her husband."[136] In response, the *Borelli* majority contended that "[i]f the rule denying compensation for support originated from considerations peculiar to women, this has no bearing on the rule's gender-neutral application today."[137]

Yet whether explicitly sex-specific or officially sex-neutral, the prohibitions on interspousal litigation continue to operate to women's systematic disadvantage. Wives are more likely than husbands to be subject to marital violence.[138] Wives are more likely than husbands to be performing domestic labor and seeking compensation for that work.[139] Wives are more likely than husbands to need economic support in marriage, in part because married women's disproportionate domestic labor can hinder their wage-earning in the market. In short, the prohibitions on suits between spouses are still more likely to prevent a woman from initiating a suit that she would like to bring.

These prohibitions, moreover, can have a cumulative effect on women's bargaining power and material resources in marriage and after it, helping to ensure that many wives accumulate few separate economic assets during marriage even as they perform household work that diminishes their earning potential in the market. Think of a married woman who stays home to care for children. She cannot make an enforceable agreement with her husband to be compensated for her household labor. She also has no directly enforceable right to support. In other words, any cash she receives from her husband during their marriage is likely to be a matter of voluntary agreement, not enforceable contract. Of course, a woman may divorce her husband if he provides her with little or no cash. Divorcing women who report that their husbands severely restricted their access to cash appear in the case law, recounting that their husbands denied them independent access to bank accounts,[140] doled out "$20 at a time" for groceries,[141] or doled out too little cash to cover household expenses.[142] But a woman may be disinclined to pursue divorce for a variety of financial, cultural, religious, personal, or other reasons. Indeed, a woman who has spent her married life focused on raising children rather than developing her earning capacity in the market is repeatedly disadvantaged under a divorce regime that presupposes, yet does not actually safeguard, women's economic and legal equality.

Many studies have found that divorce is economically disastrous for the average woman and her children, while the average man's financial well-being after divorce is much more stable or even somewhat improved. Lenore Weitzman's pathbreaking early study of no-fault divorce in California found that "divorced men experience[d] an average 42 percent rise in their standard of living in the first year after the divorce, while divorced women (and their children) experience[d] a 73 percent decline."[143] Subsequent researchers have uncovered flaws in Weitzman's methodology and convincingly disputed the extremity of her findings.[144] But a wave of scholarship confirms the general trend that Weitzman highlighted.[145]

Divorce law systematically disadvantages spouses who pursue life courses that are conventionally associated with white, middle-class women. As Chapter 2 discussed, courts overwhelmingly refuse to recognize human capital as a form of marital or community property subject to distribution at divorce. This means that a wage-earning spouse may keep for himself the value of the human capital he accumulated during marriage. Human capital, and the associated ability to earn money in the future, is frequently the most important economic asset present in a marriage. The exclusion of human capital from marital or community property often means that a divorcing couple has little marital or community property to divide at all, as many married couples have little or no savings and sometimes substantial debts.[146] Judges also rarely award alimony, and long-term alimony is virtually nonexistent.[147] Some states even impose a statutory time limit on alimony awards.[148] In addition, most children live with their mother after divorce.[149] In theory, child support payments could compensate custodial parents for the economic burdens associated with raising children. But courts often set child support awards too low and respond inadequately to widespread underpayment.[150] In sum, a wife who stayed home with children is likely to be left at divorce with a diminished capacity to earn income, no property claim on her husband's future income stream, little chance of receiving alimony, primary responsibility for raising the children, and half of the often meager, sometimes nonexistent, savings and assets that the couple managed to accumulate during marriage.

Terry Martin Hekker, who stayed home to raise five children, published a bestselling book in 1979, *Ever Since Adam and Eve,* that celebrated the joys of life as "a wife, a mother, a homemaker."[151] Years later, Hekker's husband informed her on their fortieth wedding anniversary that he wanted to divorce. She wrote in the *New York Times* in 2006 about what happened next: "He got to take his girlfriend to Cancun, while I got to sell my engagement ring to pay the roofer. When I filed my first nonjoint tax return, it triggered the shocking notification that I had become eligible for food stamps. The judge had awarded me alimony that was less than I was used to getting for household expenses, and now I had to use that money to pay bills I'd never seen before: mortgage, taxes, insurance and car payments. And that princely sum was awarded for only four years, the judge suggesting that I go for job training when I turned 67. Not only was I unprepared for divorce itself, I was utterly lacking in skills to deal with the brutal aftermath."[152] Hekker published a new book in 2009, entitled *Disregard First Book*.[153]

The Domestic Relations Exception to Federal Diversity Jurisdiction

Let's turn to the law on where spouses may sue each other, another arena in which doctrine from coverture persists. As Chapter 1 discussed, the Supreme Court in 1859 reasoned from coverture in creating the domestic relations exception to federal diversity jurisdiction. The Court devised the exception on the premise that it was generally impossible for a husband and wife to have diversity of citizenship because coverture disabled a married woman from establishing a separate legal residence from her husband, no matter where she actually lived. Although the "logic" behind the creation of the domestic relations exception no longer counts as such, the exception remains in place and keeps cases involving the issuance of a divorce, alimony, or child custody decree out of federal court.

The domestic relations exception is important for both men and women. Federal diversity jurisdiction is meant to protect out-of-state litigants from the potential parochial biases of another state's courts,[154] and the exception means that this protection is unavailable in a large number of cases.

In addition, the domestic relations exception may have particularly negative consequences for women and for men challenging dominant gender roles. States' own gender bias task forces have consistently found that state judicial systems remain biased against women's claims.[155] This systemic bias suggests that litigation in state courts may be highly risky for women, especially in cases where the stakes are as high and the gendered issues as prominent as they are in litigation involving divorce, alimony, and child custody decrees. At the same time, some commentators (discussed more in Chapter 4) have argued that state courts deciding contested custody cases remain biased against men who would like to assume childcare responsibilities conventionally assigned to women. Women, and men seeking to perform typically female work, may thus have particularly strong reasons for wanting a choice between federal and state courts, so that they can avoid state courts if they wish and pursue at least the possibility of better treatment in federal courts—even if there is no guarantee that federal courts will be free from gender bias either.[156]

More Legal Leniency for the Infliction of Injury Within Marriage

Finally, consider how the legal system continues to treat the infliction of injury more leniently when injury occurs within marriage. We could focus here on spousal assault and battery, where criminal prohibitions exist in every state yet remain chronically and disproportionately under-enforced.[157] But marital rape exemptions provide perhaps the most stunning example of the persistent imprint of coverture and the harm that it still causes women.

At common law, a husband was absolutely exempt from prosecution for raping his wife. Courts and treatises throughout the nineteenth century routinely endorsed the marital rape exemption. They acknowledged that unwanted sex harmed wives. But they reasoned that protecting husbands from liability for marital rape fit smoothly within a common law regime that legally subordinated wives to husbands and denied married women the right to make many enforceable decisions.[158]

These historical arguments no longer sound convincing, and commentators sometimes assume that states have abolished their marital rape exemptions. They declare that "[b]y the late 1980s, one of the last strongholds of the male-ownership model of marriage—the idea that a woman's body was her husband's sexual property—was erased as feminists invented and wrote into law the concept of 'marital rape.'"[159] They announce that "[n]o longer does marriage mean that a wife's identity—her name and her domicile, for example—is totally linked to her husband's. Nor does marriage give a husband license to violate his wife's bodily integrity."[160]

Yet at least twenty-three states retain some form of a marital rape exemption. These states criminalize a narrower range of conduct if committed within marriage,[161] impose less serious penalties on the marital rape they do recognize,[162] and/or create special procedural obstacles to marital rape prosecutions.[163]

The Supreme Court's emerging sex discrimination jurisprudence, along with the modern feminist movement's critique of marital rape exemptions, helped pushed states in the 1970s and 1980s to rephrase their marital rape exemptions in facially sex-neutral language, so that the exemptions now shield "spouses" rather than husbands from marital rape prosecution.[164] But the functional impact of a facially sex-neutral marital rape exemption (the contemporary formulation) and an explicitly sex-specific exemption (the common law version) is essentially the same. All available evidence indicates that marital rape is virtually always committed by husbands against wives. Indeed, I have been able to locate just a handful of cases in which a woman may have come to the attention of American law enforcement authorities for raping an adult man.[165] Only a few more examples of adult female-on-adult male rape have been reported in the psychiatric literature[166] or in child support cases (where a father reports that he was raped and argues that he should not have to support the resulting child for that reason).[167] It is possible to predict with almost perfect accuracy that marital rape cases will involve husbands as the "spouses" who continue to receive legal protection when they commit marital rape and wives as the "spouses" left unprotected when they are subject to acts that the law would otherwise treat as serious crimes. As a matter of practice, marital rape exemptions continue to define a man's rights in marriage to include sexual control over his wife. The best available empirical studies report that marital rape is both widespread[168] and extremely damaging, frequently causing even more trauma than rape outside of marriage.[169]

The canonical narrative about coverture's demise treats history as safely in the past. But doctrines and principles from coverture continue to shape modern family law in ways that still operate to undermine women's equal status. In declaring family law's repudiation of its common law roots, the story of coverture's end obscures the current state of the law and diverts attention from asking whether, when, and why the persistent manifestations of coverture's legacy, ranging from prohibitions on interspousal litigation, to the domestic relations exception to federal diversity jurisdiction, to marital rape exemptions, should remain in place.

The Status to Contract Story

A second canonical story repeatedly invoked to describe historical transformations in family law's regulation of adults contends that family law has shifted from status to contract. Some form of this story dates at least as far back as 1861, when Henry Sumner Maine famously announced "that the movement of the progressive societies has hitherto been a movement *from Status to Contract*."[170] Status rules establish legal rights, privileges, obligations, and limitations and make them unalterable by private agreement. Contract rules permit individuals to structure their own legal relationships if they prefer not to rely on the default positions the state sets. The descriptive claim in the status to contract story is that contract rules now dominate family law where status rules once did. The normative premise of the story is that the move from status to contract is an improvement.

The status to contract story is linked to the canonical narrative about coverture's demise. Common law coverture consisted of an interlocking system of status rules. When legislatures or courts replaced an aspect of coverture with a contract rule, that served to reduce the prevalence of status rules in family law.

However, the status to contract story exists in some tension with the canonical narrative stressing family law's separation from the market. The premise of the market rejection narrative, which Chapter 2 discussed, is that family law renounces and repudiates market principles that dominate other legal arenas and accordingly constrains how individuals may organize their family lives. In contrast, the status to contract narrative maintains that individuals are now free to order their family relationships as they see fit, which presumably means that individuals will have legal support if they choose to structure their family relationships according to market norms. Yet courts, lawmakers, and commentators have not addressed this tension between two canonical narratives about family law, and both narratives persist simultaneously.

For instance, many (although of course not all)[171] scholars repeat, reinforce, and rely on the status to contract narrative. One scholar has declared that "[m]odern family law has steadily moved toward contract as its governing principle."[172] Another scholar has reported that "[t]rends shifting modern family law toward contract as its governing principle are putting an end to the traditional status regime."[173] A third has announced that "[i]n virtually all doctrinal areas, private norm creation and private decision making have supplanted state-imposed rules and structures for governing family-related behavior."[174] A fourth scholar has stated that there has "been a shift in family law from public ordering to private ordering."[175] A fifth has remarked that "Maine was more right than he knew and probably more right than he wanted to be."[176] A

a shift away from detailed legal regulations, legal and rights-based terms

sixth has explained that "[n]owhere has modern law's shift from status to contract been more apparent than in family law."[177]

Scholars recounting the status to contract story frequently focus on the law of marriage. They explain that there has been "a dejuridification of marriage,"[178] that in "the law of marriage, scholars have come to understand our legal rules as resting mainly on imputed bargains that are susceptible to alteration by actual bargains,"[179] that "marriage was privatized decades ago,"[180] that "the law does not ban spouses from creating almost any kind of relationship that satisfies them,"[181] that "[m]any commentators have noted that marriage itself has evolved from a relationship based on status to one regulated by contract,"[182] that "[t]he trend from state control to private ordering within marriage is pervasive," that "[t]here are few state-prescribed obligations associated with marriage, and fewer still that cannot be altered by the parties,"[183] that "the contractual nature of the modern law of marriage is indisputable."[184]

While some version of the status to contract story is over a hundred and fifty years old, more recent accounts of the story often contend or suggest that the pace of change became faster or more noticeable in the last decades of the twentieth century. For example, one scholar explained in 1980 that "[a]n accelerated movement from status to contract is discernible in the realm of family relations."[185] Another scholar reported in 1992 that "[a] preference for private over public ordering has characterized the development of family law over the past quarter century."[186] A scholar stated in 1994 that "[w]ithin the past thirty years, family law has permitted the creation and operation of families to become increasingly a matter of negotiation and choice. As between adults, this shift nears completion."[187] In 2001, a scholar described the decades after World War II as a time when "[t]he concept of marriage as an institution of the state and a determinant of status was being converted to one predominantly governed by individual choices and agreements—the view of marriage as a contract."[188] A scholar observed in 2008 that "[a]lthough Maine made his observation more than a century ago, the transitions of the past fifty years seem to have followed his prediction to an extent that might have surprised even Maine. The law has largely abandoned the moral discourse that once surrounded marriage and divorce, and the status norms that once defined the rights and obligations of husbands and wives."[189]

The status to contract story, although not embraced by every family law scholar, is nonetheless so much a part of the family law canon and its outlines are so well-worn into the fabric of family law literature that scholars recounting the narrative tend to rely on the same examples. Scholars explaining family law's past immersion in status rules frequently employ as their quintessential illustration the Supreme Court's statement in *Maynard v. Hill* (1888) that when people marry "a relation between the parties is created which they cannot change."[190] *Maynard's* pronouncement came twenty-seven years after Maine had already declared family law's movement from status to contract, but the discrepancy typically goes unnoted. Scholars describing the current contractualization of family law, in turn, most often cite the lack of legal constraints on an individual's choice of marital partner[191]—exemplified by the Supreme Court's decision in *Loving v. Virginia* (1967),[192] the availability of no-fault divorce,[193] the enforceability of prenuptial agreements,[194] and the enforceability of agreements between nonmarital partners.[195]

As these accounts note, there are areas of family law that have become more contractualized than they once were. *Loving* gave individuals more control over decisions about whom to marry. It struck down once widespread prohibitions on interracial marriage that were still in place in sixteen states in 1967.[196] *Loving* has since become canonical in family law. Judicial opinions condemn and reject legal arguments if they suggest that *Loving* was wrongly decided.[197] *Loving* is celebrated as a pivotal and foundational moment in books,[198] articles,[199] symposia,[200] a documentary film,[201] a television movie,[202] and annual "Loving Day" celebrations throughout the United States that mark the anniversary of the Supreme Court's decision.[203]

Indeed, *Loving* operates as a dual canonical marker. First, it is deployed as a symbol of family law's transformation from status to contract. As early as 1969, a scholar identified *Loving* as part of "a profound consensus in American society that the state and the law should say as little as possible about who can marry whom. All would agree," this scholar asserted, "with the conviction that marriage is and should remain the most intimate, personal, and legally unsupervised contract known to the law."[204] Second, *Loving* is also invoked as a sign of family law's triumph over racial inequality—another systemic injustice that family law has supposedly left safely behind in the past. As one scholar observed, "*Loving's* dominant legacy has been the simple narrative sketched by the founders of Loving Day: a story about prejudice overcome."[205] *Loving* is canonically taken to stand for the proposition that family law has conquered racial inequality by providing individuals with greater choices, thus theoretically rendering moot the need for more structural reforms.

The "no-fault revolution" in divorce law, which is discussed more below, gave individuals more control over decisions about whether to get divorced. Divorce was available only for cause throughout much of the twentieth century, with cause defined narrowly under state law and rendered difficult to establish. In contrast, every state now makes some form of no-fault divorce available, meaning that a person who wants a divorce for his own reasons may eventually secure a divorce. The enforceability of prenuptial agreements and the enforceability of agreements between nonmarital partners, discussed in Chapter 2, similarly give individuals more ability to control the economic consequences of ending marital or nonmarital relationships.

Persistent Status Rules

Yet notwithstanding these canonical examples of contractualization, the status to contract story overstates its descriptive account of change over time and underdefends its normative assumption of progress. Descriptively, the narrative diverts attention and debate away from the continued importance of status rules in shaping family law. Consider, for example, some of the status rules that control entry to marriage, regulate ongoing marriages, or govern parent-child relationships.

States still impose many unwaivable and nonnegotiable restrictions on marriage formation and the choice of marital partners, preventing marriages even where all parties would like to wed. As of this writing, same-sex couples may marry in only seventeen states and the District of Columbia.[206] Prohibitions on same-sex marriage have attracted enormous attention recently because of the reform efforts of the gay rights movement. Yet there are other deeply rooted prohibitions on marriage formation that draw remarkably little notice in family law.

Every state prohibits polygamous marriages,[207] imposes age restrictions on marriage,[208] and bars marriages between some relatives.[209] Virtually the only time that these restrictions on marriage formation attract attention within family law is in the context of debates in which both sides assume that the restrictions are justified and beyond reconsideration. Courts,[210] judges,[211] lawmakers,[212] and scholars[213] defend same-sex marriage prohibitions by comparing them to prohibitions on polygamous, incestuous, or child marriage, or condemn same-sex marriage prohibitions by contrasting them with prohibitions on polygamous, incestuous, or child marriage.

Status rules regulating the rights of mentally disabled or mentally ill people to marry draw even less scrutiny. Sometimes these rules operate simply to keep people without the capacity to consent from marrying. But at least ten states impose statutory prohibitions or restrictions on marriages involving a mentally disabled or mentally ill person that go beyond a basic requirement that the person be capable of consent and want to marry.[214] In Kentucky, for example, a marriage "[w]ith a person who has been adjudged mentally disabled by a court of competent jurisdiction" "is prohibited and void,"[215] and people who aid or abet such marriages are subject to criminal penalties.[216]

Several states use significantly less precise and more pejorative language to describe the disabled or ill people targeted by state restrictions on marriage formation, leaving unclear who exactly has their rights limited and why. In Vermont, a marriage with "an idiot or lunatic" is voidable.[217] Rather than define either of those terms directly, Vermont law (unhelpfully) provides that "[t]he word 'lunatic' . . . shall extend to persons of unsound mind other than idiots."[218] In West Virginia, "[m]arriages solemnized when either of the parties" "[w]as an insane person, idiot or imbecile" "are voidable and are void from the time they are so declared by a judgment order of nullity."[219] In Tennessee, "[n]o [marriage] license shall be issued when it appears that the applicants or either of them is at the time drunk, insane or an imbecile."[220] A United States District Court has explained without apparent qualm that requiring couples in Tennessee to obtain their marriage licenses from a county clerk so that the clerk can enforce this provision "protects the State against recognizing marriages that are contrary to the public interest."[221] In Pennsylvania, "[n]o marriage license may be issued if either of the applicants for a license is weak minded, insane, of unsound mind or is under guardianship as a person of unsound mind unless the court decides that it is for the best interest of the applicant and the general public to issue the license and authorizes the issuance of the license."[222]

Family law similarly devotes little attention to status rules regulating and restricting the rights of people with sexually transmitted diseases to marry, although at least six states have such rules in place. Nebraska law provides that "[n]o person who is afflicted with a venereal disease shall marry in this state."[223] West Virginia law states that "[m]arriages solemnized when either of the parties" "[w]as afflicted with a venereal disease" "are voidable and are void from the time they are so declared by a judgment order of nullity."[224] New Jersey law provides that "[n]o marriage license shall be issued when, at the time of making an application therefor, either applicant is infected with a venereal disease in a communicable stage."[225] Ohio law states that "[n]o marriage license shall be granted when either of the applicants . . . is infected with syphilis in a form that is communicable or likely to become communicable."[226]

California and Vermont have statutes that subject people with venereal diseases to criminal penalties for marrying. California law provides that "any person infected with a venereal disease in an infectious state who knows of the condition and who marries or has sexual intercourse, is guilty of a misdemeanor."[227] Vermont law states that "[a] person, having been told by a physician that he or she was infected with gonorrhea or syphilis in a stage which is or may become communicable to a marital partner, or knowing that he or she is so infected, who marries, without assurance and certification from a legally qualified practitioner of medicine and surgery or osteopathy that he or she is free from such disease in a stage which is or may become communicable to the marital partner shall be imprisoned not less than two years or fined not less than $500.00, or both."[228]

Indeed, the persistent variety of status rules restricting marriage formation is striking. For instance, at least two states restrict the right of divorced people to remarry. Wisconsin law provides that "[i]t is unlawful for any person, who is or has been a party to an action for divorce in any court in this state, or elsewhere, to marry again until 6 months after judgment of divorce is granted, and the marriage of any such person solemnized before the expiration of 6 months from the date of the granting of judgment of divorce shall be void."[229] Marriages that run afoul of this statute have been declared void in Wisconsin courts.[230]

Alabama law empowers judges to decide "whether the party against whom the judgment of divorce is made [will] be permitted to marry again" at all. If an Alabama judge "affirmatively disallow[s]" a divorced person from remarrying, the judge may later decide, "upon motion and proper proof, to allow the moving party to marry again, as justice may seem to require."[231] The constitutionality of this law is questionable, but the Alabama Court of Civil Appeals in 1995 did not appear to find the statute overly troubling, explaining that "[t]he statute simply allows the trial court, on a case-by-case basis, in a divorce proceeding, the discretionary authority to prohibit a party from remarriage if that prohibition serves to effectuate a legitimate state interest, and is appropriate in light of the peculiar facts and circumstances of the case."[232] The court held that "[t]herefore, the statute, when narrowly applied, despite its imprecisions, is a permissible exercise of this State's power to regulate marriage and the family."[233] Alabama law also provides that "[w]hen a judgment has been entered granting a divorce in this state, the court shall order that neither party shall again marry, except to each other, until 60 days after the judgment is entered."[234]

At least one state restricts the right of people on probation or parole to marry. Delaware law states that "[a] marriage is prohibited, and is void from the time its nullity is declared by a court of competent jurisdiction at the instance of the innocent party, if either party thereto is . . . [o]n probation or parole from any court or institution, unless such person first files with the clerk of the peace to whom such person makes application for a marriage license a written consent to such person's proposed marriage from the chief officer of such court or institution or from someone who is appointed by such officer to give such consent, and unless in other respects the applicant may lawfully marry."[235]

Status rules also continue to impose important limitations on the legal structure of ongoing marital relationships, establishing significant benefits and burdens tied to marriage that spouses have no right to alter. All of the family law that this chapter just examined in exploring the continuing influence of coverture principles takes the form of status rules. A husband and wife cannot come to an enforceable agreement to waive a marital rape exemption, or to abide by an interspousal contract for domestic services, or to bring their divorce suit to federal court, or to forgo interspousal tort immunity, or to adjust the doctrine of necessaries.

Status rules are even more prevalent in the law governing parent-child relationships. Agreements between parents or prospective parents about a minor child's care, custody, visitation, or support are voidable and not binding on courts.[236] Courts will not enforce contracts in which one parent agreed not to seek any child support payments from the other parent,[237] or agreed not to seek judicial modification of child support payments,[238] or agreed not to seek custody of a child,[239] or agreed to surrender parental rights in exchange for the other parent's agreement to accept a reduced payment for child support arrearages,[240] or agreed to surrender parental rights in exchange for the other parent's agreement to receive no child support at all.[241] Minor children themselves are generally unable to make binding contracts with anyone, including a parent.[242]

In sum, a descriptive problem with the canonical status to contract story is that it tends to treat status rules as anomalies. The story obscures family law's persistent reliance on status rules and takes focus away from examining the status rules that remain in place.

Potential Disadvantages of Contract Rules

Normatively, the status to contract story appears to presume that contract rules are preferable to status rules. Scholars who endorse this story themselves or note its popularity within legal academia describe "[t]he transition from status-based relations to social arrangements organized mainly around contract" as "a shift from unquestioned traditional forms to rationally contrived ones" and "a progressive step toward freeing ourselves from the yoke of traditional gender relations and achieving a just, egalitarian society."[243] They declare that "[m]arriage law has evolved far toward recognizing the need for private choice and the untenableness of uniform public policy as a strategy for governing the conduct and obligations of intimacy."[244] They conclude that "the changing purpose and function of both marriage and the family support the idea that contractual ordering will best meet the social goals of a stable, happy, personally fulfilling environment."[245] They explain that "[t]he liberal ideal that individuals have fundamental rights, and should freely choose to make of their lives what they wish supports private ordering."[246] They report that "[m]ost would consider the move from 'status' to 'contract' 'a good thing.'"[247]

The progress narrative about the shift from status to contract diverts attention from the disadvantages that can be associated with particular contract rules, especially when the contracting parties have unequal bargaining power. For example, as some scholars have observed, the transition from fault-based to no-fault divorce appears to have made divorce even more economically devastating for many women and their children. One reason is that the availability of unilateral no-fault divorce makes it much easier for a married person to obtain a divorce without his spouse's cooperation.

Under the fault-based divorce regime, divorce was available only when a legally innocent person could prove that her spouse had committed a specific marital fault, such as adultery, desertion, cruelty, drunkenness, or felony conviction.[248] As the Tennessee Supreme Court explained in

1955, divorce was "not a matter to be worked out for the mutual accommodation of the parties in whatever manner they may desire, or in whatever manner the Court may deem to be fair and just under the circumstances. It is conceived as a remedy for the innocent against the guilty."[249]

If an innocent spouse refused to seek a divorce, the other spouse could not obtain a divorce, no matter how faulty his marital behavior. A person who wanted a divorce from a legally "faultless" spouse had to secure the spouse's agreement that one party would sue the other for divorce and contend (whether with actual or falsified evidence) that the defendant spouse had committed marital fault.

Fault-based divorce doctrine formally prohibited cooperation between spouses to establish fault.[250] In practice, however, obtaining a fault-based divorce often required cooperation between spouses. Indeed, periodic scandals and investigative reports revealed that husbands and wives sometimes participated in elaborately choreographed charades designed to fabricate evidence of the husband's adultery.[251]

One famous 1934 series in the *New York Sunday Mirror* was entitled, "I Was the 'Unknown Blonde' in 100 New York Divorces! By a Professional Co-Respondent."[252] The series explained how some husbands and wives worked together to circumvent New York's restrictive divorce laws, with the wife hiring a private detective who would by prearrangement "discover" the husband in a "'compromising position'" with another woman. The other woman actually worked for the detective agency or the wife's divorce lawyer, but the wife's divorce suit would identify the alleged paramour as "an 'unknown woman'" and use her presence to obtain the divorce that husband and wife had agreed to seek.[253]

Dorothy Jarvis wrote the *Sunday Mirror* series after more than two years as "a professional co-respondent—the 'unknown blonde' of more than one hundred uncontested divorce suits in the courts of New York City."[254] Jarvis explained that "[i]n the case where a husband and wife mutually agree to disagree—and mutually arrange between themselves such matters as alimony settlement and the custody of children, if any—there is actually a minimum of ordeal under the system now generally practiced."[255]

In return for such cooperation, wives might receive more favorable divorce settlements from their husbands.[256] Courts would also sometimes compensate wives for their husbands' marital faults with alimony payments and disproportionate property awards,[257] although the proportion of alimony awards appears never to have been high.[258]

Under unilateral no-fault divorce, a spouse can simply sue for divorce on his own. A husband who wants a divorce does not need to secure his wife's cooperation or to compensate her for that cooperation in a divorce settlement. Once in court, moreover, neither spouse will count as the wronged party entitled to judicial awards of compensation for the wrong, whether that would take the form of receiving a disproportionately large share of the couple's assets or a disproportionately small share of the couple's debts. Many wives lost real bargaining power and prerogatives in the transition to no-fault.[259] Some spouses even argued in court (unsuccessfully) that applying no-fault divorce laws to people who married under the fault-based regime infringed on an innocent spouse's vested rights.[260]

The no-fault divorce regime still has some undeniable advantages over its predecessor, which locked people into unhappy marriages and created strong incentives for fraud. But simply applauding contract rules misses the costs that can be associated with a move from status to contract, particularly for the weaker party. The loud cheers for contracting can divert attention from considering the possibility that legal arrangements should be adjusted in order to mitigate the costs of contract rules so that the economic consequences of divorce are more equivalent for women and men. For example, the legal system could preserve the important premise that the decision whether to divorce is in the hands of individuals rather than the state—which reflects basic contract principles—but still focus more attention on improving the legal defaults that apply when a married couple has not negotiated an individual contract to govern the terms of their divorce, considering whether and how those defaults might be reformed to ensure a fairer distribution of benefits and burdens, assets and liabilities.

Status or Contract or Neither

The canonical status to contract story celebrates an overstated status to contract transition. Yet the real issue for family law is whether legal decisionmakers should implement any particular family law policy as a status rule, a contract rule, or not at all. Policymakers need to deliberate about this choice in each specific instance because the advantages and disadvantages of each option are likely to vary across contexts.

Sometimes using unwaivable status rules may be the most sensible decision. For example, status rules can sometimes protect individuals against unfair or unconscionable bargains, help people who have limited or no capacity to contract, shield third parties from harm, and/ or vindicate important societal interests that extend beyond the parties immediately involved or impacted, including societal interests in equality, justice, liberty, dignity, respect, caregiving, health, and safety.

Of course, decisionmakers may disagree in some cases about what constitutes an unfair or unconscionable bargain, or about who has an impaired capacity to contract, or about whether third parties will be harmed, or about when a contract rule would infringe upon important societal interests. But these are exactly the sorts of debates that policymakers should be having. And in at least some cases, the evidence will tilt heavily in one direction.

For instance, there are good reasons for making child support obligations unwaivable. This status rule helps protect individual children from potential financial hardship, and it also furthers society's pressing moral, social, cultural, political, and economic interests in ensuring that children receive sufficient support. Children lack the capacity to adequately protect themselves through contract, and the consequences of unwisely waiving a right to child support can be dire. Moreover, an adult who seeks to waive a child's right to support may be placing her own interests above the child's needs, albeit perhaps unwittingly. For example, a custodial parent may be prioritizing her desire to sever all contact with the noncustodial parent, even though the child would benefit from connecting with and receiving support from both parents.

Similarly, there are manifest reasons for making prohibitions on marital violence, child abuse, and child neglect unwaivable. These prohibitions are meant to provide basic legal protections to extremely vulnerable people. They also reflect and reinforce society's interest in preventing and penalizing violence and cruelty, for reasons of public policy, public health, public safety, distributive justice, and more.

In contrast, sometimes it may be wiser to use contract rules to give consenting adults more freedom to arrange their family lives as they see fit. For instance, the case for permitting same-sex marriage seems to me to be overwhelming. In my view, no legitimate public interests are served by denying that choice. Moreover, prohibiting same-sex marriage undermines societal interests in equality, dignity, and respect, as well as liberty and autonomy, by treating gay people as second-class citizens.

Sometimes the objections to a family law policy are compelling, whether the policy is implemented as a status rule or a contract rule. For example, I would object to a marital rape exemption whether the exemption appeared in its current form as an unwaivable status rule or as a contract rule permitting couples to agree in advance that the ordinary prohibitions in rape law will not apply to their marriage. Legal protection from rape is too fundamental to individual safety, liberty, equality, dignity, and respect to be bargained away. Moreover, society as a whole has an overriding interest in prohibiting rape for reasons of justice, safety, liberty, equality, dignity, and respect, whether rape occurs in or out of marriage. Rather than legalizing marital rape exemptions in status or contract form, the better approach is to enact status rules that embody the opposite substantive policy choice, mandating that criminal law treat marital rape as seriously as rape outside of marriage.

Family law's canonical stories about historical transformations in the regulation of adults tend to depict family law's problems as safely in the past. These stories claim that family law was once grounded in married women's coverture, but has eradicated this legacy, that family law was once dominated by status rules, but no longer. Both canonical stories misdescribe modern family law, overstating change over time and overlooking continuity. Family law still reflects the persistent imprint of coverture, to women's systematic detriment. Status rules continue to be abundant in family law, and contract rules can also have disadvantages. The canonical narratives about coverture's demise and the replacement of status with contract direct decisionmakers away from exploring and assessing family law as it actually is and from considering the questions that the canonical stories presume are answered. Decisionmakers cannot treat coverture's legacy as a problem in family law's history, but not in its present. The pressing questions to consider are about whether, when, and why family law should keep the persistent manifestations of coverture's legacy in place. Decisionmakers cannot assume that family law has evolved beyond status rules and that contract rules are necessarily better than status rules. The pressing question to consider is what are the costs and benefits of implementing any specific family law policy in status or contract form.

4

A PROGRESS NARRATIVE FOR CHILDREN

[T]he child's welfare is the "paramount consideration."
—*In re J.P.* (Utah Supreme Court 1982)[1]

Family law's canonical progress narrative about historical transformations in the regulation of children contends that family law once accorded parents almost property-like authority over their minor children, but now prioritizes children's best interests. The story insists descriptively that family law has sharply separated itself from past practices, shedding a common law tradition that employed property norms to guide the law of parenthood and that granted parents (especially fathers) rights of custody and control that were strong enough to be the virtual equivalent of property rights. It maintains that adults have reordered the legal system so that judges, legislators, and other legal authorities now treat children's interests as paramount.

The story assumes normatively that family law's regulation of the parent-child relation should prioritize children's interests. The canonical narrative does not contend that children have or should have all the rights and liberties accorded to adults. It is not a status to contract story. But the narrative celebrates the supposed rejection of common law principles that prioritized parental prerogatives and the asserted triumph of a legal regime privileging children's interests.

Modern courts have embraced descriptions of family law that emphasize how the field has distanced itself from common law parental prerogatives in order to put children's interests first. One court reported that "[p]rior to [the twentieth century], children were little more than chattels of their parents and the public be damned if they protested the parental abuse or neglect as they could use them as they saw fit."[2]

Another court explained that "[t]he law long ago abandoned the view that children are essentially chattels of their parents without independent legal rights."[3] A third stated that "[t]he parental right or preference doctrine originated with the concept that a parent's right in his child was like that of a property owner in his chattel. This in turn led to the assumption that the interests of the parents, not the child, were of paramount consideration." The court announced in 1981 that "[i]n recent years, the focus has been on the child's interests."[4]

On such judicial accounts, "a child is no longer considered as a chattel of a parent and where there is a conflict between the interests of the parent and the child, the 'best interests' of the child should prevail."[5] "[A]ssumptions inherited from feudal law that a parent has the same possessory interests over a child as he does over some sort of chattel" are "antiquated." "Blind adherence to a parental right approach inhibits adequate consideration of the best interests of the child, which must be viewed as the primary concern of the law."[6] "In the family law setting, the best interests of the child are of paramount importance."[7] "[W]hat is in the best interest of the children . . . is the paramount concern in all family law cases."[8]

Indeed, judges have been proclaiming for decades that—in the 1921 language of Juvenile Court Judge Ben B. Lindsey—"the trend of civilization would at times seem to bring a reversal of the ancient doctrine of the ownership of the child by the parent to the ownership of the parent by the child."[9] The Missouri Supreme Court in 1949 linked the children's best interests story with the canonical narrative about coverture's demise, declaring that "[i]t is as repellent to our present-day thinking to regard a child as the chattel or servant of his parent as it is to regard a wife as the chattel of her husband."[10]

Some scholars also stress that family law no longer accepts the common law's privileging of parental prerogatives and now prioritizes children's interests, or they note the dominance of this way of understanding the field. For instance, one scholar reported that "[u]nder ancient law, children, being economic assets, were viewed as private property, owned and controlled by the father. . . . Under modern law, however, the property element of parental rights has been discredited—kept alive, as one commentator states, only in the courts' denials of the notion."[11] A second scholar observed that "[t]oday—perhaps more so than at any time in our history—courts and commentators hold that parents' rights are secondary to children's interests."[12] She explained

that "[w]hile the legal system of the feudal era accorded a family patri-
arch the right to bind his children as he saw fit, that time has long since
passed. Today, parents' rights are thought to derive from—and to be
limited by—their children's interests. Family law has thus moved consistently in the direction of a child-centered view of parental entitlements."[13]
A third scholar stated that "[c]hildren have recently emerged from hundreds of years of property status to be considered as persons."[14] Another
reported that "by the twentieth century, historians suggest, the concept
of parental obligations as an outgrowth of divinely conferred paternal
ownership and control of children had given way to that of parental
trusteeship in the child's 'best interests,'"[15] and noted that "we hear
modern family law speak in terms of the child as an individual whose
best interest is its focal point."[16] Still another scholar observed that "[i]t
is commonplace to report . . . that 'best interests of the child' is the pervasive mantra of American family law—a standard that seems to pop
up for almost every doctrinal question."[17]

Yet change in family law's treatment of the parent-child relationship
has not been nearly as dramatic or far-reaching as stories about the
modern preeminence of children's interests might suggest. Family law
continues to protect wide-ranging parental prerogatives in many arenas,
even when the prerogatives conflict with children's interests. Indeed,
courts take these parental prerogatives to be so fundamental that they
have embedded many of them within constitutional law.

I do not contend in this chapter that family law should necessarily
privilege children's interests everywhere and all the time. While narratives recounting the subordination of parental prerogatives often appear
to presume the normative superiority of prioritizing children's interests,
I do not. Instead, this chapter explores how stories about the triumph of
children's best interests can divert attention from examining how family
law actually regulates the parent-child relationship and from considering the normative question that still faces the field: Where should
family law prioritize parental prerogatives, and where, how, and to what
extent does family law's continued deference to parental rights over
children's interests need to be reformed?

The Children's Best Interests Narrative

The central example in the children's best interests narrative focuses on
the law governing custody disputes between two parents. Common law

courts after the American Revolution granted fathers legal custody of children born within marriage and mothers legal custody of children born outside of marriage (although poor mothers could find it very difficult as a practical matter to keep their illegitimate children if unable to support them adequately).[18] These custody rules were designed to operate as a matter of parental right and responsibility, with little regard for the quality of the personal relationship between a parent and child. William Blackstone, whose *Commentaries on the Laws of England* (1765) was extremely influential in the United States, declared that a legitimate child was within "the empire of the father," "for a mother, as such, is entitled to no power, but only to reverence and respect."[19] Tapping Reeve's *Law of Baron and Femme* (1816), the first family law treatise published in the United States, agreed that "[m]others, during coverture," had "no legal authority of their own."[20] Following in this direction, a New York court explained in 1836 that where "differences unfortunately exist between the parents, the right of the father is preferred to that of the mother."[21] The New Jersey Supreme Court reported in 1849 "that the father, as head of the family, is entitled to the custody and control of his legitimate child."[22] A judge announced in 1842 that a husband had legal custody of his legitimate child because "he is the legal head of the whole family, wife and children inclusive; and I have heard it urged from no quarter that he should be brought under subjection to a household democracy. All will agree, I apprehend, that such a measure would extend the right of suffrage quite too far."[23]

Over the course of the nineteenth century, however, reformers and mothers increasingly criticized the common law doctrine granting fathers custody of legitimate children. Where common law judges and treatise writers had defended this doctrine in the language of paternal authority, reformers condemned the doctrine by invoking the ideas of nurture and nature and linking the two concepts with motherhood. Reformers contended that granting fathers custody of legitimate children disregarded children's need for nurturing care and mothers' naturally superior capacity to provide such nurture. Their argument gained force as increasing industrialization took America's economy further away from its agrarian roots. It drew on related changes in dominant cultural understandings of children that began to deemphasize children's economic value as sources of labor for their fathers and to understand children as sources of economic expense requiring tremendous amounts of caretaking, especially from mothers working without pay in their own homes.[24]

The nineteenth-century woman's rights movement, for instance, embraced this line of argument for changing child custody laws, relying on prevalent assumptions about mothers and children as justifications for giving women the chance to win custody of their legitimate children. Elizabeth Cady Stanton, the movement's leading theorist, asserted that "[n]ature has clearly made the mother the guardian of the child; but man, in his inordinate love of power, does continually set nature and nature's laws at open defiance." She condemned "the law [that] gives the children to the father; no matter what his character or condition."[25] Ernestine L. Rose, another prominent woman's rights advocate, declared that "[c]hildren always depend more on the tender, watchful care of the mother, than of the father. Whether from nature, habit, or both, the mother is much more capable of administering to their health and comfort than the father, and therefore she has the best right to them."[26]

Nineteenth-century courts endorsed such arguments about woman's nature and children's nurture in opinions that began to favor mothers over fathers in custody disputes about marital children who were young, female, and/or ill. To be sure, mothers did not win the custodial rights over legitimate children that fathers had enjoyed. A woman's custody claims were always contingent on stringent judicial assessments of her behavior and character. Moreover, the transformation in mothers' prospects for securing custody focused on limited categories of legitimate children, who were understood to require greater maternal care, who were not (or would never be) ready to begin training for the social roles of adult men, and who were likely to provide little economic value to their fathers. Indeed, one irony of the case law, which frequently spoke about children's welfare, is that courts were most inclined to award women custody over children who were economic burdens, even though women were much less likely than men to have access to wealth or market work for supporting such children.

That said, mothers' custodial claims to their legitimate children did expand appreciably. Judges explained that "[d]uring the age of nurture [the children's mother] is the most appropriate and fit person to watch over and take care of them."[27] "[E]ven a Court of common law will not go so far as to hold nature in contempt, and snatch helpless, puling infancy from the bosom of an affectionate mother, and place it in the coarse hands of the father."[28] Courts granted mothers custody when children were "of tender years, or of feeble and delicate health, and where the necessity of maternal care is evident," while placing children with their fathers when "the child has arrived at an age at which it becomes important to determine upon its course of education and mental training in reference to its future business and establishment in life."[29]

Judges and legislators developed and elaborated these "tender years" doctrines through much of the twentieth century. Some state codes explicitly provided that a mother "shall have custody of her child, everything else being equal, unless the child has reached the age which necessitates a particular education or preparation for its life work."[30] Some courts applied "a presumption that the child's well being is better safeguarded in the hands of the mother" to state statutes that formally granted parents equal rights to custody. These courts would "customarily award the custody of a child of tender years to its mother unless she is so physically or morally deficient that its welfare would not be served by doing so."[31]

Twentieth-century judges often assumed that tender years doctrines were too commonsensical—too "natural" in the frequent rhetoric of the judicial opinions—to require explanation or defense. A California appellate court reported in 1942 that "[i]t is not open to question, and indeed it is universally recognized, that the mother is the natural custodian of her young."[32] The Idaho Supreme Court declared in 1951 that it "need[ed] no argument to support" the "conclusion" that "all other considerations being equal, a child of tender age or a girl of even more mature years can and will be reared, trained and cared for best by its mother."[33] As late as 1973, the Pennsylvania Supreme Court contended without elaboration that "the wisdom of the ages" supported "the rule that in the absence of compelling reasons to the contrary, a mother has the right to the custody of her children over any other person, particularly so, where the children are of tender years."[34]

Judges that did attempt to justify tender years doctrines explained that women were inherently more able, more willing, and more available to raise young children. Their opinions envisioned maternal love, care, nurture, and self-sacrifice as secondary sex characteristics, traits that helped define women as women and that fundamentally distinguished mothers from fathers. The Washington Supreme Court declared in 1916 that an orientation toward children was not optional for women and was not present, or much less present, with men: "Mother love is a dominant trait in even the weakest of women, and as a general thing surpasses the paternal affection for the common offspring, and, moreover, a child needs a mother's care even more than a father's."[35] The

Wisconsin Supreme Court in 1921 similarly stressed that women, unlike men, were eager to subordinate their own interests to those of their children or perhaps simply had no interests distinct from their children's needs. The court explained "that only a mother can give" the "constant ministration required during the period of nurture" "because in her alone is duty swallowed up in desire; in her alone is service expressed in terms of love. She alone has the patience and sympathy required to mold and soothe the infant mind in its adjustment to its environment. The difference between fatherhood and motherhood in this respect is fundamental, and the law should recognize it unless offset by undesirable traits in the mother."[36] Four decades later, the Minnesota Supreme Court was still certain "[t]hat there is no substitute for the love, companionship, and guidance of a good mother hardly needs any argument." The court presumed that fathers focused on obligations and opportunities outside the domestic sphere, while a mother "has the time and opportunity of providing care and comfort to children at times when normally the father is away from home."[37] Indeed, a Maryland appellate court stated as late as 1972 that greater maternal investment in children was a natural fact preceding culture, conscious thought, or choice: "The so-called 'preference' for the mother as the custodian particularly of younger children is simply a recognition by the law, as well as by the commonality of man, of the universal verity that the maternal tie is so primordial that it should not lightly be severed or attenuated. The appreciation of this visceral bond between mother and child will always be placed upon the balance scales and, all else being equal or nearly so, will tilt them."[38]

In the 1970s, however, the rise of the modern women's rights movement, the emergence of a fathers' rights movement, and the flourishing of social science literature concluding that men and women were equally capable of good parenting, prompted greater scrutiny and criticism of tender years doctrines. Reformers contended that tender years doctrines disserved the interests of mothers, fathers, and children alike, disproportionately pushing women to assume the burdens of custody and stigmatizing mothers who did not have custody of their children,[39] excluding fathers who wanted custody from the opportunity to undertake that responsibility,[40] and denying some children access to the best custodial arrangement for them by placing them with their mothers when their fathers would be better custodial parents.[41] For the first time, moreover, the United States Supreme Court began striking down some explicitly sex-based family law rules as unconstitutional sex discrimination.[42]

These developments helped drive state legislatures and courts to re-phrase their custody laws and doctrines in sex-neutral language. State courts holding that tender years doctrines were unconstitutional for "relying on gender as a determining factor"[43] stressed that the doctrines were "predicated upon traditional or stereotypic roles of men and women in a marital union"[44] and denied "evenhanded treatment"[45] to "loving fathers."[46] Other state courts abandoned tender years doctrines on the ground that such doctrines were inconsistent with deciding cus-tody disputes between parents based on children's best interests. Courts explained that tender years doctrines "tend[] to obscure the basic tenet in custody cases which overrides all others, the best interests of the chil-dren. The real issue is not the sex of the parent but which parent will do better in raising the children. Resolution of that issue depends upon what the evidence actually reveals in each case, not upon what someone predicts it will show in many cases."[47] "Surely, it is not asking too much to demand that a court, in making a determination as to the best interest of a child, make the determination upon specific evidence relating to that child alone."[48]

Today, state statutes and judicial opinions routinely explain that nei-ther mothers nor fathers are categorically favored in custody contests between parents. They declare that courts will decide custody disputes between parents in accordance with the "best interests of the child." Some state legislatures have codified wide-ranging lists of factors for courts to consider in making this determination, while other legislatures provide little elaboration.[49]

Scholarly accounts of child custody law commonly emphasize the rise of the child's best interests standard. Indeed, one book is entitled *From Father's Property to Children's Rights: The History of Child Custody in the United States*.[50] It recounts "a dramatic shift away from fathers' common law rights to custody and control of their children toward a modern emphasis on the best interests of the child."[51] Two other scholars have explained that "[t]he parental rights premise of ear-lier law, which regarded a child as property, has given way to a new approach that minimizes parental prerogatives" and "emphasizes the best interest of the child."[52] A fourth scholar has reported that "in resolving issues of custody. . . . all states expect courts to make the children's interests the sole focus of their attention. The parents' interests are to be ignored."[53]

Persistent Parental Prerogatives

The law on custody disputes between parents has evolved in the direction of focusing more on children's welfare. But declarations that family law's regulation of the parent-child relation is now organized around children's best interests can nonetheless significantly overstate the changes in family law over time.

First, the adjudication of custody disputes between parents does not center on a child's interests as much as stories reporting family law's prioritization of children suggest. As an initial matter, courts' custody decisions may deviate in practice from official doctrine, whether because some judges silently choose not to prioritize children's best interests or because some judges interpret children's best interests in ways that are so infused with gendered bias that judges become distracted from focusing on which custody arrangement will actually be best for a child. Some commentators[54] and fathers' rights advocates[55] contend that judges purporting to apply a child's best interests standard in custody disputes between parents continue in practice to favor mothers systematically, whether or not there is evidence that the mother will be a better custodial parent. Some commentators maintain that judges purporting to apply a child's best interests standard in custody disputes between parents really judge mothers more harshly than fathers, punishing women if they fail to meet society's high expectations for mothers, while rewarding men if they exceed society's low expectations for fathers.[56]

These charges about how judges act in practice are controversial and intensely contested.[57] But even the declared law in custody disputes between parents sometimes diverges from prioritizing a child's best interests.

Consider *Palmore v. Sidoti* (1984),[58] where the United States Supreme Court instructed a state court resolving a custody dispute between parents to ignore possible harm to the child. Linda and Anthony Sidoti, both white, divorced in 1980, and the divorce court awarded Linda custody of the couple's three-year-old daughter, Melanie. In 1981, however, Anthony sought to obtain custody on the ground that Linda was living with an African American man, Clarence Palmore, Jr., whom she soon married.[59] A Florida court granted Anthony custody, explaining that Melanie would "'suffer from . . . social stigmatization'" if she remained with her mother.[60] The United States Supreme Court decided to review the state court's judgment[61]—another notable example of federal involvement in family law to add to the ones that Chapter 1 considered. The Supreme Court agreed that "[t]here is a risk that a child living with a stepparent of a different race may be subject to a variety of pressures and stresses not present if the child were living with parents of the same racial or ethnic origin." But the Court held that the Equal Protection Clause prohibited courts from considering "the reality of private biases and the possible injury they might inflict" on Melanie because of prejudiced reactions to her mother's interracial marriage. Even if "acknowledged racial prejudice" meant that Melanie would be better off living with her father, courts were not to take Linda's interracial marriage into account in making a custody determination.[62]

My point here is not that the Court decided *Palmore* incorrectly. As I will discuss more below, my own view is that the case was rightly decided. If Melanie's interests actually conflicted with societal interests in countering racial prejudice (I am skeptical that this was really so as a factual matter), I agree with the Court's decision to prioritize the latter goal in this case. Yet *Palmore* does represent a vivid illustration of how even the law on custody disputes between parents—the core example for the children's best interests narrative—can explicitly depart from privileging the child's best interests above other considerations.

Second, and more importantly, custody disputes between parents are not the most useful measure of whether family law prioritizes children's interests over parental prerogatives because these disputes do not directly pose a conflict between the rights of parents and children. A court literally *cannot* use deference to parental prerogatives to decide a custody dispute between parents because each parent is entitled to those prerogatives. Employing a child's best interests standard in parental custody disputes helps resolve cases that a commitment to parental prerogatives is unable to resolve now that family law has abandoned explicit categorical preferences for fathers or mothers.

When parental prerogatives and children's interests actually conflict, family law continues to adhere closely to common law patterns in repeatedly prioritizing parental prerogatives. Let's examine parents' custody rights in more detail and also consider parents' rights to inflict corporal punishment, to control their children's labor, to control their children's education, and to enjoy immunity from tort liability for injuring their children.

Custody

The law of child custody is the central illustration in the story reporting the legal supremacy of children's best interests, yet a large portion of child custody law continues to privilege parents' rights over children's interests where the two conflict. Indeed, child custody law still frequently treats parental prerogatives as "natural." Recall that reformers and courts advocating tender years doctrines invoked prevailing ideas about women's nature as reasons to award mothers custody of some legitimate children. Modern courts upholding parental prerogatives persistently refer to legal parents (sex-neutral) as "natural parents." The phrase is striking because the people granted the rights of "natural parents" include legal parents whose relationship with their children originated through adoption, which is manifestly a legal process rather than a natural one. But the implication of the "natural parents" language is that family law is simply recognizing and respecting preexisting, unchangeable facts, rather than making choices among alternatives. In reality, courts are actively defining, defending, and enforcing the rights of legal parents in ways that continue to prioritize parental prerogatives. Courts are describing parents' rights over their children as "natural" when courts are simultaneously constructing and enforcing these rights through law.

Custody Disputes Between Legal Parents and People Who Are Not Legal Parents. Today, as at common law,[63] many courts adjudicating custody disputes between a legal parent and another adult who is not a legal parent do not prioritize placing the child in the custody arrangement that will best serve the child's interests, even when the person contesting custody with a legal parent is another relative, the child's longtime caregiver, or both. Instead, courts commonly focus on whether the legal parent is fit, while defining fitness to mean that the person's parenting satisfies a minimal standard of basic adequacy. The Massachusetts Supreme Judicial Court observed that "[w]e have repeatedly held that the ties of affection which exist between a child and a person who has had custody of the child must yield to the desires of the parents to raise the child in a fit environment."[64] The court stressed that "[u]nfit is a 'strong word,' and that determination should not be reached easily."[65] The South Dakota Supreme Court similarly reported that "[i]n legal contests between a parent and a non-parent for the custody of a child the threshold question is: Is the parent unfit to have custody of the child? . . . Without unfitness being established, there is no necessity to look to the best interest of the child."[66] The Wisconsin Supreme Court "conclude[d] that the 'best interests of the child' is not the proper standard in custody disputes between a natural parent and a third party."[67]

Indeed, modern courts have constitutionalized parents' custodial rights, adding force to parental prerogatives that courts once protected just as a matter of common law. The North Carolina Court of Appeals explained that "[a]bsent a finding of unfitness or neglect by the natural parent, a best interest of the child test would violate the parent's constitutional rights."[68] The Kansas Supreme Court struck down a statute providing that "[i]f the trial court determines that the best interests of the child will be served by placing it with third persons, the court may do so."[69] The Kansas court declared that "a natural parent's right to the custody of his or her children is a fundamental right which may not be disturbed by the state or by third persons, absent a showing that the natural parent is unfit."[70]

Visitation Disputes Between Legal Parents and People Who Are Not Legal Parents. Courts adjudicating visitation disputes between legal parents and people who are not legal parents also frequently prioritize parental prerogatives over children's interests when the two conflict.[71] Some courts do not consider whether visitation would be in a child's interests before rejecting a visitation petition from a former same-sex partner who helped raise the child from birth or infancy, but never obtained legal status as a parent.[72] The New York Court of Appeals explained that "[t]o allow the courts to award visitation—a limited form of custody—to a third person would necessarily impair the parents' right to custody and control."[73] The Maryland Court of Appeals refused to apply a child's best interests standard, holding that "where visitation or custody is sought over the objection of the parent, before the best interest of the child test comes into play, the *de facto* parent must establish that the legal parent is either unfit or that exceptional circumstances exist."[74] Hostility toward same-sex relationships may have influenced some judicial decisions about visitation disputes between former same-sex partners, but some courts have also refused to apply a best interests of the child standard in cases where former stepparents sought to visit their former stepchildren.[75]

Indeed, a plurality of the United States Supreme Court concluded in *Troxel v. Granville* (2000)[76] that a Washington state statute authorizing courts to "'order visitation rights for any person when visitation may serve the best interest of the child'"[77] was unconstitutional as applied where a Washington Superior Court had granted a nonparent visitation petition under the statute without according "any material weight" to the mother's determination of her children's best interests.[78] The Superior Court had given two paternal grandparents the right to visit with their granddaughters for one weekend per month, one week in the summer, and four hours on each grandparent's birthday. This was less visitation than the grandparents had sought after their son's death, but more than the one short visit per month plus some holidays that the children's mother wanted to allow.[79] The *Troxel* plurality insisted that awarding the grandparents visitation based simply on a judicial determination of the children's best interests "was an unconstitutional infringement on [the mother's] fundamental right to make decisions concerning the care, custody, and control of her two daughters."[80]

Involuntary Termination of Parental Rights. In the same vein, the governing standard in cases considering whether to involuntarily terminate a parent's legal rights, which permanently severs a parent's right to custody, is not whether termination would promote the child's best interests. The Supreme Court's due process jurisprudence indicates that termination proceedings must focus instead on whether the state has proven that the parent is so "clear[ly] and convincing[ly]"[81] unfit that it is fair to the parent to terminate parental rights because the parent has essentially forfeited his claim to the child. This inquiry into parental "unfitness"[82] is related to the child's interests, but not the same. The Court has declared that "the focus emphatically is not on" the child in a proceeding to decide whether to terminate a parent's rights. "The factfinding [in a parental rights termination proceeding] does not purport— and is not intended—to balance the child's interest in a normal family home against the parents' interest in raising the child. Nor does it purport to determine whether the natural parents or the foster parents would provide the better home. Rather, the factfinding hearing pits the State directly against the parents. The State alleges that the natural parents are at fault. . . . Victory by the State not only makes termination of parental rights possible; it entails a judicial determination that the parents are unfit to raise their own children."[83]

In re J.P., the Utah Supreme Court decision that supplied this chapter's epigraph, followed this direction. It struck down a state "statute authorizing the juvenile court to 'decree an involuntary termination of all parental rights' solely on the basis of a finding that 'such termination will be in the child's best interest.'"[84] The court concluded that the statute violated both the federal and the Utah state constitutions because "the right of a parent not to be deprived of parental rights without a showing of unfitness, abandonment, or substantial neglect is so fundamental to our society and so basic to our constitutional order."[85] The court's certainty in its constitutional judgment reflected its basic commitment to an understanding of parental rights "root[ed] in history and the common law,"[86] an understanding that the court described as natural. The court explained that "[t]he integrity of the family and the parents' inherent right and authority to rear their own children have been recognized as fundamental axioms of Anglo-American culture, presupposed by all our social, political, and legal institutions. . . . This parental right transcends all property and economic rights. It is rooted not in state or federal statutory or constitutional law, to which it is logically and chronologically prior, but in nature and human instinct."[87]

Notably, the Utah court sought to reconcile its judgment that parental termination decisions cannot turn on a child's best interests with family law's canonical narrative about children's status. The court stated that "[w]e perceive no incompatibility between the parental rights defined in the present case and the principle that the child's welfare is the 'paramount consideration.'"[88] The court explained that contending that children's welfare was paramount did not actually mean that considerations about a child's interests came first in a parental termination case. Instead, it meant only that parents' rights over their children were not unlimited when parents' conduct was extremely poor: "The principle that 'the welfare of the child is the paramount consideration' means that parental rights, though inherent and retained, are not absolute; that the state, as *parens patriae,* has the authority and obligation to assume a parental role after the natural parent has been shown to be unfit or disfunctional; and that parental prerogatives cannot, at that extreme point, frustrate the state in discharging its duty."[89]

Other state courts similarly maintain that a parent's rights cannot be involuntarily terminated unless the parent is unfit, while defining fitness to mean bare adequacy as a parent. As the Indiana Supreme Court explained, "[c]hildren are not taken from the custody of their parents because there is a better or the 'best' place for them. They are taken because the present place in the custody of their parents is wholly inadequate for their very survival."[90] The Maine Supreme Judicial Court reported that "in termination of parental rights proceedings, the court's focus must be on the Department's allegations of parental unfitness. Only if the court is convinced that the State has proven one or more of the factors demonstrating that the parents cannot safely provide care for their children does the court consider the children's best interests."[91] The New York Court of Appeals declared that "[s]o long as the parental rights have not been forfeited by gross misconduct or other behavior evincing utter indifference and irresponsibility, the natural parent may not be supplanted."[92]

As these features of child custody law illustrate, family law continues to give parents tremendous power over their children even when parental prerogatives conflict with a child's best interests. Indeed, the United States Supreme Court itself has acknowledged that "'the best interests of the child' is not the legal standard that governs parents' or guardians' exercise of their custody: So long as certain minimum requirements of child care are met, the interests of the child may be subordinated to the interests of other children, or indeed even to the interests of the parents or guardians themselves."[93]

Consider some other examples that highlight the law's persistent protection of parental prerogatives.

Corporal Punishment

Parents have a wide-ranging right to inflict corporal punishment, and the contours of that right have changed little since the nineteenth century. The common law upheld a parent's prerogative to physically chastise his child. Judges and legal commentators endorsed physical chastisement as a means of maintaining a child's obedience to his parent's authority and never required a parent to establish that the chastisement was in the child's best interests. The exact scope of a parent's common law right of correction varied modestly over time, but was always substantial. By the end of the nineteenth century, a majority of common law courts held that a parent could inflict reasonable or moderate correction on his child and rarely convicted a parent for exceeding the bounds of reasonableness or moderation.[94]

Today, all states and the federal government still recognize a parent's authority to impose corporal punishment on his child.[95] At least twenty-nine states and the District of Columbia have codified a parent's right to inflict "reasonable" corporal punishment.[96] At least thirteen states have codified a parent's right to impose corporal punishment in slightly different terms. These states protect all parental corporal punishment that is "ordinary,"[97] or not "excessive,"[98] or not "unnecessarily severe,"[99] or not "cruel and inhuman,"[100] or that inflicts less than a certain threshold of physical or mental injury.[101] Similarly, the federal Victims of Child Abuse Act, which requires various professionals to report suspected child abuse,[102] provides that "discipline administered by a parent or legal guardian to his or her child" does not constitute child abuse so long as "it is reasonable in manner and moderate in degree and otherwise does not constitute cruelty."[103]

Surveys find that most American parents inflict corporal punishment on their children,[104] and most American adults support the corporal punishment of children. A nationally representative survey in 2012 found that "77 percent of men, and 65 percent of women 18 to 65 years old agreed that a child sometimes needs a 'good hard spanking.'"[105] Some American parents believe that corporal punishment of children is biblically condoned or even biblically required.[106]

The legal commitment to a parent's right to inflict corporal punishment, and parents' widespread employment of this prerogative, persist although pediatric and psychological studies overwhelmingly conclude that corporal punishment does not benefit children and can harm them. Researchers have repeatedly found that corporal punishment can inflict physical damage; undermine trust, confidence, self-esteem, and mental health; impair the quality of the parent-child relationship; contribute to delinquent, counterproductive, and antisocial behavior; and increase the chances that the child will be violent and will accept violence as an adult.[107]

Child Labor

Child labor laws also continue to privilege parental prerogatives. The common law granted a parent (particularly a father) almost absolute authority over his child's labor.[108] Modern regulation of child labor has modified rather than broken from this common law regime. A parent still retains significant control over his child's work simply because of the parent's status as a parent and regardless of whether the parent is acting in his child's interests.

State child labor laws authorize parents employing their children to place their children in occupations that the law otherwise considers too dangerous for minors and to put their children to work at ages when employment is otherwise prohibited.[109] Many state laws also give parents legal control over their minor children's earnings.[110]

Federal law grants parents who employ their children more power than other employers may exercise over their employees, and it allows parents to consent to their children's exemption from important labor protections. For example, the National Labor Relations Act does not protect a person working for his parent,[111] which means that the act does not give such workers the right to organize, join unions, or bargain collectively.[112]

Federal law gives parents particularly expansive control over their children's labor in the agricultural arena. Americans often assume that farmwork is bucolic, healthy, and character building, and celebrate farming as central to America's yeoman roots and identity. Yet farming is one of the most dangerous occupations in the United States, with a high fatality rate.[113] The federal government's National Institute for Occupational Safety and Health reported that from "1995 through 2002, 907 youth died on farms (8.4 deaths/100,000 youth)" and identified "13% of these deaths" as "work-related."[114] A child working for his parent on the parent's farm is not protected by federal minimum wage and maximum hour requirements,[115] by the federal prohibition on child labor before the age of twelve,[116] or by the federal ban on employing children under sixteen in "particularly hazardous" occupations.[117] A parent may authorize his child to work anywhere in agriculture at the age of twelve or thirteen[118] and may authorize a child younger than twelve to work on many farms that the parent does not own,[119] even though federal law generally prohibits agricultural labor until a child reaches fourteen.[120] A child who works on the same farm that employs his parent is also often excluded from federal minimum wage and maximum hour protections.[121]

In September 2011, the Obama Administration proposed new regulations to govern child labor in agriculture,[122] the first major proposed reforms in decades.[123] These proposed regulations were spurred by years of research documenting the risks that farm labor can create for child workers. For instance, the Department of Labor explained in introducing the proposed rules "that agricultural workers aged 15 to 17 have a risk of fatality that is 4.4 times as great as the risk for the average 15- to 17-year-old worker."[124] "[D]uring the 1990s, while only about four percent of all working youth were employed in agriculture, they experienced over 40 percent of the youth occupational fatalities."[125]

The proposed limits on child labor focused on types of farmwork that federal regulators identified as particularly hazardous for children. Among other provisions, the proposed rules sought to protect children from severe or even fatal accidents and illnesses by prohibiting workers younger than sixteen from operating most heavy farm machinery,[126] handling or applying pesticides,[127] working in silos or manure pits,[128] picking tobacco,[129] and participating "in animal husbandry practices that inflict pain upon the animal and/or are likely to result in unpredictable animal behavior."[130] Despite the well-documented dangers of these jobs for child workers, federal law required the Department of Labor to structure its proposed limitations on child labor so that "[t]he proposed agricultural revisions would impact only hired farm workers and in no way compromise the statutory child labor parental exemption involving children working on farms owned or operated by their parents."[131]

Critics contended nonetheless that the proposed rules would unduly interfere with parents' control over their children's labor. Senator Mitch McConnell of Kentucky declared that " '[t]he informed, common sense decisions of parents should take precedence over those of unelected bureaucrats thousands of miles away. Family farming is a tradition in Kentucky and these proposals set a dangerous precedent for the federal government's intrusion into family matters.' "[132] Senator Jerry Moran of Kansas similarly warned that "[t]he government now is trying to tell farmers and ranchers, 'We know what's best for your children, and what they should and should not be doing.' "[133] Michigan State Representative Paul Muxlow insisted that "[t]he federal government has no place intruding on family farms and parental rights in this manner."[134]

This opposition was successful. The Department of Labor announced in April 2012 that it was withdrawing its proposed child labor regulations, stating that " '[t]he Obama administration is firmly committed to promoting family farmers and respecting the rural way of life, especially the role that parents and other family members play in passing those traditions down through the generations.'"[135]

Education

Parents similarly continue to exert enormous control over their children's education. The legal system authorizes parents to choose which schools their children will attend—whether public or private, secular or religious, coeducational or sex-segregated, outside a parent's home or within it—and to select schools that promote values the children do not share.

Education helps prepare children for adult citizenship, and its economic, social, and political importance for both individuals and the state has only grown over time. But the Supreme Court has repeatedly viewed the question of school choice through the lens of parental rights. The Court's decisions take it to be a matter of common sense deeply rooted in American traditions that parents have wide-ranging authority over their children, and the decisions then embed that common law understanding of parental prerogatives into constitutional law. This aspect of the Court's case law emerged early in precedents that the Court continues to endorse, and it still structures constitutional law to this day.

Meyer v. Nebraska (1923)[136] emphasized parents' rights over their children in striking down a Nebraska law that prohibited the teaching in schools of any modern language other than English to a child who had not completed eighth grade.[137] *Meyer* explained that the liberty the Fourteenth Amendment guarantees includes "[w]ithout doubt" the right "to marry, establish a home and bring up children, to worship God according to the dictates of his own conscience, and generally to enjoy those privileges long recognized at common law as essential to the orderly pursuit of happiness by free men."[138] The Court concluded that the Nebraska Legislature had attempted to materially interfere "with the power of parents to control the education of their own."[139]

Pierce v. Society of Sisters (1925)[140] stressed parental control over children even more emphatically in striking down an Oregon law that required parents to send their children to public schools when the children were between eight and sixteen and had not completed eighth grade.[141] The Court held that the statute "unreasonably interferes with

the liberty of parents and guardians to direct the upbringing and education of children under their control," declaring that "[t]he child is not
the mere creature of the State; those who nurture him and direct his
destiny have the right, coupled with the high duty, to recognize and
prepare him for additional obligations."[142]

The Court in both *Meyer* and *Pierce* did not think it was relevant to
inquire into which schools or classes the children themselves wished to
attend. The Court has emphasized this aspect of the opinions in more
recent years, noting in 1979 that "[w]e cannot assume that the result
in *Meyer v. Nebraska* and *Pierce v. Society of Sisters* would have been
different if the children there had announced a preference to learn
only English or a preference to go to a public, rather than a church,
school."[143]

Several state legislatures have enacted statutes since *Meyer* and *Pierce*
providing that even a parent who chooses to send his child to public
school can nonetheless remove his child from specific school programs
that the parent disfavors. For instance, New Hampshire law "[r]equire[s]
school districts to adopt a policy allowing an exception to specific course
material based on a parent's or legal guardian's determination that the
material is objectionable."[144] Texas law provides that "[a] parent is entitled to remove the parent's child temporarily from a class or other school
activity that conflicts with the parent's religious or moral beliefs if the
parent presents or delivers to the teacher of the parent's child a written
statement authorizing the removal of the child from the class or other
school activity."[145]

In fact, parents can sometimes remove their children from school
entirely in an effort to train the children in the parents' religious beliefs,
even though the exercise of that parental choice will restrict the children's future prospects and options. The Supreme Court in *Wisconsin v.
Yoder* (1972)[146] permitted Amish parents in Wisconsin to remove their
children from school after eighth grade although Wisconsin's compulsory education law required school attendance until age sixteen.[147] The
Amish parents' decision to end their children's formal education dramatically altered the opportunities open to these children, and that was
the Amish parents' explicit intent. Taking the children from school after
eighth grade pushed the children toward Amish life paths that emphasize "manual work and self-reliance and the specific skills needed to
perform the adult role of an Amish farmer or housewife."[148] At the same
time, the early termination of the children's formal education made

other choices requiring more extensive schooling harder to imagine, much less pursue. People who left school after eighth grade would have less opportunity in their formative years to learn about alternatives to the Amish way of life. Moreover, they likely would be ill-prepared if they decided as adults to depart from the Amish community and to pursue work beyond farming, carpentry, or housewifery.[149]

Nevertheless, the *Yoder* litigation and the Court's opinion allowing Amish parents to take their children from school focused remarkably little attention on the children's interests, desires, or concerns. Only one of the Amish children at issue, Frieda Yoder, even testified during the course of the lawsuit, reporting that she wished to end her formal education because of her Amish faith. Both sides in the litigation ignored the other Amish children, who were never asked whether and why they wanted to leave school after eighth grade.[150] The *Yoder* Court sided with the Amish parents regardless, explaining that the "primary role of the parents in the upbringing of their children is now established beyond debate as an enduring American tradition."[151]

State and federal courts in more recent years have relied on *Yoder* in upholding parents' rights to remove their children from schools outside the home in order to "homeschool" their children and accordingly exercise more control (whether for better or for worse) over whom their children interact with and what their children learn. For instance, the Michigan Supreme Court in 1993 relied on *Yoder* in holding that it was unconstitutional for Michigan's compulsory education law to limit homeschooling to instructors who were certified teachers, when the state applied that limitation to parents whose religious convictions prohibited the use of certified teachers.[152] The California Court of Appeal in 2008 explained that one reason it interpreted California's compulsory education law to allow homeschooling, including by people without teaching credentials, was to avoid "constitutional difficulty" under *Yoder*.[153] The North Carolina Supreme Court in 1985 similarly interpreted North Carolina's compulsory school attendance law to permit "home instruction as a means of education" in part to avoid "serious questions" about the law's constitutionality under "the principles enunciated in *Yoder* and *Pierce*."[154]

The United States Court of Appeals for the Ninth Circuit relied on *Yoder* in a 1997 decision about homeschooling that both protected parental prerogatives and also suggested the enormous amounts of unpaid female labor on which homeschooling frequently depends. The court concluded that a public school district violated a public school principal's constitutional rights when the district decided not to renew the principal's contract as a principal and to offer him reassignment to a teaching position because the principal announced that for religious reasons he was thinking about removing his eight school-age children from public school to homeschool them. The principal planned on continuing to work full-time. The eight school-age children, ages seven to sixteen, would be at home with his wife, who was also caring for their four younger siblings.[155]

Parental Tort Immunity

Notwithstanding the canonical narrative reporting the progressive triumph of children's best interests over parental prerogatives, parents' rights have actually grown stronger in some contexts over time. Until the late nineteenth century, no state recognized the doctrine of parental tort immunity, which shields parents from tort liability for intentionally or negligently injuring their children. The Mississippi Supreme Court created this doctrine in 1891 as a means of upholding parental authority and discretion. The court declared that "so long as the parent is under obligation to care for, guide, and control, and the child is under reciprocal obligation to aid and comfort and obey," "[t]he peace of society, and of the families composing society, and a sound public policy, designed to subserve the repose of families and the best interests of society, forbid to the minor child a right to appear in court in the assertion of a claim to civil redress for personal injuries suffered at the hands of the parent."[156]

Courts throughout the nation followed by adopting their own doctrines of parental tort immunity,[157] and today at least twenty-five states recognize some form of the immunity. For comparison, recall from Chapter 3 that just seven states retain some form of interspousal tort immunity.

Louisiana exempts a parent from tort liability if he exercises legal control over his child. It provides by statute that "[t]he child who is not emancipated cannot sue: (1) Either parent during the continuance of their marriage, when the parents are not judicially separated; or (2) The parent who is entitled to his custody and control, when the marriage of the parents is dissolved, or the parents are judicially separated."[158]

More commonly, states with parental tort immunity doctrines limit the parental conduct that may be the basis of a child's suit.[159] In *Blake v. Blake,* for instance, the Georgia Court of Appeals held that the doctrine of parental tort immunity prevented children injured through their father's allegedly negligent driving from suing their father in tort.[160] In *Pavlick v. Pavlick,* the Virginia Supreme Court held that parental tort immunity exempted a father from tort liability even if his alleged negligence was responsible for his infant child's death.[161]

Courts enforcing doctrines of parental tort immunity often explain that they are acting to protect "parental authority,"[162] to uphold parental "discipline and control,"[163] and to maintain "parental freedom in the exercise of authority and discretion."[164] With these doctrines, state courts have actually augmented the legal rights that parents exercise over their children at common law.

In sum, stories recounting the legal supremacy of children's best interests can significantly overstate the changes in family law over time. Of course, parents do not have unlimited rights over their children. Parents who seriously harm their children through abuse or neglect may be subject to criminal liability and to the involuntary termination of their parental rights. But parents have retained important aspects of their common law rights and have sometimes actually expanded upon their rights at common law. Family law continues to prioritize parental prerogatives, even when those prerogatives conflict with children's interests.

Where Is Family Law's Continued Deference to Parental Prerogatives Appropriate and Where Does It Need Reform?

My point in offering this account of family law's present structure is not to establish that a child's best interests should always be the controlling standard in family law's regulation of the parent-child relationship. Canonical stories about the subordination of parental prerogatives tend to presume the normative desirability of privileging children's interests, and some academics have similarly argued that children's interests should be consistently prioritized.[165] But there sometimes may be good reasons for not employing a child's best interests standard.

Children, especially young children, are dependent on adults to define, debate, and defend their interests. As a practical matter, this means that prioritizing children's best interests can enhance the power and control of adults wielding legal authority. These adults may be officially acting in a child's interests, but they are also identifying what those interests are.

Judging whether a particular decision or course of action promotes a child's best interests may sometimes, perhaps frequently, be too difficult for a court, legislature, or administrative agency to determine. Applying a child's best interests standard in circumstances that exceed the institutional competence of legal decisionmakers can foster ungrounded and unpredictable legal action without sufficient compensating benefit or, worse, encourage decisions that simply reflect the personal preferences and values of judges, legislators, or administrators. As a Supreme Court Justice noted, "[t]his Court more than once has adverted to the fact that the 'best interests of the child' standard offers little guidance to judges, and may effectively encourage them to rely on their own personal values."[166]

The litigation in *Troxel* (the grandparent visitation case discussed above) appears to provide a striking illustration of this tendency. The Washington Superior Court judge in *Troxel* explicitly relied on his own personal experiences and memories in concluding that it was in the children's best interests to have one week of visitation in the summer with their grandparents. The judge explained: "'I look back on some personal experiences. . . . We always spen[t] as kids a week with one set of grandparents and another set of grandparents, [and] it happened to work out in our family that [it] turned out to be an enjoyable experience. Maybe that can, in this family, if that is how it works out.'"[167]

There is also the related danger that a state empowered to restructure families in the name of protecting children, even when ill-equipped to judge a child's interests, may unfairly target parents whom state actors already disfavor for reasons unconnected to children's welfare, such as animus against people of color, sexual minorities, or other disempowered or marginalized groups, or simple discomfort with parents who pursue unconventional lifestyles. Consider *Painter v. Bannister,*[168] a 1966 decision in which the Iowa Supreme Court was apparently so uncomfortable with a father's "Bohemian" lifestyle that it took the highly unusual step of awarding custody to grandparents over a fit parent.

Mark Painter's mother died in a car accident and his father, Harold Painter, asked Mark's maternal grandparents, Margaret and Dwight Bannister, to care for Mark temporarily. About a year and a half after Mark moved in with the Bannisters, Harold had remarried and he wanted Mark to live with him again. When the Bannisters refused, Harold sued to regain custody and lost.[169] The Iowa Supreme Court's opinion awarding custody to the grandparents strongly suggested the judges' disapproval of the father's "romantic, impractical and unstable" lifestyle.[170] The court stressed that "[t]he Bannister home provides Mark with a stable, dependable, conventional, middle-class, middlewest background and an opportunity for a college education and profession, if he desires it. It provides a solid foundation and secure atmosphere."[171] In contrast, the court's opinion emphasized that "the kind of life Mark would be exposed to in the Painter household. . . . would be unstable, unconventional, arty, Bohemian, and probably intellectually stimulating."[172] (Readers may be interested to learn that Harold ultimately regained custody of Mark in 1968, after Margaret Bannister decided not to challenge the custody suit that Harold brought in California while Mark was visiting him there.)[173]

In addition, parents usually, although not always, have more individualized knowledge about their children than any other adult possesses and a more powerful desire to do what is best for their children. A parent's intense familiarity with and commitment to his child commonly makes him better situated and more able than an outside legal decision-maker to assess the child's best interests.

Moreover, sometimes using a child's best interests standard may fail to adequately capture all the societal interests legitimately at stake. For instance, the Supreme Court's *Palmore* opinion ignored the social stigmatization a child might experience living with a parent who had married interracially because the Court did not want to accommodate racial prejudice, a stance designed to make us all better off in the long run. *Palmore* also sought to give real life to the Court's justly celebrated *Loving* decision. Striking down interracial marriage prohibitions would lose much of its practical meaning if marrying interracially could cost a parent custody of her children.

My point then is not that family law should always place a child's best interests above all else, but that the children's best interests story, like the family law canon's other progress narratives, concentrates on trumpeting family law's supposed distance from its past, rather than scrutinizing family law's present. It directs attention away from family law as it is actually organized.

Important aspects of parents' common law prerogatives remain firmly in place. Courts and legislatures continue to give parents enormous power over their children, including when parents' rights are not necessarily consistent with their children's best interests. Indeed, courts have frequently taken common law parental prerogatives to be so commonsensical and so foundational to American law and society that they have embedded many of these prerogatives in constitutional law.

Legal authorities continue to describe family law as a field that treats children's interests as paramount without focusing on the ways in which that narrative's picture obscures some of family law's actual contours. Judges and legislators, along with scholars and family members, need to spend more time thinking about and debating the real question that family law confronts: Where is it appropriate to prioritize parental prerogatives over children's interests, and where, how, and to what extent does family law's continued deference to parental prerogatives need to be reformed? For instance, are there ways to modify or adjust the tremendous control that parents exercise over their children's custody, education, employment, punishment, and safety that would allow the legal system to better uncover, comprehend, respect, and protect children's individual needs, without creating more problems for children or for society than they solve? Can the legal system identify situations in which a parent's ability or willingness to advance his child's interests is likely to be unusually impaired? Can the legal system identify situations in which a child is likely to be particularly capable of understanding, articulating, and explaining her own interests, whether because of the child's age, maturity, or for some other reason?

Family law's canonical progress narratives insist that the field has evolved to keep pace with progressive reform. These narratives draw on some undeniable changes in family law over time, changes that have frequently benefited less powerful family members. But family law's progress narratives overstate the extent and nature of family law's historical transformations, obscuring continuity. Too often, these stories envision reform as a project already accomplished. They can divert attention from examining family law as it actually is and from asking whether, when, and why current practices should remain in place.

III

WHAT'S MISSING
FROM THE FAMILY LAW CANON?

So far, this book has considered what is contained within the family law canon. We have explored narratives, stories, examples, and ideas that judges and legislators, as well as commentators and advocates, repeatedly invoke to explain family law and its guiding principles, to understand the issues that family law confronts, and to make decisions about family law's future course.

But the power of family law's canon is also visible in what the canon excludes and ignores. Legal authorities describing, enacting, and implementing family law devote little attention to many family relationships and routinely ignore the family law governing the poor. Decisionmakers often treat these exclusions as if they were commonsensical and beyond the need for explicit acknowledgment, much less justification.

This part examines two of the most notable omissions from the family law canon. Chapter 5 explores family law's overwhelming focus on marriage, parenthood, and (sometimes) their functional equivalents, to the frequent neglect of other family ties. Chapter 6 considers the poor's absence from the family law canon.

5

SIBLING TIES AND OTHER
NONCANONICAL FAMILY RELATIONSHIPS

Hardly a week goes by that I'm not presented with a proposed parenting plan that separates siblings.

—Judge Anne Kass (1998)[1]

Family law has long revolved around marriage and parenthood. From the earliest decades of the United States republic, legal treatises on the family focused almost entirely on what modern Americans would call the nuclear family and indeed on just two specific relationships within that nucleus: the legal bonds between husbands and wives and between parents and children. Treatise writers surveying what was then known as the law of domestic relations announced in their very titles that they covered "The Law of Baron and Femme" or "Husband and Wife" and the law of "Parent and Child," without mentioning ties between other family members.[2] As a leading history of family law noted, "the traditional categories of domestic-relations law" are "matrimony and parenthood."[3] The common law of the family was to a remarkable extent actually the common law of marriage and parenthood. It reflected and expressed the judgment that these were the family relationships that mattered much more than any others, certainly for the law and at least by implication for life outside the law as well. (Perhaps unsurprisingly, historians have discovered that nuclear family forms predominated even in colonial-era America.)[4]

In more recent years, courts, legislatures, and commentators have begun to direct more attention to relationships that are the (more or less) functional equivalents of marriage and parenthood, such as non-marital cohabitation and de facto parenthood. This development is unsurprising as marriage rates have declined in the United States,[5] and the proportion of children who are not living with two legal parents has escalated.[6]

However, debates about nonmarital cohabitation and de facto parenthood still routinely take legal marriage and parenthood as their frames of reference and orienting points. Lawmakers, jurists, and commentators discuss and deliberate about the extent to which the legal regulation of nonmarital cohabiting relationships should resemble the legal regulation of marriage. For example, courts often treat some types of property that either spouse acquired during marriage as jointly owned and distribute this property between the spouses at divorce. Considerable debate about nonmarital cohabiting relationships focuses on whether and when courts should similarly treat some types of property that either partner acquired during the relationship as jointly owned and subject to court-ordered distribution at dissolution.[7] Similarly, courts disagree and deliberate about whether and when an adult who has been caring for a child should be granted some or all of the rights and responsibilities associated with legal parenthood.[8] These are debates about relationships that are the functional equivalents of legal marriage or legal parenthood, but they still revolve around marriage or parenthood as their reference points.

Family law's persistent orientation around marriage and parenthood is such a standard feature of the field that the lack of attention devoted to other family relationships generally goes without explicit notice, operating mostly as an assumed premise. For instance, one book designed to introduce law students to family law begins by observing that "[i]n its traditional sense, family law, also called domestic relations law, involves the legal relationships between husband and wife and parent and child as a social, political, and economic unit. In recent years, the boundaries of family law have grown to encompass legal relationships among persons who live together but are not married—so-called nontraditional families."[9] As this description of the field suggests, family law devotes remarkably little attention to considering how to regulate and protect relationships other than marriage, parenthood, and sometimes their functional equivalents.

Illustrations of family law's tight focus on marriage and parenthood abound in both federal and state family law.[10] For instance, federal law allows certain undocumented immigrants living in the United States to avoid deportation and become lawfully admitted for permanent residence if deportation "would result in exceptional and extremely unusual hardship to the alien's spouse, parent, or child, who is a citizen of the United States or an alien lawfully admitted for permanent residence."[11] The Family and Medical Leave Act (FMLA) entitles eligible employees to up to twelve weeks of unpaid leave a year because of the birth or adoption of a child, or to care for a spouse, child, or parent with a serious health condition.[12] These laws protect marital and parent-child relationships, but extend no protection to other family ties.

Indeed, family law's focus on marriage and parenthood is so intense that the legal system generally does not impose financial support obligations on family members other than spouses, parents, and adult children. Whatever one thinks about this as a policy matter, the decision is striking in light of the strong cultural, political, and legal traditions in the United States preferring private rather than public means of responding to need. Moreover, governments have concrete fiscal incentives to compel family members to support their relatives so that indigent people do not need to rely on public assistance. Yet relatives other than spouses, parents, and adult children typically do not owe each other financial support as a matter of law. Only a few states have enacted (and then radically underenforced) laws requiring grandparents, grandchildren, or siblings to provide financial support if the recipient relative is needy and unable to support himself and the payer relative is able to provide support.[13]

The fact that legal support obligations focus so tightly on spouses, parents, and children may, in turn, help further reinforce family law's interest in marriage and parenthood. Family law has understood marriage and parenthood as relationships in which people are supposed to support each other financially so that the state does not have to provide such support. But the law has not conceived of other family ties in those terms, and legal decisionmakers may accordingly believe that governments reap fewer economic returns from the protection and maintenance of relationships beyond marriage and parenthood.

Yet myriad family bonds beyond marriage and parenthood can be central to family life and to the flourishing of family members. One reason that relationships with siblings, grandparents, grandchildren, aunts, uncles, nieces, nephews, cousins, and other noncanonical relatives are important is that sometimes these relationships function as substitutes for marriage or, more commonly, for legal parenthood. For instance, one problem with the current hardship exception for avoiding deportation is that this exception is not available to immigrants who have established relationships with citizens that are the functional equivalents of marriage or parenthood. Deporting these immigrants may inflict as much hardship on a citizen as deporting a legal spouse, parent, or child. Yet the Supreme Court has made clear that the hardship exception to deportation protects only legalized marital and parent-child relationships. In *Immigration and Naturalization Service v. Hector* (1986), an aunt who was raising her two American nieces while living illegally in the United States unsuccessfully attempted to invoke a prior version of the hardship exception, but the Court explained that "Congress has specifically identified the relatives whose hardship is to be considered."[14]

Noncanonical family relationships can also be important sources of support, love, stability, nurturing, care, and comfort, even when these relationships are not functioning as substitutes for marriage or parenthood. For example, the FMLA provision discussed above covers functional parenting relationships, but does not facilitate caregiving in relationships beyond marriage and (legal or functional) parenthood. The FMLA defines parent for its purposes as "the biological parent of an employee or an individual who stood in loco parentis to an employee when the employee was a son or daughter."[15] It defines son or daughter to mean "a biological, adopted, or foster child, a stepchild, a legal ward, or a child of a person standing in loco parentis."[16] Federal regulations implementing FMLA specify that "[p]ersons who are 'in loco parentis' include those with day-to-day responsibilities to care for and financially support a child, or, in the case of an employee, who had such responsibility for the employee when the employee was a child. A biological or legal relationship is not necessary."[17] This aspect of the FMLA constitutes an important instance where functional parents have secured some of the rights associated with legal parenthood. But this FMLA provision does not give employees the right to take unpaid leave to care for anyone who falls outside the act's definition of spouse, parent, or child.[18]

The Sibling Relationship as an Example of a Noncanonical Family Tie

Family law's tight focus on marriage, parenthood, and sometimes their functional equivalents leaves out many family relationships. The breadth of this exclusion is enormous. Examining the legal treatment of one noncanonical family bond, whose marginalization in family law is particularly notable, can provide a foundation for better understanding the consequences of family law's narrowness.

The sibling relationship offers a striking illustration of a crucial, yet legally neglected, family tie. I do not contend that the sibling relationship is necessarily the most important noncanonical family relationship. In any given family, bonds between grandparents and grandchildren, between aunts and nieces, between cousins, or between other relatives, may be more pivotal. In any event, attempting to rank the significance of noncanonical family ties probably makes little sense.

That said, the sibling relationship constitutes a rich example on which to focus. Siblings have the potential to be extraordinarily significant in each other's lives, providing intimacy, support, love, joy, connectedness, care, and caretaking. At the same time, sibling bonds are probably less likely than family ties that span generations to become the functional equivalents of parent-child relationships. The lack of legal attention devoted to sibling ties is also particularly remarkable because minor siblings are commonly part of each other's nuclear families. Family law devotes almost all its attention to the nuclear family, but not to this aspect of it.

The law governing children's family relationships dwells almost exclusively on children's ties with their parents rather than children's ties with their siblings, making only modest, scattered, and unsystematic efforts to safeguard sibling relationships when they are in jeopardy. Siblings who have lived together for years are sometimes separated at adoption or parental divorce or death with no right to contact each other, communicate, or visit. Siblings who are separated early on may have no opportunity and no right even to learn of each other's existence. This chapter uses the example of sibling relationships to explore family law's treatment of noncanonical family ties and to consider some of the reform possibilities and choices that emerge when we expand family law's focus beyond marriage and parenthood.

The Significance of Siblings

A burgeoning social science literature on the significance of sibling relationships can help inform our thinking about the legal regulation of sibling ties. This literature is not as extensive as social science work on marriage and parenthood; family law's orientation around marriage and parenthood helps steer scholarly attention in those directions. Nonetheless, the literature on siblings makes clear that the sibling relationship is potentially one of life's most important connections.

Siblings can know and support each other from their earliest years through their final ones. The relationship between two siblings, which begins with the birth of the younger sibling and can continue until a sibling dies, is often the longest-lasting relationship that a person ever experiences. Most people have a living sibling until the end or nearly the end of their lives and remain in contact with their siblings throughout.[19] A sibling relationship can last for decades longer than the relationship between a parent and child, which typically ends with the parent's death when the child still has many years left, or the relationship between spouses, who usually do not meet until adulthood. Sarah and Bessie Delany, two sisters with an especially long-lasting and close relationship, wrote a joint memoir when Sarah was 103 and Bessie was 101. Sarah contended that the two sisters "probably know each other better than any two human beings on this Earth."[20]

Strong bonds between siblings can develop remarkably early in life. Many children spend more time with their siblings than with anyone else, except (sometimes) a parent.[21] Moreover, siblings provide children with an opportunity to experience an intimate family relationship that tends to be much more egalitarian than that between parent and child[22] and that operates to at least some extent outside of parental view.[23] The emotional importance of the sibling relationship can motivate even very small children to understand their siblings extremely well. Children as young as sixteen to eighteen months can comfort their siblings and empathize with them. Two- and three-year-olds can recognize and discuss their siblings' abilities, emotions, plans, and desires.[24]

Siblings who grow up together accumulate a store of shared memories and experiences that can shape each sibling individually and establish a foundation for their lifelong relationships with each other.[25] Indeed, sibling relationships can be so formative that they often create groundwork and patterns for other close relationships that siblings develop, such as with a romantic partner, spouse, or child.[26]

Sibling relationships can be especially important when other family relationships falter, weaken, change, or end. Children with absent, dysfunctional, or warring parents often forge extraordinarily close and intense sibling bonds that provide the children with solace, nurturing, caretaking, and secure emotional attachments.[27] Adult siblings commonly rely on each other for psychological and material support when a parent becomes ill or dies, when a marriage ends, or during other times of family crisis.[28] Elderly siblings frequently provide each other with comfort, security, companionship, belonging, connectedness, and sometimes material help and caregiving.[29] Many elderly people report that they feel closer to their siblings than to any other family members except their own children.[30] Sibling relationships can be particularly significant later in life when spouses have died and children have left or become preoccupied with other responsibilities.[31]

Elderly siblings who have not maintained affectionate relationships with their brothers and sisters often identify this absence as a source of tremendous regret and loss.[32] Siblings are most likely to develop and sustain strong bonds if they have early, close, frequent, and extended contact in childhood.[33] Closeness in sibling relationships rarely originates in adulthood.[34]

Siblings Ignored

Despite the potential significance and value of sibling bonds, however, sibling relationships have attracted remarkably little legal attention. Legal decisionmakers often overlook sibling ties, and the law frequently provides little protection to sibling relationships at times when they are vulnerable to disruption or legal termination.

The relegation of sibling relationships to the peripheries of family law reaches back to the common law and reflects again the common law's sustained influence on modern family law. Common law courts and scholars endlessly discussed, debated, developed, and deployed the law of marriage and parenthood, while addressing siblings rarely. The common law recognized sibling relationships, but infrequently considered siblings beyond a few legal contexts, such as incest prohibitions barring siblings from sexual or marital relationships with each other[35] or intestacy doctrine specifying the circumstances under which a sibling could inherit when a person died without a will.[36] Without explicit discussion, the common law assumed that the sibling tie was a legally marginal relationship.

Legal consideration of siblings is still fragmentary. Family law scholars have written little about sibling relationships,[37] and the law's protection for sibling ties remains unsystematic and incomplete. To the extent that legislatures have protected sibling relationships at all, they tend to treat that protection more as a legislative gift bestowed at the discretion of lawmakers than as a recognition of the legitimate claims of siblings.

The legal treatment of sibling relationships between minor children is particularly striking. Childhood is the crucial period for forming and solidifying sibling bonds. Moreover, children are systematically more vulnerable than adults to both government and private action that harms them or simply ignores their interests, which makes the availability of legal protection for children's relationships especially important. Yet family law envisions children almost entirely in terms of their relationships with adults—their parents—rather than in terms of their relationships with other children—their siblings. This is still another example to add to the ones Chapter 4 discussed of how family law privileges parental prerogatives over children's potentially conflicting interests.

Consider how family law deals with sibling relationships between children at moments when those relationships are most likely to be threatened, such as when siblings are facing adoption, parental divorce, or a parent's death. (Parents in an intact marriage can also keep siblings apart,[38] but that appears to be much less common.) Reviewing current law in some depth uncovers some of the places where legislatures and courts confront key choices about whether and how to protect sibling relationships and illustrates some of the ways in which existing law too often fails to safeguard sibling bonds.

Adoption. Adoption can separate siblings and legally terminate their relationship. When siblings separated by adoption have had the opportunity to write about their experiences or to speak with the media about their lives, they have emphasized the "pain,"[39] "'sad[ness],'"[40] and "complete shock"[41] that such a separation can inflict. One sixteen-year-old, whose brother was adopted away in the early 1990s at the age of six,[42] wrote three years after his adoption that she thought of her brother "every day—so much that it hurts. It hurts the most when his birthday passes. He's getting older without me."[43] She had no right to contact her brother, to visit him, or to know where he lived. Her brother's adoptive parents had never responded to her request that they permit visits. Indeed, the adoptive parents had changed her brother's first and last name, and she did not know either.[44] Another woman, the oldest of four sisters separated for adoption in 1989 when they were thirteen, eight, four, and three, reported eleven years later that finding her sisters "'was something I dreamed of and cried myself to sleep over many nights.'"[45]

One of the woman's sisters said that after the separation "'[e]very night I would cry and pray; all I ever wanted was my sisters.'"[46]

Some people who were separated from their siblings by adoption have spent decades attempting to locate their siblings again. One man, unable to discover any information about his adopted away sister, checked the personal ads in his city's newspapers "'[e]very day for about 30 years'" in the hope of discovering news of her.[47] One family "'put ads to [their adopted away sister] in the newspaper, like 'Happy 32nd birthday. Wish we knew who you were,''" in the hope of attracting their sister's attention.[48] A woman who finally found her adopted away siblings after thirty-one years explained: "'I was determined to find my sister and brother because I remembered them and I loved them. Because they're my sister and brother.'"[49] Another woman, who searched for her adopted away sister for more than forty years, recounted "that as the oldest sibling, she ha[d] always dreamed of finding her sister."[50] A man who looked for his two adopted away sisters for twenty years described life without his sisters as "'like a circle that wasn't complete.'"[51] One of his sisters reported after the siblings were reunited that finding her brother "'filled a hole in [her] heart.'"[52] The other sister explained "'[t]hat missing piece of the puzzle is gone now. Now, we've got our brother back.'"[53]

Even adopted children who do not know if they have biological siblings express a strong desire to discover whether they have such siblings, to meet their siblings, and to have ongoing relationships with them.[54]

People who learn in adulthood that they have a biological sibling who was adopted into another family often begin extensive searches for their brother or sister. They can spend hours or years "searching the Internet and writing e-mails," employing lawyers,[55] "filling out forms and waivers,"[56] or seeking the help of newspaper publicity.[57] Although it can be difficult, some siblings who find one another for the first time as adults manage to develop close relationships, "exchang[ing] thousands of e-mails,"[58] "getting together about once a week,"[59] "'talk[ing] every day,'"[60] or "talk[ing] twice a day."[61]

Perhaps unexpectedly, the world of assisted reproductive technology (ART) also provides evidence of how powerful the desire to know one's biological siblings can be. Many people conceived through ART with the use of donor gametes have made great efforts to discover whether they have biological half-siblings through a common donor parent, to find those siblings, and to build relationships with them, overcoming obstacles created by an ART system that is often not structured to facilitate or even recognize those connections.[62]

Adoption law historically did not create a "presumption" in favor of keeping siblings together,[63] much less impose an "affirmative duty" on states to do so.[64] If siblings were adopted into separate families, moreover, the law considered their relationship severed and made no provision for contact, visitation, or even the opportunity to learn of a sibling's existence. The operative premise was that biological siblings were legally connected through their relationships with a shared parent or parents. Once a child's legal relationship with her birth parents ended, siblings no longer had any legally recognized tie to each other. Indeed, one sign of how marginal the sibling relationship has been to historical understandings of adoption is that several leading histories of adoption in the United States do not even list siblings, brothers, or sisters in their indexes.[65]

Although there has been some important reform in recent years, adoption law's attempts to protect sibling relationships remain relatively modest and sporadic. We can start with the law governing whether siblings available for adoption are placed in the same adoptive home and then turn to how the law treats siblings who are separated by adoption.

Federal law and the law of some states display some concern about placing siblings together for adoption. For instance, federal law conditions some federal funding on a state's agreement to make "reasonable efforts" "to place siblings removed from their home in the same . . . adoptive placement, unless the State documents that such a joint placement would be contrary to the safety or well-being of any of the siblings." The law does not elaborate on what "reasonable efforts" means or specify the documentation that states must produce to separate siblings.[66] Moreover, a United States District Court has held that this law creates no privately enforceable rights.[67] It is unclear what impact, if any, the federal law has had on how states actually treat siblings.

The state statutes and regulations that have been promulgated thus far vary in their declared approaches to placing siblings for adoption. Some states employ the "reasonable efforts" language also used in federal law. Arizona provides that the state "shall make reasonable efforts to place" a child available for adoption "with the child's siblings," "unless a court determines that . . . the placement . . . would be contrary to the child's or a sibling's safety or well-being."[68] Missouri simply provides that adoption agencies "shall make reasonable efforts to place siblings together."[69] Other states employ different language, while ultimately leaving the question of whether siblings will be placed together to the judgment of adoption agency officials. In New York, "[m]inor siblings or half-siblings who are free for adoption must be placed together in a prospective adoptive family home unless the [agency] determines" "after a careful assessment" according to specified criteria "that such placement would be detrimental to the best interests of one or more of the children."[70] "Factors to be considered in making a determination of whether siblings or half-siblings may be placed separately must include, but are not limited to: (i) the age differences among the siblings; (ii) the health and developmental differences among the siblings; (iii) the emotional relationship of the siblings to each other; (iv) the individual service needs of the siblings; and (v) the attachment of the individual siblings to separate families/locations."[71] Massachusetts provides that "[s]iblings shall be placed in the same . . . adoptive home unless the [agency] documents a written explanation in the children's record as to why such placement is not in the best interest of the children."[72]

In addition, most state law on the placement of siblings for adoption focuses exclusively on siblings who are available for adoption at the same time. Few states address situations in which one or more siblings have already been adopted and another sibling subsequently becomes available for adoption. The statutes that do cover this situation range widely in the protection they offer to sibling relationships. Consider the law in West Virginia, Florida, and Illinois. West Virginia and Florida provide that the state must notify a parent who has adopted one sibling if another sibling becomes available for adoption,[73] while Illinois law provides that the state will "make a good faith effort to" provide such notification.[74] If the first sibling's adoptive parent would like to adopt the second sibling, West Virginia specifies that the state may keep the siblings apart only by presenting a court with "clear and convincing evidence" that the adoption would be contrary to the best interests of one or both siblings.[75] Somewhat less protectively for sibling relationships, Florida provides that an adoption application from the first sibling's adoptive parent "will be given the same consideration as an application for adoption by a relative."[76] Illinois law does not create a preference in favor of the first sibling's adoptive parent, but instead instructs the state Department of

Children and Family Services to consider at least eight factors in deciding who should adopt the second sibling, one of which is "the family ties between the child and the child's relatives, including siblings."[77]

When siblings are adopted by different parents, many states treat the sibling relationship as legally terminated. Legal attention remains tightly focused on the connection between parent and child. For instance, the West Virginia Supreme Court has reported that "[t]he right to sibling visitation does not apply in adoption cases."[78] Virginia law provides that except in adoptions by a new spouse of a birth or adoptive parent, siblings "shall, by final order of adoption, be divested of all legal rights and obligations in respect to the child including the right to petition any court for visitation with the child."[79]

With little apparent effect to date, federal law conditions some federal funding on a state's agreement to make "reasonable efforts"—a term again left undefined—"to provide for frequent visitation or other ongoing interaction between the siblings [separated by adoption], unless that State documents that frequent visitation or other ongoing inter-action would be contrary to the safety or well-being of any of the siblings."[80]

Some state statutes mention visitation or communication between siblings separated by adoption, but most of these laws impose no requirements on adoptive parents and confer no rights on siblings. One common pattern is for state laws that discuss postadoption sibling contact to focus on advice and encouragement. For instance, Iowa requires adoption agencies to "[e]ncourage prospective adoptive parents to plan for facilitating postadoption contact between the child and the child's siblings." Iowa also requires adoption agencies to "[p]rovide prospective adoptive parents with information regarding the child's siblings" and "information regarding the importance of sibling relationships to an adopted child."[81] California law does the same,[82] and case law in California makes clear that neither adoption agencies nor courts in California have the authority to compel an adoptive parent to permit visitation between siblings separated by adoption.[83] Colorado law similarly limits itself. It instructs courts hearing adoption petitions to "inquire as to whether the adoptive parents have received counseling regarding children in sibling groups maintaining or developing ties with each other" and states that "if the adoptive parents are willing, the court may encourage reasonable visitation among the siblings when visitation is in the best interests of the child or the children."[84] Maine law provides that the state "shall make reasonable efforts to establish agreements with prospective adoptive parents that provide for reasonable contact between an adoptive child and the child's siblings when the [state] believes that the contact will be in the children's best interests."[85] Washington instructs courts reviewing and approving agreements to adopt a child from foster care to "encourage the adoptive parents, birth parents, foster parents, kinship caregivers, and the department [of social and health services] or other supervising agency to seriously consider the long-term benefits to the child adoptee and siblings of the child adoptee of providing for and facilitating continuing postadoption contact between siblings."[86]

Other state laws permit courts to issue orders providing for postadoption sibling contact, but only if adoptive parents agree. For example, Indiana authorizes courts issuing adoption decrees to order "specific postadoption contact for an adopted child who is at least two (2) years of age with a pre-adoptive sibling," but only if "each adoptive parent consents to the court's order for postadoption contact privileges" and "the court determines that the postadoption contact would serve the best interests of the adopted child."[87] Louisiana law similarly provides that courts may approve agreements that adoptive parents have made for postadoption sibling contact if "[t]he child has an established, significant relationship with [the child's sibling] to the extent that its loss would cause substantial harm to the child" and "[t]he preservation of the relationship would otherwise be in the best interest of the child."[88] Tennessee law explicitly states that "[t]he adoptive parents of a child shall not be required by any order of the adoption court to permit visitation by any other person." Adoptive parents in Tennessee may, "in their sole discretion," decide to allow sibling visitation or other sibling contact. But even if adoptive parents agree "to permit visitation or contact," their agreement does not give siblings "any enforceable rights."[89]

Only a few states permit courts to order postadoption sibling contact over an adoptive parent's objection. Florida law authorizes courts to order postadoption sibling communication or contact for a child adopted from the custody of the state "[i]f the court determines that the child's best interests will be served by postadoption communication or contact." "Statements of the prospective adoptive parents" are one factor that courts must consider in deciding whether to order postadoption sibling communication or contact, but not the only factor.[90] After an adoption takes place, an adoptive parent in Florida may petition at any time for review of a sibling communication or contact order. "[T]he court may order the communication or contact to be terminated or modified, as the court deems to be in the best interests of the adopted child; however, the court may not increase contact between the adopted child and siblings . . . without the consent of the adoptive parent or parents."[91] Nevada authorizes courts in adoption proceedings to grant siblings "a reasonable right to visit" the adopted child in cases where the siblings were previously granted "a similar right" while the child was "in the custody of an agency which provides child welfare services."[92] Arkansas law provides that "[s]ibling visitation shall not terminate if the adopted child was in the custody of the Department of Human Services and had a sibling who was not adopted by the same family and before adoption the circuit court in the juvenile dependency-neglect or families-in-need-of-services case has determined that it is in the best interests of the siblings to visit and has ordered visitation between the siblings to occur after the adoption."[93]

In addition, a few states give siblings themselves the right to seek postadoption contact with each other. For example, Massachusetts permits "[a]ny child over 12 years of age [to] request visitation with siblings who . . . have been adopted in a foster or adoptive home other than where the child resides."[94] When a child is being adopted by a stepparent, Vermont permits the child's sibling to request postadoption visitation or communication. Vermont authorizes courts to grant the request if it is in the adopted child's best interests, taking into account "any objections to the requested order by the adoptive stepparent and the stepparent's spouse."[95] A sibling in New Jersey may petition for postadoption visitation and receive it if she can prove "by a preponderance of the evidence that visitation is necessary to avoid harm to the" brother or sister who has been adopted away from her.[96] Maryland law provides that "[a]ny siblings who are separated due to a[n] . . . adoptive placement may petition a court, including a juvenile court with jurisdiction over one or more of the siblings, for reasonable sibling visitation rights." Maryland instructs a court considering such a petition to "weigh the relative interests of each child and base its decision on the best interests of the children promoting the greatest welfare and least harm to the children."[97]

Even where they do exist, however, laws authorizing siblings to seek postadoption visitation and laws empowering courts to order such visitation over an adoptive parent's objection may be struck down as unconstitutional or substantially narrowed by judges in order to save their constitutionality.

The Supreme Court's current constitutional jurisprudence on children's family relationships revolves tightly around the parent-child bond. As Chapter 4 observed, the Court has protected parents' rights of custody and control over their children even when parents are intent on excluding other relatives. The Court's plurality opinion in *Troxel v. Granville* (2000) concluded that a state nonparent visitation statute was unconstitutional as applied where a state court relied on the statute in granting a visitation petition from two grandparents without according "any material weight" to the mother's determination of her children's best interests.[98] The *Troxel* plurality was convinced that the mother's "fundamental right to make decisions concerning the care, custody, and control of her two daughters" had been infringed upon in this case,[99] although the plurality explicitly chose not to settle "whether the Due Process Clause requires all nonparental visitation statutes to include a showing of harm or potential harm to the child as a condition precedent to granting visitation."[100]

In my view, the Supreme Court's constitutional decisionmaking could benefit from a much more systematic exploration of the value of noncanonical family relationships. The Court has only rarely focused on family ties beyond marriage and parenthood.[101] As the Court's case law is now organized, laws authorizing postadoption sibling visitation without an adoptive parent's agreement may unconstitutionally impinge upon the strong vision of parental autonomy that the *Troxel* plurality endorsed, at least unless courts or legislatures substantially modify these statutes.

Since *Troxel,* some state supreme courts have upheld nonparent visitation statutes after interpreting the statutes to include a requirement that judges accord special weight to a parent's assessment of her child's best interests.[102] These decisions suggest that at least some courts might be willing to uphold postadoption sibling visitation statutes after similarly interpreting those statutes to give special weight to a parent's judgment about her child's best interests.

Other state supreme courts have further constrained nonparent visitation laws since *Troxel.* For instance, some courts have held that nonparent visitation statutes must both give special weight to a parent's assessment of her child's best interests and also require the nonparent plaintiff who is seeking visitation to demonstrate that denying visitation would harm the child whose visitation is sought. Some of these decisions have read a requirement to show harm into nonparent visitation statutes,[103] while other decisions have struck down nonparent visitation statutes for failing to include such a requirement.[104] This line of case law augments protections for parental prerogatives. But if given the opportunity to litigate, at least some plaintiffs seeking postadoption visitation with a sibling should be able to establish that denying visitation would significantly harm the plaintiff's sibling.

Parental Divorce or Death. Let's turn to parental divorce and then consider a parent's death, which can sometimes have similar consequences for sibling relationships. Siblings whose parents divorce are still legally recognized as siblings. But parental divorce can leave siblings in separate households and threaten the maintenance of functioning ties between siblings, at a time when children often have more need than ever for support and stability in their sibling relationships.[105]

Some siblings who were separated after their parents' divorce have publicly described the hurt and loss that they experienced. One woman recounted her separation from her brother this way: "'When I was little . . . my mom and dad had a divorce and my brother and I were split. The father took him and my mother took me. It's hard at 5 years old to be playing with your brother all this time and all of a sudden he's gone and you can't see him and talk to him.'"[106] Another woman wrote that she "was left with a broken heart" after her divorcing parents separated their children, with her father getting custody of her and her mother getting custody of her sister and brother.[107] A third woman's parents separated when she was an infant. Her mother took her, and her father took her sister. When she learned of her sister's existence five years later, she "recall[ed] feeling a combination of anger, hurt, frustration, and powerlessness in being denied a sibling relationship for so long."[108]

Divorce courts in every state will sometimes split custody of siblings between parents so that some siblings live with one parent and other siblings live with the second parent. One study of contested custody cases found that courts awarded split custody 14.2% of the time when the mother requested joint physical custody and the father requested sole physical custody, that courts awarded split custody 7.5% of the time when each parent requested sole physical custody, and that courts awarded split custody 3.1% of the time when the mother requested sole physical custody and the father requested joint physical custody.[109]

Another study of child custody awards found that "[s]plit custody was awarded in 13 percent of the disputed cases but in only 4 percent of the couples without a formal dispute."[110]

Sometimes courts ordering split custody are attempting to resolve custody battles between two parents who each want custody of all their children. Sometimes courts accept split custody plans that one parent has advocated or that both parents support and perhaps have already implemented upon separating. Split custody can appeal to a parent as a way of distributing the financial burdens and psychological benefits of childrearing. Alternatively or in addition, split custody can appeal to a parent who feels closer ties to some of his children rather than others. For instance, split custody often operates along sex-based lines, with mothers receiving custody of girls and fathers receiving custody of boys.[111] Anne Kass, a family court judge in Albuquerque, New Mexico, reported that "[h]ardly a week goes by that [she is] not presented with a proposed parenting plan that separates siblings. Often the division is along gender lines—dads take sons, moms take daughters. Sometimes the division is based on age—dad takes the older child, mom the little one."[112] Judge Kass recounted one case that "involved a dad who insisted on taking the younger of his two sons—the one who looked just like dad. The boys were 18 months apart in age. Within a year of separation, the older boy had become a 'failure-to-thrive' child. Failure-to-thrive is the label for a physical condition that is the result of emotional injury. Children who develop it stop growing physically."[113] In each of these scenarios, parents and/or courts sometimes envision split custody as a way of promoting strong relationships between parents and the children left in their custody, even as this arrangement may harm or disregard sibling ties.

Judge Kass was personally concerned about split custody, and she reported that "Albuquerque family court judges reject parenting plans that separate siblings unless a child psychologist talks to the family and approves the separation."[114] But in general, courts often do not address split custody systematically or consistently.

Some courts appear to impose no presumptions against split custody at divorce. They split the custody of siblings when that is "desirable,"[115] "reasonable,"[116] or "best,"[117] or they treat the separation of siblings as just one factor among many for a court to take into account in determining custody.[118] Some state statutes similarly include a child's relationship with siblings as one factor for courts to consider in deciding custody.[119]

Other courts have announced varying presumptions against split custody, requiring what they deem to be "exceptional" circumstances,[120] "overwhelming"[121] or "strong need,"[122] or "compelling"[123] or "overriding reasons."[124] However, courts apply these declared standards with virtually unfettered discretion, remarkable inconsistency, and frequently questionable logic.

A presumption against split custody that sounds strict in theory often means much less in practice. For instance, Kansas is a rare state with a statute explicitly addressing split custody. The law provides that "[i]n an exceptional case, the court may order a residential arrangement in which one or more children reside with each parent and have parenting time with the other."[125] But the Kansas Court of Appeals has interpreted this statutory language so that the reference to exceptionality appears to impose no additional constraints on courts, holding that "when the district court makes a finding, supported by substantial competent evidence, that divided custody is in a child's best interests, the court has met the requirement of establishing an 'exceptional case.' "[126]

Similarly, the arguments that some parents advance for split custody arrangements along sex-based lines, and that some courts endorse, accept, or tolerate, can reflect deeply gendered understandings about the skills and preferences that each sex will and should develop and even about which children are most valuable. Parents and/or courts can present these arguments with little analysis or reflection about the sex roles and sex-based hierarchy that they assume, enforce, and perpetuate. Indeed, modern arguments for sex-based split custody arrangements can sometimes evoke recollections of tender years doctrines, which courts and legislatures officially repudiated in the 1970s and 1980s as inconsistent with constitutional prohibitions on sex discrimination and with children's best interests. Recall from Chapter 4 that these doctrines rested on the cultural premise that gendered differences between women and men were stark, unchanging, and invariable, making mothers "naturally" more suited to raise daughters and less suited to raise sons.

In re Marriage of Pundt (1996)[127] suggests how a parent's arguments for sex-based split custody may be infused with gendered reasoning. This case revolved around a custody dispute between Jeanice and Ricky Pundt. Jeanice sought custody of all three of the couple's children, while Ricky sought custody of his son, Derrick, but not his two daughters, Danielle and Devin.[128] "Jeanice testified she felt Ricky was polarizing the family along gender lines. She stated Ricky favored Derrick and did not exhibit much interest in the girls. She felt that while in Ricky's care, Derrick began to exhibit more of a disparaging attitude towards the girls. She testified the girls missed Derrick, and she felt it would be better not to separate the children."[129] Ricky's own testimony appeared to support Jeanice's account in some respects. Ricky singled out Derrick as "his best friend."[130] Ricky did not explain why his daughters did not qualify for that status, but Ricky stressed that he and Derrick shared conventionally masculine pastimes, stating that "he and Derrick had similar interests, such as watching sports and playing basketball."[131] The Iowa Court of Appeals awarded Ricky custody of Derrick despite Jeanice's concerns.[132]

In *Harris v. Harris* (1994),[133] at least one court appeared to endorse gendered arguments for sex-based split custody arrangements. This case centered on a custody dispute between Gina and Frank Harris over their children, Cole and Marissa. A Vermont family court awarded custody of Cole to his father and custody of Marissa to her mother.[134] As the Vermont Supreme Court noted on appeal, "[i]n rendering its decision, the family court suggested that Cole had a natural affinity for his father, who teaches him 'things a young boy should know,'"[135] including instruction in "fishing, hunting, and softball."[136] The family court's language suggested that this court had a gendered understanding of what boys "'should know'" and which parent was "natural[ly]" best situated to teach a boy those important lessons.

The Vermont Supreme Court in *Harris* did not endorse the family court's language, but the supreme court also did not appear eager to systematically examine the gendered nature of the family court's reasoning. The supreme court swiftly announced that it did "not interpret [the family court's] comments in this regard as an indication it applied a preference that Cole remain with his father because he was a boy" and insisted that the family court had not violated a Vermont statute that formally disestablished a tender years doctrine by prohibiting courts from "'apply[ing] a preference for one parent over the other because of the sex of the child [or] the sex of a parent.'"[137]

Half-Siblings. Half-siblings are especially likely to be separated at divorce or when their shared parent dies.[138] Half-siblings who grow up together can develop extremely close relationships. They often do not distinguish between full and half-siblings, thinking about each other just as sisters and brothers. In contrast, half-siblings with little contact in childhood tend to have more distant relationships in adulthood and to think about each other in ways that emphasize their different histories rather than their shared ties.[139]

Custody law frequently adds obstacles to the development of close ties between half-siblings. While some courts considering split custody extend the same protections to full and half-sibling relationships,[140] many courts will not apply their presumptions against splitting custody of full siblings to cases involving half-siblings. These latter decisions treating half-siblings differently sometimes seem to assume that half-sibling relationships are necessarily less close or significant than full sibling relationships.[141] More explicitly, courts refusing to create presumptions against splitting half-siblings prioritize fairness between parents over the promotion of sibling relationships. These courts note that a presumption against separating half-siblings would favor the custody claims of the half-siblings' common parent and insist that this "ironclad advantage"[142] "would be blatantly unfair to"[143] the other parent or parents involved in a custody dispute. They assume, without apparently considering the possibility of an alternative, that equity between parents disputing custody takes precedence over fostering relationships between half-siblings subject to such disputes.

When half-siblings are separated into the homes of different parents, the half-siblings often have no right to visit each other over a parent's objection. State visitation statutes frequently offer no help to siblings. By 2000, every state had enacted laws providing for some type of grandparent visitation.[144] But the passage of grandparent visitation statutes appears to have been driven less by a broad commitment to expanding family law's focus beyond marriage and parenthood and more by the extraordinary lobbying efforts and political power of groups promoting the interests of older Americans, such as the AARP. Thomas Downey, a member of Congress who advocated for grandparent visitation rights, noted candidly in 1991 the "well-known fact that seniors are the most active lobby in this country, and when it comes to grandparents there is no one group more united in their purpose."[145] Congress designated 1995 "the 'Year of the Grandparent.'"[146] Siblings and other noncanonical relatives do not come close to garnering this level of political support. Many states limit their nonparent visitation laws to grandparents and do not permit other relatives, such as siblings, to seek visitation. Even within these nonparent visitation statutes, the premise that family law revolves around marriage and parenthood remains powerful.

Several suits seeking visitation with a half-sibling over a parent's objection have failed because the state provided no sibling visitation statute. Court decisions rejecting these suits prioritize "parental authority,"[147] "[a] parent's right to associate with and make decisions concerning the care, custody and control of his or her children,"[148] "the right of parents to raise their children as they see fit."[149] The courts start from the premise that parents have a right to exclude nonparents, including siblings, from visitation with a child and refuse to disturb that premise without statutory authorization.[150]

Some half-siblings have been unable to secure rights to visit each other even in states with sibling visitation statutes.[151] Legislatures often strictly limit these laws in the interest of minimizing infringement on "parental authority,"[152] permitting suits for sibling visitation over a parent's objection only where parent-child relationships have already been affected by death, divorce, separation, or judicial supervision. One half-sibling lost a visitation suit because the state statute (since repealed) authorized sibling visitation over a parent's objection only if at least one of the siblings at issue had a deceased parent.[153] Another half-sibling lost a visitation suit because the state statute authorized sibling visitation over a parent's objection only in cases where the sibling whose visitation was sought either had a deceased parent or had parents who were divorced or living separately.[154] A third half-sibling lost a visitation suit because the state statute authorized sibling visitation over a parent's objection only if both siblings were dependent children already under the jurisdiction of the juvenile court.[155]

In re Victoria C. involved a half-sibling plaintiff who fell outside Maryland's sibling visitation statute because that law applies only to minor siblings.[156] Victoria was sixteen when she initiated her suit, but nineteen by the time the Maryland Court of Special Appeals decided her case in November 2012.[157] (As of this writing, the case is before Maryland's highest court, which has not yet issued a decision on the merits.)[158]

Victoria's mother died.[159] Until March 2009, when Victoria was fifteen, she lived with her father, George, his wife, Kieran, and their children, Lance (then three years old) and Evan (then eighteen months).[160] The Court of Special Appeals tersely explained that in March 2009 "Victoria went to live with her aunt [in Texas] after an abuse allegation against George was sustained."[161] Victoria returned from Texas a year later, but George and Kieran would not let Victoria live in the family home or visit Lance and Evan, whom she had not seen since leaving for Texas.[162] Victoria went into foster care and filed suit, seeking visitation with Lance and Evan.[163]

The Court of Special Appeals held that an adult sibling was legally no different from any other "third part[y] seeking visitation."[164] This meant that the court would safeguard George's and Kieran's "constitutionally protected, fundamental liberty interest in the care, custody, and control of their children"[165] by requiring Victoria to prove either that George and Kieran were unfit parents or that there were "exceptional circumstances" demonstrating that denying visitation would have "a significant deleterious effect" on Lance and Evan.[166] The court found that Victoria had failed to satisfy either requirement and accordingly did not consider whether visitation with Victoria would be in Lance's and Evan's best interests.[167]

In part, this holding suggests (as the judicial decisions discussed in Chapter 4 also do) how leniently courts define parental fitness. George had abused his daughter, and Kieran had been the other adult in the household. The two then refused to allow Victoria back into their home, left her with no alternative better than foster care, and denied her contact with her brothers. But Victoria's counsel apparently concluded nonetheless that it would not be possible to establish that George and Kieran were unfit parents to Lance and Evan, and Victoria did not even raise that argument.[168]

Victoria's legal defeat also illustrates how narrowly the Court of Special Appeals defined the "exceptional circumstances" that could justify sibling visitation over a parent's objection. George and Kieran conceded that Victoria had close and caring relationships with her brothers when the three siblings lived together.[169] Yet the court concluded that Victoria had not proven that denying visitation would harm Lance and Evan, in part because George and Kieran had shut Victoria out for so long that the boys now had diminished (in Lance's case) or no (in Evan's case) memories of her.[170]

Of course, denying visitation did unquestionably harm Victoria. She "testified that she had been close to her siblings before she left home and, since she had been unable to see them, '[i]t has been like a hold, kind of. I just—I miss them. They were an entire section of my life.'"[171] However, the court stressed that "[w]hile it may be true that Victoria has suffered unfortunate and regrettable harm, harm suffered by an adult as the result of a denial of visitation with minor children is not a consideration in a court's exceptional circumstances analysis."[172]

It is also important to note that even siblings who fall within a state visitation statute may face constitutional obstacles under a jurisprudence that is riveted on parent-child relationships. In *Herbst v. Swan* (2002),[173] Jeana Herbst, who was already an adult, sought visitation under a California sibling visitation law with her six-year-old half-brother, Jake Herbst. Jeana's and Jake's father had died, and Jake's mother, Charlene Swan, objected to visitation between the half-siblings.[174] The California Court of Appeal held that granting Jeana's petition for visitation would be inconsistent with the *Troxel* plurality's understanding of "the fundamental liberty interest of a parent," as the petition "suggest[ed] no compelling facts to overcome the presumption that [Swan] is acting with the best interests of Jake in mind."[175]

In sum, the legal vulnerability of sibling relationships has attracted insufficient attention. Yet sibling relationships can be enormously significant, providing care, love, support, joy, connectedness, intimacy, and nurture. A legal regime that fails to adequately safeguard sibling relationships can impose tremendous costs on people who lose opportunities to develop and maintain bonds with their siblings.

Reexamining Family Law from the Perspective of Noncanonical Relationships

Questioning family law's reflexive focus on marriage, parenthood, and sometimes their functional equivalents helps direct our attention to the legal treatment of noncanonical family members like siblings. It encourages us to think systematically about how best to reform the law's regulation and protection of noncanonical family ties. Lawmakers and judges, as well as scholars, advocates, and family members, should all participate in this process of reexamining family law. Thinking about how to protect and promote noncanonical family bonds is as complicated and multifaceted, and involves as many choices, trade-offs, and decisions, as thinking about how to protect and promote marital or parental relationships. Even if everyone were to agree that noncanonical family ties merit more legal support and safeguarding, difficult, complex, and potentially divisive questions would still remain about how best to accomplish this goal, in what ways, under what circumstances, and at what costs. In the interest of sparking dialogue and debate, this chapter concludes by exploring some potential policy reforms that come into view when considering family law through the lens of sibling relationships.

Adoption

Let's return to adoption, starting again with the issue of whether siblings who are available for adoption at the same time are placed in the same adoptive home. As this chapter has observed, current law on sibling placement at adoption, where it exists, varies with too little evidence of systematic deliberation or discussion. Some states require adoption agencies to make "reasonable efforts" to place siblings together, while others instruct adoption agencies that they must place siblings together unless the agency determines that a joint adoptive placement would be contrary to at least one child's best interests. States can consider both of these policies in more depth and with more care than they have shown to date, and states might also examine alternative policy choices.

For instance, states exploring or enacting a policy that would require reasonable efforts from adoption agencies to place siblings together could think more systematically about what constitutes reasonable efforts. The appeal of a reasonable efforts standard from the standpoint of providing more protection to sibling relationships is that this standard seems designed to encourage joint placement of siblings, while avoiding the imposition of too many costs on adoption agencies or the addition of too much delay on adoptive placements. But the potential danger for sibling relationships with requiring only "reasonable efforts" is that such a requirement may mean little in practice and may simply validate adoption agency operations as they are, rather than pushing agencies to do more to place siblings together. States seeking to capture the benefits of a reasonable efforts standard, while minimizing the standard's pitfalls, might think about how to provide greater guidance to adoption agencies as the agencies look for "reasonable" ways to keep siblings together. For example, one reform that states might implement without imposing additional expense or delay on adoptions would be to specify that adoption agencies cannot (as they sometimes have)[176] overlook or exclude a fit prospective adoptive parent interested in adopting a sibling group simply because the prospective parent is unmarried, gay, or already has other children in his household. States might also consider defining reasonable efforts to require adoption agencies to conduct out-of-state searches for potential adoptive parents, if necessary to find a shared adoptive placement for a sibling group. This latter strategy would impose costs on agencies and possibly delay some adoptions, but it would have the considerable advantage of reaching a much larger pool of potential adoptive parents.

Similarly, states instructing adoption agencies that they must place siblings together unless the agency determines that a joint adoptive placement would be contrary to at least one child's best interests could think more systematically about how to elaborate their policies in ways that would promote and protect sibling relationships. Most crucially, state law might seek to structure agency decisionmaking about whether a joint adoptive placement would be against a sibling's best interests, in an effort to ensure that agency practice reflects a real commitment to keeping siblings together. For instance, state law might provide that an adoption agency cannot conclude that a joint adoptive placement would be against a sibling's best interests without documenting in writing all of the reasons for and against separating the siblings. State law might provide that an agency cannot decide against seeking a joint sibling placement unless at least two different experts who have had sustained interaction with the siblings agree with this approach.

States committed to safeguarding sibling relationships in adoption could also consider policies that would be more protective of sibling ties than any of the laws enacted to date. For example, state statutes could require adoption agencies to place siblings in the same adoptive home when siblings are available for adoption at the same time, unless the agency can present a court with a preponderance of evidence (or even with clear and convincing evidence) that placing siblings together would be contrary to at least one sibling's best interests. Such a standard would be more protective of sibling ties and would give courts considerable leverage in monitoring agency behavior. At the same time, subjecting adoption agencies to judicial oversight in the interest of safeguarding sibling relationships would likely demand important trade-offs by imposing additional expenses on agencies and delaying the adoptive placement of some children.

States can additionally explore whether to apply the same protective rules and standards to sibling adoptions regardless of whether the siblings at issue have ever lived together.[177] Without question, the case for keeping siblings together is most compelling when siblings have already developed functioning relationships with each other. But whether children have had the opportunity to live together is almost always the product of adult decisions, rather than children's own choices. States focused on protecting sibling relationships might conclude that, even if siblings have not been able to live together to date, the fact of their biological connection creates a unique foundation for the development of lifelong intimacy and everyday functional ties that the law should not surrender lightly. Indeed, we have seen that adopted children commonly report that they want these connections with their biological siblings. Siblings separated by adoption often make great efforts to find each other and develop ongoing relationships, even when they have never lived together.

Let's turn to the situation of a child who becomes available for adoption after the child's sibling has already been adopted. Few states have any statutes on this topic, but it is an important one that all states should address. There are three basic issues for states to consider: how to inform the adoptive parents of one sibling that another sibling is available for adoption, how to encourage the first sibling's adoptive parents to seek adoption of the second sibling, and how to treat the first sibling's adoptive parents when they decide that they would like to adopt the second sibling.

First, consider the notification of the first sibling's adoptive parents. States might explore strategies to make notification more effective in leading to the placement of siblings together and to mitigate the costs associated with notification. For instance, one way to make notification more effective might be to require state adoption officials to contact the first sibling's adoptive parents not only when a second sibling becomes available for adoption, but also when a second sibling enters the foster care system or experiences other changes making it reasonably likely that the second sibling will become available for adoption. This practice would facilitate placing a second sibling who does go into foster care with the parents who have already adopted the first sibling. One way to make notification less costly from the state's perspective, while imposing only minimal costs on adoptive parents, would be to require adoptive parents to keep the contact information they provided to the state updated over time. If the state cannot reach the first sibling's adoptive parents with the contact information that the parents provided, state law might permit state adoption officials to access preexisting state databases on driver's licenses, voter registration, and the like, to facilitate finding updated contact information.

Second, consider the provision of encouragement. A relatively simple possibility for states to consider would be to require state adoption officials to provide the first sibling's adoptive parents with information about the importance of sibling ties and to encourage these parents to consider adopting the second sibling. States could do even more to promote joint adoptive placements, albeit at significantly greater expense, by establishing that any subsidies that are available to an adoptive parent who adopts a sibling group all at once are also available to an adoptive parent who has already adopted one sibling and adopts another sibling later. For instance, New York law provides for an adoption subsidy in some cases where "the child is the sibling or half-sibling of a child already adopted and it is considered necessary that such children be placed together."[178]

Third, consider what happens when the first sibling's adoptive parents decide that they would like to adopt the second sibling as well. The sparse state law on this subject currently ranges widely, from a requirement that the state must place siblings together unless the state can present a court with clear and convincing evidence that joint adoption would be contrary to at least one sibling's best interests, to a policy providing that the sibling tie is just one of many factors that state adoption officials will consider in placing the second sibling. States need to focus on this issue and to weigh the costs and benefits of various alternatives. The advantages of placing siblings together seem clear. Joint placement provides siblings with the best opportunity to enhance or develop their connections with each other and to enjoy the potential lifelong significance and value of sibling bonds. The costs of placing siblings together, in a situation where there is a fit adoptive parent eager to raise the sibling group, are less immediately apparent and could usefully be elaborated before states decide against employing a standard that prioritizes joint sibling placement.

The next issue that states need to explore is how to treat siblings who are separated by adoption. Here again, a range of options emerges when family law focuses on sibling relationships. At the more modest end of the spectrum, states could require adoption agencies to speak with adoptive parents about the importance of sibling ties and encourage adoptive parents to permit and facilitate contact, communication, and visitation between siblings. State law could direct adoption agencies to work individually with adoptive parents to help parents establish a schedule and routine of sibling visitation, phone calls, electronic communication, and the like. Adoption agencies could also help parents anticipate and respond to logistical difficulties, such as those created when siblings live a considerable distance apart.

In addition, more states could encourage prospective adoptive parents to enter into express written agreements before adoption that describe the sibling contact, communication, and visitation that the parents will allow and facilitate after adoption. Such agreements may make parents less likely to raise subsequent objections to sibling contact, communication, and visitation, even if the agreements are never litigated, much less judicially enforced.

A significantly more demanding approach to protecting sibling relationships would be to give siblings separated by adoption an enforceable right to contact, communication, and visitation even over a parent's objection, unless a court determines that such a connection would be contrary to the best interests of one or more siblings. The argument in favor of such a policy is that enforceable postadoption sibling rights are worth their intrusion on parental autonomy because of how important and valuable sibling relationships can be. However, legislatures may be unwilling to limit parental prerogatives in this way, and courts may be even less willing to uphold such a limit. In light of *Troxel,* postadoption sibling contact statutes presumably will have to specify that courts must give "material weight" to a parent's assessment of her child's best interests.[179] In at least some states, these laws will probably also have to include a requirement that the plaintiff demonstrate that denying contact would harm the plaintiff's sibling.

Another policy possibility for states to consider in more detail concerns whether and how to use sibling registries to enable siblings separated by adoption to contact each other when they reach the age of majority. These registries are not a substitute for contact in childhood, the most crucial period for forming sibling ties. But they represent a relatively small infringement on the autonomy of adoptive parents and thus may be more politically and judicially acceptable.

At least thirty-six states currently have some form of sibling registry for adopted children and their siblings.[180] However, states could think about a variety of potential reforms in the interest of protecting sibling ties. First, many states collect information about a child's biological family, including siblings, as the biological family exists at the moment of the child's adoption, but devote little, if any, attention to keeping that information current.[181] States could explore whether and how to implement procedures for updating an adopted child's biographical information when another biological sibling is born or identified. States could also consider requiring adoptive parents to keep the contact information for their adopted children current at least until the children turn eighteen.

Second, states could think about revising their procedures for distributing the information they collect. For instance, more states could enact "confidential intermediary" sibling registries that help willing brothers and sisters find each other, even if one sibling is unaware of the registry. Some state sibling registries now operate just as passive "mutual consent" registries that connect two siblings separated by adoption only if both have discovered the registry and requested contact information for each other.[182] These passive registries tend to be ineffectual, with very low matching rates. For example, approximately 8,500 adoptees, birth parents, and siblings registered in Texas by 2008, but the Texas registry made just one or two matches of any family members each month.[183] Almost 24,000 adoptees, 5,700 birth parents, and 1,100 siblings registered in New York by 2009, but the New York registry made just 100 to 200 matches of any family members a year.[184]

Confidential intermediary registries, which at least twenty states have enacted in some form, allow one sibling to initiate the connection process. When a person joins one of these registries seeking contact information about a sibling, the registry uses a confidential intermediary to search for the sibling, ask her if she would like to connect, and distribute contact information if the sibling agrees.[185] Unsurprisingly, these more active registries appear to be more effective in matching willing siblings than registries that wait passively for mutual consent. A study of the Georgia Adoption Reunion Registry for adoptees, birth parents, and siblings tracked the eighty searches that the registry both initiated and concluded during the one-year period from October 1, 1998, to September 30, 1999. Most of these searches (76%) led to a reunion, 15% led to the discovery that the searched-for family member had died, and 5% ended with the searched-for family member denying consent to be contacted. Only three searches ended with the registry unable to locate the searched-for family member.[186]

States could also think about whether their registries will be open to siblings separated by adoption, even if the siblings' biological parents have not agreed to the siblings' use of the registry. Some state sibling registries currently give biological parents substantial control over the access that siblings have to each other. For instance, Minnesota's confidential intermediary system specifies that the state "shall provide services to adult genetic siblings" only "if there is no known violation of the confidentiality of a birth parent or if the birth parent gives written consent."[187] Oregon law states that "[a]n adult adoptee or the adoptive parent of a minor or deceased adoptee may not request a search for a genetic sibling of the adoptee if there was a previous search for a birth parent of the adoptee and the birth parent did not want to make contact with the adult adoptee or adoptive parent."[188] Nevada's passive mutual consent registry provides that if two siblings separated by adoption join the registry and consent to share contact information with each other, the state may distribute the information only if "written consent for the release of such information is given by the natural parent."[189]

With little apparent discussion or debate, such laws prioritize continued parental prerogatives over biological children, including adopted away children, and represent another example of how family law views children through the lens of their relationships with their parents. States are not necessarily wrong to prioritize parental prerogatives in this way, but that decision has real costs and deserves to be the subject of substantial deliberation. The prerogatives that some registries accord to parents can come at the expense of denying some siblings separated by adoption the opportunity to connect when each sibling would like to do so. Siblings rarely have any role in the decision to separate them through adoption. Laws granting parents significant power over sibling registries make it more difficult for siblings to exercise control over whether they reunite after adoption.

Beyond sibling registries, legislators could think about establishing default rules that promote the distribution of information rather than relying on siblings to know to ask for it. For example, states could create a default rule providing that when every member of a group of siblings separated by adoption has reached the age of majority, the state will send each sibling basic, nonidentifying information about the other siblings. Siblings could contact the state in advance if they wanted to opt out of receiving any information and of having their information distributed. When siblings did not opt out, the notification would alert siblings to each other's existence and ask them if they were interested in sharing their identifying information and in receiving their siblings' identifying information. Such a regime would represent more active state intervention to encourage sibling relationships among adults without any initial prompting by one of the siblings. But it would enable siblings whose information the state has collected at the time of an adoption to find one another in adulthood even if no sibling is aware of a sibling registry or knows that he has biological brothers or sisters.

Third, the federal government could enact legislation that would coordinate all state sibling registries into a combined database in order to help people who do not know which state's registry might have information about them and/or their siblings. The Senate passed a bill in 1997 to create "a National Voluntary Mutual Reunion Registry,"[190] but the bill died in the House of Representatives after a subcommittee of the House Ways and Means Committee held a hearing on the measure.[191] Some legislators objected to the proposed federal registry on the ground that "family law is best left to the States."[192] However, evaluating the proposed federal registry on its own merits, without canonical assumptions that family law should or must be local, reveals a strong case for federal participation. A federal database combining state registries would provide crucial coordination to enable states to better effectuate their preexisting policies, coordination that states have been unable to arrange on their own. Some legislators criticizing the proposed federal registry also cited privacy concerns.[193] But both passive and confidential intermediary state registries appear to have dealt successfully with privacy concerns by requiring a family member's consent before sharing her contact information, suggesting that a federal registry combining state registries would be able to respect privacy as well.[194]

Parental Divorce, Dissolution, or Death

Let's turn to siblings separated by divorce, the dissolution of their parent's nonmarital relationship, or a common parent's death. Legislators and courts have canonically understood these events as transformative moments in marital, nonmarital, and parental relationships. But as we have seen, these events may also profoundly transform sibling relationships.

The appropriate legal treatment of split custody requires more sustained discussion and debate. At present, the law on split custody of siblings varies widely and haphazardly between states and from case to case. Some states have no presumption at all against split custody, while other states impose at least nominally exacting standards disfavoring the separation of siblings. Some judicial decisions rigorously oppose split custody, while other decisions interpret seemingly strict presumptions against separating siblings much more loosely. Split custody can give parents an additional way to share the benefits and burdens of child-rearing, but this custody arrangement can come at a tremendous cost to sibling relationships.

States need to think more rigorously about how to regulate split custody, considering both the range of alternatives that states have already adopted and additional possibilities that would be more protective of sibling ties. For instance, a significantly more protective possibility for regulating whether and when to split custody would be for state legislation to require a parent seeking to split custody of siblings at divorce or the end of a nonmarital relationship to present a court with clear and convincing evidence that placing siblings together would be contrary to the best interests of at least one of the children. Similarly, state law could require courts ordering split custody over a parent's objection to explain why there is clear and convincing evidence that placing siblings together would be contrary to at least one child's best interests.

Even if states decide that such a standard is unduly hostile to split custody and adopt a less strict presumption against split custody, or no presumption at all, state legislatures and courts could focus much more systematically on how to assess and safeguard children's interests when split custody is at issue. For instance, states could think more about how much, if any, weight courts should give to a child's own views about splitting the custody of siblings. Similarly, state legislators could think about instructing judges to be particularly wary of splitting custody along sex-based lines because of the danger that such splits might reinforce gendered understandings about children's interests and about which children are most valuable to which parents.

Another issue that states can explore in focusing on whether and when to split custody concerns whether to apply the same presumptions against separation to full siblings and half-siblings. A strict presumption against separating half-siblings favors the custody claims of the half-siblings' common parent and disfavors custody claims from a parent related to only one half-sibling. Courts and legislatures concerned about fairness between parents may accordingly be unwilling to implement a presumption against separating half-siblings. But the counterargument is that half-sibling relationships can be as close and valuable as relationships between full siblings, especially if half-siblings have the opportunity to grow up together. Family law typically prioritizes parental relationships over sibling bonds with little deliberation; lawmakers and judges often seem to act as if privileging parental ties is the only possible result. Yet children are systematically more vulnerable than adults, and they commonly have fewer material and psychological resources available to them in maintaining relationships with family members living in other households.

A subsidiary issue for states to consider in regulating whether and when to split custody involves splitting custody of half-siblings when that is necessary to keep each half-sibling with at least one parent. For instance, suppose a man and woman, both with children from previous marriages, marry each other, have children together, and then divorce. Unless the children from this most recent marriage can evenly rotate between their parents' custody, which may be impossible for children attending school, at least some half-siblings will need to live apart if every child is to reside with one parent. Or suppose half-siblings are living with their common parent and their common parent dies. Some might argue that the law should keep half-siblings together in this situation, even though that means some children will be living separately from any parent. The contrary view, however, is that such a policy would inappropriately discount the parent-child relationship.

The next issue that states need to explore is how to treat siblings whose custody is split at divorce, the end of a nonmarital relationship, or a parent's death. At the least, state legislatures and courts could encourage parents splitting custody to make explicit written parenting agreements that specify the sibling contact, communication, and visitation that parents will allow and facilitate. Here, as with adoption, express agreements may discourage parents from raising subsequent objections to siblings maintaining their relationships, even when the agreements are never subject to litigation or judicial enforcement.

A further issue for states to consider is whether full or half-siblings separated by divorce, the end of a nonmarital relationship, or a parent's death will have an enforceable right to contact, communication, and visitation even over a parent's objection, unless a court determines that such connection would be contrary to the best interests of one or more siblings. Such a right would protect and promote sibling relationships, albeit at the cost of some infringement on parental prerogatives. In light of the constitutional constraints that *Troxel* appears to impose, states that decide to create such an enforceable right to sibling contact, communication, and visitation should specify that courts will give "material weight" to a parent's assessment of her child's best interests.[195] States with judiciaries that have been particularly protective of parental prerogatives should also specify that a plaintiff must demonstrate that denying contact would harm the plaintiff's sibling.

Family law's tight focus on marriage, parenthood, and (sometimes) their functional equivalents has directed legal decisionmakers away from exploring how the law should safeguard and promote other familial ties. Yet noncanonical family relationships can also be central to family life and to the flourishing of family members, providing care, love, joy, support, stability, connectedness, and nurture. Examining the law's treatment of these relationships brings a wealth of potential reforms into view.

The reform possibilities that this chapter has considered suggest just some of the myriad policy choices that emerge when we free ourselves from the reflexive assumption that family law should be oriented around only marriage, parenthood, and their equivalents. These possibilities and many others need to be discussed and debated by legislators, regulators, and judges, as well as scholars, advocates, and family members, who have so far given sporadic and uneven attention to noncanonical family relationships. Family law's narrow focus on marriage and parenthood, inherited from the common law and then endlessly replicated, has constrained critical thinking in family law for too long.

6

FAMILY LAW FOR THE POOR

> The fact that some families may choose to remove a capped child from their home in order to avoid the effects of the family cap does not give the rule coercive effect and make it unconstitutional.
>
> —*N.B. v. Sybinski* (Indiana Court of Appeals 2000)[1]

The poor are also noticeably absent from the family law canon. Fifteen percent of the United States population—46.5 million people—lived in poverty in 2012, even using the federal government's very restrictive definition of poverty.[2] Poor people are marked by class and also by race, sex, marital status, and age. People of color, women, unmarried parents, and children are all disproportionately likely to be impoverished.[3] In 2012, non-hispanic whites constituted 62.8% of the United States population, but only 40.7% of the people in poverty.[4] That same year, 30.9% of "families with a female householder" lived in poverty, compared to 16.4% of "families with a male householder" and 6.3% of "married-couple families."[5] All told, 21.8% of the children in the United States—16.1 million children—lived in poverty in 2012.[6] Supplementing these statistics, moreover, are cultural assumptions that often envision the poor as a group consisting of unmarried women of color and their children.[7]

Family law's canonical narratives do not touch on poverty, whether in recounting family law's exceptionalism or celebrating family law's progress over time. They do not assert that family law has conquered problems of poverty, making no claim of success equivalent to the canonical contention that the field has left the legacy of common law coverture behind. Instead, with no canonical progress narrative about the poor available, courts and lawmakers describing, explaining, enacting, and implementing family law systematically fail to consider the legal regulation of poor families. The family these legal authorities have in mind is not poor.

In part, this exclusion of the family law governing the poor reflects the canonical insistence on family law's localism that Chapter 1 examined. Much of the law regulating poor families is federal. However, there is also another phenomenon at work, involving both federal and state law. Legislators and jurists routinely take family law and welfare law to be entirely separate categories. When judges and lawmakers identify legal regulation as falling within welfare law, they presume that the regulation cannot also be part of family law.

Yet much of welfare law is family law as well. Many of the statutes, regulations, and judicial opinions now classified exclusively within welfare law structure the creation and dissolution of legally recognized family relationships and/or determine important rights and responsibilities that turn on family status.

The exclusion of welfare law from the family law canon has helped obscure the sharp bifurcation in family law between the legal principles and presumptions governing poor families and the legal principles and presumptions governing other families. Courts and legislatures regulating the rights and responsibilities of family members generally stress the government's interests in protecting familial privacy, deferring to parental judgment, and reducing disruption of family relationships. As this book has discussed, one can plausibly dispute whether the law should support such far-reaching parental prerogatives or whether the government cites its interests in protecting familial privacy and maintaining existing family arrangements too frequently in cases where more active restructuring of family life would better serve the interests of less powerful family members. But such debates notwithstanding, legal authorities regulating more affluent families continually reference principles of privacy, respect, and deference.

Yet legal authorities embrace diametrically opposed norms in regulating poor families. Family law for the poor is explicitly premised on scrutiny of family life, suspicion of parental judgment, and enthusiastic interference in family relations. The poor's family law frequently operates to constrain or deny household decisionmaking, rather than to support and facilitate it.

Canonical accounts of family law that focus narrowly on the legal regulation of families considered financially self-reliant and omit reference to welfare law have helped legislators and judges to avoid discussing, much less defending, this divide between family law for the poor and family law for everyone else. At least a few scholars (unfortunately too few) have observed over the years that poor families are often subject to legal regulations very much at odds with those governing more affluent families. But what Jacobus tenBroek called the "Dual System of Family Law" in a landmark 1964 article on California has nonetheless persisted without legal authorities acknowledging or explaining this bifurcation in family law.[8] Recognizing that welfare law can also be family law makes clear that poor families are subject to a radically different family law and that lawmakers and courts need to defend and justify the differences, or eliminate them.

The Supreme Court's Exclusion of Welfare Law from Its Family Law Jurisprudence

We can begin exploring the contrast between the family law governing the poor and the rest of family law by examining the Supreme Court's jurisprudence. As a general matter, the Court is anxious to declare its constitutional commitment to safeguarding " 'the private realm of family life which the state cannot enter,' "[9] "freedom of personal choice in matters of family life,"[10] "the right of the individual, married or single, to be free from unwarranted governmental intrusion,"[11] a "privacy right [that] encompasses and protects the personal intimacies of the home, the family, marriage, motherhood, procreation, and child rearing."[12]

As this book has explored, the law pervasively regulates family relationships. Notwithstanding the Court's oft-repeated notion that there is a " 'private realm of family life which the state cannot enter,' " family life is not a preserve cordoned off from law. To the contrary, the legal system (including the Supreme Court itself) always plays a role in deciding who counts as a family member and in determining the rights and responsibilities that family members have, even if the role the law sometimes plays is to establish that family members are entitled to keep government officials from stopping or observing some of their activities. But the Court's constitutional opinions frequently stress the idea that there is an area of family life where the state cannot go, and the Court routinely cites that notion in structuring the forms of government regulation it permits.

Notably, for instance, the Court has upheld and strengthened parental prerogatives in the opinions Chapter 4 considered and in many others. It has insisted upon—indeed celebrated—parents' rights to make decisions about how to raise their children without second-guessing by government officials, even where officials or the children themselves might prefer different choices. The Court has explained that "constitutional interpretation has consistently recognized that the parents' claim to authority in their own household to direct the rearing of their children is basic in the structure of our society."[13] "The statist notion that governmental power should supersede parental authority in *all* cases because *some* parents abuse and neglect children is repugnant to American tradition."[14]

Yet the Court has repeatedly assumed that general constitutional principles governing family law do not apply to welfare law, refusing to treat welfare law as family law even where welfare law creates important rights and responsibilities tied to family status. The Court has protected the bifurcation between the legal treatment of poor families and other families as a matter of constitutional law. What's more, the Court has accepted the divide as a matter of common sense beyond the need for explication. Consider *Dandridge v. Williams,*[15] *Wyman v. James,*[16] *Lyng v. Castillo,*[17] and *Bowen v. Gilliard,*[18] four crucial cases that many family law casebooks ignore entirely.[19]

Dandridge (1970) nicely exemplifies how the Court presumes that welfare law cannot be family law and cannot be subject to the constitutional constraints that the Court otherwise applies to legal regulation of the family. *Dandridge* upheld a Maryland regulation that limited the welfare grant any family could receive. No matter how large the family or how great the family's need, the family could collect no more than $250 in welfare payments a month ($240 in some parts of Maryland).[20] This meant that families with five or more children received no additional aid to help support the fifth child or subsequent children.[21]

The Maryland regulation was a manifest example of family law. It made children's eligibility for aid turn on their family status. A child received more aid per capita if she had and lived with fewer siblings and less aid per capita if she had and lived with too many siblings.[22]

Moreover, the maximum grant regulation had a clear impact on family life and the structure of family relationships. The regulation placed tremendous pressure on impoverished parents to break up their large families, by removing children for whom the family did not receive any additional aid and placing those children in other, smaller households that would be eligible to receive welfare payments for the children's support.[23] Maryland did not dispute "that, despite the strong desire to keep their families together, [plaintiffs] in this case were having great difficulty in doing so because of the limitations on their grants."[24]

The maximum grant regulation also discouraged procreation by parents receiving or potentially in future need of welfare, as having too many children would trigger Maryland's limit on benefits. Indeed, one of Maryland's stated purposes for the regulation was "providing incentives for family planning."[25] Not surprisingly, Maryland characterized its regulation as creating incentives to use contraception, rather than as discouraging childbearing. The state presumably deemphasized the disciplinary and punitive aspects of its regulation to make the rule seem more politically appealing and less constitutionally vulnerable. But the flip side of an incentive to use birth control is that the maximum grant regulation created powerful disincentives for poor people to have more children.

Yet the *Dandridge* Court saw no need to apply constitutional precedents about protecting family life from government overreaching or to reason about the case in family law terms. The Court acknowledged that the Maryland maximum grant regulation gave parents an incentive to break up their families and separate siblings. But the Court dismissed that effect on family relations as legally irrelevant, while simultaneously attempting to discount the harm associated with such a family division. The Court explained that "even if a parent should be inclined to increase his per capita family income by sending a child away, the federal law requires that the child, to be eligible for [welfare] payments, must live with one of several enumerated relatives. The kinship tie may be attenuated but it cannot be destroyed."[26]

The *Dandridge* Court presumed that this case was not part of family law. On the Court's account, the maximum grant regulation was simply an example of "state regulation in the social and economic field."[27] Of course, the maximum grant rule—like family law more generally—*did* regulate and structure social and economic relations. But *Dandridge* characterized the maximum grant rule as just socioeconomic regulation in order to contend that the rule was constitutionally no different from any routine law governing fiscal policy, the type of government action that the Court has been uninterested in interfering with since the New Deal.[28] This meant that Maryland could escape the more exacting constitutional scrutiny that the Court typically applies to laws regulating family life and family structure. The state was free to regulate as it wished without judicial "second-guess[ing],"[29] subject only to the same minimal constitutional review that the Court applies to any ordinary "state regulation of business or industry."[30]

Dandridge quickly upheld Maryland's regulation under this undemanding standard, which requires only that the regulation rationally advance at least one legitimate government interest. The Court ignored Maryland's expressed interest in creating incentives for contraception, which arguably might not have qualified as a legitimate state interest and in any event would have directed attention to the regulation's impact on intimate family decisions. Instead, the Court focused on "the State's legitimate interest in encouraging employment and in avoiding discrimination between welfare families and the families of the working poor" and concluded that the maximum grant regulation "rationally" furthered that interest.[31]

Wyman (1971) was similarly grounded on the premise that welfare law cannot be family law. This decision upheld New York statutes and regulations that conditioned welfare benefits on the recipient permitting welfare officials to visit her home without a warrant or any individualized evidence that wrongdoing had been committed.[32] New York stressed that one reason it imposed this mandatory home visit requirement was so that state officials could inspect the home of every welfare recipient for evidence of child abuse, which might lead the state to seek to remove children from their parents' custody.[33]

New York's categorical suspicion of the parenting skills of welfare recipients contrasted sharply with the state's treatment of other parents. New York assumed that parents not receiving welfare were fit, and the state protected the privacy and autonomy of these parents without complaint. State officials did not attempt to search for evidence of child abuse in the homes of parents not receiving welfare unless officials already had probable cause to believe that the parents were abusive.[34] This is unsurprising given how much support family law generally gives to parental prerogatives and how reluctant family law is to undercut those prerogatives. Nonetheless, New York insisted that state officials needed to visit the homes of all welfare recipients to search for signs of child abuse, even where the state had no evidence that any abuse was occurring.[35] New York also noted that at least fifteen other states similarly conditioned welfare benefits on mandatory home visits.[36]

The Supreme Court has a long tradition of protecting homes against government searches unless government agents have satisfied the requirements of the Fourth Amendment by obtaining a valid search warrant.[37]

Supreme Court opinions before *Wyman* celebrate "the precious interest of privacy summed up in the ancient adage that a man's house is his castle"[38] and declare that "[a]t the very core [of the Fourth Amendment] stands the right of a man to retreat into his own home and there be free from unreasonable governmental intrusion."[39] Court opinions after *Wyman* similarly announce that "the sanctity of private dwellings [is] ordinarily afforded the most stringent Fourth Amendment protection,"[40] that "[i]t is axiomatic that the physical entry of the home is the chief evil against which the wording of the Fourth Amendment is directed,"[41] that "the Fourth Amendment has drawn a firm line at the entrance to the house,"[42] that "[t]he Fourth Amendment embodies this centuries-old principle of respect for the privacy of the home."[43] Notwithstanding the references to castles in the Supreme Court's case law (as well as in legal scholarship),[44] the Court has stressed that Fourth Amendment protection for privacy at home extends to rich and poor alike, insisting that "[w]e have, after all, lived our whole national history with an understanding of the ancient adage that a man's house is his castle to the point that the poorest man may in his cottage bid defiance to all the forces of the Crown."[45] *Wyman* itself noted that "over the years the Court consistently has been most protective of the privacy of the dwelling."[46]

Yet the *Wyman* Court concluded without apparent hesitation that the Fourth Amendment posed no obstacle to scrutinizing the homes and parenting practices of welfare recipients. *Wyman* held that New York's mandatory home visits did not constitute searches within the meaning of the Fourth Amendment. The Court suggested that this conclusion was "seemingly obvious and simple."[47] It briefly offered two supporting arguments.

The *Wyman* Court's first argument understated the investigatory nature of the mandatory home visits. This line of reasoning was in considerable tension with other aspects of the case. Recall that New York contended that it needed the mandatory home visits in order to search for signs of child abuse, a process that presumably could lead to criminal charges if state officials found evidence of abuse. Yet the Court nonetheless described the visits as "both rehabilitative and investigative," insisting that "this latter aspect . . . is given too broad a character and far more emphasis than it deserves if it is equated with a search in the traditional criminal law context."[48]

Wyman's second argument for why the visits were not searches stressed that a welfare recipient could refuse to allow welfare officials to enter her home. The Court "note[d] . . . that the visitation in itself is not forced or compelled, and that the beneficiary's denial of permission is not a criminal act. If consent to the visitation is withheld, no visitation takes place. The aid then never begins or merely ceases, as the case may be. There is no entry of the home and there is no search."[49]

The Court's decision to justify the home visits in the language of consent is striking because of how little choice welfare recipients actually exercised. As the Court itself conceded, "the average beneficiary might feel she is in no position to refuse consent to the visit."[50] Indeed, such a refusal would result in the loss of life-sustaining benefits for the welfare recipient and her children. The *Wyman* Court elsewhere in its opinion described the New York City Department of Social Services as "the agency that provides [plaintiff Barbara James] and her infant son with the necessities for life."[51] Under such circumstances, a welfare recipient's right to refuse a home visit was a formal premise of the state's regulatory regime, but not a practical reality. *Wyman* defined liberty in negative terms—as the freedom to decline to cooperate with the welfare system. Yet for an impoverished mother like James, the freedom to deny welfare officials admittance to her home was nothing more than the freedom to lose the means of keeping that home for herself and her child.

Wyman also contended that even if the mandatory home visits did constitute searches within the meaning of the Fourth Amendment, the searches were constitutional because they were "not unreasonable."[52] The Court's conclusion appeared to presuppose (without explicit acknowledgment) that state regulation of parents receiving welfare can reasonably start with an assumption of bad parenting rather than parental fitness and can begin with inspection rather than privacy. Where family law generally presumes (for better or for worse) that parents will look after their children best when state supervision is limited, the *Wyman* Court started from the premise that welfare law is outside of family law's boundaries and untethered to family law's governing principles. *Wyman* depicted parents and children on welfare as having warring interests, with all children on welfare needing close state supervision that parents might oppose. The Court explained that welfare law "is concerned about any possible exploitation of the child."[53] And *Wyman* declared that "[t]he dependent child's needs are paramount, and only with hesitancy would we relegate those needs, in the scale of comparative values, to a position secondary to what the mother claims as her rights."[54]

Lower courts in the years since *Wyman* have repeatedly relied on the Supreme Court's opinion to uphold county welfare programs that explicitly or functionally condition welfare benefits on the applicants submitting to home visits by government officials without warrants or individualized evidence of wrongdoing.[55]

The Supreme Court's decision in *Lyng* (1986) also treated welfare law as strictly separate from family law. In this case, the Court upheld a federal law that determined eligibility and benefit levels for the food stamp program by generally treating parents, children, and siblings who lived together as a single household, regardless of whether the parents, children, and siblings customarily purchased and prepared their food together. The law did not treat other relatives or unrelated people who lived together as a single household unless they actually did customarily purchase and prepare food together.[56]

This was practically important because food stamp benefits vary based on the size of the beneficiary's household, with people in smaller households receiving larger benefits per person.[57] Before Congress enacted the law at issue in *Lyng*, parents, children, and siblings who lived together could be part of separate households for purposes of the food stamp program if they bought and prepared food separately.[58]

The reasons why parents, children, and siblings might live together, but shop and cook separately, reflected the intimate details of family life. For instance, poor families might shop and cook separately because they did not have the time and the control over their work schedules needed to shop and cook together. Alternatively or in addition, poor people forced by economic circumstances to double up in the same homes with relatives might want to keep functioning as separate family units to the extent possible.

When Congress changed the food stamp law, it explicitly cited its fiscal interests in conserving funds.[59] However, the *Lyng* opinion also suggested ways in which the new law implicitly assumed middle-class norms of family life that expect close relatives living together to have the practical means and the personal inclination to shop and cook together. The Court stated that "Congress could reasonably determine that close relatives sharing a home—almost by definition—tend to purchase and prepare meals together while distant relatives and unrelated individuals might not be so inclined."[60] The Court observed that "Congress might have reasoned that it would be somewhat easier for close relatives—again, almost by definition—to accommodate their living habits to a federal policy favoring common meal preparation than it would be for more distant relatives or unrelated persons to do so."[61]

The federal law establishing that the food stamp program would generally treat parents, children, and siblings who lived together as a single household was a clear example of family law, determining important legal benefits and burdens based on family status. It meant that when these relatives lived in the same home, but shopped and cooked separately, they would receive smaller food stamp benefits per person than other equally poor people who were in the same situation, yet not close family members. Indeed, sometimes the new law meant that parents, children, siblings would not be eligible for food stamps benefits at all, when they would have been eligible for benefits if they were not so closely related. The Court itself acknowledged that "the loss or reduction of benefits will impose a severe hardship on a needy family, and may be especially harmful to the affected young children for whom an adequate diet is essential."[62]

Here too, however, the Court refused to apply its constitutional precedents about cabining the government's ability to rearrange family life. The Court held that "the statutory classification" the food stamp law drew between parents, children, and siblings, and all other persons living together but shopping and cooking separately, did not " 'directly and substantially' interfere with family living arrangements and thereby burden a fundamental right."[63] *Lyng* recognized—without qualm—that the food stamp law gave parents, children, and siblings reason "to accommodate their living habits to a federal policy favoring common meal preparation."[64] But the Court dismissed constitutional objections to the food stamp law. It relied again on the language of choice, focusing on the formal liberty that poor people retained to resist the food stamp law's organizing premises. The Court stressed that the law did "not order or prevent any group of persons from dining together."[65] With that noted, the Court subjected the law to the same minimal review for rationality that the Court applies to any ordinary form of economic regulation.[66]

Here too, the freedom of choice that the food stamp law left open to poor people was more theoretical than real. Some poor parents, children, and siblings living together, but shopping and cooking separately, had no available means of mitigating the harshness of the federal food stamp law. They could not afford to separate into different households to increase their food stamp benefits, and they could not reduce their food expenses by cooking together because the reasons they cooked and ate separately were not realistically changeable, such as working at different times. These parents, children, and siblings simply had less money for food and less food available to them because of their status as close relatives living together.[67]

For parents, children, and siblings who could alter their family structure, the food stamp statute gave them a powerful incentive to either separate into different homes or rearrange their family lives and lived relationships with each other so that relatives residing in the same home shopped and cooked together and could actually benefit from the economies of scale that federal law conclusively presumed existed. In theory, these relatives had the "choice" not to comply with how Congress thought they should, or assumed they would, shop and cook. But if they actually exercised that choice, they likely would be left—adults and growing children alike—without access to adequate nutrition.

Bowen (1987) similarly reflected the Court's presumption that welfare law is outside of family law. This decision upheld a federal statute providing that government determinations of eligibility for welfare benefits would "take into account, with certain specified exceptions, the income of all parents, brothers, and sisters living in the same home."[68] Before Congress enacted this statute in 1984, some children in a family could receive welfare benefits, while others did not. A typical situation in which this occurred was where an impoverished mother was living with her children, who were half-siblings to each other. At least one child did not need welfare benefits because she received support payments from her noncustodial father, while at least one other child was without resources and in need of welfare because she received no support payments from her noncustodial father.[69]

The new statute meant that if one child in a household received support payments, the government would consider the amount of that child support to be income for the whole family in determining whether and to what extent the family was eligible for welfare benefits. Some families lost most or all of their welfare benefits when the government reclassified one child's support payments as household income. When a family was still eligible for welfare, moreover, the government required the custodial parent to transfer to the state the right to receive any child support payments that a noncustodial parent made for a child in the household.[70]

The statute was yet another significant example of how welfare law can simultaneously be family law. The law made a child's eligibility for welfare benefits turn on whether the child lived with parents or siblings who had some income. If a child had no such relatives, a child with no money of his own was eligible for maximum welfare benefits. If a child had such relatives, a child with no money of his own was eligible for smaller benefits or no benefits at all.

The statute also made a child's ability to keep child support payments for his own use turn on whether the child's co-resident parents and siblings had sufficient income from outside the welfare program to support themselves. Children could use their child support payments for themselves when they lived with parents and siblings who had sufficient non-welfare income. Indeed, as Chapter 5 discussed, siblings generally have no legal obligation to support one another. However, children living with indigent parents and siblings had their child support rights assigned to the state to reimburse the state for welfare payments made to support the entire household.

Continuing a theme in welfare law, the statute placed enormous economic pressure on impoverished custodial parents to send some of their children away, separating the children from siblings and their primary parent. If siblings with some money, such as support payments, lived in different households from siblings with no money, then the siblings with some money would be able to keep that money for their own support, and the parent and siblings without money would be able to receive some or more welfare benefits.

One *Bowen* plaintiff, a mother of four, received some child support payments for two of her children and no child support for the other two. When welfare law changed to treat those child support payments as income available to the whole household, the family was no longer eligible for welfare benefits. However, the mother was unable to actually support five people on the child support payments she received for two children. The mother sent the child receiving the largest child support payments to live with that child's father—separating her daughter from three half-siblings and her primary parent—in order to be able to keep receiving welfare benefits for the other three children.[71]

In addition, the statute created reasons to stop paying child support, at least from the perspective of some noncustodial parents. The law conclusively presumed that support paid for one child would also be used to support that child's co-resident full or half-siblings, even if those siblings were biologically unrelated and legally unconnected to the person paying the support. A noncustodial parent who did not want to support someone else's children might be disinclined to keep paying support. Another *Bowen* plaintiff, a mother of two half-siblings, reported that her son's father had stopped paying child support and stopped visiting his son after the father discovered that the welfare system treated his son's support payments as income for the whole household.[72]

The statute also meant that child support payments did not make the intended beneficiaries much better off economically. If a noncustodial parent paid child support for a child living with an indigent parent, the government used almost all of that money to reimburse itself for the welfare payments it was making to the household. The government left the family with only $50 more per month than the family would have had if the noncustodial parent had paid no child support at all.[73] *Bowen* acknowledged that "some noncustodial parents stopped making their support payments because they believed that their payments were helping only the State, and not their children."[74]

Yet here too, the Court would not think about this welfare law as family law, despite the law's striking intervention into parent-child and sibling relationships. Instead, the Court relied again on the language of choice. *Bowen* stressed that poor parents had made decisions about how to rearrange their family lives to respond to the law, and the Court did not emphasize the severe constraints that the statute imposed on those decisions. *Bowen* asserted "[t]hat some families may decide to modify their living arrangements in order to avoid the effect of the amendment, does not transform the amendment into an act whose design and direct effect are to intrude on choices concerning family living arrangements."[75]

Having declared that poor people could still choose to arrange their family lives as they saw fit (no matter the dire consequences), *Bowen* treated the welfare law just like any other "[g]overnmental decision[] to spend money to improve the general public welfare in one way and not another."[76] The Court reviewed the law simply for "rationality" and held that the statute rationally advanced Congress's interests in conserving funds and "in distributing benefits among competing needy families in a fair way."[77]

In sum, the Supreme Court has long treated family law and welfare law as strictly separate fields organized around diametrically opposed principles. Welfare law frequently determines crucial rights and responsibilities that family members have because of their family status. But the Court's opinions refuse to apply standard constitutional norms about the family to the family law of the poor. The Court does not attempt to reconcile its welfare law decisions with its constitutional jurisprudence on the family because it approaches welfare cases with the premise that welfare law is not family law. Welfare has no place in the Court's canonical understanding of family law.

The Legislative Bifurcation Between Family Law for the Poor and Family Law for Everyone Else

The Supreme Court's constitutional jurisprudence parallels and enables a legislative bifurcation between the family law governing most families and the family law governing poor families. This stark divide is evident in myriad examples of federal and state law. Consider the contrast between Social Security, which is not typically associated with poor families, and Temporary Assistance for Needy Families (TANF), the most prominent federal-state welfare program.

Both Social Security and TANF provide redistributive benefits to family members whose primary wage earner is dead, incapacitated, or not working. Yet Social Security is organized around norms respecting privacy and autonomy that generally govern family law. TANF—created in the federal Personal Responsibility and Work Opportunity Reconciliation Act of 1996, but substantially modeled on earlier welfare programs[78]—reflects the highly investigatory, instrumental, and interventionist premises common in regulating poor families.

Social Security

The federal Social Security system does not supervise the behavior of family members. As Chapter 1 explored, Social Security provides benefits to the dependent minor children, dependent parents, and current, surviving, or divorced spouses of primary beneficiaries. The Social Security system distributes these family member benefits based solely on the recipient's family status. The people collecting family member benefits need not have contributed to the Social Security system at all, and primary beneficiaries do not pay more into the Social Security system if they have children, parents, or spouses who are or will be eligible for family member benefits.[79] In total, a primary beneficiary and his family members are generally able to collect up to about 150 to 180% of the money that the primary beneficiary is entitled to receive on his own.[80]

One theory sometimes advanced for why it is appropriate to distribute Social Security benefits to family members who may not have paid into the Social Security system themselves is that these family members helped put the primary beneficiary in a position to earn income and pay Social Security taxes, for instance by providing the primary beneficiary with domestic or childcare services.[81] Nonetheless, the Social Security Administration makes no attempt to scrutinize family life or to ensure that Social Security recipients have performed their family roles and responsibilities well or even adequately. A spouse may have given the primary beneficiary no help at all and a parent may have been neglectful, but they are still entitled to collect Social Security benefits by virtue of their status as family members of the primary beneficiary.

In important respects, Social Security is a redistributive scheme that responds to economic need in families in which the main or only bread-winner has stopped working or died. As the Supreme Court has noted, the Social Security program is designed "to provide dependent members of a wage earner's family with protection against the hardship occasioned by the loss of the insured's earnings."[82] Many families receive more money from the Social Security program than the members of the family collectively paid in Social Security taxes.[83]

However, receiving Social Security is not culturally taken to be a sign of economic dependence or need. Instead, Social Security is popularly characterized as a benefit that successful and self-reliant husbands, fathers, and sons (and less frequently, wives, mothers, and daughters)[84] have earned for themselves and their families through their employment.[85] Accordingly, the Social Security system, operating on principles implicitly understood yet never fully explained, conforms to norms conventionally associated with family law.

Other Redistributive Family Law Programs for Families Not Considered Poor

The Social Security program's interest in avoiding individualized inspection of family relationships and disruption of family life is typical of redistributive family law programs directed at families who are not considered poor. Government programs for families regarded as economically self-sufficient tend to respect family law norms of deference and privacy, even when distributing financial aid. They assume that family members are acting appropriately and that family life is functioning smoothly. For instance, federal veterans' benefits law provides for benefits to a veteran's surviving spouse, child, or parent without scrutinizing the quality of the relationship the family member had with the veteran.[86] The federal income tax code gives parents tax deductions for dependent children, yet the Internal Revenue Service does not attempt to verify that parents are meeting their responsibilities well or using the money saved on taxes for their children's benefit.[87] The tax code also allows parents to claim these deductions for all of their dependent children, no matter how many children a parent has.[88]

These government programs regulate families understood to be middle class or wealthier. Indeed, these programs help make their beneficiaries middle class. First, they help provide beneficiaries with the necessary resources to maintain middle-class status. Redistributive programs for families who are not considered poor are frequently more generous than welfare programs for the impoverished. Moreover, the very fact that the government treats their family relationships with respect helps mark the beneficiaries of programs like Social Security as middle class.

Temporary Assistance for Needy Families (TANF)

In contrast, TANF is directed at poor children and their caregivers. Like poor people more generally, TANF recipients are marked by their (lack of) income and also by their age, sex, marital status, and race. An estimated 3,067,764 children received TANF in an average month in 2009, along with approximately 973,580 adults.[89] Most of these adults were women, with men constituting just 14.1% of adult recipients.[90] Only 14% of the adults receiving TANF were married and living with their spouses.[91] While 35% of the adults and 26.1% of the children receiving TANF in 2009 were white, people of color were disproportionately likely to receive TANF.[92] Moreover, scholars have found that welfare recipients are often assumed to be people of color, so that references in political and popular discourse to welfare are sometimes meant to be implicit references to people of color and are understood in those terms.[93]

TANF regulates family rights and responsibilities with a radically different governing logic from the family law directed at more affluent families. A guiding premise of the TANF program is that the government's provision of TANF benefits entitles the government to inspect individual family relationships and to employ blunt and punitive measures in seeking to change their course.

The TANF program vigorously evaluates the caregiver relatives receiving TANF benefits and conditions aid on the caregivers' ability to satisfy government standards. Social Security and other government programs directed at more affluent families assume that parents have been successful, even when they or their family members are receiving government benefits. TANF assumes that parents have been unsuccessful and need detailed government guidance. For example, federal law authorizes states to impose "individual responsibility plan[s]" that require TANF recipients to perform specific parental obligations, such as "keep[ing] school age children . . . in school, immuniz[ing] children, [and] attend[ing] parenting and money management classes."[94] Another federal provision permits states to sanction a TANF "family that includes an adult who . . . fails to ensure that the minor dependent children of such adult attend school as required by the law of the State in which the minor children reside."[95]

At least sixteen states currently enforce "learnfare" requirements that condition a family's receipt of some or all TANF benefits on children's regular school attendance.[96] At least twelve states enforce "medfare" or "shotfare" requirements that condition a family's receipt of some or all TANF benefits on children's immunizations.[97] Such requirements assume that parents receiving TANF, unlike parents benefiting from family law programs not directed at the poor, cannot be trusted to care for their children well.

Learnfare and medfare laws seek to track the daily activities of TANF parents and to respond with swift retribution to any deviation from prescribed parental behavior in ways that penalize not only the parents, but their children as well. A parent receiving TANF, who is usually subject to strict work requirements that dominate her schedule,[98] may have little practical ability to control whether her child attends school, especially when the child is a teenager. Moreover, the reasons that a child on TANF is not attending school may have little to do with family life. Yet learnfare laws treat truancy as proof of bad parenting and react by punishing the entire family—parents, truant children, and non-truant children alike. The term learnfare, which at least four states employ in their statutes,[99] emphasizes the benefits for children of regular school attendance, but not the costs to children if they lose subsistence benefits because of their or their siblings' truancy. Similarly, a parent receiving TANF may not have effective access to healthcare. Yet so-called medfare or shotfare laws—the terms are too unappealing to appear in the statutes themselves—take incomplete immunization to be evidence of parental failure and respond by subjecting the whole impoverished family, children included, to more financial deprivation.

Family Caps. Still more strikingly, federal law also allows states to adopt "family cap provisions" within their TANF programs.[100] These family caps, which at least eighteen states currently impose in some form,[101] deny or limit TANF benefits to children conceived while their parents were already receiving TANF.

A few examples illustrate how family caps work. New Jersey's TANF program provides that a family of two will ordinarily receive up to $322 a month, a family of three will ordinarily receive up to $424 a month, and a family of four will ordinarily receive up to $488 a month.[102] These meager benefits are supposed to cover a family's basic subsistence needs, although they are extremely unlikely to do so in practice. New Jersey has not increased its grant levels for TANF (or the predecessor program) for over a quarter century, not even adjusting grant levels for inflation.[103] New Jersey's family cap means that a family that enters TANF with two people is still limited to just $322 a month if another child is born, $102 less than New Jersey itself otherwise thinks necessary for three people's subsistence. A family that enters TANF with three people is still limited to just $424 a month if another child is born, $64 less than New Jersey otherwise thinks necessary for four people's subsidence.[104]

Mississippi's TANF program is significantly stingier than even New Jersey's. It provides that a family of two will ordinarily receive up to $146 a month, a family of three will ordinarily receive up to $170 a month, and a family of four will ordinarily receive up to $194 a month. Mississippi's family cap means that a family that enters TANF with two people is still limited to just $146 a month if another child is born, $24 less than even Mississippi otherwise thinks necessary for three people's subsidence. A Mississippi family that enters TANF with three people is still limited to just $170 a month if another child is born, $24 less than Mississippi otherwise thinks necessary for four people's subsistence.[105]

Family law generally encourages childbearing or attempts to stay out of individuals' childbearing decisions.[106] Such policies hold even where more children will mean more expense for government programs, whether in the form of more Social Security beneficiaries, more federal tax deductions for dependent children, or more students requiring free public education. The legal system does at times push poor women toward childbearing. For instance, the Supreme Court has upheld federal and state laws that deny poor women access to abortions under Medicaid.[107] Yet birth-promoting norms are also sometimes reversed for family law directed at the poor.

States explicitly acknowledge that their family caps are designed to dissuade parents receiving TANF from having any more children. The New Jersey Department of Health and Human Services described the decision to have a child while receiving welfare as " 'irresponsible and not socially desirable.' "[108] Indiana praised its family cap for "provid[ing] incentives for family planning."[109] Delaware law "declare[s it] to be the legislative intent that public assistance be administered, to the extent practicable, in such a way that . . . recipients are not encouraged to have additional children while receiving public assistance."[110]

Some states have endorsed family caps as disincentives to reproduction without elaborating on the reasons why the state does not want TANF recipients to have more children. However, Mississippi Governor Kirk Fordice explained in supporting the enactment of his state's family cap that he took the birth of more children on TANF to be categorically undesirable because he assumed that these children would have inadequate and irresponsible parents and would burden rather than contribute to society. Fordice contended that a family cap law would reduce " 'the continual production of children that nobody seems to want to take responsibility for raising' " and get " 'right to the root cause of crime in Mississippi' " by lowering the number of children born to teenage mothers.[111] The governor's " 'continual production' " language seemed to suggest that mothers receiving TANF were threatening social welfare by having torrents of children. In fact, families receiving TANF contained an average of just 1.8 recipient children in 2009.[112]

There is some evidence that family caps do sometimes affect childbearing decisions, but not in the way that the often ardently antiabortion supporters of family caps predicted.[113] One study of 8393 women receiving welfare in New Jersey found that women who were subject to the state's family cap had a birthrate that was 8.25% lower than women in a control group not subject to the family cap, meaning that women subject to the cap had 2.2 fewer births per thousand women. However, women who were subject to the state's family cap also had an abortion rate that was approximately 12% higher than women in the control group, meaning that women subject to the cap had 3.2 more abortions per thousand women. The findings together suggest that the rate of pregnancy was actually slightly higher in the group of women subject to the family cap.[114] Other studies focused on birthrates,[115] or on both birth and abortion rates,[116] find that family cap laws do not have an effect.

On every account, though, many parents have additional children while receiving TANF despite the existence of family cap laws. When this occurs, family caps operate by punishing not only the parents who have made childbearing decisions that the state disfavors, but also their children who have no control over their parents' choices. States may praise the incentives against childbearing that family caps create for parents and disregard the harm that family caps inflict on parents on the ground that parents "chose" to bear those costs. But the penalties that family caps impose fall most directly on children, who manifestly have no choice in the matter. Family caps treat an impoverished child who was born to a parent receiving TANF at the time of conception much less favorably than another child with the same needs and resources who was born to a parent not receiving TANF at the time of conception. The distinction is based solely on the child's familial connection to his parent. And it is punitive. A parent can no longer be discouraged from bearing this child; the child already exists in the world.

A United States General Accounting Office study compiling data for an average month in 2000 from twenty states with family cap laws found that about 9% of the families receiving TANF, about 108,000 families, received smaller cash benefits than they would have received if their states did not have family caps. If a two-person family had one additional child while on TANF, the now three-person family received about 20% less in cash benefits than the family would have received for its subsidence without a family cap. About 12% of the families who continued to have children while on TANF had at least two additional children while on TANF, likely creating an even larger gap between a family's benefits and its subsidence needs.[117]

Mothers report that the enforcement of family caps "has imposed an extreme financial hardship on their families and left them without adequate food, shelter and other necessities."[118] Courts and legislatures often state that a parent will not be found neglectful based on the parent's poverty alone.[119] Nonetheless, it seems likely that family caps, which further constrict already paltry TANF benefits, have contributed to more parents being judged neglectful because their children lacked basic necessities. Indeed, some research finds that reducing a family's welfare benefits significantly increases the chances that the family will come to the attention of government authorities investigating child maltreatment.[120]

States with family caps contend that having more children while receiving TANF is undesirable, in part on the theory that parents already receiving TANF will be unable to care adequately for additional children. But then family caps help make that so, by denying parents the resources they need to care for their children.

One of the only ways that a parent who has had an additional child while on TANF can avoid the imposition of a family cap is by sending her youngest child to live elsewhere, apart from parents and siblings. Family caps place impoverished parents under stark economic pressure to surrender their babies to foster care or to send their babies to live with other relatives, who in at least seven family cap states will be able to receive TANF benefits for the child because they are not responsible for the child's birth.[121] Some researchers have found that family caps appear to "increase the number of children living in out-of-home care."[122]

One oddity in the official explanations for family caps is that states have sometimes contended that their family caps foster family stability. *N.B. v. Sybinski* (2000),[123] an unsuccessful constitutional challenge to Indiana's family cap,[124] provides a striking example. The state's family cap did not apply when a child conceived on TANF lived with neither parent,[125] yet Indiana asserted in defending the constitutionality of its family cap that the state's goal in implementing the cap was "to promote self-sufficiency, *family stability,* and personal responsibility."[126] States are probably motivated to make such claims in an attempt to reconcile family caps with the welfare system's occasionally declared, if inconsistently honored, commitment to family preservation. One "stated intention" of Indiana's welfare program was " 'to keep families together.' "[127] In fact, however, family caps can promote the dissolution of families by structuring aid so that impoverished parents bearing children while on TANF can secure subsistence benefits for their youngest children only by sending those children to live away from parents and siblings.

Nonetheless, federal and state courts have consistently upheld the constitutionality of family cap laws under rational basis review, refusing to apply constitutional precedents focused on protecting family members and family life. The opinions—which many family law casebooks predictably ignore as they are canonically classified outside of family law[128]—have common themes.

First, courts recognize that either the explicit purpose or the expected outcome of family caps is to discourage childbearing by women receiving welfare.[129] However, courts accept deterring childbirth by women on welfare as a legitimate state interest. Indeed, some judges appear to endorse that interest themselves. The Indiana Court of Appeals declared that "[t]he State has a legitimate interest in encouraging welfare recipients to act responsibly in child bearing,"[130] with the court apparently agreeing that the responsible decision for welfare recipients is the decision not to have more children. The United States District Court for the District of New Jersey stated that "it cannot be gainsaid that the Family Cap sends a message that recipients should consider the static level of their welfare benefits before having another child, a message that may reasonably have an ameliorative effect on the rate of out-of-wedlock births that only foster the familial instability and crushing cycle of poverty currently plaguing the welfare class."[131] The court's statement suggested that children born to parents receiving welfare inflicted harm on society and their families both, miring their families in poverty as part of a long-term "welfare class."

Second, courts reviewing family cap laws conclude that the caps do not infringe upon women's constitutionally protected reproductive rights. Courts acknowledge that "[i]t is well-settled that decisions about family composition, conception and childbirth fall into a constitutionally protected zone of privacy."[132] Yet they find that a state's willingness, even eagerness, to affect women's childbearing decisions by placing intense economic pressure on impoverished women not to have more children is insufficient to impair women's reproductive freedom.

Most courts stress in reaching this conclusion that family caps do not legally compel anyone to have an abortion or to stop bearing children. Here again, judges utilize the language of choice. Courts contend that caps do "not hinder one's exercise of protected choices,"[133] do "not attempt to fetter or constrain the welfare mother's right to bear as many children as she chooses,"[134] do "not deprive [TANF recipients] of the right to have children,"[135] do "not place a direct legal obstacle in the path of a woman's decision to have additional children,"[136] do "not deprive women of the right or the ability to have children,"[137] do "not directly effect a woman's fundamental right to become pregnant,"[138] and do leave "the decision to bring a child to term or to have an abortion . . . wholly with the woman."[139] These arguments highlight the absence of formal requirements to avoid childbearing. But they disregard the functional constraints—as concrete and unyielding in many cases as legal prohibitions—that family caps place on reproduction and are meant to place on reproduction.

Some courts also emphasize that family caps do not reduce the amount of cash benefits that a family receives if that family has an additional child while on welfare. "In other words," these courts blithely conclude, a family cap "does nothing to bar [a welfare] recipient from conceiving and/or bringing to term an additional child."[140] "Rather than burdening the procreative choice of [welfare recipients, a family cap] is neutral with respect to that choice."[141] These arguments stress again the choices that remain formally open to women receiving TANF, while ignoring the punitive force of family caps that keep a family's cash benefits constant while the family's subsistence needs increase.

Third, courts flatly deny that family caps punish children for the behavior of their parents. This claim is legally important because the United States Supreme Court's constitutional jurisprudence purports to protect children from government action that penalizes them for their parents' conduct. The Supreme Court has explained that punishing children for what their parents have done "is illogical and unjust," "contrary to the basic concept of our system that legal burdens should bear some relationship to individual responsibility or wrongdoing," and "an ineffectual—as well as an unjust—way of deterring the parent."[142] As the Court has observed, "children can affect neither their parents' conduct nor their own status."[143]

The lower courts' contention that family caps do not punish children rests on the assumption that capped children (children conceived while their parents were already receiving TANF) share in the welfare payments that go to their families.[144] This assumption is probably accurate, but it is irrelevant and nonresponsive. One would expect a parent who keeps her youngest, capped child with her to use some of her TANF benefits to care for her youngest child, even though the parent receives no TANF aid for that youngest child. Indeed, a parent who did not give all her children some access to the family's resources would be committing child neglect. Yet this point does not actually address how family cap laws punish children.

Family caps penalize children—the capped children and their siblings alike—by giving them less aid than another family with the same size and needs *solely* because of a parent's disfavored conduct in having another child while already receiving TANF. Courts never account for why this distinction between capped and uncapped families does not constitute punishing children for their parents' behavior, and a satisfactory argument along those lines is difficult to imagine. For all the judicial discussion of the "choices" that family caps leave open to parents, children have no control over their parents' procreative decisions, yet bear the brunt of family caps nonetheless.

Judicial opinions upholding family caps concede that the imposition of a family cap can leave an impoverished family in even more desperate straits. One court observed that "it cannot be denied that the less money a poor woman has available the more difficult it will be for her to house and feed her children."[145] Another court simply "assume[d] that, when necessary, [the state] will insure the health and safety of families in need" by, for instance, providing shelter to families rendered homeless.[146]

Fourth, courts accept that family caps "strengthen the family unit"[147] or "strengthen and stabilize the family unit."[148] This contention presupposes that poor families will be stronger and more stable with fewer children. One could perhaps question that starting assumption. It is certainly not applied to wealthier parents, whom state actors do not criticize for having more children. But in any event, the contention is blind to how family caps undermine the strength and stability of families once a new child is born. Family caps weaken and strain family life by further constricting the already meager means that a poor family has to purchase basic necessities.

Moreover, family caps can place impoverished parents under tremendous pressure to send their youngest children to live elsewhere, so that the children can receive benefits to cover their subsistence needs. Courts either ignore altogether this pressure to break up families or they discount the pressure and dismiss its importance by stressing that poor parents retain formal control over their decisions about how to respond to family caps because the caps do not legally "require that capped children be removed from the home."[149] The Indiana Court of Appeals in *N.B. v. Sybinski* noted that "the family cap may have some incidental effect on family structure," but quickly insisted that "[t]he fact that some families may choose to remove a capped child from their home in order to avoid the effects of the family cap does not give the rule coercive effect and make it unconstitutional."[150] On this account, sending a child to live elsewhere so the child can access the basic necessities of life is evidence that a parent has made a choice, rather than a sign that the parent believes she has no other choice available to her.

At this point, the outcome in the family cap cases should perhaps be unsurprising. Poor families, with little cultural or political power, face extreme difficulty with both legislatures and the judiciary. Yet family caps create extraordinarily significant burdens tied to family status, and the courts' persistent refusal in reviewing these laws to apply or actively engage with constitutional precedents designed to protect families and family members from government overreaching remains striking.

The exclusion of welfare law from the family law canon has helped judges and lawmakers avoid addressing why such radically different rules govern familial rights and responsibilities in poor families. The crucial unexplored question is not about how much welfare the government should supply, a topic that has been repeatedly debated. To be sure, welfare programs like TANF are remarkably stingy. The underprovision of aid to the poor both reflects and helps produce the poor's persistent vulnerability. It appears to be an enduring feature of the American legal system.

That said, the key question that welfare's exclusion from canonical understandings of family law obscures is why the provision of welfare, no matter how stingy, should cause the legal principles governing family relations to reverse course so dramatically. Why should the law sustain two separate and diametrically opposed normative regimes for governing families whose application turns on whether money is transferred in certain stigmatized forms? For example, why should and why can programs like TANF impose family caps or condition aid on warrantless inspections of parents' homes, when family law otherwise attempts to support parental autonomy and reduce disruption of family relationships—even when distributing financial benefits? Judges and lawmakers have hardly begun to frame this question, much less answer it. They assume, generally without explicit acknowledgment, that programs like TANF are not part of family law and that the guiding principles legal authorities apply to family law as a matter of public policy and constitutional law necessarily do not apply to welfare law.

In all likelihood, it would be politically unpopular to remake welfare law to be more in accord with general family law principles. Bringing welfare law into alignment with the family law applied to more affluent people would mean, for instance, that welfare programs would assume that poor parents are raising their children well unless there is individualized evidence to the contrary and that welfare law would provide financial benefits to poor families in ways designed to support rather than rearrange family life. But even if restructuring welfare law would be politically difficult, that does not explain why it is constitutionally acceptable to use welfare law to penalize children because their parents conceived them while receiving welfare, or to condition welfare benefits on warrantless inspections of parents' homes, or to construct welfare programs so that they create tremendous economic pressures to separate children from their parents.

Recognizing that welfare law can also be family law brings family law's divergent treatment of poor families to the foreground. It reveals the systematic disjunction between how family law regulates poor families and other families as a divide that requires explanation and justification, or elimination.

CONCLUSION

Recasting the Family Law Canon

> Common sense is not what the mind cleared of cant sponta-
> neously apprehends; it is what the mind filled with presup-
> positions . . . concludes.
>
> —Anthropologist Clifford Geertz (1983)[1]

By definition, the family law canon is difficult to alter. The canon consists of deeply rooted, widely held ways of thinking about family law
and its guiding principles that gain strength from their repeated invocation. Much of the family law canon's power lies in its ability to operate
at the level of common sense, so that canonical narratives and modes of
understanding the field appear to require no explanation or reexamination. Changing the canon requires revising fundamental, embedded
assumptions about family law that legal decisionmakers are accustomed
to acting upon with little, if any, question or qualm. Legislators and
judges, as well as scholars, lawyers, and family members, reason within
the family law canon and reproduce the canon intergenerationally, instructing new generations to think about family law as their predecessors do.

However, recognizing the need for change is the first step to reforming
the family law canon. As we have seen, canonical ideas about family law
often misdescribe the field, misdirect critical analysis, and misshape the
policy choices that decisionmakers pursue. The family law canon diverts
attention from key questions facing the field, shielding the subject of
family law in superficially appealing, but distorted and misleading, narratives. This book has highlighted three central arenas in which the
family law canon needs recasting.

The first arena for reform concerns how to understand family law's relationship to the rest of the law. Courts and lawmakers repeatedly describe family law as starkly set apart from other legal fields. One canonical narrative insists that family law is a rare outpost of localism in an age when the federal government regulates almost every other area of life. A second narrative contends that family law rejects ordinarily dominant market rules and economic exchanges. But family law resembles other legal fields much more closely than these narratives suggest. Canonical stories assuming family law's exceptionalism mischaracterize the field, divert attention away from important questions that family law confronts, and distort the decisions that judges and legislators reach. The key questions for family law are not about whether the federal government should be involved in family law at all. Federal family law has long been pervasive. The relevant questions for family law are about whether any particular family law measure is substantively desirable on its own merits and about which level (or levels) of government is best situated to carry out that specific policy. Similarly, the pressing questions for family law are not about whether the law should permit and enforce economic exchanges within the family. Family law already allows and upholds extensive economic exchanges between family members. Indeed, such exchanges are essentially unavoidable. Instead, the relevant questions for family law are about when the law should enforce economic exchanges between family members, how, why, to what ends, and with what consequences.

A second arena for reform centers on canonical understandings of family law's relationship to its past. Where narratives about family law exceptionalism tend to present the field as a haven of stability in a world otherwise undergoing frenetic change, family law's canonical progress narratives promise that family law has nonetheless kept pace with progressive reform. These progress narratives suggest that family law's support for normatively problematic practices is safely in the past, announcing the demise of common law coverture, the progression from status to contract, and the reorganization of family law around children's best interests. Yet family law's canonical progress narratives significantly overstate change over time. Important doctrines and principles from common law coverture persist, status rules remain central to family law, contract rules can have their own disadvantages, and family law often continues to prioritize parental prerogatives over children's interests where the two conflict. The family law canon's progress narratives can divert attention from scrutinizing family law's present and from exploring whether, when, how, why, and to what extent family law might still operate to perpetuate injustice and subordination. Family law needs to shift focus away from celebrating the supposed repudiation of the past, to ask pressing, live questions about how family law might still need to change in order to eradicate coverture's legacy, about the advantages and disadvantages of employing status rules or contract rules to implement family law policy in any specific context, and about the extent to which family law's persistent privileging of parents' rights over children's interests should be revised.

A third arena for reform centers on what the family law canon excludes and ignores. Legal decisionmakers describing, explaining, and enacting family law pay little attention to many family relationships and routinely ignore the family law governing the poor. Family law's overwhelming focus on marriage, parenthood, and (sometimes) their functional equivalents takes attention away from considering how to regulate and safeguard other family relationships, such as sibling ties. Yet noncanonical family bonds can be invaluable to family life and to the flourishing of family members. Exploring the law's present regulation of these noncanonical relationships brings an abundance of reform possibilities into view. Similarly, the exclusion of welfare law from the family law canon obscures the diametrically opposed treatment that family law accords to poor families compared to other families, making it easier for this bifurcation in family law to persist without acknowledgment or explanation. Recognizing that welfare law can also be family law makes clear that poor families are subject to a radically different family law and that decisionmakers need to defend and justify the differences, or eradicate them.

In sum, family law's canon is in tremendous need of recasting. Family law helps structure all of our lives, whether as family members, individuals, or participants in society. Yet family law is canonically organized and understood in ways that take precious time, attention, and energy away from critical questions, problems, and choices confronting the field.

Legislators, regulators, judges, scholars, lawyers, and family members should all play a role in the reform process. All these groups shape and are shaped by the family law canon. But it is useful to distinguish among the various actors who create and maintain the canon, and the various contexts in which the canon is reinforced and perpetuated, in thinking about concrete mechanisms for changing the canon.

Lawmakers and judges have the most control over family law's canon, for reasons that turn on the differences between a legal canon and a literary one. The content of a literary canon is largely in the hands of academics, who decide what they will teach, what they will write about, and what they consider exemplary work. In contrast, the content of a legal canon is mainly within the dominion of legal authorities. Judges, legislators, and regulators wield the most power to decide both what the law is and what counts as a convincing argument in a judicial opinion, legislative debate, or regulatory dispute. Their decisions, statutes, and regulations have the force of law, even if some scholars, practitioners, litigants, or individual citizens disagree with them. For this reason, however, it may be more difficult to change how legal authorities understand family law.

The specific institutional hurdles associated with altering what lawmakers and jurists think and do suggest that an effort to reshape family law's canon may be most successful if the effort begins with scholars and the process by which they transmit the family law canon to students, successors, peers, and legal decisionmakers. Scholars, who are self-consciously engaged in studying family law and not insulated by the authority to make law, may be the group easiest to reach first on the path to changing what legal authorities think and do.

Family law scholarship, courses, and casebooks provide an invaluable opportunity to subject the family law canon to more inspection and debate and to advance the process of altering it. There are some wonderful academics working in family law, and scholars can contribute to changing the family law canon by joining this book's project and generating more writing about family law that critiques and contests its canonical narratives. Some family law scholars have already written in ways that reflect doubts about some of family law's canonical stories. These scholars should be natural allies in this book's project to recast the canon, even if they have not thought about themselves or their work in those terms before. However, other scholars (or sometimes the same scholars at different times) have repeated and relied on canonical ideas about family law. One goal of this book is to encourage academics to rethink that scholarly pattern.

Revising the teaching of family law may be even more important. The family law canon is transmitted and reproduced intergenerationally, as one generation's work and words describe and explain the field to the next. Changing the canon requires intervening in that process of intergenerational transfer. Family law teachers are well situated to use their courses to help students—who are future lawyers, lawmakers, judges, scholars, and their aides and clerks—examine family law from new perspectives and think about the subject in new ways. But scholars have not focused on the idea that family law has a canon and hence have not strategized about how to disrupt the intergenerational transmission of canonical ideas about the field.

Challenging family law's canon in our teaching means that when we encounter a canonical premise about family law in a judicial opinion, legal brief, legislative debate, political forum, regulatory document, news story, scholarly article, or classroom remark, we should not repeat it without reflection or even pass over it without comment. Instead, we need to subject these canonical assumptions to explicit critical evaluation and discussion. Family law teachers should help their students learn how canonical ideas about family law have shaped the ways in which legal authorities understand the subject. We should ask our students to think about how lawmaking, adjudication, political discourse, academic dialogue, and ordinary conversation about family law could be altered if judges, lawmakers, and other legal actors did not rely so frequently on dominant accounts of family law that misrepresent the field.

Challenging the family law canon also means teaching aspects of family law that the field canonically overlooks or ignores. Family law courses should consider not only marriage, parenthood, and their functional equivalents, but also the legal treatment of siblings, grandparents, grandchildren, aunts, uncles, nieces, nephews, cousins, and other noncanonical relatives. Family law courses should examine not only the family law applied to people considered middle class or wealthier, but also the legal regulation of poor people's familial rights and responsibilities. Family law courses should explore not only state law, but also the breadth, range, and importance of federal family law.

More generally, challenging the family law canon means not confining family law courses to a traditional curriculum focused on state law governing marriage, divorce, family property, child custody, child support, and adoption. These topics are unquestionably important to family law. But they offer too limited a window into the field when studied by themselves. As we have seen, family law pervades state and federal statutes, judicial decisions, and regulations. It runs through and intersects with myriad other areas of law, including tort law, contract law, property law, constitutional law, criminal law, tax law, employment law, labor law, immigration law, citizenship law, international relations law, military law, welfare law, social benefits law, public health law, education law, housing law, bankruptcy law, intellectual property law, agricultural law, Native American law, evidence law, personal jurisdiction law, and more. A single course cannot realistically hope to cover every aspect of family law in all of its richness, variety, and detail. But a family law course can make the scope, significance, and extent of family law clear. Students studying family law need to understand the depth, reach, pervasiveness, and variety of the field.

As importantly, students who never take a class officially designated as a family law course should understand and recognize the family law that falls within the subject matter of other courses. These students should learn how their legal careers may frequently engage them with family law, even if they never work with legal materials that a traditional family law course would include. In the real world, family law overlaps with many other areas of the law. Law schools should not treat family law as an intellectual silo disconnected from the rest of the curriculum.

Recasting the family law canon is a long and demanding project. But uncovering and understanding the canon's misdescription and misdirection is the first step on the path to reform. We need to challenge the answers that the family law canon presumes and to ask questions that the canon never considers. We need to reimagine family law.

NOTES

ACKNOWLEDGMENTS

INDEX

NOTES

Introduction

1. Planned Parenthood of Se. Pa. v. Casey, 505 U.S. 833, 851 (1992) (citation and internal quotation marks omitted); see also Smith v. Org. of Foster Families for Equal. & Reform, 431 U.S. 816, 842 (1977); Moore v. City of E. Cleveland, 431 U.S. 494, 499 (1977) (plurality opinion).

2. See Robert C. LaFountain et al., Nat'l Ctr. for State Courts, *Examining the Work of State Courts: An Analysis of 2010 State Court Caseloads* 13–17 (2012).

3. See, e.g., Harold Bloom, *The Western Canon: The Books and School of the Ages* (1994); J.M. Balkin and Sanford Levinson, "The Canons of Constitutional Law," 111 *Harv. L. Rev.* 963 (1998).

4. For an early and influential recognition of the tendency to describe history as a story of steady progress, see H. Butterfield, *The Whig Interpretation of History* (1931).

I. Family Law Exceptionalism

1. Martha Albertson Fineman, "What Place for Family Privacy?," 67 *Geo. Wash. L. Rev.* 1207, 1207 (1999).

2. Lee E. Teitelbaum, "Placing the Family in Context," 22 *U.C. Davis L. Rev.* 801, 801 (1989).

3. Janet Halley and Kerry Rittich, "Critical Directions in Comparative Family Law: Genealogies and Contemporary Studies of Family Law Exceptionalism," 58 *Am. J. Comp. L.* 753, 754 (2010).

1. Federalism and the Family

1. 133 S. Ct. 2675, 2691 (2013) (quoting In re Burrus, 136 U.S. 586, 593–94 (1890)).

2. I first introduced my definition of family law in a law review article. See Jill Elaine Hasday, "The Canon of Family Law," 57 *Stan. L. Rev.* 825, 871 (2004). Several family law scholars have subsequently found my definition helpful and used it in their own work. See, e.g., Kerry Abrams, "Immigration Law and the Regulation of Marriage," 91 *Minn. L. Rev.* 1625, 1629 n.1 (2007); Ann Laquer Estin, "Sharing Governance: Family Law in Congress and the States," 18 *Cornell J.L. & Pub. Pol'y* 267, 272 n.20 (2009); Meredith Johnson Harbach, "Is the Family a Federal Question?," 66 *Wash. & Lee L. Rev.* 131, 134 n.8 (2009); Shani King, "The Family Law Canon in a (Post?) Racial Era," 72 *Ohio St. L.J.* 575, 579 n.13 (2011); David B. Thronson, "Custody and Contradictions: Exploring Immigration Law as Federal Family Law in the Context of Child Custody," 59 *Hastings L.J.* 453, 457 n.24 (2008).

3. Trammel v. United States, 445 U.S. 40, 50 (1980); see also Mansell v. Mansell, 490 U.S. 581, 587 (1989); Thompson v. Thompson, 484 U.S. 174, 186 (1988); Moore v. Sims, 442 U.S. 415, 435 (1979); Williams v. North Carolina, 325 U.S. 226, 233 (1945); De la Rama v. De la Rama, 201 U.S. 303, 307 (1906); Barber v. Barber, 62 U.S. (21 How.) 582, 584 (1859).

4. Hillman v. Maretta, 133 S. Ct. 1943, 1950 (2013).

5. Sosna v. Iowa, 419 U.S. 393, 404 (1975); see also Zablocki v. Redhail, 434 U.S. 374, 398 (1978) (Powell, J., concurring in the judgment).

6. De Sylva v. Ballentine, 351 U.S. 570, 580 (1956).

7. United States v. Windsor, 133 S. Ct. 2675, 2691 (2013) (quoting In re Burrus, 136 U.S. 586, 593–94 (1890)); see also Elk Grove Unified Sch. Dist. v. Newdow, 542 U.S. 1, 12 (2004); Boggs v. Boggs, 520 U.S. 833, 848 (1997); Rose v. Rose, 481 U.S. 619, 625 (1987); McCarty v. McCarty, 453 U.S. 210, 220 (1981); Hisquierdo v. Hisquierdo, 439 U.S. 572, 581 (1979); Ohio ex rel. Popovici v. Agler, 280 U.S. 379, 383 (1930); Simms v. Simms, 175 U.S. 162, 167 (1899).

8. Santosky v. Kramer, 455 U.S. 745, 770 (1982) (Rehnquist, J., dissenting) (footnote omitted).

9. Mary Ann Mason, *The Equality Trap* 77 (1988).

10. Anne C. Dailey, "Federalism and Families," 143 *U. Pa. L. Rev.* 1787, 1790 (1995).

11. Robert A. Destro, "Law and the Politics of Marriage: *Loving v. Virginia* After 30 Years Introduction," 47 *Cath. U. L. Rev.* 1207, 1226 (1998).

12. Naomi R. Cahn, "Models of Family Privacy," 67 *Geo. Wash. L. Rev.* 1225, 1230 n.30 (1999).

13. Margaret Ryznar and Anna Stepień-Sporek, "To Have and To Hold, for Richer or Richer: Premarital Agreements in the Comparative Context," 13 *Chap. L. Rev.* 27, 30 (2009).

14. Martin Guggenheim, *What's Wrong with Children's Rights* 81 (2005).

15. Theresa M. Beiner, "Female Judging," 36 *U. Tol. L. Rev.* 821, 832 (2005).

16. Ellen Kandoian, "Cohabitation, Common Law Marriage, and the Possibility of a Shared Moral Life," 75 *Geo. L.J.* 1829, 1831 (1987).

17. Samuel Green and John V. Long, *Marriage and Family Law Agreements* § 1.10, at 13 (1984).

18. Lynn D. Wardle and Laurence C. Nolan, *Fundamental Principles of Family Law* 29 (2d ed. 2006).

19. Harry D. Krause et al., *Family Law: Cases, Comments, and Questions* 20–21 (7th ed. 2013).

20. 41 *Am. Jur.* 2d "Husband and Wife" § 45 (2005).

21. Violence Against Women Act of 1994, Pub. L. No. 103-322, § 40,302, 108 Stat. 1902, 1941 (codified at 42 U.S.C. § 13981 (2006)), invalidated by United States v. Morrison, 529 U.S. 598, 601–02 (2000).

22. Defense of Marriage Act, Pub. L. No. 104-199, § 3, 110 Stat. 2419, 2419 (1996) (codified at 1 U.S.C. § 7 (2012)), invalidated by United States v. Windsor, 133 S. Ct. 2675, 2696 (2013).

23. 514 U.S. 549 (1995).

24. See U.S. Const. art. I, § 8, cl. 3.

25. See Wickard v. Filburn, 317 U.S. 111, 118–29 (1942).

26. See *Lopez,* 514 U.S. at 551.

27. See id. at 564.

28. Id.

29. Id. at 564–65.

30. Id. at 565.

31. Id. (citation omitted).

32. Id. at 585 (Thomas, J., concurring).

33. Id. at 624 (Breyer, J., dissenting) (citations omitted).

34. See, e.g., *The Federalist No. 80,* at 478 (Alexander Hamilton) (Clinton Rossiter ed., 1961).

35. See U.S. Const. art. III, § 2, cl. 1.

36. 28 U.S.C. § 1332(a) (2006) (emphasis added).

37. Ankenbrandt v. Richards, 504 U.S. 689, 703 (1992).

38. Id. at 704.

39. United States v. Lopez, 514 U.S. 549, 564 (1995).

40. See 439 U.S. 572, 573 (1979).

41. Id. at 581 (quoting In re Burrus, 136 U.S. 586, 593–94 (1890)).

42. 481 U.S. 619, 625 (1987).

43. 62 U.S. (21 How.) 582 (1859).

44. See id. at 588–93; id. at 600–03 (Daniel, J., dissenting).

45. See id. at 592–94, 597–98 (majority opinion). A later Supreme Court case held that a wife who lived in a separate state from her husband would be treated as a legal domiciliary of the state she lived in for purposes of filing a divorce suit in that state's courts. See Cheever v. Wilson, 76 U.S. (9 Wall.) 108, 123–24 (1870).

46. *Barber,* 62 U.S. (21 How.) at 584.

47. Id. at 601 (Daniel, J., dissenting).

48. See In re Burrus, 136 U.S. 586, 593–94 (1890).

49. See, e.g., Ohio ex rel. Popovici v. Agler, 280 U.S. 379, 382–83 (1930); De la Rama v. De la Rama, 201 U.S. 303, 307–08 (1906); Simms v. Simms, 175 U.S. 162, 167–68 (1899); Cheely v. Clayton, 110 U.S. 701, 705 (1884).

50. 504 U.S. 689, 694 (1992).

51. See id. at 695–97, 700–01.

52. Id. at 700.

53. See id. at 691, 694–95, 704.

54. See id. at 693–94.

55. Id. at 694–95; see also id. at 703; id. at 715 (Blackmun, J., concurring in the judgment).

56. Id. at 704 (majority opinion).

57. See Elk Grove Unified Sch. Dist. v. Newdow, 542 U.S. 1, 12–13 (2004).

58. See Marshall v. Marshall, 547 U.S. 293, 299, 305–08 (2006).

59. Violence Against Women Act of 1994, Pub. L. No. 103-322, § 40,302, 108 Stat. 1902, 1941 (codified at 42 U.S.C. § 13981 (2006)), invalidated by United States v. Morrison, 529 U.S. 598, 601–02 (2000).

60. Defense of Marriage Act, Pub. L. No. 104-199, § 3, 110 Stat. 2419, 2419 (1996) (codified at 1 U.S.C. § 7 (2012)), invalidated by United States v. Windsor, 133 S. Ct. 2675, 2696 (2013).

61. See *Morrison,* 529 U.S. at 601–02.

62. 42 U.S.C. § 13981(a)–(b) (2006).

63. See id. § 13981(c).

64. See S. 2754, 101st Cong. § 301(a)(1) (1990); H.R. Rep. No. 103-711, at 385 (1994) (Conf. Rep.); S. Rep. No. 103-138, at 48, 55 (1993); S. Rep. No. 102-197, at 35 (1991).

65. See H.R. Rep. No. 103-711, at 385; S. Rep. No. 103-138, at 54; S. Rep. No. 102-197, at 53.

66. See, e.g., S. Rep. No. 103-138, at 54; S. Rep. No. 102-197, at 53.

67. H.R. Rep. No. 103-711, at 385; see also id. at 385–86.

68. S. Rep. No. 103-138, at 49; S. Rep. No. 102-197, at 43, 48.

69. S. 2754 § 301(a)(3); see also H.R. Rep. No. 103-711, at 385.

70. See S. Rep. No. 103-138, at 64; S. Rep. No. 102-197, at 62; S. Rep. No. 101-545, at 51 (1990).

71. See 42 U.S.C. § 13981(a) (2006); see also H.R. Rep. No. 103-711, at 385.

72. See Brief of Law Professors as Amici Curiae in Support of Petitioners at 13 & n.18, United States v. Morrison, 529 U.S. 598 (2000) (Nos. 99-5, 99-29).

73. 529 U.S. 598.

74. See id. at 602.

75. See id. at 602, 604.

76. See S. Rep. No. 103-138, at 41 (1993); S. Rep. No. 102-197, at 37 (1991).

77. S. 2754, 101st Cong. § 301(a)(2) (1990); see also H.R. Rep. No. 103-711, at 385 (1994) (Conf. Rep.).

78. See 42 U.S.C. § 13981(d)(2)(B) (2006).

79. *Violence Against Women: Victims of the System: Hearing on S. 15 Before the Senate Comm. on the Judiciary,* 102d Cong. 317 (1992) (statement of Conference of Chief Justices); *Crimes of Violence Motivated by Gender: Hearing Before the Subcomm. on Civil and Constitutional Rights of the House Comm. on the Judiciary,* 103d Cong. 82 (1994) (statement of Conference of Chief Justices).

80. *Crimes of Violence Motivated by Gender: Hearing Before the Subcomm. on Civil and Constitutional Rights of the House Comm. on the Judiciary,* supra note 79, at 84 (statement of Conference of Chief Justices).

81. William H. Rehnquist, "Chief Justice's 1991 Year-End Report on the Federal Judiciary," *Third Branch* (Office of Legislative & Pub. Affairs, Admin. Office of the U.S. Courts, Washington, D.C.), Jan. 1992, at 1, 3 [hereinafter Rehnquist, "Year-End Report"]; see also Remarks of Chief Justice Rehnquist, reprinted in 138 Cong. Rec. 6186, 6186 (1992); Report of the Proceedings of the Judicial Conference of the United States (Sept. 23–24, 1991), reprinted in *Crimes of Violence Motivated by Gender: Hearing Before the Subcomm. on Civil and Constitutional Rights of the House Comm. on the Judiciary,* supra note 79, at 74, 75.

82. *Violence Against Women: Victims of the System: Hearing on S. 15 Before the Senate Comm. on the Judiciary,* supra note 79, at 315, 317 (statement of Conference of Chief Justices); *Crimes of Violence Motivated by Gender: Hearing Before the Subcomm. on Civil and Constitutional Rights of the House Comm. on the Judiciary,* supra note 79, at 82–84 (statement of Conference of Chief Justices).

83. See Report of the Proceedings of the Judicial Conference of the United States (Sept. 23–24, 1991), supra note 81, at 75.

84. Report of the Judicial Conference Ad Hoc Committee on Gender-Based Violence 7 (Sept. 1991) (unpublished manuscript, on file with author).

85. Rehnquist, "Year-End Report," supra note 81, at 3; see also Remarks of Chief Justice Rehnquist, reprinted in 138 Cong. Rec. 6186, 6186 (1992).

86. Judith Resnik, "'Naturally' Without Gender: Women, Jurisdiction, and the Federal Courts," 66 *N.Y.U. L. Rev.* 1682, 1749 (1991); see also Naomi R. Cahn, "Family Law, Federalism, and the Federal Courts," 79 *Iowa L. Rev.* 1073, 1097–111 (1994).

87. E.g., Violence Against Women Act of 1991, S. 15, 102d Cong. § 301(d)(1).

88. See, e.g., Violence Against Women Act of 1993, H.R. 1133, 103d Cong. § 301(e)(1).

89. See Violence Against Women Act of 1993, S. 11, 103d Cong. § 302(d)(2)(A) (as amended by Judiciary Committee), reprinted in S. Rep. No. 103-138, at 2, 30 (1993). For the final codification of this provision, see 42 U.S.C. § 13981(d)(2)(A) (2006).

90. S. 11 § 302(d)(1), reprinted in S. Rep. No. 103-138, at 30 (emphasis added). For the final codification, see 42 U.S.C. § 13981(d)(1).

91. S. Rep. No. 103-138, at 64.

92. Id. at 51.

93. See id. at 40.

94. Ruth Shalit, "Caught in the Act," *New Republic,* July 12, 1993, at 12, 14 (quoting Senator Orrin Hatch) (emphasis added).

95. S. 11 § 302(e)(4), reprinted in S. Rep. No. 103-138, at 30. For the final codification, see 42 U.S.C. § 13981(e)(4).

96. See S. 11 § 301(e)(3), reprinted in S. Rep. No. 103-138, at 30. For the final codification, see 42 U.S.C. § 13981(e)(3).

97. See Violence Against Women Act of 1994, Pub. L. No. 103-322, § 40,302, 108 Stat. 1902, 1941.

98. See Bergeron v. Bergeron, 48 F. Supp. 2d 628, 631 (M.D. La. 1999); Doe v. Doe, 929 F. Supp. 608, 615–16 (D. Conn. 1996).

99. See *Bergeron,* 48 F. Supp. 2d at 635–36; Seaton v. Seaton, 971 F. Supp. 1188, 1190–91, 1194 (E.D. Tenn. 1997); Brzonkala v. Va. Polytechnic & State Univ., 935 F. Supp. 779, 793 (W.D. Va. 1996), aff'd sub nom. Brzonkala v. Va. Polytechnic Inst. & State Univ., 169 F.3d 820 (4th Cir. 1999) (en banc), aff'd sub nom. United States v. Morrison, 529 U.S. 598 (2000).

100. See *Brzonkala,* 169 F.3d at 826, 843.

101. See id. at 838, 842–43, 854, 859, 888; see also id. at 896 (Wilkinson, C.J., concurring); id. at 899 (Niemeyer, J., concurring); id. at 930 (Motz, J., dissenting).

102. For an insightful discussion of this conflict, see Judith Resnik, "The Programmatic Judiciary: Lobbying, Judging, and Invalidating the Violence Against Women Act," 74 *S. Cal. L. Rev.* 269, 269–78 (2000).

103. See 529 U.S. at 609, 614–15.

104. See, e.g., id. at 613.

105. Id. at 615–16.

106. Id. at 617–18.

107. Defense of Marriage Act, Pub. L. No. 104-199, § 3, 110 Stat. 2419, 2419 (1996) (codified at 1 U.S.C. § 7 (2012)), invalidated by United States v. Windsor, 133 S. Ct. 2675, 2696 (2013).

108. See Goodridge v. Dep't of Pub. Health, 798 N.E.2d 941, 948, 969 (Mass. 2003).

109. See Pam Belluck, "Hundreds of Same-Sex Couples Wed in Massachusetts," *N.Y. Times,* May 18, 2004, at A1.

110. In addition to Massachusetts, see Del. Code Ann. tit. 13, § 129 (Supp. 2013); D.C. Code § 46-401 (LexisNexis 2012); Haw. Rev. Stat. § 572-1; 750 Ill. Comp.

Stat. Ann. 5/201 (West); Me. Rev. Stat. Ann. tit. 19-A, § 650-A (Supp. 2013); Md. Code Ann., Fam. Law § 2-201 (LexisNexis 2012); Minn. Stat. § 517.01 (Supp. 2013); N.H. Rev. Stat. Ann. § 457:1-a (LexisNexis Supp. 2012); N.Y. Dom. Rel. Law § 10-a (McKinney Supp. 2013); R.I. Gen. Laws § 15-1-1 (2013); Vt. Stat. Ann. tit. 15, § 8 (2010); Wash. Rev. Code Ann. § 26.04.010 (West Supp. 2013); Hollingsworth v. Perry, 133 S. Ct. 2652, 2668 (2013); Kerrigan v. Comm'r of Pub. Health, 957 A.2d 407, 412 (Conn. 2008); Varnum v. Brien, 763 N.W.2d 862, 872 (Iowa 2009); Garden State Equal. v. Dow, 79 A.3d 1036, 1039 (N.J. 2013); Griego v. Oliver, __ P.3d __ (N.M. 2013). Federal district courts in Oklahoma and Utah have held that the same-sex marriage prohibitions in those states violate the United States Constitution. Oklahoma and Utah are appealing these decisions, however, and as of this writing same-sex couples are not permitted to marry in either state. See Bishop v. United States ex rel. Holder, __ F. Supp. 2d __ (N.D. Okla. 2014); Kitchen v. Herbert, __ F. Supp. 2d __ (D. Utah 2013), stay granted, __ S. Ct. __ (2014).

111. See *Defense of Marriage Act: Hearing on H.R. 3396 Before the Subcomm. on the Constitution of the H. Comm. on the Judiciary,* 104th Cong. 32 (1996) (statement of Representative F. James Sensenbrenner, Jr.); id. at 239 (statement of Lynn D. Wardle, Professor of Law, Brigham Young University Law School); H.R. Rep. No. 104-664, at 10 (1996); 142 Cong. Rec. 17,072 (1996) (statement of Representative Frank Sensenbrenner); id. at 22,448 (statement of Senator Robert Byrd); id. at 22,454 (statement of Senator Conrad Burns).

112. See *The Defense of Marriage Act: Hearing on S. 1740 Before the S. Comm. on the Judiciary,* 104th Cong. 5 (1996) (statement of Senator Don Nickles); *Defense of Marriage Act: Hearing on H.R. 3396 Before the Subcomm. on the Constitution of the H. Comm. on the Judiciary,* supra note 111, at 32 (statement of Representative F. James Sensenbrenner, Jr.); id. at 239 (statement of Lynn D. Wardle, Professor of Law, Brigham Young University Law School); 142 Cong. Rec. 17,072 (1996) (statement of Representative Frank Sensenbrenner); id. at 22,454 (statement of Senator Conrad Burns).

113. 142 Cong. Rec. 22,453 (1996) (statement of Senator Dirk Kempthorne).

114. *The Defense of Marriage Act: Hearing on S. 1740 Before the S. Comm. on the Judiciary,* supra note 112, at 5 (statement of Senator Don Nickles).

115. See Office of the Gen. Counsel, U.S. Gen. Accounting Office, GAO/OGC-97-16, *Defense of Marriage Act* 1–2 (1997).

116. See U.S. Gen. Accounting Office, GAO-04-353R, *Defense of Marriage Act: Update to Prior Report* 1 (2004).

117. *The Defense of Marriage Act: Hearing on S. 1740 Before the S. Comm. on the Judiciary,* supra note 112, at 12 (statement of Senator Dianne Feinstein).

118. *Defense of Marriage Act: Hearing on H.R. 3396 Before the Subcomm. on the Constitution of the H. Comm. on the Judiciary,* supra note 111, at 237 (statement of Representative Michael Patrick Flanagan).

119. 142 Cong. Rec. 16,800 (1996) (statement of Representative Jerrold Nadler).

120. Id. at 16,978 (statement of Representative Neil Abercrombie); see also id. at 16,977 (statement of Representative Neil Abercrombie).

121. Id. at 16,975 (statement of Representative Sam Farr).

122. Id. at 22,457 (statement of Senator Russell Feingold); see also id. at 16,976 (statement of Representative Sheila Jackson-Lee); id. at 17,086 (statement of Representative Carolyn Maloney); id. at 17,087 (statement of Representative Peter DeFazio); id. (statement of Representative John Conyers, Jr.); id. at 22,439 (statement of Senator Edward Kennedy); id. at 22,459 (statement of Senator Charles Robb); H.R. Rep. No. 104-664, at 42–43 (1996) (dissenting views on H.R. 3396).

123. *Defense of Marriage Act: Hearing on H.R. 3396 Before the Subcomm. on the Constitution of the H. Comm. on the Judiciary,* supra note 111, at 188 (statement of Elizabeth Birch, Executive Director, Human Rights Campaign).

124. Id. at 202 (statement of Rabbi David Saperstein, Director and Counsel, Religious Action Center of Reform Judaism).

125. 142 Cong. Rec. 22,455 (statement of Senator Dianne Feinstein) (emphasis added).

126. Id. at 22,461 (statement of Senator J. Robert Kerrey).

127. Evan Wolfson and Michael F. Melcher, "Constitutional and Legal Defects in the 'Defense of Marriage' Act," 16 *QLR* 221, 221, 227 (1996).

128. Id. at 227 (emphasis and capitalization omitted).

129. Ruthann Robson, "Assimilation, Marriage, and Lesbian Liberation," 75 *Temp. L. Rev.* 709, 794–95 (2002).

130. Barbara J. Cox, "But Why Not Marriage: An Essay on Vermont's Civil Unions Law, Same-Sex Marriage, and Separate but (Un)Equal," 25 *Vt. L. Rev.* 113, 136 (2000).

131. Nadine Strossen, "The Current Assault on Constitutional Rights and Civil Liberties: Origins and Approaches," 99 *W. Va. L. Rev.* 769, 772 (1997).

132. 315 B.R. 123 (Bankr. W.D. Wash. 2004).

133. See id. at 130–31.

134. Id. at 132.

135. U.S. Const. amend. X.

136. *Kandu,* 315 B.R. at 131.

137. Id. at 132.

138. See Gill v. Office of Pers. Mgmt., 699 F. Supp. 2d 374, 377 (D. Mass. 2010), aff'd, 682 F.3d 1 (1st Cir. 2012); Massachusetts v. U.S. Dep't of Health & Human Servs., 698 F. Supp. 2d 234, 236 (D. Mass. 2010), aff'd, 682 F.3d 1 (1st Cir. 2012).

139. *Gill,* 699 F. Supp. 2d at 391.

140. *Massachusetts,* 698 F. Supp. 2d at 249 (quoting United States v. Morrison, 529 U.S. 598, 618 (2000)).

141. Id. at 250.

142. Id. at 251.

143. See Golinski v. U.S. Office of Pers. Mgmt., 824 F. Supp. 2d 968, 1002 (N.D. Cal. 2012).

144. Id. at 1000 (quoting Elk Grove Unified Sch. Dist. v. Newdow, 542 U.S. 1, 12 (2004)).

145. Id. (quoting Sosna v. Iowa, 419 U.S. 393, 404 (1975)).

146. Id. (quoting *Sosna*, 419 U.S. at 404).

147. See Pedersen v. Office of Pers. Mgmt., 881 F. Supp. 2d 294, 347 (D. Conn. 2012).

148. Id. at 345 (citation and internal quotation marks omitted).

149. Id. (quoting *Elk Grove Unified Sch. Dist.*, 542 U.S. at 12).

150. 133 S. Ct. 2675, 2696 (2013).

151. See Jeremy W. Peters, "Plaintiff, 83, Is Calm Center in a Legal and Political Storm," *N.Y. Times*, Mar. 28, 2013, at A19.

152. See *Windsor*, 133 S. Ct. at 2682–83.

153. Id. at 2689–90.

154. Id. at 2691 (citations and internal quotation marks omitted).

155. Id. (citation, internal quotation marks, and alteration marks omitted).

156. Id. (quoting In re Burrus, 136 U.S. 586, 593–94 (1890)).

157. Id. at 2693 (citation and internal quotation marks omitted).

158. Id. at 2690.

159. Id. at 2693.

160. Id. at 2692.

161. Id.

162. Id. at 2693.

163. Id. at 2696.

164. See id. at 2683, 2688, 2690, 2694.

165. Id. at 2690.

166. See id. at 2690, 2694–95.

167. Id. at 2690.

168. Santosky v. Kramer, 455 U.S. 745, 768 n.18 (1982) (citation, internal quotation marks, and alteration marks omitted).

169. 388 U.S. 1, 2, 6 & n.5, 11–12 (1967).

170. 434 U.S. 374, 375–77, 382–91 (1978).

171. 482 U.S. 78, 94–99 (1987).

172. 401 U.S. 371, 372–74 (1971).

173. See 440 U.S. 268, 270–71, 283 (1979).

174. See 421 U.S. 7, 8, 14–15 (1975).

175. See Planned Parenthood of Se. Pa. v. Casey, 505 U.S. 833, 887–88, 892–98 (1992).

176. See Griswold v. Connecticut, 381 U.S. 479, 480, 485–86 (1965).

177. See Mills v. Habluetzel, 456 U.S. 91, 99–102 (1982).

178. See Michael H. v. Gerald D., 491 U.S. 110, 113, 124, 129–30 (1989) (plurality opinion).

179. See Santosky v. Kramer, 455 U.S. 745, 747–48 (1982).

180. See Lassiter v. Dep't of Soc. Servs., 452 U.S. 18, 31–32 (1981).

181. Pierce v. Soc'y of Sisters, 268 U.S. 510, 534–35 (1925); see also Wisconsin v. Yoder, 406 U.S. 205, 231–34 (1972); Meyer v. Nebraska, 262 U.S. 390, 399 (1923).

182. See *Pierce,* 268 U.S. at 534–35.

183. See *Yoder,* 406 U.S. at 207–09.

184. See Troxel v. Granville, 530 U.S. 57, 60, 63, 65–73 (2000) (plurality opinion).

185. See Palmore v. Sidoti, 466 U.S. 429, 430, 433–34 (1984).

186. See Planned Parenthood of Se. Pa. v. Casey, 505 U.S. 833, 899 (1992) (plurality opinion).

187. See Prince v. Massachusetts, 321 U.S. 158, 159–60, 166–67, 170 (1944).

188. See Moore v. City of E. Cleveland, 431 U.S. 494, 495–96, 503–06 (1977) (plurality opinion).

189. See Sosna v. Iowa, 419 U.S. 393, 407 (1975); Williams v. North Carolina, 325 U.S. 226, 227, 229–30 (1945); Williams v. North Carolina, 317 U.S. 287, 298–99, 302–03 (1942).

190. See Kulko v. Superior Court, 436 U.S. 84, 91 (1978); Vanderbilt v. Vanderbilt, 354 U.S. 416, 418–19 (1957); May v. Anderson, 345 U.S. 528, 533–34 (1953); Kreiger v. Kreiger, 334 U.S. 555, 557 (1948); Estin v. Estin, 334 U.S. 541, 549 (1948).

191. See 495 U.S. 604, 607–08, 628 (1990) (plurality opinion).

192. See 436 U.S. at 87–88, 93.

193. See id. at 88–90.

194. Id. at 92 (quoting Int'l Shoe Co. v. Washington, 326 U.S. 310, 316 (1945)).

195. Id. at 97. For further discussion of *Kulko,* see Allan Erbsen, "Impersonal Jurisdiction," 60 *Emory L.J.* 1, 26–28 (2010).

196. See Richard H. Fallon, Jr. et al., *Hart and Wechsler's the Federal Courts and the Federal System* 607 (6th ed. 2009).

197. See Wissner v. Wissner, 338 U.S. 655, 656–61 (1950).

198. See McCarty v. McCarty, 453 U.S. 210, 211, 232–35 (1981), superseded by statute, Uniformed Services Former Spouses' Protection Act, Pub. L. No. 97-252, § 1002(a), 96 Stat. 730, 730 (1982) (codified as amended at 10 U.S.C. § 1408 (2012)).

199. See Ridgway v. Ridgway, 454 U.S. 46, 48–49, 55–56 (1981).

200. See Free v. Bland, 369 U.S. 663, 664–70 (1962).

201. See Yiatchos v. Yiatchos, 376 U.S. 306, 307–09 (1964).

202. See Hisquierdo v. Hisquierdo, 439 U.S. 572, 573, 590–91 (1979).

203. See An Act to Establish Rules of Evidence for Certain Courts and Proceedings, Pub. L. No. 93-595, 88 Stat. 1926, 1933 (1975) (enacting Fed. R. Evid. 501).

204. See Funk v. United States, 290 U.S. 371, 373, 382, 386–87 (1933).

205. See Trammel v. United States, 445 U.S. 40, 53 (1980).

206. Id.

207. Id. at 51.

208. See *Manual for Courts-Martial United States,* at IV-103 to IV-104 (2012).

209. Witt v. Dep't of the Air Force, 548 F.3d 1264, 1280 (9th Cir. 2008) (Kleinfeld, J., dissenting from denial of rehearing en banc). For examples of successful military prosecutions of adultery, see United States v. Taylor, 64 M.J. 416, 416–17 (C.A.A.F. 2007); United States v. Orellana, 62 M.J. 595, 597–98, 601 (N-M. Ct. Crim. App. 2005).

210. See Fort v. Fort, 425 N.E.2d 754, 758 (Mass. App. Ct. 1981); Lynn v. Lynn, 398 A.2d 141, 144 (N.J. Super. Ct. 1979). For a rare civilian adultery prosecution twenty years before *Lawrence,* see Commonwealth v. Stowell, 449 N.E.2d 357, 360–61 (Mass. 1983).

211. 539 U.S. 558 (2003).

212. See id. at 562–64, 578–79.

213. Id. at 572; see also id. at 590 (Scalia, J., dissenting).

214. See U.S. Dep't of Def., Instruction 1315.18, Procedures for Military Personnel Assignments para. 6.10.4 (Jan. 12, 2005); U.S. Dep't of Def., Instruction 1342.19, Family Care Plans para. 4(g) (May 7, 2010).

215. 8 U.S.C. § 1229b(b)(1) (2012).

216. Id. § 1151(b)(2)(A)(i).

217. See Office of Immigration Statistics, U.S. Dep't of Homeland Sec., *2011 Yearbook of Immigration Statistics* 18 tbl.6, 20–21 tbl.7 (2012).

218. See 8 U.S.C. § 1151(b)(2)(A)(i).

219. Hamdi ex rel. Hamdi v. Napolitano, 620 F.3d 615, 627 n.12 (6th Cir. 2010) (citation, internal quotation marks, and alteration marks omitted).

220. 8 U.S.C. § 1154(c).

221. See Rodriguez v. Immigration & Naturalization Serv., 204 F.3d 25, 26–28 (1st Cir. 2000); Faustin v. Lewis, 427 A.2d 1105, 1108 (N.J. 1981); Ramshardt v. Ballardini, 324 A.2d 69, 70–71 (N.J. Super. Ct. 1974).

222. See 8 U.S.C. §§ 1154(c), 1186a(b)(1)(A)(i), (d)(1)(A)(i)(III).

223. See id. § 1227(a)(1)(G).

224. See id. § 1325(c).

225. See 8 C.F.R. § 216.4(a)(5) (2013); see also id. §§ 204.2(a)(1)(i)(B), 216.5(e)(2).

226. *USCIS Adjudicator's Field Manual* 195–96 (2013). For earlier guides, see U.S. Citizenship & Immigration Servs., U.S. Dep't of Homeland Sec., *Fraud Referral Sheet* 2 (Sept. 30, 2004); Immigration & Naturalization Serv., U.S. Dep't of Justice, *Examinations Handbook,* at III-21 to III-22 (Oct. 1, 1988).

227. See United States v. Darif, 446 F.3d 701, 703–04 (7th Cir. 2006); United States v. Chowdhury, 169 F.3d 402, 403–05 (6th Cir. 1999); United States v. Dedhia, 134 F.3d 802, 803–04 (6th Cir. 1998).

228. See *Darif,* 446 F.3d at 703–04.

229. See Cho v. Gonzales, 404 F.3d 96, 104 (1st Cir. 2005).

230. United States v. Islam, 418 F.3d 1125, 1126–29 (10th Cir. 2005).

231. See United States v. Orellana-Blanco, 294 F.3d 1143, 1152 (9th Cir. 2002).

232. See *Chowdhury,* 169 F.3d at 403–04.

233. See 8 U.S.C. § 1101(a)(15)(K)(i) (2012).

234. Id. § 1184(d)(1).

235. See id.

236. See id. § 1184(d)(2).

237. See id. § 1409(c).

238. See id. § 1401(g).

239. See id. § 1409(a).

240. See Nguyen v. Immigration & Naturalization Serv., 533 U.S. 53, 92 (2001) (O'Connor, J., dissenting).

241. See id. at 73 (majority opinion).

242. See 131 S. Ct. 2312, 2313 (2011) (per curiam), aff'g by an equally divided Court 536 F.3d 990 (9th Cir. 2008).

243. See Intercountry Adoption Act of 2000, Pub. L. No. 106-279, § 2, 114 Stat. 825, 826 (codified at 42 U.S.C. § 14901 (2006)).

244. See 42 U.S.C. § 14911(c).

245. See id. §§ 14921–14924.

246. See id. § 14953(a).

247. See International Child Abduction Remedies Act, Pub. L. No. 100-300, § 2, 102 Stat. 437, 437 (1988) (codified at 42 U.S.C. § 11601).

248. 42 U.S.C. § 11603.

249. Indian Child Welfare Act of 1978, Pub. L. No. 95-608, 92 Stat. 3069.

250. See 25 U.S.C. § 1913(a).

251. See id. § 1913(d).

252. Id. § 1915(a).

253. Adoptive Couple v. Baby Girl, 133 S. Ct. 2552, 2557 (2013).

254. 11 U.S.C. § 523(a)(5).

255. See id. § 101(14A).

256. Id. § 523(a)(15).

257. See id. § 522(c)(1).

258. 17 U.S.C. § 101.

259. See id. §§ 203, 304.

260. See 5 U.S.C. § 8901(5), (9) (2012).

261. See id. § 8701(d).

262. See id. §§ 8101(6)–(11), 8102.

263. See Foreign Service Act of 1980, Pub. L. No. 96-465, § 814, 94 Stat. 2071, 2113 (codified as amended at 22 U.S.C. § 4054 (2006)).

264. See 38 U.S.C. §§ 101(14), 1310–1318.

265. See id. §§ 101(15), 1541–1543.

266. See id. § 103(a).

267. See 26 U.S.C. § 2(b)(2)(C).

268. See id. §§ 2(b)(2)(B), 6013(a)(1).

269. See Boyter v. Comm'r, 668 F.2d 1382, 1387 (4th Cir. 1981).

270. See 26 U.S.C. §§ 151–152.

271. See id. § 23.

272. See U.S. Gen. Accounting Office, GAO/GGD-96-175, *Tax Administration: Income Tax Treatment of Married and Single Individuals* 3 (1996).

273. See id. at 4; Mapes v. United States, 576 F.2d 896, 897–98 (Ct. Cl. 1978).

274. See Congressional Budget Office, *For Better or for Worse: Marriage and the Federal Income Tax,* at xiv, 30 (1997).

275. See Gregory Acs and Elaine Maag, Urban Institute, No. B-66, *Irreconcilable Differences?: The Conflict Between Marriage Promotion Initiatives for Cohabiting Couples with Children and Marriage Penalties in Tax and Transfer Programs* 3, 4 fig.1 (2005).

276. See James Alm and Leslie A. Whittington, "Does the Income Tax Affect Marital Decisions?," 48 *Nat'l Tax J.* 565, 566 (1995); James Alm and Leslie A. Whittington, "For Love or Money?: The Impact of Income Taxes on Marriage," 66 *Economica* 297, 297 (1999). But see David L. Sjoquist and Mary Beth Walker, "The Marriage Tax and the Rate and Timing of Marriage," 48 *Nat'l Tax J.* 547, 556 (1995).

277. See James Alm and Leslie A. Whittington, "Income Taxes and the Timing of Marital Decisions," 64 *J. Pub. Econ.* 219, 219 (1997); Sjoquist and Walker, supra note 276, at 556.

278. See Leslie A. Whittington and James Alm, "'Til Death or Taxes Do Us Part: The Effect of Income Taxation on Divorce," 32 *J. Hum. Resources* 388, 388 (1997).

279. See Druker v. Comm'r, 697 F.2d 46, 50–51 (2d Cir. 1982).

280. See Mapes v. United States, 576 F.2d 896, 897 (Ct. Cl. 1978); Barter v. United States, 550 F.2d 1239, 1240 (7th Cir. 1977) (per curiam).

281. See Boyter v. Comm'r, 668 F.2d 1382, 1382–85 (4th Cir. 1981); *Tax Treatment of Married, Head of Household, and Single Taxpayers: Hearings*

Before the H. Comm. on Ways and Means, 96th Cong. 164 (1980) (statement of Angela M. Boyter).

282. *Tax Treatment of Married, Head of Household, and Single Taxpayers: Hearings Before the H. Comm. on Ways and Means,* supra note 281, at 167 (statement of H. David Boyter).

283. "Divorced, and $18,000 Richer," *Wash. Post,* Feb. 3, 1981, at B5.

284. *Tax Treatment of Married, Head of Household, and Single Taxpayers: Hearings Before the H. Comm. on Ways and Means,* supra note 281, at 164 (statement of Angela M. Boyter).

285. *Reducing the Tax Burden: Hearings Before the H. Comm. on Ways and Means,* 105th Cong. 19 (1998) (statement of Sharon Mallory).

286. See 42 U.S.C. § 402(a) (2006).

287. See id. § 402(d).

288. See id. § 402(b), (c), (e), (f).

289. See id. § 402(d)(2).

290. See id. § 402(b)(2), (c)(2).

291. See id. § 402(e)(2)(A), (f)(2)(A).

292. See id. § 402(b)(1)(D), (c)(1)(D), (e)(1)(D), (f)(1)(D).

293. See Office of Ret. & Disability Policy, Office of Research, Evaluation, & Statistics, Soc. Sec. Admin., *Annual Statistical Supplement to the Social Security Bulletin, 2012,* at 5.18 tbl.5.A14, G.6 (2013).

294. See 42 U.S.C. § 416(b), (f).

295. See id. §§ 402(b)(1)(G), 402(c)(1)(G), 416(d)(1), 416(d)(4).

296. See id. § 402(b)(1)(C), (b)(3), (c)(1)(C), (c)(3). If the primary spouse dies, the divorced spouse is subject to the same remarriage rules applied to surviving spouses. See id. §§ 402(e)(1)(A), 402(e)(3), 402(f)(1)(A), 402(f)(3), 416(d)(2), 416(d)(5).

297. See id. § 416(c), (g); see also Weinberger v. Salfi, 422 U.S. 749, 777–85 (1975) (upholding nine-month requirement).

298. See 42 U.S.C. § 402(e)(1)(A), (e)(3), (f)(1)(A), (f)(3).

299. See id. § 402(d)(1)(B).

300. See id. § 416(h)(1)(B)(i).

301. See Hisquierdo v. Hisquierdo, 439 U.S. 572, 573–77, 579, 582–83, 585–87 (1979).

302. See Family and Medical Leave Act of 1993, Pub. L. No. 103-3, § 102, 107 Stat. 6, 9–11 (codified as amended at 29 U.S.C. § 2612(a)(1), (c) (2006 & Supp. II 2009)).

303. See 29 U.S.C. § 2612(a)(3), (c).

304. See Boggs v. Boggs, 520 U.S. 833, 840 (1997).

305. See 29 U.S.C. § 1055(c) (2006 & Supp. V 2012).

306. See Egelhoff v. Egelhoff, 532 U.S. 141, 143–50 (2001).

307. Id. at 151.

308. See 29 U.S.C. § 152(3) (2006).

309. See id. § 157.

310. See id. §§ 206–207.

311. See id. § 203(s)(2).

312. See id. § 213(a)(6)(B).

313. 42 U.S.C. § 3604.

314. Id. § 3602(k).

315. See International Parental Kidnapping Crime Act of 1993, Pub. L. No. 103-173, § 2(a), 107 Stat. 1998, 1998 (codified as amended at 18 U.S.C. § 1204).

316. See Child Protection and Obscenity Enforcement Act of 1988, Pub. L. No. 100-690, § 7512(a), 102 Stat. 4485, 4486 (codified as amended at 18 U.S.C. § 2251A).

317. See Safe Homes for Women Act of 1994, Pub. L. No. 103-322, § 40221(a), 108 Stat. 1925, 1926 (codified as amended at 18 U.S.C. § 2261(a)(1)).

318. See Child Support Recovery Act of 1992, Pub. L. No. 102-521, § 2(a), 106 Stat. 3403, 3403 (codified as amended at 18 U.S.C. § 228).

319. See Deadbeat Parents Punishment Act of 1998, Pub. L. No. 105-187, § 2, 112 Stat. 618, 618 (codified at 18 U.S.C. § 228).

320. 42 U.S.C. § 652(k).

321. See Child Abuse Prevention and Treatment and Adoption Reform Act of 1978, Pub. L. No. 95-266, 92 Stat. 205; Adoption Assistance and Child Welfare Act of 1980, Pub. L. No. 96-272, 94 Stat. 500; Howard M. Metzenbaum Multiethnic Placement Act of 1994, Pub. L. No. 103-382, 108 Stat. 4056; Small Business Job Protection Act of 1996, Pub. L. No. 104-188, §§ 1807–1808, 110 Stat. 1755, 1899–904; Adoption and Safe Families Act of 1997, Pub. L. No. 105-89, 111 Stat. 2115.

322. See Small Business Job Protection Act of 1996 § 1808 (codified at 42 U.S.C. §§ 674(d)(4), 1996b(3)).

323. See 42 U.S.C. §§ 671(a)(18), 1996b(1).

324. See id. §§ 671, 675(5).

325. See Adoption and Safe Families Act of 1997 §§ 101(a), 103(a) (codified as amended at 42 U.S.C. §§ 671(a)(15)(D), 675(5)(E)).

326. See Social Services Amendments of 1974, Pub. L. No. 93-647, 88 Stat. 2337 (1975); Child Support Enforcement Amendments of 1984, Pub. L. No. 98-378, 98 Stat. 1305; Family Support Act of 1988, Pub. L. No. 100-485, 102 Stat. 2343; Child Support Recovery Act of 1992, Pub. L. No. 102-521, 106 Stat. 3403; Ted Weiss Child Support Enforcement Act of 1992, Pub. L. No. 102-537, 106 Stat. 3531; Full Faith and Credit for Child Support Orders Act, Pub. L. No. 103-383, 108 Stat. 4063 (1994); Child Support Performance and Incentive Act of 1998, Pub. L. No. 105-200, 112 Stat. 645.

327. See 42 U.S.C. § 652(f).

328. See id. § 666(a)(5).

329. See Child Abuse Prevention and Treatment Act, Pub. L. No. 93-247, 88 Stat. 4 (1974); Child Abuse Prevention and Treatment and Adoption Reform Act of 1978, Pub. L. No. 95-266, 92 Stat. 205; Parental Kidnaping Prevention Act of 1980, Pub. L. No. 96-611, 94 Stat. 3568; Child Protection Act of 1984, Pub. L. No. 98-292, 98 Stat. 204; Child Abuse Amendments of 1984, Pub. L. No. 98-457, 98 Stat. 1749; Child Abuse Prevention, Adoption, and Family Services Act of 1988, Pub. L. No. 100-294, 102 Stat. 102; Child Abuse Prevention Challenge Grants Reauthorization Act of 1989, Pub. L. No. 101-126, 103 Stat. 764; Child Abuse, Domestic Violence, Adoption and Family Services Act of 1992, Pub. L. No. 102-295, 106 Stat. 187; Battered Women's Testimony Act of 1992, Pub. L. No. 102-527, 106 Stat. 3459; An Act To amend the State Justice Institute Act of 1984 to carry out research, and develop judicial training curricula, relating to child custody litigation, Pub. L. No. 102-528, 106 Stat. 3461 (1992); Child Abuse Prevention and Treatment Act Amendments of 1996, Pub. L. No. 104-235, 110 Stat. 3063; Prosecutorial Remedies and Other Tools to end the Exploitation of Children Today Act of 2003 (PROTECT Act), Pub. L. No. 108-21, 117 Stat. 650.

330. See Victims of Child Abuse Act of 1990, Pub. L. No. 101-647, § 226, 104 Stat. 4792, 4806 (codified at 42 U.S.C. § 13031(a)–(b)).

331. 42 U.S.C. § 13031(c)(8).

332. See Keeping Children and Families Safe Act of 2003, Pub. L. No. 108-36, § 114(b)(1)(B), 117 Stat. 800, 809 (codified at 42 U.S.C. § 5106a(b)(2)(A)(ii)).

333. See Violence Against Women Act of 1994, Pub. L. No. 103-322, § 40,302, 108 Stat. 1902, 1941 (codified at 42 U.S.C. § 13981(a)–(c)), invalidated by United States v. Morrison, 529 U.S. 598, 601–02 (2000).

334. S. Rep. No. 103-138, at 51 (1993); see also S. Rep. No. 102-197, at 49 (1991).

335. S. Rep. No. 102-197, at 43–44 (footnotes, internal quotation marks, and alteration marks omitted).

336. Defense of Marriage Act, Pub. L. No. 104-199, § 3, 110 Stat. 2419, 2419 (1996) (codified at 1 U.S.C. § 7 (2012)), invalidated by United States v. Windsor, 133 S. Ct. 2675, 2696 (2013).

337. Windsor, 133 S. Ct. at 2693.

338. See Tara Siegel Bernard and Ron Lieber, "The Costs of Being a Gay Couple Run Higher," N.Y. Times, Oct. 3, 2009, at A1.

339. Windsor, 133 S. Ct. at 2693–94.

340. See id. at 2696.

341. Id. (Roberts, C.J., dissenting) (quoting id. at 2692 (majority opinion)).

342. Id. at 2697 (Roberts, C.J., dissenting) (quoting id. at 2692 (majority opinion)).

343. Id. at 2709 (Scalia, J., dissenting).
344. Id. at 2720 (Alito, J., dissenting).

2. Family Law and Economic Exchange

1. 16 Cal. Rptr. 2d 16, 20 (Ct. App. 1993).

2. Frances E. Olsen, "The Family and the Market: A Study of Ideology and Legal Reform," 96 *Harv. L. Rev.* 1497, 1529 (1983); see also id. at 1498, 1520.

3. Judith Areen, "*Baby M* Reconsidered," 76 *Geo. L.J.* 1741, 1741 (1988).

4. Milton C. Regan, Jr., *Family Law and the Pursuit of Intimacy* 106–07 (1993).

5. Linda R. Hirshman and Jane E. Larson, *Hard Bargains: The Politics of Sex* 281 (1998).

6. Joan Williams, *Unbending Gender: Why Family and Work Conflict and What To Do About It* 118 (2000).

7. Anita L. Allen, "Surrogacy, Slavery, and the Ownership of Life," 13 *Harv. J.L. & Pub. Pol'y* 139, 147 (1990).

8. Michael Walzer, *Spheres of Justice: A Defense of Pluralism and Equality* 97 (1983); see also id. at 101–03.

9. Elizabeth Anderson, *Value in Ethics and Economics* 189 (1993); see also id. at 172, 187.

10. See Borelli v. Brusseau, 16 Cal. Rptr. 2d 16, 20 (Ct. App. 1993); Mays v. Wadel, 236 N.E.2d 180, 183 (Ind. App. Ct. 1968); Hughes v. Lord (In re Estate of Lord), 602 P.2d 1030, 1031 (N.M. 1979); Dade v. Anderson, 439 S.E.2d 353, 354–56 (Va. 1994); Reva B. Siegel, "The Modernization of Marital Status Law: Adjudicating Wives' Rights to Earnings, 1860–1930," 82 *Geo. L.J.* 2127, 2197 n.248 (1994) (collecting cases).

11. See *Borelli,* 16 Cal. Rptr. 2d at 23 (Poché, J., dissenting); Watkins v. Watkins, 192 Cal. Rptr. 54, 56 (Ct. App. 1983); Morone v. Morone, 413 N.E.2d 1154, 1156 (N.Y. 1980).

12. See Estate of Shapiro v. United States, 634 F.3d 1055, 1058–59 (9th Cir. 2011); Carroll v. Lee, 712 P.2d 923, 927 (Ariz. 1986) (en banc); Marvin v. Marvin, 557 P.2d 106, 110, 119 (Cal. 1976) (in bank); Chiba v. Greenwald, 67 Cal. Rptr. 3d 86, 92 (Ct. App. 2007); Whorton v. Dillingham, 248 Cal. Rptr. 405, 407–10 & nn.1&5 (Ct. App. 1988); *Watkins,* 192 Cal. Rptr. at 56; Wurche v. Stenzel, 75 Cal. Rptr. 856, 857–58, 860 (Ct. App. 1969); Glasgo v. Glasgo, 410 N.E.2d 1325, 1332 (Ind. Ct. App. 1980); Tyranski v. Piggins, 205 N.W.2d 595, 597, 599 (Mich. Ct. App. 1973); Kinkenon v. Hue, 301 N.W.2d 77, 79–81 (Neb. 1981); Wolf v. Mangiamele, No. A-97-284, 1998 WL 902572, at *3 (Neb. Ct. App. Sept. 15, 1998); In re Estate of Jackson, 583 N.W.2d 82, 89

(Neb. Ct. App. 1998); *Morone,* 413 N.E.2d at 1155–58; Moors v. Hall, 532 N.Y.S.2d 412, 413–15 (App. Div. 1988); Artache v. Goldin, 519 N.Y.S.2d 702, 704, 706 (App. Div. 1987); Stephan v. Shulman, 515 N.Y.S.2d 67, 69 (App. Div. 1987); Latham v. Latham, 547 P.2d 144, 144–45, 147 (Or. 1976) (in banc); Doe v. Burkland, 808 A.2d 1090, 1093–94 (R.I. 2002); Watts v. Watts, 405 N.W.2d 303, 306, 312–14 (Wis. 1987); In re Estate of Steffes, 290 N.W.2d 697, 698–709 (Wis. 1980).

13. 16 Cal. Rptr. 2d at 16.

14. See id. at 17–18.

15. See id. at 20.

16. Id.

17. Hughes v. Lord (In re Estate of Lord), 602 P.2d 1030, 1031 (N.M. 1979).

18. Dade v. Anderson, 439 S.E.2d 353, 356 (Va. 1994) (quoting Alexander v. Kuykendall, 63 S.E.2d 746, 747 (Va. 1951)).

19. See, e.g., J. Thomas Oldham, *Divorce, Separation and the Distribution of Property* § 3.03 (2013).

20. For a typical fact pattern, see DeLa Rosa v. DeLa Rosa, 309 N.W.2d 755, 758 (Minn. 1981).

21. See Lenore J. Weitzman, *The Divorce Revolution: The Unexpected Social and Economic Consequences for Women and Children in America,* at xiii, 110–11 (1985).

22. See Shirley P. Burggraf, *The Feminine Economy and Economic Man: Reviving the Role of Family in the Post-Industrial Age* 125 (1997); Theodore W. Schultz, *Investment in Human Capital: The Role of Education and of Research* 25 (1971).

23. See Jones v. Jones, 454 So. 2d 1006, 1009 (Ala. Civ. App. 1984); Nelson v. Nelson, 736 P.2d 1145, 1146 (Alaska 1987); Pyeatte v. Pyeatte, 661 P.2d 196, 201–02 (Ariz. Ct. App. 1982); In re Marriage of Olar, 747 P.2d 676, 682 (Colo. 1987) (en banc); Simmons v. Simmons, 708 A.2d 949, 951, 953 (Conn. 1998); Hernandez v. Hernandez, 444 So. 2d 35, 36 (Fla. Dist. Ct. App. 1983); In re Marriage of Weinstein, 470 N.E.2d 551, 559 (Ill. App. Ct. 1984); In re Marriage of Francis, 442 N.W.2d 59, 62 (Iowa 1989); Lovett v. Lovett, 688 S.W.2d 329, 331 (Ky. 1985); Sweeney v. Sweeney, 534 A.2d 1290, 1291 (Me. 1987); Archer v. Archer, 493 A.2d 1074, 1079–80 (Md. 1985); Drapek v. Drapek, 503 N.E.2d 946, 949 (Mass. 1987); Guy v. Guy, 736 So. 2d 1042, 1044, 1046–47 (Miss. 1999); Riaz v. Riaz, 789 S.W.2d 224, 227 (Mo. Ct. App. 1990); Ruben v. Ruben, 461 A.2d 733, 735 (N.H. 1983); Mahoney v. Mahoney, 453 A.2d 527, 529 (N.J. 1982); Muckleroy v. Muckleroy, 498 P.2d 1357, 1358 (N.M. 1972); Geer v. Geer, 353 S.E.2d 427, 431 (N.C. Ct. App. 1987); Nastrom v. Nastrom, 262 N.W.2d 487, 493 (N.D. 1978); Stevens v. Stevens, 492 N.E.2d 131, 133–35 (Ohio 1986); Hubbard v. Hubbard, 603 P.2d 747, 750 (Okla. 1979) (per curiam); Hodge v. Hodge, 520 A.2d 15, 17 (Pa.

1986); Becker v. Perkins-Becker, 669 A.2d 524, 530 (R.I. 1996); Helm v. Helm, 345 S.E.2d 720, 721 (S.C. 1986); Wehrkamp v. Wehrkamp, 357 N.W.2d 264, 266 (S.D. 1984); Saint-Pierre v. Saint-Pierre, 357 N.W.2d 250, 259–60 (S.D. 1984); Beeler v. Beeler, 715 S.W.2d 625, 627 (Tenn. Ct. App. 1986); Frausto v. Frausto, 611 S.W.2d 656, 659 (Tex. Ct. App. 1980); Martinez v. Martinez, 818 P.2d 538, 540–42 (Utah 1991); Downs v. Downs, 574 A.2d 156, 158 (Vt. 1990); Hoak v. Hoak, 370 S.E.2d 473, 474, 477 (W. Va. 1988); DeWitt v. DeWitt, 296 N.W.2d 761, 765 (Wis. Ct. App. 1980); Grosskopf v. Grosskopf, 677 P.2d 814, 822 (Wyo. 1984).

24. See O'Brien v. O'Brien, 489 N.E.2d 712, 713, 718 (N.Y. 1985).

25. Church v. Church, 630 P.2d 1243, 1246 (N.M. Ct. App. 1981).

26. See Wisner v. Wisner, 631 P.2d 115, 122 (Ariz. Ct. App. 1981); *In re Marriage of Olar*, 747 P.2d at 679–80; *Mahoney*, 453 A.2d at 531–32; *Hoak*, 370 S.E.2d at 476–77; *DeWitt*, 296 N.W.2d at 767.

27. See Washburn v. Washburn, 677 P.2d 152, 162–63 (Wash. 1984) (en banc) (Rosellini, J., dissenting); 2 Dan B. Dobbs, *Dobbs Law of Remedies: Damages-Equity-Restitution* 357, 361–74 (2d ed. 1993).

28. See *Pyeatte*, 661 P.2d at 199.

29. See id. at 201–02.

30. Id. at 207.

31. See 818 P.2d 538, 539–40 (Utah 1991).

32. Id. at 540.

33. See DeWitt v. DeWitt, 296 N.W.2d 761, 762 (Wis. Ct. App. 1980).

34. See id. at 762–63.

35. Id. at 763.

36. See id. at 765.

37. Id. at 767.

38. See 708 A.2d 949, 951–52 (Conn. 1998).

39. Id. at 956.

40. Id. (quoting Hoak v. Hoak, 370 S.E.2d 473, 478 (W. Va. 1988) (emphasis added)).

41. Id.; see also Archer v. Archer, 493 A.2d 1074, 1077 (Md. 1985).

42. See Cook v. Cook, 691 P.2d 664, 668–70 (Ariz. 1984) (en banc); Marvin v. Marvin, 557 P.2d 106, 110–16 (Cal. 1976) (in bank); Boland v. Catalano, 521 A.2d 142, 144–47 (Conn. 1987); Glasgo v. Glasgo, 410 N.E.2d 1325, 1331 (Ind. Ct. App. 1980); Tyranski v. Piggins, 205 N.W.2d 595, 596–99 (Mich. Ct. App. 1973); Hay v. Hay, 678 P.2d 672, 674 (Nev. 1984); Kozlowski v. Kozlowski, 403 A.2d 902, 906–08 (N.J. 1979); Morone v. Morone, 413 N.E.2d 1154, 1156 (N.Y. 1980); Suggs v. Norris, 364 S.E.2d 159, 162 (N.C. Ct. App. 1988); Latham v. Latham, 547 P.2d 144, 147 (Or. 1976) (in banc); Watts v. Watts, 405 N.W.2d 303, 313 (Wis. 1987); Kinnison v. Kinnison, 627 P.2d 594, 595–96 (Wyo. 1981).

43. See Norris v. Norris, 174 N.W.2d 368, 369–71 (Iowa 1970); Fincham v. Fincham, 165 P.2d 209, 211, 213 (Kan. 1946); Hilbert v. Hilbert, 177 A. 914, 919 (Md. 1935); French v. McAnarney, 195 N.E. 714, 715–16 (Mass. 1935); Crouch v. Crouch, 385 S.W.2d 288, 293 (Tenn. Ct. App. 1964); Cumming v. Cumming, 102 S.E. 572, 574 (Va. 1920); Caldwell v. Caldwell, 92 N.W.2d 356, 361 (Wis. 1958); Fricke v. Fricke, 42 N.W.2d 500, 501–02 (Wis. 1950).

44. See *Norris,* 174 N.W.2d at 370; *Crouch,* 385 S.W.2d at 293; *Fricke,* 42 N.W.2d. at 502.

45. See *Fincham,* 165 P.2d at 213; *Crouch,* 385 S.W.2d at 293; *Cumming,* 102 S.E. at 575–76.

46. See *Norris,* 174 N.W.2d at 370.

47. For early cases upholding prenuptial agreements, see In re Marriage of Dawley, 551 P.2d 323, 325, 329, 333–34 (Cal. 1976) (in bank); Burtoff v. Burtoff, 418 A.2d 1085, 1087–90 (D.C. 1980); Posner v. Posner, 233 So. 2d 381, 385 (Fla. 1970); Scherer v. Scherer, 292 S.E.2d 662, 666 (Ga. 1982); Frey v. Frey, 471 A.2d 705, 708–10 (Md. 1984); Osborne v. Osborne, 428 N.E.2d 810, 815–16 (Mass. 1981); Buettner v. Buettner, 505 P.2d 600, 603–05 (Nev. 1973); Unander v. Unander, 506 P.2d 719, 720–22 (Or. 1973). For an early case upholding a postnuptial agreement, see Capps v. Capps, 219 S.E.2d 901, 903 (Va. 1976) (per curiam).

48. See Brooks v. Brooks, 733 P.2d 1044, 1050 (Alaska 1987); In re Marriage of Pendleton and Fireman, 5 P.3d 839, 848 (Cal. 2000); Newman v. Newman, 653 P.2d 728, 731 (Colo. 1982) (en banc).

49. See *Brooks,* 733 P.2d at 1050; *Newman,* 653 P.2d at 732; In re Marriage of Boren, 475 N.E.2d 690, 694 (Ind. 1985).

50. See Am. Law Inst., *Principles of the Law of Family Dissolution: Analysis and Recommendations* 1109–15 (2002); Brian Bix, "Bargaining in the Shadow of Love: The Enforcement of Premarital Agreements and How We Think About Marriage," 40 *Wm. & Mary L. Rev.* 145, 153–58 (1998); Brian H. Bix, "Private Ordering and Family Law," 23 *J. Am. Acad. Matrim. Law.* 249, 264–70 (2010); Judith T. Younger, "Lovers' Contracts in the Courts: Forsaking the Minimum Decencies," 13 *Wm. & Mary J. Women & L.* 349, 355–428 (2007).

51. Ashby v. Ashby, 227 P.3d 246, 248 (Utah 2010).

52. See id. at 248–49.

53. Id. at 250.

54. Id. at 254.

55. See Steven McElroy, "Cruise and Holmes Still Married," *N.Y. Times,* Nov. 20, 2006, at E2.

56. See Mickey Porter, "Porter's People," *Akron Beacon J.,* Oct. 6, 2006, at A2.

57. See Lucinda Hahn, "Anna Nicole Jumps in; Vince, Jen Bail out," *Chi. Trib.,* Oct. 11, 2006, § 5, at 2.

58. Scott N. Weston and Robert J. Nachshin, *I Do, You Do . . . But Just Sign Here* 22 (2004).

59. See Ehlert v. Ehlert, No. 354292, slip op. at 1–2, 6–7 (Conn. Super. Ct. Jan. 30, 1997).

60. Me. Rev. Stat. Ann. tit. 19-A, § 606 (2012).

61. See "Mrs. Marshall Wed to Vincent Astor," *N.Y. Times,* Oct. 9, 1953, at 31.

62. See "America's Biggest Fortunes," *Fortune,* Nov. 1957, at 177, 177.

63. See "Mrs. Marshall Wed to Vincent Astor," supra note 61, at 31.

64. See Frances Kiernan, *The Last Mrs. Astor: A New York Story* 124 (2007).

65. See Jae-Ha Kim, "Split Ends," *Chi. Sun-Times,* Sept. 29, 2004, at 66; Arlene Vigoda, "Love and Marriage, Celebrity-Style," *USA Today,* Dec. 29, 2000, at 3E.

66. See Burtoff v. Burtoff, 418 A.2d 1085, 1087 (D.C. 1980).

67. See Sides v. Sides, 717 S.E.2d 472, 472 (Ga. 2011).

68. See id. at 472–73.

69. Id. at 472.

70. See Bruce Weber, "Donald and Marla Are Headed for Divestiture," *N.Y. Times,* May 3, 1997, at A27.

71. See "Divorce Begins for the Trumps," *N.Y. Times,* Aug. 12, 1997, at B6.

72. See Liz Smith and Philip Messing, "Splitsville for Perelman & Barkin: Boots Her Before Prenup Deadline," *N.Y. Post,* Jan. 20, 2006, at 3.

73. George Rush and Leo Standora, "Barkin's Heart Is Broken: 'Devastated' as Perelman Said to Be Planning Divorce," *N.Y. Daily News,* Jan. 21, 2006, at 2.

74. See Bill Zwecker, "Prenup Hastened Britney's Filing," *Chi. Sun-Times,* Nov. 9, 2006, at 50.

75. See Burtoff v. Burtoff, 418 A.2d 1085, 1087, 1090–91 (D.C. 1980).

76. See Sides v. Sides, 717 S.E.2d 472, 472–73 (Ga. 2011).

77. 37 A.3d 173 (Conn. App. Ct. 2012).

78. See id. at 175.

79. See id. at 177–78.

80. See id. at 175.

81. See id. at 176.

82. Id. at 177.

83. Id. at 178.

84. Id.

85. At least one state will not enforce reconciliation agreements. See Ohio Rev. Code Ann. § 3103.06 (LexisNexis 2008).

86. See In re Estate of Wood, No. 63,584, slip op. at 1–4 (Kan. Ct. App. Dec. 22, 1989) (per curiam).

87. Id. at 4 (citations omitted).

88. See Lindsley v. Lindsley, 387 N.Y.S.2d 840, 842–43 (App. Div. 1976).

89. See Earp v. Earp, 290 S.E.2d 739, 740–41 (N.C. Ct. App. 1982).

90. See Bowden v. Bowden, 167 P. 154, 156–57 (Cal. 1917); Braden v. Braden, 3 Cal. Rptr. 120, 122–23 (Dist. Ct. App. 1960).

91. *Braden,* 3 Cal. Rptr. at 122 (quoting trial judge's Memorandum for Judgment).

92. See Borelli v. Brusseau, 16 Cal. Rptr. 2d 16, 24 (Ct. App. 1993) (Poché, J., dissenting).

93. See Romeo v. Romeo, 418 A.2d 258, 265–66 (N.J. 1980); Penley v. Penley, 332 S.E.2d 51, 61–62 (N.C. 1985).

94. Sonnier v. Bayou Boudin & Cracklins, 597 So. 2d 1245, 1246 (La. Ct. App. 1992) (quoting trial judge).

95. 524 A.2d 1184 (D.C. 1987).

96. See id. at 1185, 1186 n.2.

97. Id. at 1185.

98. Id. at 1188 (citation and internal quotation marks omitted).

99. Id. at 1189.

100. See Noah v. Noah, 491 So. 2d 1124, 1127 (Fla. 1986); In re Marriage of Hochleutner, 633 N.E.2d 164, 168 (Ill. App. Ct. 1994); Heins v. Ledis, 664 N.E.2d 10, 16 (Mass. 1996); Perlberger v. Perlberger, 626 A.2d 1186, 1203 (Pa. Super. Ct. 1993); Ramsbottom v. Ramsbottom, 542 A.2d 1098, 1100 (R.I. 1988); Roberts v. Roberts, 835 P.2d 193, 198 (Utah Ct. App. 1992).

101. See Ariz. Rev. Stat. Ann. § 25-319(A)(3) (2007); Cal. Fam. Code § 4320(b) (West Supp. 2013); Del. Code Ann. tit. 13, § 1512(c)(6) (2009); Fla. Stat. Ann. § 61.08(2)(f) (West Supp. 2013); Ga. Code Ann. § 19-6-5(a)(6) (2010); 750 Ill. Comp. Stat. Ann. 5/504(a)(10) (West Supp. 2013); N.Y. Dom. Rel. Law § 236(B)(6)(a)(16) (McKinney 2010); Ohio Rev. Code Ann. § 3105.18(C)(1)(j) (LexisNexis Supp. 2013); Or. Rev. Stat. Ann. § 107.105(1)(d)(B) (West Supp. 2013); 23 Pa. Cons. Stat. Ann. § 3701(b)(6), (12) (West 2010); Tex. Fam. Code Ann. § 8.052(7), (9) (West Supp. 2012); Utah Code Ann. § 30-3-5(8)(a)(vii) (LexisNexis Supp. 2013); Va. Code Ann. § 20-107.1(E)(6), (12) (2008); W. Va. Code Ann. § 48-6-301(b)(11) (LexisNexis 2009); Wis. Stat. Ann. § 767.56(9) (West 2009).

102. See infra Chapter 3.

103. See Dade v. Anderson, 439 S.E.2d 353, 358 (Va. 1994) (Lacy, J., dissenting).

104. See In re Marriage of Olar, 747 P.2d 676, 680 (Colo. 1987) (en banc); In re Marriage of Weinstein, 470 N.E.2d 551, 559 (Ill. App. Ct. 1984); Drapek v. Drapek, 503 N.E.2d 946, 950 (Mass. 1987); Geer v. Geer, 353 S.E.2d 427, 431 (N.C. Ct. App. 1987); Beeler v. Beeler, 715 S.W.2d 625, 627 (Tenn. Ct. App. 1986); Downs v. Downs, 574 A.2d 156, 158–59 (Vt. 1990); Hoak v. Hoak, 370 S.E.2d 473, 478 (W. Va. 1988).

105. See Fla. Stat. Ann. § 61.075(1)(e) (West Supp. 2013); Iowa Code Ann. § 598.21(5)(e) (West Supp. 2013); N.H. Rev. Stat. Ann. § 458:16-a(II)(h) (LexisNexis 2007); N.J. Stat. Ann. § 2A:34-23.1(h) (West 2010); N.Y. Dom. Rel. Law § 236(B)(5)(d)(7); N.C. Gen. Stat. § 50-20(c)(7) (2011); Tenn. Code Ann. § 36-4-121(c)(3) (Supp. 2012); Utah Code Ann. § 30-3-5(8)(g); Vt. Stat. Ann. tit. 15, § 751(b)(5) (Supp. 2013); see also Cal. Fam. Code § 2641(a)–(b) (West 2004).

106. See Fla. Stat. Ann. § 61.075(1)(a); Iowa Code Ann. § 598.21(5)(c); N.J. Stat. Ann. § 2A:34-23.1(i); N.Y. Dom. Rel. Law § 236(B)(5)(d)(7); N.C. Gen. Stat. § 50-20(c)(6); Tenn. Code Ann. § 36-4-121(c)(5)(A); Vt. Stat. Ann. tit. 15, § 751(b)(11); O'Neill v. O'Neill, 536 A.2d 978, 984 (Conn. App. Ct. 1988); *Drapek*, 503 N.E.2d at 950.

107. See statutes cited infra notes 108–11. Georgia law does not provide for an elective share for surviving spouses. See Ga. Code Ann. § 53-4-1 (2011).

108. See Fla. Stat. Ann. § 732.2065 (West 2010); Mich. Comp. Laws Ann. § 700.2202 (West 2002); Miss. Code Ann. § 91-5-29 (2004); Neb. Rev. Stat. § 30-2313 (2008); N.D. Cent. Code § 30.1-05-01 (2010); Okla. Stat. Ann. tit. 84, § 44 (West 2013); Vt. Stat. Ann. tit. 14, § 319 (2010).

109. See Ala. Code § 43-8-70 (LexisNexis 1991); Alaska Stat. § 13.12.202 (2012); Conn. Gen. Stat. Ann. § 45a-436 (West 2004); Iowa Code Ann. § 633.238 (West Supp. 2013); Ky. Rev. Stat. Ann. § 392.080 (LexisNexis 2010); Me. Rev. Stat. Ann. tit. 18-A, § 2-201 (2012); N.J. Stat. Ann. § 3B:8-1 (West 2007); N.Y. Est. Powers & Trusts Law § 5-1.1-A(a)(2) (McKinney Supp. 2013); 20 Pa. Cons. Stat. Ann. § 2203 (West 2005); S.C. Code Ann. § 62-2-201 (2009); Utah Code Ann. § 75-2-202 (LexisNexis Supp. 2012).

110. See 755 Ill. Comp. Stat. Ann. 5/2-8(a) (West 2007); Ind. Code Ann. § 29-1-3-1 (LexisNexis 2011); Md. Code Ann., Est. & Trusts § 3-203(b) (LexisNexis 2011); Mass. Ann. Laws ch. 191, § 15 (LexisNexis 2011); Mo. Ann. Stat. § 474.160(1)(1) (West 2009); N.H. Rev. Stat. Ann. § 560:10 (LexisNexis 2006); N.C. Gen. Stat. § 30-3.1 (2011); Ohio Rev. Code Ann. § 2106.01(C) (LexisNexis 2011); Va. Code Ann. § 64.2-304 (2012); Wyo. Stat. Ann. § 2-5-101(a) (2013).

111. See Colo. Rev. Stat. § 15-11-201 (2011); Haw. Rev. Stat. § 560:2-202 (2008); Kan. Stat. Ann. § 59-6a202 (2005); Minn. Stat. § 524.2-202 (2012); Mont. Code Ann. § 72-2-221 (2011); Or. Rev. Stat. Ann. § 114.605 (West Supp. 2013); S.D. Codified Laws § 29A-2-202 (2004); Tenn. Code Ann. § 31-4-101 (2007); W. Va. Code Ann. § 42-3-1 (LexisNexis 2010).

112. See In re R.H.N., 710 P.2d 482, 486 (Colo. 1985) (en banc); In re Adoption of B.L.P., 728 P.2d 803, 805 (Mont. 1986); Holodook v. Spencer, 324 N.E.2d 338, 342 (N.Y. 1974); In re Adoption of Lay, 495 N.E.2d 9, 10 (Ohio 1986) (per curiam); In re Adoption of Blevins, 695 P.2d 556, 560 (Okla. Ct. App. 1984); In re Adoption of RMS, 253 P.3d 149, 151–53 (Wyo. 2011).

113. See infra Chapter 4.

114. See Alaska Stat. §§ 25.20.030, 47.25.230 (2012); Cal. Fam. Code § 4400 (West 2004); Cal. Penal Code § 270c (West 2008); Conn. Gen. Stat. Ann. § 53-304(a) (West 2012); Del. Code Ann. tit. 13, § 503 (2009); Ga. Code Ann. § 36-12-3 (2012); Ind. Code Ann. § 31-16-17-1 (LexisNexis 2007); id. § 35-46-1-7 (LexisNexis 2009); Iowa Code Ann. § 252.2 (West 2008); Ky. Rev. Stat. Ann. § 530.050 (LexisNexis 2008); La. Rev. Stat. Ann. § 13:4731 (2012); La. Civ. Code Ann. art. 229 (2007); Md. Code Ann., Fam. Law § 13-102 (LexisNexis 2012); Mass. Ann. Laws ch. 273, § 20 (LexisNexis 2010); Miss. Code Ann. § 43-31-25 (2009); Mont. Code Ann. §§ 40-6-214, 40-6-301 (2011); N.H. Rev. Stat. Ann. § 167:2 (LexisNexis 2010); id. § 546-A:2 (LexisNexis 2006); N.J. Stat. Ann. §§ 44:1-140 to 44:1-141, 44:4-101 to 44:4-102, 44:7-19 (West 1993); N.C. Gen. Stat. § 14-326.1 (2011); N.D. Cent. Code § 14-09-10 (2009); Ohio Rev. Code Ann. § 2919.21 (LexisNexis Supp. 2013); Or. Rev. Stat. Ann. § 109.010 (West 2003); 23 Pa. Cons. Stat. Ann. § 4603 (West 2010); R.I. Gen. Laws § 15-10-1 (2013); S.D. Codified Laws § 25-7-27 (2004); Utah Code Ann. § 17-14-2 (LexisNexis 2009); Vt. Stat. Ann. tit. 15, § 202 (2010); Va. Code Ann. § 20-88 (Supp. 2013); W. Va. Code Ann. § 9-5-9 (LexisNexis 2012).

115. Connell v. Francisco, 898 P.2d 831, 834 (Wash. 1995) (en banc).

116. Id. at 837.

117. Id.

118. Am. Law Inst., supra note 50, at 907.

119. Id. at 937.

120. Id. at 940.

121. On women's disproportionate responsibility for domestic labor, see Suzanne M. Bianchi et al., *Changing Rhythms of American Family Life* 113–15 (2006); Scott Coltrane, "Research on Household Labor: Modeling and Measuring the Social Embeddedness of Routine Family Work," 62 *J. Marriage & Fam.* 1208, 1212 (2000); Yun-Suk Lee and Linda J. Waite, "Husbands' and Wives' Time Spent on Housework: A Comparison of Measures," 67 *J. Marriage & Fam.* 328, 334 (2005).

122. See Borelli v. Brusseau, 16 Cal. Rptr. 2d 16, 17–18 (Ct. App. 1993); id. at 23 & n.2 (Poché, J., dissenting).

123. See id. at 20 (majority opinion).

124. See D.C. Code § 16-402(a) (LexisNexis 2012); Ind. Code Ann. §§ 31-20-1-1 to 31-20-1-2 (LexisNexis 2007); Mich. Comp. Laws Ann. § 722.855 (West 2011); N.Y. Dom. Rel. Law § 122 (McKinney 2010); N.D. Cent. Code § 14-18-05 (2009).

125. See Ala. Code § 26-10A-34(c) (LexisNexis 2009); Ark. Code Ann. § 9-10-201 (2009); 750 Ill. Comp. Stat. Ann. 47/10 (West 2009); id. 47/25(d)(3)–(4); Iowa Code Ann. § 710.11 (West 2003); Utah Code Ann. §§ 78B-15-803(2)

(g)–(h), 78B-15-808(1) (LexisNexis 2012); W. Va. Code Ann. § 61-2-14h(e)(3) (LexisNexis Supp. 2012).

126. See Ky. Rev. Stat. Ann. § 199.590(4) (LexisNexis 2007); La. Rev. Stat. Ann. § 9:2713 (2005); Neb. Rev. Stat. § 25-21,200 (2008); Wash. Rev. Code Ann. §§ 26.26.210(1), 26.26.230, 26.26.240 (West 2005); In re Baby M, 537 A.2d 1227, 1234–35, 1264 (N.J. 1988).

127. See Fla. Stat. Ann. § 742.15(4) (West 2010); id. § 63.212(1)(h) (West Supp. 2013); Nev. Rev. Stat. Ann. § 126.045(3) (LexisNexis 2010); N.H. Rev. Stat. Ann. § 168-B:25(V) (LexisNexis 2010); Va. Code Ann. § 20-156 (2008); id. §§ 20-160(B)(4)–(5), 20-162(A) (Supp. 2013); R.R. v. M.H., 689 N.E.2d 790, 797 (Mass. 1998).

128. See, e.g., Del. Code Ann. tit. 13, § 928(b) (2009); D.C. Code § 4-1410 (LexisNexis Supp. 2013); Fla. Stat. Ann. § 63.097 (West 2012); Kan. Stat. Ann. § 59-2121(a) (2005); Ky. Rev. Stat. Ann. § 199.590(2); Md. Code Ann., Fam. Law § 5-362(b)(2) (LexisNexis 2006); Miss. Code Ann. § 43-15-23 (2009); Mont. Code Ann. § 42-7-101(1) (2011); N.M. Stat. Ann. § 32A-5-34(B) (West 2013); N.C. Gen. Stat. § 48-10-103(a) (2011); Ohio Rev. Code Ann. § 3107.055(C) (LexisNexis Supp. 2013); Okla. Stat. Ann. tit. 10, § 7505-3.2(B) (West Supp. 2013); Utah Code Ann. § 76-7-203 (LexisNexis 2012); Vt. Stat. Ann. tit. 15A, § 7-104 (2010).

129. See, e.g., Cal. Penal Code § 273(a)–(b) (West 2008); Fla. Stat. Ann. § 63.212(1)(c); Tenn. Code Ann. § 36-1-109 (2010); Utah Code Ann. § 76-7-203; Kingsley v. State, 744 S.W.2d 191, 193 (Tex. App. 1987).

130. See In re Adoption of Stephen, 645 N.Y.S.2d 1012, 1015 (Fam. Ct. 1996); In re Adoption of Anonymous, 501 N.Y.S.2d 240, 242 (Surr. Ct. 1986).

131. See In re Adoption of Anonymous, 507 N.Y.S.2d 968, 969 (Surr. Ct. 1986).

132. See In re Adoption No. 9979, 591 A.2d 468, 473 (Md. 1991).

133. In re Baby Girl D., 517 A.2d 925, 929 (Pa. 1986).

134. See Murray Enkin et al., *A Guide to Effective Care in Pregnancy and Childbirth* 49, 54–57 (3d ed. 2000).

135. See Judith Lothian and Charlotte DeVries, *The Official Lamaze Guide*, at x (new ed. 2010).

136. *In re Baby Girl D.*, 517 A.2d at 929.

137. See Office of Tech. Assessment, U.S. Cong., *Infertility: Medical and Social Choices* 268–70, 273 (1988); Helena Ragoné, *Surrogate Motherhood: Conception in the Heart* 6, 54–55, 89, 91 (1994); Janice C. Ciccarelli and Linda J. Beckman, "Navigating Rough Waters: An Overview of Psychological Aspects of Surrogacy," 61 *J. Soc. Issues* 21, 31, 35–36 (2005); David MacPhee and Kathy Forest, "Surrogacy: Programme Comparisons and Policy Implications," 4 *Int'l J.L. & Fam.* 308, 311 (1990); Philip J. Parker, "Motivation of

Surrogate Mothers: Initial Findings," 140 *Am. J. Psychiatry* 117, 117 (1983); Nancy E. Reame and Philip J. Parker, "Surrogate Pregnancy: Clinical Features of Forty-Four Cases," 162 *Am. J. Obstetrics & Gynecology* 1220, 1220–22 (1990).

138. See Paul Sachdev, *Unlocking the Adoption Files* 21, 23, 50–51 (1989); Steven D. McLaughlin et al., "Do Adolescents Who Relinquish Their Children Fare Better or Worse than Those Who Raise Them?," 20 *Fam. Plan. Persp.* 25, 25, 32 (1988).

139. See Charles L. Baum, "The Effect of Work Interruptions on Women's Wages," 16 *Lab.* 1, 29 (2002); Joyce P. Jacobsen and Laurence M. Levin, "Effects of Intermittent Labor Force Attachment on Women's Earnings," *Monthly Lab. Rev.*, Sept. 1995, at 14, 18; Christy Spivey, "Time Off at What Price?: The Effects of Career Interruptions on Earnings," 59 *Indus. & Lab. Rel. Rev.* 119, 137 (2005).

140. See, e.g., In re Baby M, 537 A.2d 1227, 1241–42 (N.J. 1988); In re Adoption of Paul, 550 N.Y.S.2d 815, 816 (Fam. Ct. 1990).

141. See Minn. Stat. § 259.55(1)(4)(iii) (2012); Mont. Code Ann. § 42-7-101(1)(k) (2011); N.H. Rev. Stat. Ann. § 170-B:13(I)(d) (LexisNexis 2010); N.D. Cent. Code § 14-15-09(1)(j)(5)(b) (2009).

142. See Cal. Fam. Code §§ 8800(d)(1), 8801.5(c)(4) (West 2004).

143. Id. § 7962(b) (West Supp. 2013).

II. The Family Law Canon's Progress Narratives

1. See, e.g., Robert W. Gordon, "The Struggle over the Past," 44 *Clev. St. L. Rev.* 123, 129–30 (1996).

3. Progress Narratives for Adults

1. Cal. Assembly Comm. on Judiciary, Assembly Committee Report on Assembly Bill No. 530 and Senate Bill No. 252 (The Family Law Act) (Aug. 8, 1969), in 4 Legislature of the State of Cal., *Journal of the Assembly* 8053, 8062 (1969).

2. Henry Sumner Maine, *Ancient Law: Its Connection with the Early History of Society, and Its Relation to Modern Ideas* 170 (London, John Murray 1861).

3. 1 William Blackstone, *Commentaries* *430.

4. James Schouler, *Law of the Domestic Relations* 5–6 (1905).

5. See Thompson v. Thompson, 218 U.S. 611, 614–15 (1910); Norma Basch, *In the Eyes of the Law: Women, Marriage, and Property in Nineteenth-Century New York* 17, 51–55 (1982); Elizabeth Bowles Warbasse, *The Changing Legal Rights of Married Women, 1800–1861*, at 5–24 (1987);

Richard H. Chused, "Married Women's Property Law: 1800–1850," 71 *Geo. L.J.* 1359, 1365–68 (1983); Jill Elaine Hasday, "Contest and Consent: A Legal History of Marital Rape," 88 *Cal. L. Rev.* 1373, 1389–92 (2000).

6. See 1 *History of Woman Suffrage* 67–74 (Elizabeth Cady Stanton et al. eds., Ayer Co. 1985) (1881).

7. See U.S. Const. amend. XIX.

8. William Schofield, "Uniformity of Law in the Several States as an American Ideal" (pt. 2), 21 *Harv. L. Rev.* 510, 514 (1908).

9. 1 James Schouler, *A Treatise on the Law of Domestic Relations* § 4, at 5 (Arthur W. Blakemore ed., 6th ed. 1921).

10. Id.; see also Ocie Speer, *A Treatise on the Law of Married Women in Texas* 27–28 (1901).

11. See Reed v. Reed, 404 U.S. 71, 74–77 (1971).

12. United States v. Dege, 364 U.S. 51, 54 (1960).

13. United States v. Yazell, 382 U.S. 341, 351 (1966).

14. Id. at 343.

15. Dennis v. Perkins, 129 P. 165, 168 (Kan. 1913).

16. Morton v. State, 209 S.W. 644, 645 (Tenn. 1919); see also Angel v. McClean, 116 S.W.2d 1005, 1007 (Tenn. 1938).

17. Bryant v. Smith, 198 S.E. 20, 23 (S.C. 1938).

18. Merch.'s Hostess Serv. of Fla., Inc. v. Cain, 9 So. 2d 373, 375 (Fla. 1942) (en banc).

19. Follansbee v. Benzenberg, 265 P.2d 183, 189 (Cal. Dist. Ct. App. 1954).

20. Trammel v. United States, 445 U.S. 40, 52 (1980).

21. Eisenstadt v. Baird, 405 U.S. 438, 453 (1972).

22. Planned Parenthood of Se. Pa. v. Casey, 505 U.S. 833, 898 (1992); see also Orr v. Orr, 440 U.S. 268, 279–80 (1979); Stanton v. Stanton, 421 U.S. 7, 14–15 (1975).

23. In re Luby, 89 B.R. 120, 125–26 (Bankr. D. Or. 1988).

24. Burns v. Burns, 518 So. 2d 1205, 1210 (Miss. 1988) (citation and internal quotation marks omitted).

25. Boan v. Watson, 316 S.E.2d 401, 402 (S.C. 1984); see also McCall v. Bangs, 207 S.E.2d 91, 93 (S.C. 1974).

26. People v. M.D., 595 N.E.2d 702, 710 (Ill. App. Ct. 1992).

27. Robinson v. Trousdale Cnty., 516 S.W.2d 626, 631 (Tenn. 1974).

28. Immer v. Risko, 267 A.2d 481, 484 (N.J. 1970).

29. Perry v. Schwarzenegger, 704 F. Supp. 2d 921, 992–93 (N.D. Cal. 2010) (citation omitted), aff'd sub nom. Perry v. Brown, 671 F.3d 1052 (9th Cir. 2012), vacated and remanded sub nom. Hollingsworth v. Perry, 133 S. Ct. 2652 (2013).

30. See id.; Goodridge v. Dep't of Pub. Health, 798 N.E.2d 941, 967 (Mass. 2003).

31. 208 U.S. 412 (1908).

32. 335 U.S. 464 (1948).

33. 368 U.S. 57 (1961).

34. See *Muller,* 208 U.S. at 416–17, 423.

35. See id. at 418–19.

36. See id. at 418.

37. Id.

38. Id. at 422.

39. See 335 U.S. 464, 465, 467 (1948).

40. Id. at 465–66.

41. Id. at 465.

42. Id. at 466.

43. Id.

44. See 368 U.S. 57, 58, 61 (1961).

45. Id. at 61–62.

46. Id. at 62; cf. Bradwell v. State, 83 U.S. (16 Wall.) 130, 142 (1873) (Bradley, J., concurring in the judgment).

47. See Family Law Act, ch. 1608, 1969 Cal. Stat. 3314.

48. See, e.g., Herma Hill Kay, "Equality and Difference: A Perspective on No-Fault Divorce and Its Aftermath," *56 U. Cin. L. Rev.* 1, 5–14 (1987).

49. See, e.g., Cal. Assembly Comm. on Judiciary, supra note 1, at 8056–57, 8061; *Report of the Governor's Commission on the Family* 1, 26, 44 (1966).

50. See Family Law Act § 8 (enacting Cal. Civ. Code §§ 4506–4510).

51. See id. § 8 (enacting Cal. Civ. Code § 4800).

52. Id. § 8 (enacting Cal. Civ. Code § 4801(a)).

53. See Cal. Assembly Comm. on Judiciary, supra note 1, at 8053.

54. Id. at 8062.

55. See id. at 8053–54; Jerry Gillam, "Second Major Divorce Reform Bill Offered," *L.A. Times,* Feb. 18, 1969, § 1, at 22; Jerry Gillam, "Divorce Overhaul Bill Approved by Assembly," *L.A. Times,* June 19, 1969, § 1, at 3; Tom Goff, "1st Major Divorce Reform Bill Since 1872 Signed by Governor," *L.A. Times,* Sept. 6, 1969, § 1, at 1; Carlos Vásquez, State Gov't Oral History Program, Cal. State Archives, Oral History Interview with James A. Hayes 117–22 (1990) (unpublished manuscript, on file with author).

56. James A. Hayes, "California Divorce Reform: Parting Is Sweeter Sorrow," *56 A.B.A. J.* 660, 663 (1970).

57. See Family Law Act § 37.

58. See Riane Tennenhaus Eisler, *Dissolution: No-Fault Divorce, Marriage, and the Future of Women* 24–25 (1977) (citing Hayes v. Hayes, No. D700 518 (Cal. Super. Ct. Nov. 6, 1969)); "Hayes' Ex-Wife Seeks Welfare, Food Stamps," *L.A. Times,* June 6, 1975, § 1, at 29.

59. See Myrna Oliver, "Hayes Sues Former Wife to Reduce $650 Alimony," *L.A. Times*, Jan. 30, 1976, § 2, at 4; Eisler, supra note 58, at 25 (citing Interview with Janne Hayes in L.A., Cal. (Jan. 25, 1975)).

60. See Eisler, supra note 58, at 25–26, 28 (citing Respondent's Opening Points and Authorities, Order to Show Cause, Hayes v. Hayes, No. D700 518 (Cal. Super. Ct. Dec. 13, 1972)).

61. See Myrna Oliver, "Court Reduces Alimony Paid by Supervisor," *L.A. Times*, June 4, 1975, § 1, at 29; "Hayes' Ex-Wife Seeks Welfare, Food Stamps," supra note 58, at 29.

62. See Oliver, supra note 61, at 29; "Hayes' Ex-Wife Seeks Welfare, Food Stamps," supra note 58, at 29.

63. "Not Upset by Former Wife, Hayes Says," *L.A. Times*, June 10, 1975, § 1, at 25.

64. See Eisler, supra note 58, at 30 (citing Hayes v. Hayes, 2d Civil No. 45168 (Cal. Ct. App. Oct. 3, 1975)).

65. See Oliver, supra note 59, at 4.

66. See "Hayes Loses Court Bid to Alter Alimony Pact," *L.A. Times*, Mar. 30, 1976, § 1, at 24.

67. See Eisler, supra note 58, at 30 (citing Telephone Interview with Albert J. Corske, Attorney for Janne Hayes, in L.A., Cal. (Apr. 15, 1976)).

68. Kover v. Kover, 278 N.E.2d 886, 888 (N.Y. 1972).

69. Tan v. Tan, 279 N.E.2d 486, 488 (Ill. App. Ct. 1972); see also Borowitz v. Borowitz, 311 N.E.2d 292, 297–98 (Ill. App. Ct. 1974).

70. Beard v. Beard, 262 So. 2d 269, 271–72 (Fla. Dist. Ct. App. 1972) (per curiam).

71. Id. at 272; see also Spotts v. Spotts, 355 So. 2d 228, 230 (Fla. Dist. Ct. App. 1978); Thigpen v. Thigpen, 277 So. 2d 583, 585 (Fla. Dist. Ct. App. 1973); Olsen v. Olsen, 557 P.2d 604, 614–15 (Idaho 1976) (Shepard, J., dissenting); In re Marriage of Beeh, 214 N.W.2d 170, 171 (Iowa 1974).

72. Parniawski v. Parniawski, 359 A.2d 719, 721 (Conn. Super. Ct. 1976).

73. Edwardson v. Edwardson, 798 S.W.2d 941, 944–45 (Ky. 1990).

74. Volid v. Volid, 286 N.E.2d 42, 46–47 (Ill. App. Ct. 1972); see also Potter v. Collin, 321 So. 2d 128, 132 (Fla. Dist. Ct. App. 1975); Scherer v. Scherer, 292 S.E.2d 662, 665–66 (Ga. 1982); Gant v. Gant, 329 S.E.2d 106, 112 (W. Va. 1985).

75. 581 A.2d 162 (Pa. 1990).

76. See id. at 163–64.

77. See supra Chapter 2.

78. See *Simeone*, 581 A.2d at 165–67.

79. Id. at 165; see also Lebeck v. Lebeck, 881 P.2d 727, 733 (N.M. Ct. App. 1994) (quoting *Simeone*, 581 A.2d at 165).

80. *Simeone*, 581 A.2d at 165.

81. Pa. Const. art I, § 28.

82. *Simeone*, 581 A.2d at 165. For sharp criticism of *Simeone*, see id. at 168 (Papadakos, J., concurring); id. at 170–71 (McDermott, J., dissenting).

83. See Basch, supra note 5, at 158–59, 164; James Schouler, *A Treatise on the Law of the Domestic Relations* 16 (Boston, Little, Brown, & Co. 1870); Richard H. Chused, "Late Nineteenth Century Married Women's Property Law: Reception of the Early Married Women's Property Acts by Courts and Legislatures," 29 *Am. J. Legal Hist.* 3, 3 (1985); Chused, supra note 5, at 1398, 1410–11; Reva B. Siegel, "Home as Work: The First Woman's Rights Claims Concerning Wives' Household Labor, 1850–1880," 103 *Yale L.J.* 1073, 1082–83, 1142–43, 1180–81 (1994).

84. Bartrom v. Adjustment Bureau, Inc., 618 N.E.2d 1, 4 n.2 (Ind. 1993).

85. Immer v. Risko, 267 A.2d 481, 482 (N.J. 1970).

86. Robinson v. Trousdale Cnty., 516 S.W.2d 626, 632 (Tenn. 1974); see also Miller v. Monsen, 37 N.W.2d 543, 548 (Minn. 1949).

87. See, e.g., Larison v. Larison, 9 Ill. App. 27, 32 (1881); Gillespie v. Gillespie, 67 N.W. 206, 207 (Minn. 1896); William E. McCurdy, "Torts Between Persons in Domestic Relation," 43 *Harv. L. Rev.* 1030, 1037–38 (1930).

88. See Tapping Reeve, *The Law of Husband and Wife* 93 n.1 (Albany, William Gould, Jr., & Co. 4th ed. 1888); James Schouler, *A Treatise on the Law of the Domestic Relations* 77–78 (Boston, Little, Brown, & Co. 3d ed. 1882).

89. See, e.g., Austin v. Austin, 100 So. 591, 591–93 (Miss. 1924).

90. 218 U.S. 611 (1910).

91. See id. at 614, 617–18.

92. Id. at 615–16 (quoting D.C. Code § 1155, 31 Stat. 1189, 1374 (1901)).

93. Id. at 617–18.

94. Longendyke v. Longendyke, 44 Barb. 366, 368 (N.Y. Sup. Ct. 1863).

95. Lillienkamp v. Rippetoe, 179 S.W. 628, 629 (Tenn. 1915).

96. Gowin v. Gowin, 264 S.W. 529, 537 (Tex. Civ. App. 1924); see also In re Dolmage's Estate, 212 N.W. 553, 555 (Iowa 1927); Peters v. Peters, 42 Iowa 182, 183 (1875); Libby v. Berry, 74 Me. 286, 288–89 (1883); Strom v. Strom, 107 N.W. 1047, 1048 (Minn. 1906); Butterfield v. Butterfield, 187 S.W. 295, 295 (Mo. Ct. App. 1916); Wilson v. Barton, 283 S.W. 71, 71–72 (Tenn. 1926); Keister's Adm'r v. Keister's Ex'rs, 96 S.E. 315, 316–18 (Va. 1918).

97. *Keister's Adm'r,* 96 S.E. at 322 (Burks, J., concurring).

98. See Brooks v. Brooks, 119 P.2d 970, 972 (Cal. Dist. Ct. App. 1941); In re Sonnicksen's Estate, 73 P.2d 643, 645 (Cal. Dist. Ct. App. 1937); Lee v. Savannah Guano Co., 27 S.E. 159, 160 (Ga. 1896); Youngberg v. Holstrom, 108 N.W.2d 498, 502 (Iowa 1961); Bohanan v. Maxwell, 181 N.W. 683, 688 (Iowa 1921); Miller v. Miller, 42 N.W. 641, 642 (Iowa 1889); Dempster Mill

Mfg. Co. v. Bundy, 67 P. 816, 817–18 (Kan. 1902); Lewis v. Lewis, 245 S.W. 509, 511 (Ky. 1922); Foxworthy v. Adams, 124 S.W. 381, 383 (Ky. 1910); Mich. Trust Co. v. Chapin, 64 N.W. 334, 334 (Mich. 1895); Martinez v. Martinez, 307 P.2d 1117, 1119 (N.M. 1957); Tellez v. Tellez, 186 P.2d 390, 392–93 (N.M. 1947); Coleman v. Burr, 93 N.Y. 17, 24–26, 31 (1883); Whitaker v. Whitaker, 52 N.Y. 368, 371 (1873); Ritchie v. White, 35 S.E.2d 414, 415–16 (N.C. 1945); Frame v. Frame, 36 S.W.2d 152, 154 (Tex. 1931); Oates v. Oates, 33 S.E.2d 457, 460 (W. Va. 1945). For an illuminating legal history examining litigation over interspousal contracts for domestic services in the decades between the Civil War and the New Deal, see Reva B. Siegel, "The Modernization of Marital Status Law: Adjudicating Wives' Rights to Earnings, 1860–1930," 82 *Geo. L.J.* 2127, 2181–96 (1994).

99. See *Brooks,* 119 P.2d at 972; *Foxworthy,* 124 S.W. at 383; *Ritchie,* 35 S.E.2d at 415; *Oates,* 33 S.E.2d at 460.

100. See Borelli v. Brusseau, 16 Cal. Rptr. 2d 16, 20 (Ct. App. 1993); Dep't of Human Res. v. Williams, 202 S.E.2d 504, 506–07 (Ga. Ct. App. 1973); State v. Bachmann, 521 N.W.2d 886, 888 (Minn. Ct. App. 1994); Church v. Church, 630 P.2d 1243, 1250 (N.M. Ct. App. 1981); Kuder v. Schroeder, 430 S.E.2d 271, 273 (N.C. Ct. App. 1993).

101. *Lee,* 27 S.E. at 160.

102. See *Brooks,* 119 P.2d at 972; *Lee,* 27 S.E. at 160; *Youngberg,* 108 N.W.2d at 502; *Bohanan,* 181 N.W. at 688; *Dempster Mill Mfg. Co.,* 67 P. at 817–18; *Mich. Trust Co.,* 64 N.W. at 334; *Martinez,* 307 P.2d at 1119; *Tellez,* 186 P.2d at 392–93; *Coleman,* 93 N.Y. at 24–25, 31; *Whitaker,* 52 N.Y. at 371; *Ritchie,* 35 S.E.2d at 416; *Frame,* 36 S.W.2d at 154; *Oates,* 33 S.E.2d at 460.

103. See Decker v. Kedly, 148 F. 681, 681–82 (9th Cir. 1906); Joel Prentiss Bishop, *Commentaries on the Law of Marriage and Divorce* 32 (Boston, Little, Brown & Co. 1852); 1 William T. Nelson, *A Treatise on the Law of Divorce* 5 (Chicago, Callaghan & Co. 1895); Schouler, supra note 83, at 56–57.

104. See Eames v. Sweetser, 101 Mass. 78, 80 (1869).

105. See Fischer v. Brady, 94 N.Y.S. 25, 26 (Sup. Ct. 1905) (per curiam); Gill v. Read, 5 R.I. 343, 345–46 (1858); Homer H. Clark, Jr., *The Law of Domestic Relations in the United States* § 6.3, at 189–92 (1968); John F. Kelly, *A Treatise on the Law of Contracts of Married Women* § 21, at 164–78 (Jersey City, F.D. Linn & Co. 1882); James Schouler, *A Treatise on the Law of the Domestic Relations* §§ 63–71, at 101–19 (Boston, Little, Brown, & Co. 5th ed. 1895).

106. See Clark, supra note 105, § 6.3, at 190; Kelly, supra note 105, § 21, at 167.

107. See Jordan Marsh Co. v. Hedtler, 130 N.E. 78, 79 (Mass. 1921); Gimbel Bros. v. Pinto, 145 A.2d 865, 867 (Pa. Super. Ct. 1958).

108. See Sharpe Furniture, Inc. v. Buckstaff, 299 N.W.2d 219, 224 (Wis. 1980).

109. See Graves v. Graves, 36 Iowa 310, 313 (1873); *Eames,* 101 Mass. at 80–81; *Gill,* 5 R.I. at 345.

110. See, e.g., Cal. Fam. Code § 914(a) (West 2004); Colo. Rev. Stat. § 14-6-110 (2011); Conn. Gen. Stat. Ann. § 46b-37(b) (West 2009); Haw. Rev. Stat. § 510-8(h) (2008); 750 Ill. Comp. Stat. Ann. 65/15(a)(1) (West 2009); Iowa Code Ann. § 597.14 (West 2001); Mass. Ann. Laws ch. 209, § 1 (LexisNexis 2011); Mont. Code Ann. § 40-2-106 (2011); N.Y. Jud. Ct. Acts Law § 412 (McKinney 2008); N.D. Cent. Code § 14-07-08(3) (2009); Ohio Rev. Code Ann. § 3103.03(C) (LexisNexis Supp. 2013); Okla. Stat. Ann. tit. 43, § 209.1 (West 2001); Or. Rev. Stat. Ann. § 108.040(1) (West Supp. 2013); 23 Pa. Cons. Stat. Ann. § 4102 (West 2010); S.D. Codified Laws § 25-7-2 (2004); Tex. Fam. Code Ann. § 2.501(b) (West 2006); Va. Code Ann. § 55-37 (2012); Wash. Rev. Code Ann. § 26.16.205 (West Supp. 2013); Wyo. Stat. Ann. § 20-1-201 (2013); Davis v. Baxter Cnty. Reg'l Hosp., 855 S.W.2d 303, 305–06 (Ark. 1993); Bartrom v. Adjustment Bureau, Inc., 618 N.E.2d 1, 8 (Ind. 1993); St. Francis Reg'l Med. Ctr., Inc. v. Bowles, 836 P.2d 1123, 1128 (Kan. 1992); Hawley v. Hawley, 904 S.W.2d 584, 585–86 (Mo. Ct. App. 1995); Cheshire Med. Ctr. v. Holbrook, 663 A.2d 1344, 1345–47 (N.H. 1995); Jersey Shore Med. Ctr.-Fitkin Hosp. v. Estate of Baum, 417 A.2d 1003, 1005 (N.J. 1980); Med. Bus. Assocs., Inc. v. Steiner, 588 N.Y.S.2d 890, 890 (App. Div. 1992); N.C. Baptist Hosps., Inc. v. Harris, 354 S.E.2d 471, 472–74 (N.C. 1987); Landmark Med. Ctr. v. Gauthier, 635 A.2d 1145, 1152 (R.I. 1994); Richland Mem'l Hosp. v. Burton, 318 S.E.2d 12, 13 (S.C. 1984); Kilbourne v. Hanzelik, 648 S.W.2d 932, 934 (Tenn. 1983); sources cited infra note 111.

111. See Ky. Rev. Stat. Ann. § 404.040 (LexisNexis 2010); Neb. Rev. Stat. § 42-201 (2008); Nev. Rev. Stat. Ann. §§ 123.090, 123.110 (LexisNexis 2010); Swogger v. Sunrise Hosp., Inc., 496 P.2d 751, 752 (Nev. 1972) (per curiam); Marshfield Clinic v. Discher, 314 N.W.2d 326, 327–31 (Wis. 1982).

112. See Brewer v. Brewer, 66 So. 2d 450, 451 (Ala. 1953); Wright v. Wright, No. CN90-7815, 1990 WL 255821, at *2–3 (Del. Fam. Ct. Nov. 29, 1990); Austin v. Austin, 124 N.Y.S.2d 900, 901–02 (App. Div. 1953) (per curiam); Smith v. Smith, 92 N.E.2d 418, 418–19 (Ohio Ct. App. 1949); Commonwealth v. George, 56 A.2d 228, 231 (Pa. 1948); Shilling v. Shilling, 575 A.2d 145, 147 (Pa. Super. Ct. 1990); Commonwealth ex rel. Gauby v. Gauby, 289 A.2d 745, 746–47 (Pa. Super. Ct. 1972); McGuire v. McGuire, 59 N.W.2d 336, 342 (Neb. 1953).

113. Va. Code Ann. § 55-37.

114. See 1990 WL 255821, at *1.

115. Id. at *1–2.

116. See id. at *1.

117. Id. at *2.

118. Id. at *1.

119. See id.

120. Id. at *2.

121. Id. at *1.

122. Id. at *3.

123. Id. at *2.

124. See id. at *3.

125. 59 N.W.2d 336 (Neb. 1953).

126. Id. at 336–37.

127. See id. at 338.

128. Id. at 337.

129. See id. at 337–38.

130. See id. at 337.

131. Id. at 337–38.

132. Id. at 342.

133. See Ga. Code Ann. § 19-3-8 (2010); La. Rev. Stat. Ann. § 9:291 (2008); Nogueira v. Nogueira, 444 N.E.2d 940, 941 (Mass. 1983); Brown v. Brown, 409 N.E.2d 717, 718–19 (Mass. 1980); Cook v. Hanover Ins. Co., 592 N.E.2d 773, 775–76 (Mass. App. Ct. 1992); Rupert v. Stienne, 528 P.2d 1013, 1017 (Nev. 1974); Tevis v. Tevis, 400 A.2d 1189, 1192 (N.J. 1979); Stoker v. Stoker, 616 P.2d 590, 592 (Utah 1980); Richard v. Richard, 300 A.2d 637, 641 (Vt. 1973).

134. Douglas D. Scherer, "Tort Remedies for Victims of Domestic Abuse," 43 S.C. L. Rev. 543, 565 (1992) (footnote omitted).

135. See Fla. Farm Bureau Ins. Co. v. Gov't Employees Ins. Co., 387 So. 2d 932, 934 (Fla. 1980); Principal Cas. Ins. Co. v. Blair, 500 N.W.2d 67, 68–70 (Iowa 1993); State Farm Fire & Cas. Co. v. White, 993 S.W.2d 40, 43 (Tenn. Ct. App. 1998); Shannon v. Shannon, 442 N.W.2d 25, 35 (Wis. 1989).

136. 16 Cal. Rptr. 2d 16, 21 (Ct. App. 1993) (Poché, J., dissenting) (citations omitted).

137. Id. at 20 (majority opinion).

138. See Bureau of Justice Statistics, U.S. Dep't of Justice, *Female Victims of Violence* 1–2, 4 (2009).

139. See supra Chapter 2.

140. See Spires v. Spires, 743 A.2d 186, 188 & n.2 (D.C. 1999).

141. Massey v. Massey, 807 S.W.2d 391, 399 (Tex. Ct. App. 1991).

142. See Myers v. Myers, No. L-99-1168, slip op. at 3 (Ohio Ct. App. Mar. 31, 2000); see also In re Estate of Collins, 3 Pa. D. & C.5th 34, 40–41 (C.P. Bucks Cnty. 2008).

143. Lenore J. Weitzman, *The Divorce Revolution: The Unexpected Social and Economic Consequences for Women and Children in America* 323 (1985).

144. See, e.g., Saul D. Hoffman and Greg J. Duncan, "What *Are* the Economic Consequences of Divorce?," 25 *Demography* 641, 644 (1988); Richard R.

Peterson, "A Re-Evaluation of the Economic Consequences of Divorce," 61 *Am. Soc. Rev.* 528, 529–35 (1996).

145. See, e.g., Karen C. Holden and Pamela J. Smock, "The Economic Costs of Marital Disruption: Why Do Women Bear a Disproportionate Cost?," 17 *Ann. Rev. Soc.* 51, 53 (1991); Matthew McKeever and Nicholas H. Wolfinger, "Reexamining the Economic Costs of Marital Disruption for Women," 82 *Soc. Sci. Q.* 202, 207, 215 (2001); Barbara R. Rowe and Jean M. Lown, "The Economics of Divorce and Remarriage for Rural Utah Families," 16 *J. Contemp. L.* 301, 319, 322, 324–25 (1990); Pamela J. Smock, "The Economic Costs of Marital Disruption for Young Women over the Past Two Decades," 30 *Demography* 353, 366–67 (1993).

146. See, e.g., Juliet B. Schor, *The Overspent American: Upscaling, Downshifting, and the New Consumer* 6–7, 11–12, 19–20, 72 (1998); Elizabeth Warren and Amelia Warren Tyagi, *The Two-Income Trap: Why Middle-Class Mothers and Fathers Are Going Broke* 8–10, 110–13 (2003); Marsha Garrison, "The Economic Consequences of Divorce," 32 *Fam. & Conciliation Cts. Rev.* 10, 11 (1994).

147. See, e.g., Timothy S. Grall, U.S. Census Bureau, U.S. Dep't of Commerce, *Support Providers: 2002*, at 6 (2005); Gordon H. Lester, Bureau of the Census, U.S. Dep't of Commerce, Ser. P-60, No. 173, *Child Support and Alimony: 1989*, at 12 (1991); Yoram Weiss and Robert J. Willis, "Transfers Among Divorced Couples: Evidence and Interpretation," 11 *J. Lab. Econ.* 629, 637–39, 644 (1993).

148. See Cal. Fam. Code § 4320(*l*) (West Supp. 2013); Del. Code Ann. tit. 13, § 1512(d) (2009); Ind. Code Ann. § 31-15-7-2(3) (LexisNexis 2007); Me. Rev. Stat. Ann. tit. 19-A, § 951-A(2)(A) (2012); Mass. Ann. Laws ch. 208, § 49(b) (LexisNexis Supp. 2013); Or. Rev. Stat. Ann. § 107.407 (West Supp. 2013); Tex. Fam. Code Ann. § 8.054 (West Supp. 2012); Utah Code Ann. § 30-3-5(8)(j) (LexisNexis Supp. 2013).

149. See U.S. Census Bureau, U.S. Dep't of Commerce, *Custodial Mothers and Fathers and Their Child Support: 2007*, at 2, 4 (2009).

150. See id. at 8–9; Marsha Garrison, "The Goals and Limits of Child Support Policy," in *Child Support: The Next Frontier* 16, 17 (J. Thomas Oldham and Marygold S. Melli eds., 2000); Elaine Sorensen, "A National Profile of Nonresident Fathers and Their Ability to Pay Child Support," 59 *J. Marriage & Fam.* 785, 793 (1997).

151. Terry Hekker, *Ever Since Adam and Eve* 11 (1979).

152. Terry Martin Hekker, "Paradise Lost (Domestic Division)," *N.Y. Times,* Jan. 1, 2006, § 9, at 9.

153. Terry Martin Hekker, *Disregard First Book* (2009).

154. See supra Chapter 1.

155. See supra Chapter 1.

156. For some studies of gender bias in federal courts, see D.C. Circuit Task Force on Gend., Race & Ethnic Bias, *The Gender, Race, and Ethnic Bias Task Force Project in the D.C. Circuit* (1995); *The Effects of Gender in the Federal Courts: The Final Report of the Ninth Circuit Gender Bias Task Force* (1993); "Report of the Second Circuit Task Force on Gender, Racial, and Ethnic Fairness in the Courts," 1997 *Ann. Surv. Am. L. 9.*

157. See, e.g., Dep't of Research & Analysis, State Bar of Tex., *The Gender Bias Task Force of Texas Final Report* 66–78 (1994); *Gender and Justice in the Courts: A Report to the Supreme Court of Georgia by the Commission on Gender Bias in the Judicial System* 1–50 (1991); Neil Websdale, *Rural Woman Battering and the Justice System: An Ethnography* 91–158 (1998).

158. See Hasday, supra note 5, at 1392–406, 1464–74, 1504.

159. E. J. Graff, *What Is Marriage For?* 222–23 (1999).

160. Sanford N. Katz, *Family Law in America* 7 (2003).

161. See, e.g., Alaska Stat. § 11.41.432 (2012); Ariz. Rev. Stat. Ann. § 13-1407(D) (2010); Cal. Penal Code §§ 261–262 (West 2008); Conn. Gen. Stat. Ann. §§ 53a-65(2)–(3), 53a-70b(b) (West 2012); Idaho Code Ann. § 18-6107 (Supp. 2013); Iowa Code Ann. § 709.4(1)–(2) (West 2003); Ky. Rev. Stat. Ann. § 510.035 (LexisNexis Supp. 2012); La. Rev. Stat. Ann. § 14:93.5 (2012); Md. Code Ann., Crim. Law § 3-318 (LexisNexis 2012); Mich. Comp. Laws Ann. § 750.520*l* (West 2004); Minn. Stat. § 609.349 (2012); Miss. Code Ann. § 97-3-99 (2006); Nev. Rev. Stat. Ann. § 200.373 (LexisNexis 2012); N.H. Rev. Stat. Ann. § 632-A:2 (LexisNexis Supp. 2012); Ohio Rev. Code Ann. §§ 2907.01(L), 2907.02 (LexisNexis 2010); Okla. Stat. Ann. tit. 21, § 1111 (West Supp. 2013); R.I. Gen. Laws §§ 11-37-1(9), 11-37-2 (2002); S.C. Code Ann. § 16-3-658 (2003); S.D. Codified Laws § 22-22-7.4 (2006); Wash. Rev. Code Ann. §§ 9A.44.010(3), 9A.44.050, 9A.44.060, 9A.44.100 (West 2009); W. Va. Code Ann. § 61-8B-1(6) (LexisNexis 2010); Wyo. Stat. Ann. § 6-2-307(a) (2013).

162. See, e.g., Va. Code Ann. §§ 18.2-61(C), 18.2-67.1(C), 18.2-67.2(C) (Supp. 2013).

163. See, e.g., S.C. Code Ann. § 16-3-658.

164. See statutes cited supra notes 161–63.

165. See Hasday, supra note 5, at 1494–95 & nn.444–45.

166. See id. at 1495 & n.446.

167. See S.F. v. State ex rel. T.M., 695 So. 2d 1186, 1187–89 (Ala. Civ. App. 1996).

168. See David Finkelhor and Kersti Yllo, *License To Rape: Sexual Abuse of Wives* 6–7 (1985); Diana E. H. Russell, *Rape in Marriage* 1–2 (rev. ed. 1990); Patricia Tjaden and Nancy Thoennes, U.S. Dep't of Justice, *Extent, Nature, and Consequences of Intimate Partner Violence: Findings from the National Violence Against Women Survey* 9–10, 13 (2000).

169. See, e.g., Raquel Kennedy Bergen, *Wife Rape: Understanding the Response of Survivors and Service Providers* 59–61 (1996); Finkelhor and Yllo, supra note 168, at 117–38; Russell, supra note 168, at 190–205; David Finkelhor and Kersti Yllo, "Rape in Marriage: A Sociological View," in *The Dark Side of Families: Current Family Violence Research* 119, 126–27 (David Finkelhor et al. eds., 1983); Patricia Mahoney, "High Rape Chronicity and Low Rates of Help-Seeking Among Wife Rape Survivors in a Nonclinical Sample: Implications for Research and Practice," 5 *Violence Against Women* 993, 993–94 (1999); Mark A. Whatley, "For Better or Worse: The Case of Marital Rape," 8 *Violence & Victims* 29, 33–34 (1993).

170. Maine, supra note 2, at 170.

171. See, e.g., Ira Mark Ellman, "'Contract Thinking' Was *Marvin*'s Fatal Flaw," 76 *Notre Dame L. Rev.* 1365, 1367 (2001).

172. Milton C. Regan, Jr., *Family Law and the Pursuit of Intimacy* 35 (1993); see also Lawrence M. Friedman, *Private Lives: Families, Individuals, and the Law* 6 (2004).

173. Jean L. Cohen, *Regulating Intimacy: A New Legal Paradigm* 184 (2002).

174. Jana B. Singer, "The Privatization of Family Law," 1992 *Wis. L. Rev.* 1443, 1444.

175. Laurence C. Nolan, "Legal Strangers and the Duty of Support: Beyond the Biological Tie—But How Far Beyond the Marital Tie?," 41 *Santa Clara L. Rev.* 1, 34 (2000).

176. Mary Ann Glendon, *The New Family and the New Property* 43 (1981).

177. William N. Eskridge, Jr., *Gaylaw: Challenging the Apartheid of the Closet* 271 (1999); see also Bruce C. Hafen, "The Family as an Entity," 22 *U.C. Davis L. Rev.* 865, 868, 897 (1989).

178. Mary Ann Glendon, *Abortion and Divorce in Western Law* 63–64 (1987).

179. John H. Langbein, "The Contractarian Basis of the Law of Trusts," 105 *Yale L.J.* 625, 630 (1995) (footnote omitted).

180. William N. Eskridge Jr., "Family Law Pluralism: The Guided-Choice Regime of Menus, Default Rules, and Override Rules," 100 *Geo. L.J.* 1881, 1948 (2012).

181. Stephen J. Morse, "Family Law in Transition: From Traditional Families to Individual Liberty," in *Changing Images of the Family* 319, 339 (Virginia Tufte and Barbara Myerhoff eds., 1979).

182. Margaret Ryznar and Anna Stepień-Sporek, "To Have and To Hold, for Richer or Richer: Premarital Agreements in the Comparative Context," 13 *Chap. L. Rev.* 27, 37 (2009).

183. Elizabeth S. Scott and Robert E. Scott, "A Contract Theory of Marriage," in *The Fall and Rise of Freedom of Contract* 201, 203 (F.H. Buckley ed., 1999).

184. Id. at 236; see also Anne C. Dailey, "Federalism and Families," 143 *U. Pa. L. Rev.* 1787, 1830 (1995); Jennifer Wriggins, "Marriage Law and Family Law: Autonomy, Interdependence, and Couples of the Same Gender," 41 *B.C. L. Rev.* 265, 277 (2000).

185. Walter Otto Weyrauch, "Metamorphoses of Marriage," 13 *Fam. L.Q.* 415, 417 (1980).

186. Singer, supra note 174, at 1567.

187. Janet L. Dolgin, "The Family in Transition: From *Griswold* to *Eisenstadt* and Beyond," 82 *Geo. L.J.* 1519, 1560 (1994).

188. Alicia Brokars Kelly, "The Marital Partnership Pretense and Career Assets: The Ascendancy of Self over the Marital Community," 81 *B.U. L. Rev.* 59, 67 (2001).

189. Ann Laquer Estin, "Golden Anniversary Reflections: Changes in Marriage After Fifty Years," 42 *Fam. L.Q.* 333, 334–35 (2008); see also "The Course of Change in Family Law 1978–79," 5 *Fam. L. Rep.* 4013, 4015 (1979); Sean Hannon Williams, "Postnuptial Agreements," 2007 *Wis. L. Rev.* 827, 828.

190. 125 U.S. 190, 211 (1888). For use of *Maynard* in telling the status to contract story, see Regan, supra note 172, at 10; Eskridge, supra note 180, at 1903–04; Singer, supra note 174, at 1456; Cynthia Starnes, "Divorce and the Displaced Homemaker: A Discourse on Playing with Dolls, Partnership Buyouts and Dissociation Under No-Fault," 60 *U. Chi. L. Rev.* 67, 106–07 (1993).

191. See Cohen, supra note 173, at 185; Herbert Jacob, *Silent Revolution: The Transformation of Divorce Law in the United States* 7 (1988); Regan, supra note 172, at 37; Eskridge, supra note 180, at 1905–10.

192. 388 U.S. 1 (1967).

193. See Cohen, supra note 173, at 185; Janet L. Dolgin, *Defining the Family: Law, Technology, and Reproduction in an Uneasy Age* 35–36 (1997); Joanna L. Grossman and Lawrence M. Friedman, *Inside the Castle: Law and the Family in 20th Century America* 209 (2011); Regan, supra note 172, at 38; Dolgin, supra note 187, at 1560–61; Eskridge, supra note 180, at 1894, 1919–23; Estin, supra note 189, at 335; Scott and Scott, supra note 183, at 204; Singer, supra note 174, at 1445.

194. See Cohen, supra note 173, at 185; Dolgin, supra note 193, at 36; Grossman and Friedman, supra note 193, at 209; Katz, supra note 160, at 7; Harry D. Krause and David D. Meyer, *Family Law in a Nutshell* 14–15 (5th ed. 2007); Regan, supra note 172, at 37; Dolgin, supra note 187, at 1560; Eskridge, supra note 180, at 1894, 1916–19; Estin, supra note 189, at 335; Scott and Scott, supra note 183, at 203–04; Singer, supra note 174, at 1460; "Developments

in the Law: The Law of Marriage and Family," 116 *Harv. L. Rev.* 1996, 2078 (2003).

195. See Cohen, supra note 173, at 186; Dolgin, supra note 193, at 36; Regan, supra note 172, at 40; Singer, supra note 174, at 1449–51.

196. See *Loving,* 388 U.S. at 2, 6 & n.5, 11–12.

197. See, e.g., Planned Parenthood of Se. Pa. v. Casey, 505 U.S. 833, 847–48 (1992); Bowers v. Hardwick, 478 U.S. 186, 210 (1986) (Blackmun, J., dissenting); id. at 216 (Stevens, J., dissenting).

198. See, e.g., Loving v. Virginia *in a Post-Racial World: Rethinking Race, Sex, and Marriage* (Kevin Noble Maillard and Rose Cuison Villazor eds., 2012); Phyl Newbeck, *Virginia Hasn't Always Been for Lovers: Interracial Marriage Bans and the Case of Richard and Mildred Loving* (2004); Peter Wallenstein, *Tell the Court I Love My Wife: Race, Marriage, and Law—An American History* (2002).

199. See, e.g., Carol Sanger, Introduction to *Family Law Stories* 1, 1 (Carol Sanger ed., 2008); Lynn D. Wardle, "*Loving v. Virginia* and the Constitutional Right to Marry, 1790–1990," 41 *How. L.J.* 289, 289 (1998).

200. See Symposium, "Commemorating *Loving v. Virginia,*" 51 *How. L.J.* ix (2007); Symposium, "Forty Years of *Loving*: Confronting Issues of Race, Sexuality, and the Family in the Twenty-First Century," 76 *Fordham L. Rev.* 2669 (2008); Symposium, "Intimacy, Race, Marriage, and the Meanings of Equality: Perspectives on the 40th Anniversary of *Loving v. Virginia,*" 2007 *Wis. L. Rev.* 239; Symposium, "Law and the Politics of Marriage: *Loving v. Virginia* After Thirty Years," 12 *BYU J. Pub. L.* 201 (1998); Symposium, "Law and the Politics of Marriage: *Loving v. Virginia* After 30 Years," 47 *Cath. U. L. Rev.* 1207 (1998); Symposium, "Law and the Politics of Marriage: *Loving v. Virginia* After Thirty Years," 41 *How. L.J.* 215 (1998).

201. See *The Loving Story* (HBO 2012).

202. See *Mr. and Mrs. Loving* (Showtime 1996).

203. See Editorial, "Loving Day: When Race Matters Less," *Phila. Inquirer,* June 12, 2008, at A22; Neely Tucker, "Mildred Loving Followed Her Heart and Made History," *Wash. Post,* May 6, 2008, at C1, C8.

204. Robert F. Drinan, "American Laws Regulating the Formation of the Marriage Contract," 383 *Annals Am. Acad. Pol. & Soc. Sci.* 48, 49 (1969).

205. Angela Harris, Foreword to Loving v. Virginia *in a Post-Racial World: Rethinking Race, Sex, and Marriage,* supra note 198, at xv, xviii.

206. See supra Chapter 1.

207. See, e.g., Ariz. Const. art. 20, para. 2; Idaho Const. art. I, § 4; N.M. Const. art. XXI, § 1; Okla. Const. art. I, § 2; Utah Const. art. III, § 1; Cleveland v. United States, 329 U.S. 14, 16, 18–19 (1946); Reynolds v. United States, 98 U.S. 145, 164–67 (1879); Potter v. Murray City, 760 F.2d 1065, 1067 (10th Cir. 1985); Brown v. Buhman, 947 F. Supp. 2d 1170, 1234 (D. Utah 2013); Barlow v.

Blackburn, 798 P.2d 1360, 1361 (Ariz. Ct. App. 1990); State v. Holm, 137 P.3d 726, 730 (Utah 2006); State v. Green, 99 P.3d 820, 822, 834 (Utah 2004).

208. See Moe v. Dinkins, 533 F. Supp. 623, 629 (S.D.N.Y. 1981), aff'd, 669 F.2d 67, 68 (2d Cir. 1982) (per curiam); In re Barbara Haven, 86 Pa. D. & C. 141, 141–45 (Orphans' Ct. 1953).

209. See Muth v. Frank, 412 F.3d 808, 810 (7th Cir. 2005); Singh v. Singh, 569 A.2d 1112, 1121 (Conn. 1990); State v. Sharon H., 429 A.2d 1321, 1328 (Del. Super. Ct. 1981); Marriage of MEW & MLB, 4 Pa. D. & C.3d 51, 59 (C.P. Allegheny Cnty. 1977); Rhodes v. McAfee, 457 S.W.2d 522, 524 (Tenn. 1970).

210. See Goodridge v. Dep't of Pub. Health, 798 N.E.2d 941, 965, 969 & n.34 (Mass. 2003); Lewis v. Harris, 908 A.2d 196, 206–08 & n.10 (N.J. 2006).

211. See Lawrence v. Texas, 539 U.S. 558, 590 (2003) (Scalia, J., dissenting); Kerrigan v. Comm'r of Pub. Health, 957 A.2d 407, 523 n.14 (Conn. 2008) (Zarella, J., dissenting).

212. See *Federal Marriage Amendment (The Musgrave Amendment): Hearing on H.R.J. Res. 56 Before the Subcomm. on the Constitution of the House Comm. on the Judiciary*, 108th Cong. 39 (2004) (statement of Rep. King); 142 Cong. Rec. 16,971 (1996) (statement of Rep. Largent); id. at 17,089 (statement of Rep. Hyde); see also Baehr v. Miike, 23 Fam. L. Rep. (BNA) 2001, 2011 (Haw. Cir. Ct. 1996).

213. See *Defense of Marriage Act: Hearing on H.R. 3396 Before the Subcomm. on the Constitution of the House Comm. on the Judiciary*, 104th Cong. 88 (1996) (statement of Hadley Arkes, Edward Ney Professor of Jurisprudence and American Institutions, Amherst College); William N. Eskridge, Jr., *The Case for Same-Sex Marriage: From Sexual Liberty to Civilized Commitment* 145 (1996); Evan Gerstmann, *Same-Sex Marriage and the Constitution* 104 (2004); Sherif Girgis et al., *What Is Marriage?* 18–20, 51–52, 56–57, 68, 74, 76, 78–80, 86, 90 (2012); David L. Chambers, "Polygamy and Same-Sex Marriage," 26 *Hofstra L. Rev.* 53, 60 (1997); James M. Donovan, "Rock-Salting the Slippery Slope: Why Same-Sex Marriage Is Not a Commitment to Polygamous Marriage," 29 *N. Ky. L. Rev.* 521, 557 (2002); Sarah Barringer Gordon, "Chapel and State: Laws Written in the 19th Century to Prevent Polygamy Are Thwarting the Efforts of Today's Same-Sex Marriage Advocates," *Legal Aff.*, Jan./Feb. 2003, at 46, 46; Maura I. Strassberg, "Distinctions of Form or Substance: Monogamy, Polygamy and Same-Sex Marriage," 75 *N.C. L. Rev.* 1501, 1622 (1997); Lynn D. Wardle, "Legal Claims for Same-Sex Marriage: Efforts to Legitimate a Retreat from Marriage by Redefining Marriage," 39 *S. Tex. L. Rev.* 735, 749 (1998).

214. See Conn. Gen. Stat. Ann. § 46b-29 (West 2009); Ky. Rev. Stat. Ann. §§ 402.020(1)(a), 402.990(2) (LexisNexis 2010); Minn. Stat. § 517.03(2)

(2012); N.J. Stat. Ann. § 37:1-9 (West 2002); 23 Pa. Cons. Stat. Ann. § 1304(c) (West 2010); R.I. Gen. Laws § 15-1-5(2) (2013); S.C. Code Ann. § 20-1-10(A) (Supp. 2012); Tenn. Code Ann. § 36-3-109 (2010); Vt. Stat. Ann. tit. 15, § 512 (2010); W. Va. Code Ann. § 48-3-103(a)(3)(A) (LexisNexis 2009).

215. Ky. Rev. Stat. Ann. § 402.020(1)(a).

216. See id. § 402.990(2).

217. Vt. Stat. Ann. tit. 15, § 512.

218. Id. § 514(e); see also Klittner v. Steiner, 610 A.2d 149, 149 (Vt. 1992).

219. W. Va. Code Ann. § 48-3-103(a).

220. Tenn. Code Ann. § 36-3-109 (2010).

221. Becker v. Judd, 646 F. Supp. 2d 923, 925 (M.D. Tenn. 2009).

222. 23 Pa. Cons. Stat. Ann. § 1304(c) (West 2010).

223. Neb. Rev. Stat. § 42-102 (2008).

224. W. Va. Code Ann. § 48-3-103(a).

225. N.J. Stat. Ann. § 37:1-9 (West 2002); see also Lewis v. Harris, No. MER-L-15-03, slip op. at 60–61 (N.J. Super. Ct. Law Div. Nov. 5, 2003), aff'd, 875 A.2d 259 (N.J. Super. Ct. App. Div. 2005), aff'd in part & modified in part, 908 A.2d 196 (N.J. 2006).

226. Ohio Rev. Code Ann. § 3101.06 (LexisNexis 2008).

227. Cal. Health & Safety Code § 120600 (West 2012).

228. Vt. Stat. Ann. tit. 18, § 1105 (2012).

229. Wis. Stat. Ann. § 765.03(2) (West 2009).

230. See In re Estate of Toutant, 633 N.W.2d 692, 697–700 (Wis. Ct. App. 2001); Falk v. Falk, 462 N.W.2d 547, 547–48 (Wis. Ct. App. 1990).

231. Ala. Code § 30-2-8 (LexisNexis 2011).

232. G.G. v. R.S.G., 668 So. 2d 828, 831 (Ala. Civ. App. 1995) (per curiam).

233. Id. at 831–32.

234. Ala. Code § 30-2-10; see also Ex parte Rawls, 953 So. 2d 374, 387 (Ala. 2006).

235. Del. Code Ann. tit. 13, § 101(b) (2009).

236. See, e.g., Edwardson v. Edwardson, 798 S.W.2d 941, 946 (Ky. 1990); State Dep't of Human Servs. ex rel. K.A.G. v. T.D.G., 861 P.2d 990, 994 (Okla. 1993).

237. See Perkinson v. Perkinson, 989 N.E.2d 758, 760, 762 (Ind. 2013); Houck v. Ousterhout, 861 So. 2d 1000, 1001–02 (Miss. 2003); Thomas B. v. Lydia D., 886 N.Y.S.2d 22, 27 (App. Div. 2009); Tiokasin v. Haas, 370 N.W.2d 559, 562 (N.D. 1985); *State Dep't of Human Servs. ex rel. K.A.G.*, 861 P.2d at 992–93, 995; Huck v. Huck, 734 P.2d 417, 419 (Utah 1986); Kelley v. Kelley, 449 S.E.2d 55, 56 (Va. 1994); Chen v. Warner, 695 N.W.2d 758, 762 n.2 (Wis. 2005).

238. See Guille v. Guille, 492 A.2d 175, 178–79 (Conn. 1985); Wood v. Propeck, 728 N.W.2d 757, 758 (Wis. Ct. App. 2007).

239. See In re Marriage of Rife, 878 N.E.2d 775, 778–79 (Ill. App. Ct. 2007); In re Custody of Neal, 393 A.2d 1057, 1059 (Pa. Super. Ct. 1978).

240. See White v. Laingor, 746 N.E.2d 150, 152 (Mass. 2001).

241. See Taylor v. Taylor, 623 S.E.2d 477, 478–79 (Ga. 2005); Monmouth Cnty. Div. of Soc. Servs. for D.M. v. G.D.M., 705 A.2d 408, 409–10, 415 (N.J. Super. Ct. Ch. Div. 1997).

242. See *Restatement (Second) of Contracts* § 14 (1981).

243. Carmel Shalev, *Birth Power: The Case for Surrogacy* 18–19 (1989).

244. Marjorie Maguire Shultz, "Contractual Ordering of Marriage: A New Model for State Policy," 70 *Cal. L. Rev.* 204, 291 (1982).

245. Gregg Temple, "Freedom of Contract and Intimate Relationships," 8 *Harv. J.L. & Pub. Pol'y* 121, 153 (1985).

246. Robert H. Mnookin, "Divorce Bargaining: The Limits on Private Ordering," 18 *U. Mich. J.L. Reform* 1015, 1018 (1985).

247. Brian Bix, "Bargaining in the Shadow of Love: The Enforcement of Premarital Agreements and How We Think About Marriage," 40 *Wm. & Mary L. Rev.* 145, 162 (1998).

248. See Nelson Manfred Blake, *The Road to Reno: A History of Divorce in the United States* 7–8 (1962); Isabel Drummond, *Getting a Divorce* 71 (1931); Michael Grossberg, *Governing the Hearth: Law and the Family in Nineteenth-Century America* 251 (1985).

249. Brown v. Brown, 281 S.W.2d 492, 498 (Tenn. 1955); see also 1 Joel Prentiss Bishop, *New Commentaries on Marriage, Divorce, and Separation* § 56, at 23–24 (Chicago, T.H. Flood & Co. 1891); Nelson, supra note 103, at 18; W.C. Rodgers, *A Treatise on the Law of Domestic Relations* 3 (Chicago, T.H. Flood & Co. 1899); Schouler, supra note 83, at 22–23.

250. See Fuchs v. Fuchs, 64 N.Y.S.2d 487, 489 (Sup. Ct. 1946).

251. See Ass'n of the Bar of the City of N.Y., *Report of the Special Committee on the Improvement of the Divorce Laws* 1 (1950); Comm. on Law Reform, Ass'n of the Bar of the City of N.Y., *Report on the Proposal to Amend the Civil Practice Act by Providing for Grounds Additional to Adultery for Absolute Divorce* 1–2 (1945); Hubert J. O'Gorman, *Lawyers and Matrimonial Cases: A Study of Informal Pressures in Private Professional Practice* 20–21 (1963); Walter Gellhorn, "The Administration of Laws Relating to the Family in the City of New York," in *Children and Families in the Courts of New York City* 17, 285–86 (1954).

252. Dorothy Jarvis, "I Was the 'Unknown Blonde' in 100 New York Divorces!: By a Professional Co-Respondent," *N.Y. Sunday Mirror,* Feb. 18, 1934, Magazine, at 10.

253. Id.

254. Id.

255. Id. at 11.

256. See Martha Albertson Fineman, *The Illusion of Equality: The Rhetoric and Reality of Divorce Reform* 32–33, 196 n.46 (1991); Glendon, supra note 178, at 81–82; Allen M. Parkman, *No-Fault Divorce: What Went Wrong?*, at xii (1992); Weitzman, supra note 143, at 8–9, 14, 366; Kay, supra note 48, at 28 n.118; "The Course of Change in Family Law 1978–79," supra note 189, at 4015.

257. See Fineman, supra note 256, at 56.

258. See Charles E. Welch, III and Sharon Price-Bonham, "A Decade of No-Fault Divorce Revisited: California, Georgia, and Washington," 45 *J. Marriage & Fam.* 411, 415 tbl.2 (1983).

259. For an empirical study, see H. Elizabeth Peters, "Marriage and Divorce: Informational Constraints and Private Contracting," 76 *Am. Econ. Rev.* 437, 452–53 (1986).

260. See Ryan v. Ryan, 277 So. 2d 266, 273–74 (Fla. 1973); id. at 277–78 (Roberts, J., dissenting); Gleason v. Gleason, 256 N.E.2d 513, 519 (N.Y. 1970).

4. A Progress Narrative for Children

1. 648 P.2d 1364, 1377 (Utah 1982).

2. In re Westerville, No. 12114 (Mich. Prob. Ct. 1976), reprinted in Westerville v. Kalamazoo Cnty. Dep't of Soc. Servs., 534 F. Supp. 1088 app. at 1102 (W.D. Mich. 1982).

3. Commonwealth v. Ogin, 540 A.2d 549, 554 (Pa. Super. Ct. 1988); see also In re D.T., 35 Pa. D. & C.4th 454, 461 (C.P. Dauphin Cnty. 1996) (quoting this passage).

4. In re Christina L., 173 Cal. Rptr. 722, 728 (Ct. App. 1981) (citations omitted).

5. Bailey v. Lombard, 420 N.Y.S.2d 650, 654 (Sup. Ct. 1979).

6. In re Catherine S., 347 N.Y.S.2d 470, 477 (Fam. Ct. 1973).

7. In re Marriage of Wieldraayer, No. 59429-0-I, slip op. at 6 (Wash. Ct. App. Dec. 22, 2008) (per curiam).

8. Wilder-Newland v. Kessinger, 967 N.E.2d 558, 565 (Ind. Ct. App. 2012); see also Goodridge v. Dep't of Pub. Health, 798 N.E.2d 941, 972 (Mass. 2003) (Greaney, J., concurring); Bennett v. Jeffreys, 356 N.E.2d 277, 281 (N.Y. 1976).

9. Ben B. Lindsey, "The Parenthood of the State," in Nat'l Educ. Ass'n of the U.S., *Addresses and Proceedings of the Fifty-Ninth Annual Meeting Held at Des Moines, Iowa July 3–8 1921*, at 42, 42 (1921).

10. Mennemeyer v. Hart, 221 S.W.2d 960, 962 (Mo. 1949).

11. Katharine T. Bartlett, "Rethinking Parenthood as an Exclusive Status: The Need for Legal Alternatives When the Premise of the Nuclear Family Has Failed," 70 *Va. L. Rev.* 879, 886 n.49 (1984) (citation omitted).

12. Marsha Garrison, "Law Making for Baby Making: An Interpretive Approach to the Determination of Legal Parentage," 113 *Harv. L. Rev.* 835, 893–94 (2000).

13. Id. at 864 (footnotes omitted).

14. Stuart N. Hart, "From Property to Person Status: Historical Perspective on Children's Rights," 46 *Am. Psychologist* 53, 53 (1991).

15. Barbara Bennett Woodhouse, "'Who Owns the Child?': *Meyer* and *Pierce* and the Child as Property," 33 *Wm. & Mary L. Rev.* 995, 1038–39 (1992).

16. Barbara Bennett Woodhouse, "Hatching the Egg: A Child-Centered Perspective on Parents' Rights," 14 *Cardozo L. Rev.* 1747, 1811 (1993).

17. Brian H. Bix, *The Oxford Introductions to U.S. Law: Family Law* 11 (2013); see also Stephen J. Morse, "Family Law in Transition: From Traditional Families to Individual Liberty," in *Changing Images of the Family* 319, 321 (Virginia Tufte and Barbara Myerhoff eds., 1979); Irma S. Russell, "Within the Best Interests of the Child: The Factor of Parental Status in Custody Disputes Arising from Surrogacy Contracts," 27 *J. Fam. L.* 585, 618 n.104 (1989).

18. See, e.g., Holly Brewer, *By Birth or Consent: Children, Law, and the Anglo-American Revolution in Authority* 281–85 (2005); Holly Brewer, "The Transformation of Domestic Law," in 1 *The Cambridge History of Law in America* 288, 302–04, 313–14 (Michael Grossberg and Christopher Tomlins eds., 2008).

19. 1 William Blackstone, *Commentaries* *441.

20. Tapping Reeve, *The Law of Baron and Femme* 295 (New Haven, Oliver Steele 1816).

21. People ex rel. Ordronaux v. Chegaray, 18 Wend. 637, 642 (N.Y. Sup. Ct. 1836).

22. State v. Stigall, 22 N.J.L. 286, 288 (1849).

23. People ex rel. Barry v. Mercein, 3 Hill 399, 420 (N.Y. Sup. Ct. 1842) (Cowen, J.).

24. See Jill Elaine Hasday, "Parenthood Divided: A Legal History of the Bifurcated Law of Parental Relations," 90 *Geo. L.J.* 299, 318–28 (2002).

25. Elizabeth Cady Stanton, *Address to the Legislature of New-York* 14–15 (Albany, Weed, Parsons & Co. 1854).

26. Ernestine L. Rose, The Second National Convention in Worcester (Oct. 15 & 16, 1851), in 1 *History of Woman Suffrage* 237, 241 (Elizabeth Cady Stanton et al. eds., Ayer Co. 1985) (1881).

27. Commonwealth v. Maxwell, 6 Monthly L. Rep. 214, 218 (Mass. 1843).

28. Helms v. Franciscus, 2 Bland 544, 563 (Md. Ch. 1830).

29. In re Gregg, 5 N.Y. Legal Observer 265, 267–68 (N.Y. Super. Ct. 1847); see also Anonymous, 55 Ala. 428, 432–33 (1876); State v. King, 1 Ga. Dec. 93, 95–96 (Super. Ct. 1841); McKim v. McKim, 12 R.I. 462, 464–65 (1879); State ex rel. Paine v. Paine, 23 Tenn. (4 Hum.) 523, 536–37 (1843).

30. Washburn v. Washburn, 122 P.2d 96, 100 (Cal. Dist. Ct. App. 1942) (citing Cal. Civ. Code § 138).

31. Wojnarowicz v. Wojnarowicz, 137 A.2d 618, 620 (N.J. Super. Ct. Ch. Div. 1958) (citing N.J. Stat. Ann. § 9:2–4).

32. *Washburn*, 122 P.2d at 100.

33. Brashear v. Brashear, 228 P.2d 243, 246 (Idaho 1951) (citation and internal quotation marks omitted).

34. Commonwealth ex rel. Lucas v. Kreischer, 299 A.2d 243, 245 (Pa. 1973) (citations omitted).

35. Freeland v. Freeland, 159 P. 698, 699 (Wash. 1916); see also Ex parte Alderman, 73 S.E. 126, 128 (N.C. 1911); Bruce v. Bruce, 285 P. 30, 37 (Okla. 1930).

36. Jenkins v. Jenkins, 181 N.W. 826, 827 (Wis. 1921).

37. Meinhardt v. Meinhardt, 111 N.W.2d 782, 784–85 (Minn. 1961).

38. Kirstukas v. Kirstukas, 286 A.2d 535, 538 (Md. Ct. Spec. App. 1972); see also Green v. Green, 188 So. 355, 356 (Fla. 1939); Hines v. Hines, 185 N.W. 91, 92 (Iowa 1921); Tuter v. Tuter, 120 S.W.2d 203, 205 (Mo. Ct. App. 1938); Ellis v. Johnson, 260 S.W. 1010, 1012 (Mo. Ct. App. 1924); People ex rel. Sinclair v. Sinclair, 86 N.Y.S. 539, 541 (App. Div. 1904); Cox v. Cox, 532 P.2d 994, 996 (Utah 1975); Mullen v. Mullen, 49 S.E.2d 349, 354 (Va. 1948).

39. See Cathy J. Jones, "The Tender Years Doctrine: Survey and Analysis," 16 *J. Fam. L.* 695, 737–38 (1977–78).

40. See id. at 738; Allan Roth, "The Tender Years Presumption in Child Custody Disputes," 15 *J. Fam. L.* 423, 440 (1976–77).

41. See Henry H. Foster and Doris Jonas Freed, "Life with Father: 1978," 11 *Fam. L.Q.* 321, 341–42 (1978); Jones, supra note 39, at 738; Ralph J. Podell et al., "Custody—To Which Parent?," 56 *Marq. L. Rev.* 51, 52–53 (1972); David H. Radcliff, "Pennsylvania Child Custody: The Tender Years Doctrine—Reason or Excuse?," 81 *Dick. L. Rev.* 775, 776 (1976–77).

42. See Kirchberg v. Feenstra, 450 U.S. 455, 456 (1981); Orr v. Orr, 440 U.S. 268, 270–71 (1979); Stanton v. Stanton, 429 U.S. 501, 501, 503 (1977) (per curiam); Stanton v. Stanton, 421 U.S. 7, 14–15, 17 (1975); Weinberger v. Wiesenfeld, 420 U.S. 636, 637–39 (1975); Stanley v. Illinois, 405 U.S. 645, 658 (1972).

43. Pusey v. Pusey, 728 P.2d 117, 119 (Utah 1986).

44. Commonwealth ex rel. Spriggs v. Carson, 368 A.2d 635, 639 (Pa. 1977).

45. State ex rel. Watts v. Watts, 350 N.Y.S.2d 285, 290 (Fam. Ct. 1973).

46. Ex parte Devine, 398 So. 2d 686, 696 (Ala. 1981).

47. In re Marriage of Bowen, 219 N.W.2d 683, 688 (Iowa 1974).

48. Bazemore v. Davis, 394 A.2d 1377, 1383 (D.C. 1978) (en banc); see also Johnson v. Johnson, 564 P.2d 71, 75 (Alaska 1977).

49. See, e.g., Alaska Stat. § 25.20.060(a)–(b) (2012); Ark. Code Ann. § 9-13-101(a)(1)(A) (Supp. 2013); Ind. Code Ann. § 31-14-13-2 (LexisNexis 2007); Mass. Ann. Laws ch. 208, § 31 (LexisNexis 2011); N.Y. Dom. Rel. Law § 240(1)(a) (McKinney Supp. 2013); N.C. Gen. Stat. § 50-13.2(a) (Supp. 2012); Or. Rev. Stat. Ann. § 107.137 (West Supp. 2013).

50. Mary Ann Mason, *From Father's Property to Children's Rights: The History of Child Custody in the United States* (1994).

51. Id. at xiii. For a description of nineteenth-century family law in similar terms, see Michael Grossberg, *Governing the Hearth: Law and the Family in Nineteenth-Century America* 234–35 (1985).

52. Jessica Pearson and Maria A. Luchesi Ring, "Judicial Decision-Making in Contested Custody Cases," 21 *J. Fam. L.* 703, 703 (1982–83).

53. David L. Chambers, "Rethinking the Substantive Rules for Custody Disputes in Divorce," 83 *Mich. L. Rev.* 477, 499 (1984); see also Judith T. Younger, "Responsible Parents and Good Children," 14 *Law & Ineq.* 489, 497 (1996).

54. See Am. Law Inst., *Principles of the Law of Family Dissolution: Analysis and Recommendations* 308 (2002); Julie E. Artis, "Judging the Best Interests of the Child: Judges' Accounts of the Tender Years Doctrine," 38 *Law & Soc'y Rev.* 769, 769, 771, 783, 798 (2004).

55. See Jeffery M. Leving and Kenneth A. Dachman, *Fathers' Rights: Hard-Hitting & Fair Advice for Every Father Involved in a Custody Dispute* 26–29, 35 (1997); William Haddad, Introduction to Mel Roman and William Haddad, *The Disposable Parent: The Case for Joint Custody* 1, 3–4 (1978); Roman and Haddad, supra, at 40.

56. See Am. Law Inst., supra note 54, at 308; Allison Blackwell Lee, Law as a Process of Power: Construction and Application of Gender Bias in Custody Litigation 50, 99–100 (June 17, 1993) (unpublished M.A. thesis, University of North Carolina at Chapel Hill) (on file with author).

57. For some empirical studies, see Eleanor E. Maccoby and Robert H. Mnookin, *Dividing the Child: Social and Legal Dilemmas of Custody* 103, 153–54 (1992); Stephen J. Bahr et al., "Trends in Child Custody Awards: Has the Removal of Maternal Preference Made a Difference?," 28 *Fam. L.Q.* 247, 250–51, 267 (1994); Suzanne Reynolds et al., "Back to the Future: An Empirical Study of Child Custody Outcomes," 85 *N.C. L. Rev.* 1629, 1659–60, 1667 (2007); Laura E. Santilli and Michael C. Roberts, "Custody Decisions in Alabama Before and After the Abolition of the Tender Years Doctrine," 14 *Law & Hum. Behav.* 123, 126, 134 (1990).

58. 466 U.S. 429 (1984).

59. See id. at 430–31.

60. Id. at 431 (emphasis and citation omitted).

61. See id. at 430.

62. Id. at 433.

63. See, e.g., Harper v. Tipple, 184 P. 1005, 1007 (Ariz. 1919); Hernandez v. Thomas, 39 So. 641, 645 (Fla. 1905); Ex parte Kailer, 255 P. 41, 42 (Kan. 1927); State ex rel. Herrick v. Richardson, 40 N.H. 272, 275 (1860); People ex rel. Trainer v. Cooper, 8 How. Pr. 288, 293 (N.Y. Sup. Ct. 1853); Armstrong v. Stone, 50 Va. (9 Gratt.) 102, 107 (1852); Rust v. Vanvacter, 9 W. Va. 600, 612 (1866).

64. Freeman v. Chaplic, 446 N.E.2d 1369, 1376 (Mass. 1983).

65. Id. at 1373 (citation omitted).

66. In re Guardianship of Sedelmeier, 491 N.W.2d 86, 87 (S.D. 1992); see also Webb v. Webb, 546 So. 2d 1062, 1066 (Fla. Dist. Ct. App. 1989).

67. Barstad v. Frazier, 348 N.W.2d 479, 482 (Wis. 1984).

68. Brewer v. Brewer, 533 S.E.2d 541, 548 (N.C. Ct. App. 2000); see also Owenby v. Young, 579 S.E.2d 264, 266–67 (N.C. 2003); Petersen v. Rogers, 445 S.E.2d 901, 905 (N.C. 1994).

69. Sheppard v. Sheppard, 630 P.2d 1121, 1127 (Kan. 1981).

70. Id.

71. See, e.g., Finck v. O'Toole, 880 P.2d 624, 627–28 (Ariz. 1994) (en banc); In re Marriage of Freel, 448 N.W.2d 26, 26–28 (Iowa 1989).

72. See Guardianship of Z.C.W. & K.G.W., 84 Cal. Rptr. 2d 48, 50–51 (Ct. App. 1999); West v. Superior Court, 69 Cal. Rptr. 2d 160, 162–64 (Ct. App. 1997); Wakeman v. Dixon, 921 So. 2d 669, 669–70, 673 (Fla. Dist. Ct. App. 2006) (per curiam); Kazmierazak v. Query, 736 So. 2d 106, 110 (Fla. Dist. Ct. App. 1999); Music v. Rachford, 654 So. 2d 1234, 1234–35 (Fla. Dist. Ct. App. 1995) (per curiam); In re C.B.L., 723 N.E.2d 316, 320–21 (Ill. App. Ct. 1999); Janice M. v. Margaret K., 948 A.2d 73, 74–75 (Md. 2008); Alison D. v. Virginia M., 572 N.E.2d 27, 29 (N.Y. 1991) (per curiam); In re Thompson, 11 S.W.3d 913, 919, 923 (Tenn. Ct. App. 1999); In re Wells, 373 S.W.3d 174, 177–78 (Tex. Ct. App. 2012); Jones v. Barlow, 154 P.3d 808, 809–10 (Utah 2007); Titchenal v. Dexter, 693 A.2d 682, 690 (Vt. 1997).

73. *Alison D.*, 572 N.E.2d at 29.

74. *Janice M.*, 948 A.2d at 87.

75. See O'Dell v. O'Dell, 629 So. 2d 891, 891–92 (Fla. Dist. Ct. App. 1993); Meeks v. Garner, 598 So. 2d 261, 261–62 (Fla. Dist. Ct. App. 1992); In re Marriage of Engelkens, 821 N.E.2d 799, 803–06 (Ill. App. Ct. 2004); In re Marriage of Halvorsen, 521 N.W.2d 725, 729 (Iowa 1994); Pruitt v. Payne, 14 So. 3d 806, 810–11 (Miss. Ct. App. 2009); Strauss v. Tuschman, 216 P.3d 370, 373 (Utah Ct. App. 2009); In re Parentage of M.F., 228 P.3d 1270, 1272–74 (Wash. 2010) (en banc); see also Lubinski v. Lubinski, 761 N.W.2d 676, 681–82 (Wis. Ct. App. 2008).

76. 530 U.S. 57 (2000) (plurality opinion).

77. Id. at 61 (citation omitted).

78. Id. at 72.

79. See id. at 60–61, 71.

80. Id. at 72.

81. Santosky v. Kramer, 455 U.S. 745, 747–48 (1982).

82. Quilloin v. Walcott, 434 U.S. 246, 255 (1978) (citation and internal quotation marks omitted); *Santosky,* 455 U.S. at 760 n.10.

83. *Santosky,* 455 U.S. at 759–60; see also id. at 772–73 (Rehnquist, J., dissenting); M.L.B. v. S.L.J., 519 U.S. 102, 121 (1996); DeBoer v. DeBoer, 509 U.S. 1301, 1302 (1993) (Stevens, Circuit Justice).

84. 648 P.2d 1364, 1374 (Utah 1982).

85. Id. at 1375.

86. Id.

87. Id. at 1373.

88. Id. at 1377.

89. Id.

90. In re Miedl, 425 N.E.2d 137, 141 (Ind. 1981).

91. In re Scott S., 775 A.2d 1144, 1151 (Me. 2001).

92. In re Adoption of L., 462 N.E.2d 1165, 1169 (N.Y. 1984) (citations omitted); see also In re Appeal in Pima Cnty., 575 P.2d 310, 314 (Ariz. 1978) (in banc); Adoption of Kelsey S., 823 P.2d 1216, 1236 (Cal. 1992) (in bank); In re Heather B., 11 Cal. Rptr. 2d 891, 904 (Ct. App. 1992); In re Petition of Doe, 638 N.E.2d 181, 182–83 (Ill. 1994); In re Baby M, 537 A.2d 1227, 1252 (N.J. 1988); Corey L. v. Martin L., 380 N.E.2d 266, 270 (N.Y. 1978); In re Kody D.V., 548 N.W.2d 837, 841 (Wis. Ct. App. 1996).

93. Reno v. Flores, 507 U.S. 292, 304 (1993); see also Ginsberg v. New York, 390 U.S. 629, 639 (1968).

94. See Hasday, supra note 24, at 310–11, 314–17.

95. See, e.g., Doe v. Heck, 327 F.3d 492, 522–23 (7th Cir. 2003); G.C. v. R.S., 71 So. 3d 164, 165–67 (Fla. Dist. Ct. App. 2011) (per curiam); In re J.P., 692 N.E.2d 338, 345–47 (Ill. App. Ct. 1998); Willis v. State, 888 N.E.2d 177, 180–84 (Ind. 2008); State v. Arnold, 543 N.W.2d 600, 602–04 (Iowa 1996); State v. Wade, 245 P.3d 1083, 1088–91 (Kan. Ct. App. 2010); In re Welfare of the Children of N.F. & S.F., 749 N.W.2d 802, 810 (Minn. 2008); N.J. Div. of Youth & Family Servs. v. P.W.R., 11 A.3d 844, 853–56 (N.J. 2011); Raboin v. N.D. Dep't of Human Servs., 552 N.W.2d 329, 334–35 (N.D. 1996); Clark v. Clark, 683 N.E.2d 800, 802–03 (Ohio Ct. App. 1996); Chronister ex rel. Morrison v. Brenneman, 742 A.2d 190, 192–93 (Pa. Super. Ct. 1999).

96. See Ala. Code § 13A-3-24(1) (LexisNexis 2005); Alaska Stat. § 11.81.430(a)(1) (2012); Ariz. Rev. Stat. Ann. § 13-403(1) (2010); Ark. Code Ann. § 5-2-605(1) (Supp. 2011); Cal. Welf. & Inst. Code § 300(a) (West 2008);

Colo. Rev. Stat. § 18-1-703(1)(a) (2012); Conn. Gen. Stat. Ann. § 53a-18(1) (West 2012); Del. Code Ann. tit. 11, § 468(1) (2007); D.C. Code § 16-2301(23) (B)(i) (LexisNexis Supp. 2013); Haw. Rev. Stat. § 703-309(1) (2008); Ind. Code Ann. § 31-34-1-15(1) (LexisNexis 2007); La. Rev. Stat. Ann. § 14:18(4) (2007); Me. Rev. Stat. Ann. tit. 17-A, § 106(1) (Supp. 2012); Md. Code Ann., Fam. Law § 4-501(b)(2) (LexisNexis Supp. 2012); Mich. Comp. Laws Ann. § 750.136b(9) (West Supp. 2013); Minn. Stat. § 609.06(1)(6) (2012); Miss. Code Ann. § 43-21-105(m) (Supp. 2012); Mo. Ann. Stat. § 210.110(1) (West 2010); N.H. Rev. Stat. Ann. § 627:6(I) (LexisNexis Supp. 2012); N.Y. Penal Law § 35.10(1) (McKinney 2009); N.D. Cent. Code § 12.1-05-05(1) (2012); Or. Rev. Stat. Ann. § 161.205(1)(a) (West); S.C. Code Ann. § 63-7-20(4)(a) (2010); S.D. Codified Laws § 22-18-5 (2006); Tenn. Code Ann. § 39-15-401(d) (1) (Supp. 2012); Tex. Fam. Code Ann. § 261.001(1)(C) (West Supp. 2012); Utah Code Ann. § 76-2-401 (LexisNexis 2012); Wash. Rev. Code Ann. § 26.44.015 (West Supp. 2013); Wis. Stat. Ann. § 939.45(5) (West 2005); Wyo. Stat. Ann. § 14-3-202(a)(ii) (2013).

97. Okla. Stat. Ann. tit. 21, § 844 (West 2002).

98. 705 Ill. Comp. Stat. Ann. 405/2-3(2)(v) (West Supp. 2013); Nev. Rev. Stat. Ann. § 432B.150 (LexisNexis 2011); Ohio Rev. Code Ann. § 2919.22(B) (3) (LexisNexis Supp. 2013); R.I. Gen. Laws § 40-11-2(1)(i)–(ii) (Supp. 2012); W. Va. Code Ann. § 49-1-3(1) (LexisNexis Supp. 2012).

99. N.J. Stat. Ann. § 9:6-1 (West 2002).

100. Kan. Stat. Ann. § 21-5602(a)(3) (Supp. 2012).

101. See Fla. Stat. Ann. § 39.01(2) (West Supp. 2013); Ga. Code Ann. § 19-15-1(3)(A) (Supp. 2012); Iowa Code Ann. § 232.71B(4)(f) (West Supp. 2013); Ky. Rev. Stat. Ann. § 503.110(1) (LexisNexis 2008); 18 Pa. Cons. Stat. Ann. § 509(1) (West 1998).

102. See Victims of Child Abuse Act of 1990, Pub. L. No. 101-647, § 226, 104 Stat. 4792, 4806 (codified at 42 U.S.C. § 13031(a)–(b) (2006)).

103. 42 U.S.C. § 13031(c)(8).

104. See Michael J. MacKenzie et al., "Who Spanks Infants and Toddlers?: Evidence from the Fragile Families and Child Well-Being Study," 33 *Child. & Youth Services Rev.* 1364, 1364–65 (2011); Michael Regalado et al., "Parents' Discipline of Young Children: Results from the National Survey of Early Childhood Health," 113 *Pediatrics* 1952, 1954 (2004); Murray A. Straus and Julie H. Stewart, "Corporal Punishment by American Parents: National Data on Prevalence, Chronicity, Severity, and Duration, in Relation to Child and Family Characteristics," 2 *Clinical Child & Fam. Psychol. Rev.* 55, 59–60 (1999).

105. Child Trends DataBank, *Attitudes Toward Spanking: Indicators on Children and Youth* 2 (2013).

106. See James Dobson, *The New Dare to Discipline* 247–50 (1992).

107. See Comm. on Psychosocial Aspects of Child & Family Health, Am. Acad. of Pediatrics, "Guidance for Effective Discipline," 101 *Pediatrics* 723, 726 (1998); "Corporal Punishment in the Home: Commentary," *SCAN: Newsl. Sec. on Child Abuse & Neglect* (Am. Acad. of Pediatrics, Elk Grove Vill., Ill.), Mar. 1992, at 1, 2; Joan Durrant and Ron Ensom, "Physical Punishment of Children: Lessons from 20 Years of Research," 184 *CMAJ* 1373, 1374 (2012); Elizabeth Thompson Gershoff, "Corporal Punishment by Parents and Associated Child Behaviors and Experiences: A Meta-Analytic and Theoretical Review," 128 *Psychol. Bull.* 539, 544 (2002); Michael J. MacKenzie et al., "Spanking and Child Development Across the First Decade of Life," 132 *Pediatrics* 1118, 1121–24 (2013); Kim J. Overby, "Pediatric Health Supervision," in *Rudolph's Pediatrics* 1, 35 (Colin D. Rudolph et al. eds., 21st ed. 2003); Murray A. Straus et al., "Spanking by Parents and Subsequent Antisocial Behavior of Children," 151 *Archives Pediatrics & Adolescent Med.* 761, 761 (1997); "The Role of the Pediatrician in Violence Prevention: Findings, Recommendations, and Action Steps," 94 *Pediatrics* 579, 580 (1994); Lawrence S. Wissow and Debra Roter, "Toward Effective Discussion of Discipline and Corporal Punishment During Primary Care Visits: Findings from Studies of Doctor-Patient Interaction," 94 *Pediatrics* 587, 587 (1994).

108. See Eustice v. Plymouth Coal Co., 13 A. 975, 976 (Pa. 1888); 1 Blackstone, supra note 19, at *441.

109. See Ark. Code Ann. § 11-6-104 (2012); Cal. Lab. Code § 1394(a) (West 2011); S.D. Codified Laws § 60-12-3 (2009).

110. See Cal. Fam. Code § 7500 (West 2004); Del. Code Ann. tit. 13, § 703 (2009); Ga. Code Ann. § 19-7-1(a) (2010); Idaho Code Ann. § 32-1007 (2006); Ky. Rev. Stat. Ann. § 405.010 (LexisNexis 2010); Me. Rev. Stat. Ann. tit. 19-A, § 1651 (2012); Md. Code Ann., Fam. Law § 5-205 (LexisNexis 2006); Mo. Ann. Stat. § 453.090(3) (West 2003); Mont. Code Ann. § 40-6-221 (2011); N.J. Stat. Ann. § 9:1-1 (West 2002); N.Y. Gen. Oblig. Law § 3-109 (McKinney 2012); N.D. Cent. Code § 14-09-17 (2009); Ohio Rev. Code Ann. § 2111.08 (LexisNexis 2011); Or. Rev. Stat. Ann. § 109.030 (West 2003); R.I. Gen. Laws § 33-15.1-1(a) (2011); S.D. Codified Laws § 25-5-7 (Supp. 2013); Tenn. Code Ann. § 34-1-102(a) (2007); Tex. Fam. Code Ann. § 3.103 (West 2006); Wash. Rev. Code Ann. § 26.16.125 (West Supp. 2013).

111. See 29 U.S.C. § 152(3) (2006).

112. See id. § 157.

113. See Bureau of Labor Statistics, U.S. Dep't of Labor, *National Census of Fatal Occupational Injuries in 2011 (Preliminary Results)* 4–5 (2012).

114. Nat'l Inst. for Occupational Safety & Health, U.S. Dep't of Health & Human Servs., Pub. No. 2009-117, *Injuries to Youth on Farms and Safety Recommendations, U.S. 2006*, at 1 (2009).

115. See 29 U.S.C. § 213(a)(6)(B).

116. See id. § 213(c)(1)(A).

117. Id. § 213(c)(2).

118. See id. § 213(c)(1)(B).

119. See id. § 213(c)(1)(A).

120. See id. § 213(c)(1)(C).

121. See id. § 213(a)(6)(D).

122. See Child Labor Regulations, Orders and Statements of Interpretation; Child Labor Violations—Civil Money Penalties, 76 Fed. Reg. 54,836 (proposed Sept. 2, 2011).

123. See id. at 54,839, 54,849.

124. Id. at 54,843.

125. Id.

126. See id. at 54,852–58.

127. See id. at 54,863.

128. See id. at 54,862.

129. See id. at 54,864–65.

130. Id. at 54,859.

131. Id. at 54,836.

132. Robyn L. Minor, "Comer: Regulators Affecting Farms," *Daily News* (Bowling Green), Apr. 1, 2012, at 1A (quoting Senator Mitch McConnell).

133. Jerry Moran, Op-Ed., "Protecting the Future of Agriculture," *Agweek*, Apr. 2, 2012, at 5.

134. Paul Muxlow, Op-Ed., "Big Government Should Leave Family Farms Alone," *Times Herald* (Port Huron), Feb. 22, 2012, at 7A.

135. Child Labor Regulations, Orders and Statements of Interpretation; Child Labor Violations—Civil Money Penalties, 77 Fed. Reg. 31,549, 31,550 (May 29, 2012) (quoting Department of Labor statement from April 26, 2012).

136. 262 U.S. 390 (1923).

137. See id. at 397, 400–03.

138. Id. at 399.

139. Id. at 401.

140. 268 U.S. 510 (1925).

141. See id. at 530–31.

142. Id. at 534–35.

143. Parham v. J.R., 442 U.S. 584, 603–04 (1979) (citations omitted).

144. N.H. Rev. Stat. Ann. § 186:11(IX-c) (LexisNexis Supp. 2012).

145. Tex. Educ. Code Ann. § 26.010(a) (West 2012); see also Minn. Stat. § 120B.20 (2012); Neb. Rev. Stat. §§ 79-531 to 79-532 (2008).

146. 406 U.S. 205 (1972).

147. See id. at 207.

148. Id. at 211.

149. See id. at 224; id. at 239–40 (White, J., concurring).

150. See id. at 231 n.21 (majority opinion).

151. Id. at 232. But see id. at 245–46 (Douglas, J., dissenting in part).

152. See People v. DeJonge, 501 N.W.2d 127, 129–30, 134–44 (Mich. 1993).

153. Jonathan L. v. Superior Court, 81 Cal. Rptr. 3d 571, 591–92 (Ct. App. 2008).

154. Delconte v. State, 329 S.E.2d 636, 647 (N.C. 1985).

155. See Peterson v. Minidoka Cnty. Sch. Dist. No. 331, 118 F.3d 1351, 1354–58 (9th Cir. 1997).

156. Hewellette v. George, 9 So. 885, 887 (Miss. 1891).

157. See, e.g., McKelvey v. McKelvey, 77 S.W. 664, 664–65 (Tenn. 1903); Roller v. Roller, 79 P. 788, 788–89 (Wash. 1905).

158. La. Rev. Stat. Ann. § 9:571 (2008).

159. See Brunner v. Hutchinson Div., Lear-Siegler, Inc., 770 F. Supp. 517, 523–26 (D.S.D. 1991); Newman v. Cole, 872 So. 2d 138, 139–40, 144 (Ala. 2003) (per curiam); Fields v. S. Farm Bureau Cas. Ins. Co., 87 S.W.3d 224, 228, 231 (Ark. 2002); Terror Mining Co. v. Roter, 866 P.2d 929, 933, 936–37 (Colo. 1994) (en banc); Crotta v. Home Depot, Inc., 732 A.2d 767, 770–73 (Conn. 1999); Sears, Roebuck & Co. v. Huang, 652 A.2d 568, 572 (Del. 1995); Herzfeld v. Herzfeld, 781 So. 2d 1070, 1077, 1078 n.17, 1079 (Fla. 2001); Blake v. Blake, 508 S.E.2d 443, 444 (Ga. Ct. App. 1998); Farmers Ins. Group v. Reed, 712 P.2d 550, 551–52 (Idaho 1985); Cates v. Cates, 619 N.E.2d 715, 728–29 (Ill. 1993); Cooley v. Hosier, 659 N.E.2d 1127, 1129, 1131 (Ind. Ct. App. 1996); Smith v. Smith, 646 N.W.2d 412, 415 (Iowa 2002); Bentley v. Bentley, 172 S.W.3d 375, 377–78 (Ky. 2005); Allstate Ins. Co. v. Kim, 829 A.2d 611, 614–16 (Md. 2003); Ashley v. Bronson, 473 N.W.2d 757, 759 (Mich. Ct. App. 1991) (per curiam); Buono v. Scalia, 843 A.2d 1120, 1122 (N.J. 2004); Holodook v. Spencer, 324 N.E.2d 338, 340 (N.Y. 1974); Doe v. Holt, 418 S.E.2d 511, 512–13 (N.C. 1992); Sixkiller v. Summers, 680 P.2d 360, 360–62 (Okla. 1984); Broadwell v. Holmes, 871 S.W.2d 471, 476–77 (Tenn. 1994); Shoemake v. Fogel, Ltd., 826 S.W.2d 933, 935–36 (Tex. 1992); Pavlick v. Pavlick, 491 S.E.2d 602, 604–05 (Va. 1997); Zellmer v. Zellmer, 188 P.3d 497, 498 (Wash. 2008) (en banc); Cole v. Fairchild, 482 S.E.2d 913, 926 (W. Va. 1996).

160. See 508 S.E.2d at 444.

161. See 491 S.E.2d at 604–06.

162. *Terror Mining Co.,* 866 P.2d at 936; see also *Smith,* 646 N.W.2d at 415; *Buono,* 843 A.2d at 1122; *Shoemake,* 826 S.W.2d at 936.

163. *Blake,* 508 S.E.2d at 444; see also *Cates,* 619 N.E.2d at 729; *Zellmer,* 188 P.3d at 502.

164. *Brunner,* 770 F. Supp. at 526; see also *Crotta,* 732 A.2d at 773; *Sears, Roebuck & Co.,* 652 A.2d at 572; *Sixkiller,* 680 P.2d at 362; *Broadwell,* 871 S.W.2d at 476–77.

165. See James G. Dwyer, *The Relationship Rights of Children* 6–9 (2006).

166. Lassiter v. Dep't of Soc. Servs., 452 U.S. 18, 45 n.13 (1981) (Blackmun, J., dissenting).

167. Troxel v. Granville, 530 U.S. 57, 72 (2000) (plurality opinion) (quoting Superior Court).

168. 140 N.W.2d 152 (Iowa 1966).

169. See id. at 153, 156.

170. Id. at 154.

171. Id.

172. Id. at 156.

173. See "'Arty' Father Wins Custody of Son, 10, from Grandparents," *Chi. Trib.,* Aug. 29, 1968, at B24; "Boy in Custody Row Says He Wants to Live with Father," *L.A. Times,* Aug. 19, 1968, at 3; "Grandmother to Let Iowa Boy, 10, Decide If He Wants Father," *N.Y. Times,* Aug. 15, 1968, at 41; Hal Painter, "'Mark Is Home to Stay!,'" *Good Housekeeping,* Mar. 1969, at 110, 111, 186–89.

5. Sibling Ties and Other Noncanonical Family Relationships

1. Anne Kass, "Splitting Siblings upon Divorce," *Fairshare,* Jan. 1998, at 13, 13.

2. Tapping Reeve, *The Law of Baron and Femme; of Parent and Child; of Guardian and Ward; of Master and Servant* (New Haven, Oliver Steele 1816); James Schouler, *A Treatise on the Law of the Domestic Relations; Embracing Husband and Wife, Parent and Child, Guardian and Ward, Infancy, and Master and Servant* (Boston, Little, Brown, & Co. 1870).

3. Michael Grossberg, *Governing the Hearth: Law and the Family in Nineteenth-Century America,* at x (1985).

4. See Carole Haber and Brian Gratton, *Old Age and the Search for Security: An American Social History* 4 (1994).

5. See Rose M. Kreider and Renee Ellis, U.S. Census Bureau, U.S. Dep't of Commerce, *Number, Timing, and Duration of Marriages and Divorces: 2009,* at 4–6 (2011).

6. See *ProQuest Statistical Abstract of the United States 2014,* at 58 tbl.72 (2014); Annie E. Casey Found., *Kids Count Data Book: State Trends in Child Well-Being* 34 (2013).

7. For prominent arguments in favor of subjecting nonmarital cohabitants to such property distribution at dissolution, see Connell v. Francisco, 898 P.2d 831, 835–37 (Wash. 1995) (en banc); In re Marriage of Lindsey, 678 P.2d 328,

331–32 (Wash. 1984) (en banc); Am. Law Inst., *Principles of the Law of Family Dissolution: Analysis and Recommendations* 907–43 (2002).

8. See Smith v. Guest, 16 A.3d 920, 931–32 (Del. 2011); C.E.W. v. D.E.W., 845 A.2d 1146, 1147, 1151 (Me. 2004); Janice M. v. Margaret K., 948 A.2d 73, 74–75, 87 (Md. 2008); E.N.O. v. L.M.M., 711 N.E.2d 886, 888, 891–94 (Mass. 1999); V.C. v. M.J.B., 748 A.2d 539, 542, 551–55 (N.J. 2000); Debra H. v. Janice R., 930 N.E.2d 184, 192–94 (N.Y. 2010); T.B. v. L.R.M., 786 A.2d 913, 914, 919–20 (Pa. 2001); Rubano v. DiCenzo, 759 A.2d 959, 974–76 (R.I. 2000); Jones v. Barlow, 154 P.3d 808, 816–19 (Utah 2007); In re Parentage of L.B., 122 P.3d 161, 163, 176–77 (Wash. 2005) (en banc); In re Custody of H.S.H.-K., 533 N.W.2d 419, 421, 435–36 (Wis. 1995).

9. John DeWitt Gregory et al., *Understanding Family Law* 1 (4th ed. 2013).

10. See, e.g., Rohmiller v. Hart, 799 N.W.2d 612, 618 (Minn. Ct. App. 2011); In re Katrina E., 636 N.Y.S.2d 53, 53 (App. Div. 1996).

11. 8 U.S.C. § 1229b(b)(1) (2012).

12. See Family and Medical Leave Act of 1993, Pub. L. No. 103-3, § 102, 107 Stat. 6, 9–11 (codified as amended at 29 U.S.C. § 2612(a)(1), (c) (2006 & Supp. II 2009)).

13. See Alaska Stat. § 47.25.230 (2012); La. Rev. Stat. Ann. § 13:4731 (2012); La. Civ. Code Ann. art. 229 (2007); Miss. Code Ann. § 43-31-25 (2009); Utah Code Ann. § 17-14-2 (LexisNexis 2009); W. Va. Code Ann. § 9-5-9 (LexisNexis 2012).

14. 479 U.S. 85, 86, 88 (1986) (per curiam).

15. 29 U.S.C. § 2611(7) (2006).

16. Id. § 2611(12).

17. 29 C.F.R. § 825.122(d)(3) (2013).

18. See, e.g., Novak v. MetroHealth Med. Ctr., 503 F.3d 572, 581 (6th Cir. 2007); Krohn v. Forsting, 11 F. Supp. 2d 1082, 1092 (E.D. Mo. 1998).

19. See Jane Mersky Leder, *Brothers & Sisters: How They Shape Our Lives*, at xv, 102, 104 (1991); Victor G. Cicirelli, "Sibling Influence Throughout the Lifespan," in *Sibling Relationships: Their Nature and Significance Across the Lifespan* 267, 281 (Michael E. Lamb and Brian Sutton-Smith eds., 1982) [hereinafter Cicirelli, "Sibling Influence"]; Victor G. Cicirelli, "Sibling Relationships in Middle and Old Age," in *Sibling Relationships: Their Causes and Consequences* 47, 50–51, 61 (Gene H. Brody ed., 1996) [hereinafter Cicirelli, "Sibling Relationships"].

20. Sarah Delany and A. Elizabeth Delany with Amy Hill Hearth, *Having Our Say: The Delany Sisters' First 100 Years* 5 (1993).

21. See Judy Dunn, *Sisters and Brothers* 4 (1985); Leder, supra note 19, at xv; Don Meyer, Foreword to Peggy Gallagher et al., *Brothers & Sisters: A Special Part of Exceptional Families*, at ix, ix (3d ed. 2006).

22. See Victor G. Cicirelli, *Sibling Relationships Across the Life Span* 2 (1995); Elizabeth Fishel, *Sisters: Love and Rivalry Inside the Family and Beyond* 110, 115 (1979); Leder, supra note 19, at 3; Cicirelli, "Sibling Influence," supra note 19, at 268; Michael E. Lamb, "Sibling Relationships Across the Lifespan: An Overview and Introduction," in *Sibling Relationships: Their Nature and Significance Across the Lifespan,* supra note 19, at 1, 6; Laura M. Padilla-Walker et al., "Self-Regulation as a Mediator Between Sibling Relationship Quality and Early Adolescents' Positive and Negative Outcomes," 24 *J. Fam. Psychol.* 419, 426 (2010).

23. See Leder, supra note 19, at 63.

24. See Dunn, supra note 21, at 169–70.

25. See Stephen P. Bank and Michael D. Kahn, *The Sibling Bond,* at xv–xvii (2d ed. 1997); Dunn, supra note 21, at 162–63; Fishel, supra note 22, at 113–15; Gallagher et al., supra note 21, at xi; Leder, supra note 19, at xvi, 8, 104–05, 155; Susan Scarf Merrell, *The Accidental Bond: The Power of Sibling Relationships* 7–8, 13, 15–16, 142 (1995); Cicirelli, "Sibling Influence," supra note 19, at 268.

26. See Cicirelli, supra note 22, at 114; Leder, supra note 19, at xviii, 38, 62; Theodore Lidz, *The Person: His and Her Development Throughout the Life Cycle* 558 (rev. ed. 1983); Merrell, supra note 25, at 11–12, 14–15.

27. See Bank and Kahn, supra note 25, at xvii, 19, 64, 112–13; Dunn, supra note 21, at 159–60; Fishel, supra note 22, at 109–10; Gloria Hochman et al., Nat'l Adoption Info. Clearinghouse, *The Sibling Bond: Its Importance in Foster Care and Adoptive Placement* 3 (1992); Leder, supra note 19, at 8, 213–15, 226–27; Dorothy W. Le Pere et al., *Large Sibling Groups: Adoption Experiences* 9 (1986); Merrell, supra note 25, at 59–60, 273; Stephen Bank and Michael D. Kahn, "Intense Sibling Loyalties," in *Sibling Relationships: Their Nature and Significance Across the Lifespan,* supra note 19, at 251, 251.

28. See Cicirelli, supra note 22, at 109, 115; Dunn, supra note 21, at 159–60, 162–63; Fishel, supra note 22, at 98–99; Leder, supra note 19, at xvi–xvii; Cicirelli, "Sibling Relationships," supra note 19, at 68.

29. See Cicirelli, supra note 22, at 109, 115, 201; Dunn, supra note 21, at 162–63; Leder, supra note 19, at 104–05; Cicirelli, "Sibling Relationships," supra note 19, at 51, 55, 68.

30. See Leder, supra note 19, at 104–05; Cicirelli, "Sibling Influence," supra note 19, at 274.

31. See Bank and Kahn, supra note 25, at 13; Gallagher et al., supra note 21, at 16–17; Cicirelli, "Sibling Influence," supra note 19, at 274.

32. See Bank and Kahn, supra note 25, at xxiii.

33. See id. at 10; Dunn, supra note 21, at 158–59; Leder, supra note 19, at xvii, 81; Cicirelli, "Sibling Influence," supra note 19, at 282–83.

34. See Helgola G. Ross and Joel I. Milgram, "Important Variables in Adult Sibling Relationships: A Qualitative Study," in *Sibling Relationships: Their Nature and Significance Across the Lifespan,* supra note 19, at 225, 230.

35. See Schouler, supra note 2, at 26–27.

36. See 2 Emory Washburn, *A Treatise on the American Law of Real Property* 401–35 (Boston, Little, Brown & Co. 1862).

37. For some exceptions, see Ellen Marrus, "'Where Have You Been, Fran?': The Right of Siblings to Seek Court Access to Override Parental Denial of Visitation," 66 *Tenn. L. Rev.* 977 (1999); William Wesley Patton and Sara Latz, "Severing Hansel from Gretel: An Analysis of Siblings' Association Rights," 48 *U. Miami L. Rev.* 745 (1994); Barbara Jones, Note, "Do Siblings Possess Constitutional Rights?," 78 *Cornell L. Rev.* 1187 (1993).

38. See In re Interest of D.W., 542 N.W.2d 407, 409–10 (Neb. 1996); Weber v. Weber, 524 A.2d 498, 498 (Pa. Super. Ct. 1987).

39. Brenden Timpe, "Family Sorrow, Family Miracle," *Grand Forks Herald,* June 27, 2004, at 1A.

40. Tom Droege, "Putting the Pieces Together: East Tulsan Meets with Siblings for First Time in 13 Years," *Tulsa World,* Sept. 13, 2000, at 4 East (quoting Michelle Skelton).

41. Wunika Hicks, "I Lost My Brother to Adoption," in *The Heart Knows Something Different: Teenage Voices from the Foster Care System* 30, 31 (Al Desetta ed., 1996).

42. See id. at 31, 33.

43. Id. at 32.

44. See id. at 31–32.

45. Kim Horner, "Almost Complete: Three Sisters Reunite 11 Years After Separation—and Wonder About a Fourth," *Dall. Morning News,* Aug. 28, 2000, at 17A (quoting Misty Hayner).

46. Id. (quoting April Hartline Norris).

47. Linnet Myers, "40 Years After Adoption, Sister Finds Her Family," *Chi. Trib.,* May 25, 1990, § 2, at 3 (quoting William Wimmer).

48. Michele Lesie, "Seeking Their Past: Registry Helps Adoptees Find Origins," *Plain Dealer* (Cleveland), Nov. 23, 1996, at 1-E (quoting Theresa Emerson).

49. Stephanie Simon, "Years Apart, 14 Find They're All in Family," *Chi. Trib.,* July 6, 1990, § 2, at 1 (quoting Linda Jones).

50. Kevan Goff-Parker, "OKDHS Adoption Subsidy Employee Judy Ott Finds Long-Lost Sister After More than 40 Years," *Okla. Woman,* Sept. 2004, at 5, 5.

51. Elbert Starks III, "Search Mends Shattered Family: Siblings Are Reunited in Wadsworth Decades After Their Mother's Tragic Death Tore Them Apart," *Akron Beacon J.,* Feb. 7, 2005, at B1 (quoting Rick Panther).

52. Id. (quoting Deborah Conway).

53. Id. (quoting Wendy Miracle).

54. See Jerica M. Berge et al., "Adolescent Sibling Narratives Regarding Contact in Adoption," 9 *Adoption Q.* 81, 99 (2006).

55. Christopher Woytko, "Family Finds Long-Lost Brother," *Reading Eagle*, Aug. 31, 2007, at C2.

56. Christine Show, "Finally, Reunited: Brother and Sister Separated as Children, Adopted by Different Families, Find Each Other After Long Search," *Newsday* (Long Island), July 29, 2006, at A5.

57. See Mick Walsh, "Ohio Couple Looking for a Long-Lost Brother: May Have Been Adopted by a Columbus Family More than 50 Years Ago," *Columbus Ledger-Enquirer,* July 22, 2006, at A1.

58. Elyse Schein and Paula Bernstein, *Identical Strangers: A Memoir of Twins Separated and Reunited,* at vii (2007).

59. Valerie Schremp Hahn, "3 Sisters Separated by Adoption Are Reunited and Sharing Lives," *St. Louis Post-Dispatch,* Dec. 27, 2004, at N2.

60. Elizabeth Moore, "Sisters Get Together, 4 Decades Later: Separated by Adoption, 2 Are Reunited," *Star-Ledger* (N.J.), Nov. 17, 2002, at 27 (quoting Fran Joans).

61. Show, supra note 56, at A5.

62. See Naomi Cahn, *The New Kinship: Constructing Donor-Conceived Families* 74–81 (2013).

63. Adoption of Hugo, 700 N.E.2d 516, 524 (Mass. 1998).

64. In re Gerald J., 2 Cal. Rptr. 2d 569, 574 (Ct. App. 1991).

65. See E. Wayne Carp, *Family Matters: Secrecy and Disclosure in the History of Adoption* (1998); Ellen Herman, *Kinship by Design: A History of Adoption in the Modern United States* (2008); Barbara Melosh, *Strangers and Kin: The American Way of Adoption* (2002).

66. Fostering Connections to Success and Increasing Adoptions Act of 2008, Pub. L. No. 110-351, § 206, 122 Stat. 3949, 3962 (codified at 42 U.S.C. § 671(a)(31)(A) (Supp. II 2009)).

67. See BK v. N.H. Dep't of Health & Human Servs., 814 F. Supp. 2d 59, 64–71 (D.N.H. 2011).

68. Ariz. Rev. Stat. Ann. § 8-513(D) (Supp. 2012).

69. Mo. Code Regs. Ann. tit. 13, § 40-73.080(5)(C) (1998).

70. N.Y. Comp. Codes R. & Regs. tit. 18, §§ 421.2(e), 421.18(d)(3) (2008).

71. Id. § 421.18(d)(3).

72. 102 Mass. Code Regs. 5.08(10) (1998).

73. See Fla. Admin. Code Ann. r. 65C-16.002(4)(e) (2013); W. Va. Code Ann. § 49-2-14(d) (LexisNexis 2009).

74. 20 Ill. Comp. Stat. Ann. 505/7.4(h) (West Supp. 2013).

75. W. Va. Code Ann. § 49-2-14(e). For enforcement, see In re Carol B., 550 S.E.2d 636, 644–45 (W. Va. 2001).

76. Fla. Admin. Code Ann. r. 65C-16.002(4)(e).

77. 20 Ill. Comp. Stat. Ann. 505/7.4(h).

78. Lindsie D.L. v. Richard W.S., 591 S.E.2d 308, 312 n.3 (W. Va. 2003).

79. Va. Code Ann. §§ 63.2-1215, 63.2-1241 (2012).

80. Fostering Connections to Success and Increasing Adoptions Act of 2008, Pub. L. No. 110-351, § 206, 122 Stat. 3949, 3962 (codified at 42 U.S.C. § 671(a)(31)(B) (Supp. II 2009)).

81. Iowa Code Ann. § 232.108(6) (West Supp. 2013).

82. See Cal. Welf. & Inst. Code § 16002(e) (West Supp. 2013).

83. See In re Celine R., 71 P.3d 787, 794 (Cal. 2003); In re Daniel H., 121 Cal. Rptr. 2d 475, 481 (Ct. App. 2002).

84. Colo. Rev. Stat. § 19-5-210(7) (2012).

85. Me. Rev. Stat. Ann. tit. 22, § 4068(2) (Supp. 2012).

86. Wash. Rev. Code Ann. § 26.33.430 (West Supp. 2013); see also id. § 26.33.190(2)(c).

87. Ind. Code Ann. § 31-19-16.5-1 (LexisNexis 2007); see also id. § 31-19-16.5-4.

88. La. Child. Code Ann. art. 1269.2(A) (Supp. 2013).

89. Tenn. Code Ann. § 36-1-121(f) (2010); see also N.M. Stat. Ann. § 32A-5-35(A) (West 2013); N.Y. Dom. Rel. Law § 112-b(2) (McKinney 2010); Wash. Rev. Code Ann. § 26.33.295(2) (West Supp. 2013).

90. Fla. Stat. Ann. § 63.0427(1) (West Supp. 2013).

91. Id. § 63.0427(2).

92. Nev. Rev. Stat. Ann. § 127.171(1) (LexisNexis Supp. 2013).

93. Ark. Code Ann. § 9-9-215(c) (Supp. 2011).

94. Mass. Ann. Laws ch. 119, § 26B(b) (LexisNexis 2009). For implementation, see Adoption of Pierce, 790 N.E.2d 680, 685 (Mass. App. Ct. 2003); Adoption of Galvin, 773 N.E.2d 1007, 1009 (Mass. App. Ct. 2002).

95. Vt. Stat. Ann. tit. 15A, § 4-112(c)–(d) (2010).

96. In re D.C., 4 A.3d 1004, 1021 (N.J. 2010) (citation and internal quotation marks omitted).

97. Md. Code Ann., Fam. Law § 5-525.2(b) (LexisNexis 2006).

98. 530 U.S. 57, 72 (2000) (plurality opinion).

99. Id.

100. Id. at 73.

101. See Moore v. City of E. Cleveland, 431 U.S. 494, 504 (1977) (plurality opinion).

102. See In re Adoption of C.A., 137 P.3d 318, 319, 325–26 (Colo. 2006) (en banc); In re Visitation of M.L.B., 983 N.E.2d 583, 586–87 (Ind. 2013); Walker

v. Blair, 382 S.W.3d 862, 870–73 (Ky. 2012); Harrold v. Collier, 836 N.E.2d 1165, 1168, 1172–73 (Ohio 2005); Hiller v. Fausey, 904 A.2d 875, 887 (Pa. 2006); In re A.L., 781 N.W.2d 482, 483, 487–88 (S.D. 2010); State ex rel. Brandon L. v. Moats, 551 S.E.2d 674, 685–86 (W. Va. 2001).

103. See Roth v. Weston, 789 A.2d 431, 434, 445, 447–50 (Conn. 2002); Koshko v. Haining, 921 A.2d 171, 191–93 (Md. 2007); Blixt v. Blixt, 774 N.E.2d 1052, 1060 (Mass. 2002); Moriarty v. Bradt, 827 A.2d 203, 205, 222–23 (N.J. 2003); Neal v. Lee, 14 P.3d 547, 550 (Okla. 2000); Camburn v. Smith, 586 S.E.2d 565, 567–68 (S.C. 2003); Glidden v. Conley, 820 A.2d 197, 204–05 (Vt. 2003).

104. See Doe v. Doe, 172 P.3d 1067, 1079–80 (Haw. 2007); In re Marriage of Howard, 661 N.W.2d 183, 191–92 (Iowa 2003).

105. See Lori Kaplan et al., "Splitting Custody of Children Between Parents: Impact on the Sibling System," 74 *Families Soc'y: J. Contemp. Hum. Services* 131, 133 (1993).

106. Larry Powell, "Long-Overdue Reunion Is a Good Reason To Give Thanks," *Dall. Morning News,* Nov. 24, 1988, at 38A (quoting Janie Owens).

107. Debra Nisson, "Sisters Reunited After 23 Years," *Hous. Chron.,* June 26, 1994, at 1G.

108. Marrus, supra note 37, at 978.

109. See Eleanor E. Maccoby and Robert H. Mnookin, *Dividing the Child: Social and Legal Dilemmas of Custody* 104 tbl.5.4 (1992).

110. Stephen J. Bahr et al., "Trends in Child Custody Awards: Has the Removal of Maternal Preference Made a Difference?," 28 *Fam. L.Q.* 247, 257 (1994).

111. See, e.g., Hepburn v. Hepburn, 659 So. 2d 653, 654–55 (Ala. Civ. App. 1995); Matias v. Matias, 948 So. 2d 1021, 1022–23 (Fla. Dist. Ct. App. 2007); In re Marriage of Pundt, 547 N.W.2d 243, 244–46 (Iowa Ct. App. 1996); In re Marriage of Williams, 90 P.3d 365, 366–67 (Kan. Ct. App. 2004); Durbin v. Durbin, 226 S.W.3d 876, 880–81 (Mo. Ct. App. 2007) (per curiam); Replogle v. Replogle, 903 S.W.2d 551, 554–56 (Mo. Ct. App. 1995); Lightbody v. Lightbody, 840 N.Y.S.2d 131, 132–33 (App. Div. 2007); Harris v. Harris, 647 A.2d 309, 314 (Vt. 1994); Gooch v. Gooch, 575 S.E.2d 628, 632 (W. Va. 2002) (per curiam).

112. Kass, supra note 1, at 13.

113. Id.

114. Id.

115. BeauLac v. BeauLac, 649 N.W.2d 210, 216 (N.D. 2002).

116. In re Paternity of B.D.D., 779 N.E.2d 9, 14–15 (Ind. Ct. App. 2002).

117. Puddicombe v. Dreka, 167 P.3d 73, 78 (Alaska 2007) (citation and internal quotation marks omitted).

118. See A.B. v. J.B., 40 So. 3d 723, 729–30 (Ala. Civ. App. 2009) (per curiam); Foskett v. Foskett, 634 N.W.2d 363, 369 (Mich. Ct. App. 2001); Price v. McBeath, 989 So. 2d 444, 459 (Miss. Ct. App. 2008); Kay v. Ludwig, 686 N.W.2d 619, 630–31 (Neb. Ct. App. 2004); Gardner v. Gardner, 229 S.W.3d 747, 754 (Tex. Ct. App. 2007); Harris v. Harris, 647 A.2d 309, 313–14 (Vt. 1994); Hughes v. Gentry, 443 S.E.2d 448, 451–52 (Va. Ct. App. 1994); Blakely v. Blakely, 218 P.3d 253, 256 (Wyo. 2009).

119. See Ariz. Rev. Stat. Ann. § 25-403(A)(2) (Supp. 2012); Colo. Rev. Stat. § 14-10-124(1.5)(a)(III) (2013); D.C. Code § 16-914(a)(3)(C) (LexisNexis 2012); Idaho Code Ann. § 32-717(1)(c) (Supp. 2013); Ind. Code Ann. §§ 31-14-13-2(4)(B), 31-17-2-8(4)(B) (LexisNexis 2007); Ky. Rev. Stat. Ann. § 403.270(2)(c) (LexisNexis 2010); Minn. Stat. § 518.17(1)(a)(5) (2012); Mo. Ann. Stat. § 452.375(2)(3) (West Supp. 2013); N.J. Stat. Ann. § 9:2-4 (West 2002); N.M. Stat. Ann. § 40-4-9(A)(3) (West 2013); Va. Code Ann. § 20-124.3(4) (Supp. 2013).

120. Kan. Stat. Ann. § 23-3207(b) (Supp. 2012); In re Marriage of Williams, 90 P.3d 365, 370 (Kan. Ct. App. 2004); Lloyd v. Butts, 37 S.W.3d 603, 607 (Ark. 2001); Sykes v. Warren, 258 S.W.3d 788, 793 (Ark. Ct. App. 2007); Durbin v. Durbin, 226 S.W.3d 876, 880 (Mo. Ct. App. 2007) (per curiam).

121. Valenti v. Valenti, 869 N.Y.S.2d 266, 269 (App. Div. 2008).

122. Sanders v. Sanders, 923 So. 2d 721, 725 (La. Ct. App. 2005).

123. In re Marriage of Williams, 105 Cal. Rptr. 2d 923, 924 (Ct. App. 2001); Matias v. Matias, 948 So. 2d 1021, 1022–23 (Fla. Dist. Ct. App. 2007); In re Marriage of Pundt, 547 N.W.2d 243, 245 (Iowa Ct. App. 1996); Brawley v. Brawley, 734 So. 2d 237, 241 (Miss. Ct. App. 1999); Saintz v. Rinker, 902 A.2d 509, 513 (Pa. Super. Ct. 2006); Hathaway v. Bergheim, 648 N.W.2d 349, 352 (S.D. 2002).

124. In re Marriage of Morales, 159 P.3d 1183, 1189 (Or. Ct. App. 2007).

125. Kan. Stat. Ann. § 23-3207(b).

126. In re Marriage of Williams, 90 P.3d 365, 370 (Kan. Ct. App. 2004).

127. 547 N.W.2d 243 (Iowa Ct. App. 1996).

128. See id. at 244.

129. Id.

130. Id.

131. Id.

132. See id. at 246.

133. 647 A.2d 309 (Vt. 1994).

134. See id. at 311.

135. Id. at 314.

136. Id. at 312.

137. Id. at 314 (quoting Vt. Stat. Ann. tit. 15, § 665(c)).

138. For half-siblings separated after their shared parent's death, see J.M.W. v. C.C., 736 So. 2d 644, 645 (Ala. Civ. App. 1999); Lihs v. Lihs, 504 N.W.2d

890, 891 (Iowa 1993); Jones v. Willis, 996 So. 2d 364, 372 (La. Ct. App. 2008); Mills v. Hardy, 842 So. 2d 443, 444–45, 453 (La. Ct. App. 2003); Scruggs v. Saterfiel, 693 So. 2d 924, 925 (Miss. 1997); D.N. v. V.B., 814 A.2d 750, 751–52 (Pa. Super. Ct. 2002).

139. See Lawrence H. Ganong and Marilyn Coleman, *Remarried Family Relationships* 104 (1994); Lawrence H. Ganong and Marilyn Coleman, "Do Mutual Children Cement Bonds in Stepfamilies?," 50 *J. Marriage & Fam.* 687, 696 (1988).

140. See A.B. v. J.B., 40 So. 3d 723, 729–30 (Ala. Civ. App. 2009) (per curiam); In re Marriage of Quirk-Edwards, 509 N.W.2d 476, 480 (Iowa 1993); In re Marriage of Swenka, 576 N.W.2d 615, 618 (Iowa Ct. App. 1998); Sumrall v. Sumrall, 970 So. 2d 254, 259 (Miss. Ct. App. 2007); Saintz v. Rinker, 902 A.2d 509, 513 (Pa. Super. Ct. 2006); Van Driel v. Van Driel, 525 N.W.2d 37, 40 (S.D. 1994); In re Guardianship of BJO, 165 P.3d 442, 446 (Wyo. 2007).

141. See Middleton v. Middleton, 113 S.W.3d 625, 630 (Ark. Ct. App. 2003); Miers v. Miers, 53 S.W.3d 592, 598 (Mo. Ct. App. 2001); Chant v. Filippelli, 716 N.Y.S.2d 158, 159–60 (App. Div. 2000); Stoppler v. Stoppler, 633 N.W.2d 142, 147 (N.D. 2001); In re K.L.R., 162 S.W.3d 291, 306 (Tex. Ct. App. 2005).

142. Viamonte v. Viamonte, 748 A.2d 493, 498 (Md. Ct. Spec. App. 2000).

143. Johns v. Cioci, 865 A.2d 931, 943 (Pa. Super. Ct. 2004).

144. See Troxel v. Granville, 530 U.S. 57, 73 n.* (2000) (plurality opinion) (citing statutes).

145. *Grandparents Rights: Preserving Generational Bonds: Hearing Before the Subcomm. on Human Servs. of the H. Select Comm. on Aging,* 102d Cong. 2 (1991) (statement of Rep. Thomas Downey).

146. Joint Resolution Designating 1995 the "Year of the Grandparent," Pub. L. No. 103-368, 108 Stat. 3475, 3475 (1994).

147. Lihs v. Lihs, 504 N.W.2d 890, 892 (Iowa 1993).

148. MBB v. ERW, 100 P.3d 415, 420 (Wyo. 2004).

149. Ken R. ex rel. C.R. v. Arthur Z., 682 A.2d 1267, 1271 (Pa. 1996).

150. See Sandor v. Sandor, 444 So. 2d 1029, 1030 (Fla. Dist. Ct. App. 1984) (per curiam); *Lihs,* 504 N.W.2d at 892–93; Scruggs v. Saterfiel, 693 So. 2d 924, 926 (Miss. 1997); *Ken R. ex rel. C.R.,* 682 A.2d at 1271; D.N. v. V.B., 814 A.2d 750, 753–54 (Pa. Super. Ct. 2002); *MBB,* 100 P.3d at 420.

151. For examples of sibling visitation statutes, see Alaska Stat. § 25.20.060(a) (2012); Ark. Code Ann. § 9-13-102 (2009); Haw. Rev. Stat. § 571-46(a)(7) (West Supp. 2012); 750 Ill. Comp. Stat. Ann. 5/607 (West Supp. 2013); La. Rev. Stat. Ann. § 9:344(C)–(D) (Supp. 2013); Nev. Rev. Stat. Ann. § 125C.050(1) (LexisNexis 2010); N.H. Rev. Stat. Ann. § 169-C:19-d (LexisNexis 2010); N.Y. Dom. Rel. Law § 71 (McKinney 2010); Or. Rev. Stat. Ann. § 109.119

(West Supp. 2013); R.I. Gen. Laws §§ 15-5-24.3(b), 15-5-24.4 (2013); S.C. Code Ann. § 63-3-530(A)(44) (2010).

152. Pullman v. Pullman, 560 A.2d 1276, 1278 (N.J. Super. Ct. Ch. Div. 1988).

153. See Barger ex rel. E.B. v. Brown, 134 P.3d 905, 907 & n.1, 910 (Okla. Civ. App. 2006).

154. See *Pullman,* 560 A.2d at 1277–79 (citing N.J. Stat. Ann. § 9:2-7.1, found unconstitutional as applied in Wilde v. Wilde, 775 A.2d 535, 538 (N.J. Super. Ct. App. Div. 2001)).

155. See In re Dependency of M.J.L., 96 P.3d 996, 1000 (Wash. Ct. App. 2004).

156. See 56 A.3d 338, 344 n.1 (Md. Ct. Spec. App. 2012), cert. granted, 61 A.3d 18 (Md. 2013).

157. See id. at 341.

158. See 61 A.3d at 18.

159. See 56 A.3d at 341.

160. See id. at 341, 348.

161. Id. at 341.

162. See id. at 341, 348.

163. See id. at 341.

164. Id. at 345.

165. Id.

166. Id. at 345–46, 349 (citation and internal quotation marks omitted).

167. See id. at 346.

168. See id.

169. See id. at 341–42.

170. See id. at 348–49.

171. Id. at 341.

172. Id. at 348.

173. 125 Cal. Rptr. 2d 836 (Ct. App. 2002).

174. See id. at 837.

175. Id. at 841.

176. See Hochman et al., supra note 27, at 7; see also Act No. 98-439, H.J.R. 35, 1998 Ala. Acts 867; Miss. Code Ann. § 93-17-3(5) (Supp. 2012); Utah Code Ann. § 78B-6-117(3) (LexisNexis 2012).

177. For decisions denying postadoption sibling visitation because the siblings never had the chance to develop a relationship, see Sherman v. Hughes, 821 N.Y.S.2d 628, 629 (App. Div. 2006); In re Justin H., 626 N.Y.S.2d 479, 480 (App. Div. 1995); Hatch ex rel. Angela J v. Cortland Cnty. Dep't of Soc. Servs., 605 N.Y.S.2d 428, 429 (App. Div. 1993).

178. N.Y. Comp. Codes R. & Regs. tit. 18, § 421.24(a)(3)(iii)(b) (2010).

179. Troxel v. Granville, 530 U.S. 57, 72 (2000) (plurality opinion).

180. See statutes cited infra notes 182, 185.

181. See, e.g., Ala. Code § 26-10A-31(d)(9) (LexisNexis 2009); Conn. Gen. Stat. Ann. § 45a-746(a)(6) (West 2004); Mich. Comp. Laws Ann. § 710.27(3) (d) (West 2012).

182. See Ark. Code Ann. § 9-9-503 (2009); id. § 9-9-504 (Supp. 2011); Fla. Stat. Ann. § 63.165 (West 2012); Idaho Code Ann. § 39-259A (2011); Iowa Code Ann. § 144.43A (West 2005); Ky. Rev. Stat. Ann. § 199.575 (LexisNexis 2007); La. Child. Code Ann. art. 1270 (Supp. 2013); Me. Rev. Stat. Ann. tit. 22, § 2706-A (2004); Mo. Ann. Stat. § 453.121(9) (West Supp. 2013); Nev. Rev. Stat. Ann. § 127.007 (LexisNexis 2010); N.Y. Pub. Health Law §§ 4138-c to 4138-d (McKinney 2012); Ohio Rev. Code Ann. §§ 3107.40 to 3107.41, 3107.48 to 3107.49 (LexisNexis 2008); R.I. Gen. Laws §§ 15-7.2-6 to 15-7.2-10 (2013); S.C. Code Ann. § 63-9-780(E) (2010); Tex. Fam. Code Ann. §§ 162.414, 162.416 (West 2008); Utah Code Ann. § 78B-6-144 (LexisNexis 2012); Vt. Stat. Ann. tit. 15A, § 6-105 (2010).

183. See Wendy Koch, "As Adoptees Seek Roots, States Unsealing Records: Maine Lawmakers' Story Shows 2 Sides of Debate," *USA Today,* Feb. 13, 2008, at 1A.

184. See Akiko Matsuda, "Woman Seeking Adopted Half-Sister: Teacher Hopes Registry Inquiry Leads to Long-Sought Reunion," *J. News* (Lower Hudson Valley), Jan. 25, 2009, at 1B.

185. See Ariz. Rev. Stat. Ann. § 8-134(A)(7) (Supp. 2012); Cal. Fam. Code § 9205(g) (West Supp. 2013); Colo. Rev. Stat. § 19-5-304(1)(b)(I)(C) (2012); Conn. Gen. Stat. Ann. §§ 45a-743(3)(C), 45a-751(a) (West 2004); Del. Code Ann. tit. 13, § 962(a)(3) (2009); Ga. Code Ann. § 19-8-23(f)(5) (Supp. 2012); 750 Ill. Comp. Stat. Ann. 50/18.3a(a)–(b), (i) (West Supp. 2013); Ind. Code Ann. § 31-19-24-2 (LexisNexis Supp. 2012); Md. Code Ann., Fam. Law § 5-4B-05 (LexisNexis 2012); Mich. Comp. Laws Ann. § 710.68b (West 2012); Minn. Stat. § 259.83(1) (2012); Mont. Code Ann. §§ 42-1-103(11), 42-6-103 to 42-6-104 (2011); N.M. Stat. Ann. § 32A-5-41 (West 2013); N.C. Gen. Stat. § 48-9-104 (2011); N.D. Cent. Code § 14-15-16 (2009); Okla. Stat. Ann. tit. 10, § 7508-1.3 (West 2009); Or. Rev. Stat. Ann. §§ 109.502 to 109.504 (West 2003); Tenn. Code Ann. §§ 36-1-128 to 36-1-131 (2010); Wash. Rev. Code Ann. § 26.33.343 (West 2005); Wyo. Stat. Ann. § 1-22-203 (2013).

186. See Robert L. Fischer, "The Emerging Role of Adoption Reunion Registries: Adoptee and Birthparent Views," 81 *Child Welfare* 445, 453–54 (2002).

187. Minn. Stat. § 259.83(1).

188. Or. Rev. Stat. Ann. § 109.504(1).

189. Nev. Rev. Stat. Ann. § 127.007(3) (LexisNexis 2010); see also Ariz. Rev. Stat. Ann. § 8-134(F); Conn. Gen. Stat. Ann. § 45a-751b(e) (West Supp. 2013); Okla. Stat. Ann. tit. 10, § 7508-1.3(D).

190. S. 1487, 105th Cong. (1997).

191. For the hearing, see *Adoption Reunion Registries and Screening of Adults Working with Children: Hearing Before the Subcomm. on Human Res. of the H. Comm. on Ways and Means*, 105th Cong. (1998).

192. Id. at 36 (statement of Rep. Tom Bliley); see also id. at 40–41 (statement of Sen. Robert Bennett).

193. See id. at 36 (statement of Rep. Tom Bliley); id. at 40–41, 43 (statement of Sen. Robert Bennett); id. at 45 (statement of Rep. Jim McCrery).

194. See id. at 30, 41–42, 48–49 (statement of Sen. Carl Levin).

195. Troxel v. Granville, 530 U.S. 57, 72 (2000) (plurality opinion). For a post-*Troxel* opinion along these lines, see Lindsie D.L. v. Richard W.S., 591 S.E.2d 308, 314 (W. Va. 2003).

6. Family Law for the Poor

1. 724 N.E.2d 1103, 1109 (Ind. Ct. App. 2000).

2. See Carmen DeNavas-Walt et al., U.S. Census Bureau, U.S. Dep't of Commerce, *Income, Poverty, and Health Insurance Coverage in the United States: 2012*, at 13 (2013).

3. See id. at 13–17.

4. See id. at 13.

5. Id. at 17.

6. See id. at 15.

7. For discussion of such assumptions, see Dorothy Roberts, *Killing the Black Body: Race, Reproduction, and the Meaning of Liberty* 17–19, 207, 215, 243–45 (1997); Tonya L. Brito, "From Madonna to Proletariat: Constructing a New Ideology of Motherhood in Welfare Discourse," 44 *Vill. L. Rev.* 415, 415, 434–35 (1999); Wahneema Lubiano, "Black Ladies, Welfare Queens, and State Minstrels: Ideological War by Narrative Means," in *Racing Justice, En-Gendering Power: Essays on Anita Hill, Clarence Thomas, and the Construction of Social Reality* 323, 332–33, 335–40 (Toni Morrison ed., 1992); Lucy A. Williams, "Race, Rat Bites and Unfit Mothers: How Media Discourse Informs Welfare Legislation Debate," 22 *Fordham Urb. L.J.* 1159, 1170–74 & nn.68–69 (1995).

8. Jacobus tenBroek, "California's Dual System of Family Law: Its Origin, Development, and Present Status" (pts. 1–2), 16 *Stan. L. Rev.* 257 (1964), 16 *Stan. L. Rev.* 900 (1964).

9. Planned Parenthood of Se. Pa. v. Casey, 505 U.S. 833, 851 (1992) (quoting Prince v. Massachusetts, 321 U.S. 158, 166 (1944)); see also Smith v. Org. of Foster Families for Equal. & Reform, 431 U.S. 816, 842 (1977); Moore v. City of E. Cleveland, 431 U.S. 494, 499 (1977) (plurality opinion).

10. Santosky v. Kramer, 455 U.S. 745, 753 (1982); see also Harris v. McRae, 448 U.S. 297, 312 (1980); Cleveland Bd. of Educ. v. LaFleur, 414 U.S. 632, 639–40 (1974).

11. Eisenstadt v. Baird, 405 U.S. 438, 453 (1972) (emphasis omitted).

12. Paris Adult Theatre I v. Slaton, 413 U.S. 49, 65 (1973).

13. Ginsberg v. New York, 390 U.S. 629, 639 (1968).

14. Parham v. J.R., 442 U.S. 584, 603 (1979).

15. 397 U.S. 471 (1970).

16. 400 U.S. 309 (1971).

17. 477 U.S. 635 (1986).

18. 483 U.S. 587 (1987).

19. For examples of family law casebooks that neither discuss nor cite any of these cases, see Judith Areen et al., *Family Law: Cases and Materials* (6th ed. 2012); Homer H. Clark, Jr. and Ann Laquer Estin, *Cases and Problems on Domestic Relations* (7th ed. 2005); James Dwyer, *Family Law: Theoretical, Comparative, and Social Science Perspectives* (2012); Ira Mark Ellman et al., *Family Law: Cases, Text, Problems* (5th ed. 2010); Harry D. Krause et al., *Family Law: Cases, Comments, and Questions* (7th ed. 2013); Carl E. Schneider and Margaret F. Brinig, *An Invitation to Family Law: Principles, Process and Perspectives* (3d ed. 2006); Walter Wadlington et al., *Domestic Relations: Cases and Materials* (7th ed. 2013); Lynn D. Wardle and Laurence C. Nolan, *Fundamental Principles of Family Law* (2d ed. 2006); Walter O. Weyrauch et al., *Cases and Materials on Family Law: Legal Concepts and Changing Human Relationships* (1994).

20. See *Dandridge*, 397 U.S. at 473–75.

21. See id. at 509 & n.2 (Marshall, J., dissenting).

22. See id. at 477 (majority opinion).

23. See id.; id. at 501–02 (Douglas, J., dissenting); id. at 513–14 & n.5 (Marshall, J., dissenting).

24. Id. at 514 n.6 (Marshall, J., dissenting).

25. Id. at 484 (majority opinion).

26. Id. at 480 (footnote omitted).

27. Id. at 484.

28. See id. at 484–85.

29. Id. at 487.

30. Id. at 485.

31. Id. at 486–87.

32. See Wyman v. James, 400 U.S. 309, 310–14 (1971).

33. See id. at 339–40 (Marshall, J., dissenting).

34. See id. at 342.

35. See id. at 339–40.

36. See Jurisdictional Statement of Appellant Wyman at 14 n.*, Wyman v. James, 400 U.S. 309 (1971) (No. 69).

37. See *Wyman*, 400 U.S. at 317.

38. Miller v. United States, 357 U.S. 301, 307 (1958).

39. Silverman v. United States, 365 U.S. 505, 511 (1961); see also Gregory v. City of Chicago, 394 U.S. 111, 125 (1969) (Black, J., concurring).

40. United States v. Martinez-Fuerte, 428 U.S. 543, 561 (1976).

41. Welsh v. Wisconsin, 466 U.S. 740, 748 (1984) (citation and internal quotation marks omitted).

42. Payton v. New York, 445 U.S. 573, 590 (1980).

43. Wilson v. Layne, 526 U.S. 603, 610 (1999).

44. See Joanna L. Grossman and Lawrence M. Friedman, *Inside the Castle: Law and the Family in 20th Century America* (2011).

45. Georgia v. Randolph, 547 U.S. 103, 115 (2006) (citation, internal quotation marks, and alteration marks omitted); see also Carey v. Brown, 447 U.S. 455, 471 (1980).

46. Wyman v. James, 400 U.S. 309, 316 (1971).

47. Id. at 317.

48. Id.

49. Id. at 317–18.

50. Id. at 318.

51. Id. at 321.

52. Id. at 318.

53. Id. at 319.

54. Id. at 318.

55. See Sanchez v. Cnty. of San Diego, 464 F.3d 916, 918–23 (9th Cir. 2006); S.L. v. Whitburn, 67 F.3d 1299, 1301–03, 1307–10 (7th Cir. 1995); Smith v. L.A. Cnty. Bd. of Supervisors, 128 Cal. Rptr. 2d 700, 702, 704, 712–14 (Ct. App. 2002).

56. See Lyng v. Castillo, 477 U.S. 635, 636, 643 (1986).

57. See id. at 640 n.4.

58. See id. at 636 n.1.

59. See id. at 640–42 & nn.5–6, 10.

60. Id. at 642.

61. Id. at 643.

62. Id. at 637.

63. Id. at 638 (citation omitted).

64. Id. at 643.

65. Id. at 638.

66. See id. at 639.

67. See id. at 645 (Marshall, J., dissenting) (citing S. Rep. No. 97-504, at 25 (1982)).

68. Bowen v. Gilliard, 483 U.S. 587, 589 (1987).

69. See id. at 589–92.

70. See id. at 591–94.

71. See id. at 623 (Brennan, J., dissenting).

72. See id. at 620–21.

73. See id. at 594 (majority opinion).

74. Id. at 598.

75. Id. at 601–02 (citation, internal quotation marks, and alteration marks omitted).

76. Id. at 598 (citation and internal quotation marks omitted).

77. Id. at 599.

78. See Personal Responsibility and Work Opportunity Reconciliation Act of 1996, Pub. L. No. 104-193, § 103(a), 110 Stat. 2105, 2112.

79. See 42 U.S.C. § 402(b)–(h) (2006).

80. See Soc. Sec. Admin., *Social Security: Understanding the Benefits* 13, 15 (2014); 42 U.S.C. § 403(a).

81. See Neville v. Neville, 791 N.E.2d 434, 437 (Ohio 2003).

82. Astrue v. Capato ex rel. B.N.C., 132 S. Ct. 2021, 2032 (2012) (citation, internal quotation marks, and alteration marks omitted).

83. See C. Eugene Steuerle and Stephanie Rennane, Nat'l Inst. for Health Care Mgmt., *How Lifetime Benefits and Contributions Point the Way Toward Reforming Our Senior Entitlement Programs* 1–2 (2011); Alan L. Gustman and Thomas L. Steinmeier, "How Effective Is Redistribution Under the Social Security Benefit Formula?," 82 *J. Pub. Econ.* 1, 2, 20–21, 26–27 (2001); Jeffrey B. Liebman, "Redistribution in the Current U.S. Social Security System," in *The Distributional Aspects of Social Security and Social Security Reform* 11, 12 (Martin Feldstein and Jeffrey B. Liebman eds., 2002).

84. See Office of Ret. & Disability Policy, Office of Research, Evaluation, & Statistics, Soc. Sec. Admin., *Annual Statistical Supplement to the Social Security Bulletin, 2012,* at 5.18 tbl.5.A14, G.6 (2013).

85. For accounts of how the Social Security Board helped create this cultural understanding, see Jerry R. Cates, *Insuring Inequality: Administrative Leadership in Social Security, 1935–54,* at 104 (1983); Nancy Fraser and Linda Gordon, "A Genealogy of *Dependency*: Tracing a Keyword of the U.S. Welfare State," 19 *Signs* 309, 322 (1994).

86. See 38 U.S.C. §§ 101(14)–(15), 1310–1318, 1541–1543 (2006).

87. See 26 U.S.C. §§ 151–152.

88. See id.

89. See Office of Family Assistance, U.S. Dep't of Health & Human Servs., *Temporary Assistance for Needy Families Program (TANF) Ninth Report to Congress,* at ix (2012).

90. See id. at X-73.

91. See id.

92. See id. at X-73 to X-75.

93. See, e.g., Martin Gilens, "'Race Coding' and White Opposition to Welfare," 90 *Am. Pol. Sci. Rev.* 593, 593–95, 597–98, 600–02 (1996).

94. 42 U.S.C. § 608(b)(2)(A) (2006).

95. Id. § 604(i) (Supp. II 2009).

96. See Ariz. Rev. Stat. Ann. § 46-292(S) (Supp. 2012); Ark. Code Ann. § 20-76-402(a)(10) (Supp. 2011); Fla. Stat. Ann. § 414.1251 (West 2013); Ga. Code Ann. § 49-4-192 (2009); 305 Ill. Comp. Stat. Ann. 5/4-8(a) (West 2008); Ind. Code Ann. § 12-14-2-17 (LexisNexis Supp. 2012); La. Rev. Stat. Ann. § 46:231.3 (2010); 106 Mass. Code Regs. 203.900 (1998); Miss. Code Ann. § 43-17-5(4) (Supp. 2012); Neb. Rev. Stat. § 68-1724(2)(c) (Supp. 2007); Ohio Rev. Code Ann. §§ 5107.28 to 5107.287 (LexisNexis 2011); Okla. Stat. Ann. tit. 56, § 230.65(C)(7) (West Supp. 2013); id. § 230.66 (West 2004); 62 Pa. Cons. Stat. Ann. § 405.3(a)(6)(i) (West 2010); Tenn. Code Ann. § 71-3-104(h)(2)(B)(i) (2012); Va. Code Ann. § 63.2-606 (2012); Wis. Stat. Ann. § 49.26 (West Supp. 2013).

97. See Ariz. Rev. Stat. Ann. § 46-292(T); Fla. Stat. Ann. § 414.13 (West 2013); Ga. Code Ann. § 49-4-183(b)(10) (Supp. 2011); 305 Ill. Comp. Stat. Ann. 5/4-4.1 (West 2008); La. Rev. Stat. Ann. § 46:231.4 (Supp. 2013); 106 Mass. Code Regs. 203.800 (2001); Miss. Code Ann. § 43-17-5(5); Nev. Rev. Stat. Ann. § 422A.355 (LexisNexis 2011); Okla. Stat. Ann. tit. 56, § 230.56 (West 2004); 62 Pa. Cons. Stat. Ann. § 405.3(a)(6)(ii); Tenn. Code Ann. § 71-3-104(h)(2)(B)(ii); Va. Code Ann. § 63.2-603 (2012).

98. See 42 U.S.C. § 607 (2006 & Supp. III 2010).

99. See Fla. Stat. Ann. § 414.1251; Ga. Code Ann. § 49-4-192; Ohio Rev. Code Ann. §§ 5107.28 to 5107.287; Wis. Stat. Ann. § 49.26.

100. 42 U.S.C. § 602(a)(7)(A)(iii) (2006).

101. See Ariz. Rev. Stat. Ann. § 46-292(H)–(I); 208-00-001 Ark. Code R. § 2150.1 (LexisNexis 2010); Cal. Welf. & Inst. Code § 11450.04 (West 2001); Conn. Gen. Stat. Ann. § 17b-112(d) (West Supp. 2013); 16-5000-5100 Del. Code Regs. § 3008.2 (LexisNexis 2010); Fla. Stat. Ann. § 414.115 (West 2013); Ga. Code Ann. § 49-4-186 (2009); Ind. Code Ann. § 12-14-2-5.3 (LexisNexis Supp. 2012); 106 Mass. Code Regs. 203.300 (1999); Minn. Stat. § 256J.24(6) (2012); Miss. Code Ann. § 43-17-5(1); N.J. Stat. Ann. § 44:10-61 (West Supp. 2013); Div. of Soc. Servs., N.C. Dep't of Health & Human Servs., *North Carolina's Temporary Assistance for Needy Families State Plan P.L. 104-193: The Work First Program, Effective October 1, 2010–September 30, 2013*, at 28, 39, 41; N.D. Cent. Code § 50-09-29(1)(w) (Supp. 2011); S.C. Code Ann. § 43-5-1175 (Supp. 2012); Tenn. Code Ann. § 71-3-104(i); Va. Code Ann. § 63.2-604 (2012); Wis. Stat. Ann. § 49.19(11s)(b) (West 2011).

102. See N.J. Admin. Code § 10:90-3.3 (2013).

103. See Legal Servs. of N.J. Poverty Research Inst., *Poverty Benchmarks 2013: Assessing New Jersey's Progress in Combating Poverty* 112 (2013).

104. See N.J. Stat. Ann. § 44:10-61; C.K. v. Shalala, 883 F. Supp. 991, 999 (D.N.J. 1995), aff'd sub nom. C.K. v. N.J. Dep't of Health & Human Servs., 92

F.3d 171, 179 (3d Cir. 1996); Sojourner A. v. N.J. Dep't of Human Servs., 794 A.2d 822, 827 (N.J. Super. Ct. App. Div. 2002), aff'd, 828 A.2d 306 (N.J. 2003).

105. See Miss. Code Ann. § 43-17-5(1).

106. See, e.g., Ind. Code Ann. § 16-34-1-1 (LexisNexis 1993); 18 Pa. Cons. Stat. Ann. § 3202(c) (West 2000); Planned Parenthood of Se. Pa. v. Casey, 505 U.S. 833, 872, 878, 883 (1992) (plurality opinion).

107. See Harris v. McRae, 448 U.S. 297, 300–03, 315–18, 322–26 (1980); Maher v. Roe, 432 U.S. 464, 466–67, 469–74, 478–80 (1977); see also Rust v. Sullivan, 500 U.S. 173, 177–81, 192–203 (1991); Webster v. Reprod. Health Servs., 492 U.S. 490, 499–501, 507–11 (1989); Poelker v. Doe, 432 U.S. 519, 519–21 (1977) (per curiam).

108. C.K., 883 F. Supp. at 1000 (citation and alteration marks omitted), aff'd, 92 F.3d at 180 (citation and alteration marks omitted).

109. N.B. v. Sybinski, 724 N.E.2d 1103, 1109 (Ind. Ct. App. 2000).

110. Del. Code Ann. tit. 31, § 501 (2009).

111. David A. Breaux et al., Nelson A. Rockefeller Inst. of Gov't, *First Report Form: State Capacity Study, Mississippi* 8 (1997) (quoting Governor Kirk Fordice).

112. See Office of Family Assistance, supra note 89, at x.

113. For a prominent example of antiabortion advocacy supporting the federal Personal Responsibility Act that allowed states to adopt family caps, see Gary Bauer and Phil Gramm, "Why Pro-Lifers Should Support Welfare Reform," *Wall St. J.*, Aug. 30, 1995, at A10.

114. See Radha Jagannathan and Michael J. Camasso, "Family Cap and Nonmarital Fertility: The Racial Conditioning of Policy Effects," 65 *J. Marriage & Fam.* 52, 57, 61, 63–65 (2003).

115. See Carolyn Turturro et al., Univ. of Ark. at Little Rock Sch. of Soc. Work, *Arkansas Welfare Waiver Demonstration Project: Final Report July, 1994 Through June, 1997,* at 1–2, 80, 95–96 (1997); Wendy Tanisha Dyer and Robert W. Fairlie, "Do Family Caps Reduce Out-of-Wedlock Births?: Evidence from Arkansas, Georgia, Indiana, New Jersey and Virginia," 23 *Population Res. & Pol'y Rev.* 441, 469–70 (2004); Melissa Schettini Kearney, "Is There an Effect of Incremental Welfare Benefits on Fertility Behavior?: A Look at the Family Cap," 39 *J. Hum. Resources* 295, 296–97, 318 (2004).

116. See Ted Joyce et al., "Family Cap Provisions and Changes in Births and Abortions," 23 *Population Res. & Pol'y Rev.* 475, 503–04 (2004).

117. See U.S. Gen. Accounting Office, GAO-01-924, *Welfare Reform: More Research Needed on TANF Family Caps and Other Policies for Reducing Out-of-Wedlock Births* 2–3, 13, 17, 19 (2001).

118. Sojourner A. v. N.J. Dep't of Human Servs., 828 A.2d 306, 308 (N.J. 2003).

119. See, e.g., D.C. Code § 16-2301(9)(A)(ii) (LexisNexis Supp. 2013); Fla. Stat. Ann. § 39.01(44) (West Supp. 2013); N.C. Gen. Stat. § 7B-1111(a)(2) (Supp. 2012); Wis. Stat. Ann. § 48.13(10) (West 2011); In re A.S.C., 671 A.2d 942, 948 n.7 (D.C. 1996); In re B.D.J., 728 N.E.2d 195, 202 (Ind. Ct. App. 2000).

120. See Kristen Shook, "Does the Loss of Welfare Income Increase the Risk of Involvement with the Child Welfare System?," 21 *Child. & Youth Services Rev.* 781, 785–86, 800 (1999).

121. See Cal. Welf. & Inst. Code § 11450.04(d)(3) (West 2001); 16-5000-5100 Del. Code Regs. § 3008.2 (LexisNexis 2010); Fla. Stat. Ann. § 414.115(2) (d)–(e) (West 2013); 106 Mass. Code Regs. 203.300(D)(1) (1999); Div. of Soc. Servs., N.C. Dep't of Health & Human Servs., *North Carolina's Temporary Assistance for Needy Families State Plan P.L. 104-193: The Work First Program, Effective October 1, 2010–September 30, 2013*, at 28; Va. Code Ann. § 63.2-604 (2012); Wis. Stat. Ann. § 49.19(11s)(b)(4) (West 2011).

122. Christina Paxson and Jane Waldfogel, "Welfare Reforms, Family Resources, and Child Maltreatment," 22 *J. Pol'y Analysis & Mgmt.* 85, 103 (2003); see also id. at 105, 108.

123. 724 N.E.2d 1103 (Ind. Ct. App. 2000).

124. See id. at 1105.

125. See id. at 1106, 1108.

126. Id. at 1112 (emphasis added).

127. Id. at 1106 (citation omitted).

128. See, e.g., Areen et al., supra note 19; Clark and Estin, supra note 19; Dwyer, supra note 19; Ellman et al., supra note 19; Leslie Joan Harris et al., *Family Law* (4th ed. 2010); Krause et al., supra note 19; Schneider and Brinig, supra note 19; Wadlington et al., supra note 19; Wardle and Nolan, supra note 19.

129. See C.K. v. Shalala, 883 F. Supp. 991, 1000 (D.N.J. 1995), aff'd sub nom. C.K. v. N.J. Dep't of Health & Human Servs., 92 F.3d 171, 180, 188 (3d Cir. 1996); *N.B.*, 724 N.E.2d at 1110; Sojourner A. v. N.J. Dep't of Human Servs., 794 A.2d 822, 833 (N.J. Super. Ct. App. Div. 2002), aff'd, 828 A.2d 306 (N.J. 2003).

130. *N.B.*, 724 N.E.2d at 1110.

131. *C.K.*, 883 F. Supp. at 1014.

132. Id.

133. Id.

134. Id. at 1015.

135. *N.B.*, 724 N.E.2d at 1110.

136. Sojourner A. v. N.J. Dep't of Human Servs., 794 A.2d 822, 833 (N.J. Super. Ct. App. Div. 2002), aff'd, 828 A.2d 306 (N.J. 2003).

137. Id.

138. Id. at 835.

139. *Sojourner A.*, 828 A.2d at 316.

140. C.K. v. Shalala, 883 F. Supp. 991, 1015 (D.N.J. 1995), aff'd sub nom. C.K. v. N.J. Dep't of Health & Human Servs., 92 F.3d 171 (3d Cir. 1996).

141. *C.K.*, 92 F.3d at 195.

142. Weber v. Aetna Cas. & Sur. Co., 406 U.S. 164, 175 (1972).

143. Trimble v. Gordon, 430 U.S. 762, 770 (1977).

144. See *C.K.*, 883 F. Supp. at 1013; N.B. v. Sybinski, 724 N.E.2d 1103, 1113 (Ind. Ct. App. 2000); *Sojourner A.*, 828 A.2d at 316–17.

145. Sojourner A. v. N.J. Dep't of Human Servs., 794 A.2d 822, 835 (N.J. Super. Ct. App. Div. 2002), aff'd, 828 A.2d 306 (N.J. 2003).

146. *Sojourner A.*, 828 A.2d at 317 n.8.

147. *Sojourner A.*, 794 A.2d at 834.

148. *C.K.*, 883 F. Supp. at 1013; *N.B.*, 724 N.E.2d at 1110.

149. *N.B.*, 724 N.E.2d at 1109; see also id. at 1112.

150. Id. at 1108–09.

Conclusion

1. Clifford Geertz, *Local Knowledge: Further Essays in Interpretive Anthropology* 84 (1983).

ACKNOWLEDGMENTS

I am delighted to have the opportunity to thank the many people who helped me as I wrote this book. My colleagues Brian Bix, Susanna Blumenthal, Naomi Cahn, June Carbone, Maxine Eichner, Katie Eyer, and Clare Huntington did me the tremendous favor of reading and commenting on the entire manuscript. I was fortunate to receive comments on parts of the manuscript from Eleanor Brown, Robert Levy, Barbara Welke, and the participants in numerous workshops and conferences on family law, antidiscrimination law, legal history, constitutional law, and property law. I also benefited from the superb support of the University of Minnesota Law Library staff.

This book builds on ideas that I began to develop in a series of law review articles. "The Canon of Family Law," 57 *Stanford Law Review* 825 (2004), first introduced the idea of a family law canon. Other articles have considered aspects of family law that the book explores further, including "Intimacy and Economic Exchange," 119 *Harvard Law Review* 491 (2005); "Parenthood Divided: A Legal History of the Bifurcated Law of Parental Relations," 90 *Georgetown Law Journal* 299 (2002); "Contest and Consent: A Legal History of Marital Rape," 88 *California Law Review* 1373 (2000); and "Federalism and the Family Reconstructed," 45 *UCLA Law Review* 1297 (1998). An earlier version of Chapter 5 was published as "Siblings in Law," 65 *Vanderbilt Law Review* 897 (2012).

Elizabeth Knoll, my editor at Harvard University Press, skillfully guided the book through the publication process. I am grateful for her enthusiasm and support. I also appreciate the time and care that the three reviewers for Harvard devoted to their reviews.

Lastly, I would like to give special thanks to my family. My parents, Carol and Robert Hasday, and my husband, Allan Erbsen, read the entire manuscript and encouraged me to pursue this project and all my other scholarly and personal goals. My children, Sarah, Daniel, and David, along with my brother, Michael, and sister, Lisa, inspired me to write about sibling relationships in Chapter 5. My family reminds me every day why family ties and the law governing them matter so much.

INDEX

AARP, 180
Abortion, 41–42, 213–214, 216–217
Adoption, 8–10, 13, 20, 50–51, 53, 56, 58–59, 77, 86, 88–93, 143, 163–165, 168–176, 184–191, 193, 225
Adoption and Safe Families Act, 59
Adultery, 41, 45–46, 48, 78, 128–129
Age-based restrictions on marriage, 63, 124–125
Agricultural law, 2, 21, 57, 114, 149–153, 226
Alimony, 23–25, 30, 41–42, 51, 79, 83, 104–106, 114, 117–118, 129
Alito, Samuel, 65
American Law Institute (ALI), 85–86
Anderson, Elizabeth, 68
Ankenbrandt v. Richards, 25–26
Annulment, 47, 125–127
Ashby, Dallen, 77
Ashby, Gloria, 77
Assisted reproductive technology (ART), 10, 86, 88–93, 169–170
Astor, Brooke, 78
Astor, Vincent, 78
Aunts, 5, 12, 163–165, 181, 225

Bankruptcy law, 2, 8, 34–35, 38, 45, 51, 226
Barber v. Barber, 24–25, 118
Barkin, Ellen, 79
Biology (role in family law), 41, 46, 49, 77, 164, 169–170, 186, 188–191, 207

Birth, 9, 41, 46–47, 49–50, 56, 59, 73, 77–78, 82, 89–93, 136, 144, 163, 166, 170, 172–173, 189–190, 212–218
Birth control. *See* Contraception
Blackstone, William, 99, 136
Blake v. Blake, 154–155
Boddie v. Connecticut, 41
Borelli v. Brusseau, 67, 69–70, 81–82, 87–88, 110, 115
Bowen v. Gilliard, 198, 205–207
Boyter, Angela, 54
Boyter, David, 54
Brothers. *See* Siblings
Brown v. Brown, 82–83
Burnham v. Superior Court, 42–43
Burtoff, Samuel, 78–80
Burtoff, Wilma, 78–80

California Assembly Judiciary Committee, 97, 104
Casebooks, 2, 19–20, 198, 216, 224
Castles (homes as), 201
Child abuse, 25, 59, 131, 133, 148, 155, 181–182, 198, 200–202
Child custody, 12, 20–26, 30, 33, 36, 42–43, 50–51, 58, 99, 104, 117–118, 127, 129, 131, 133, 135–147, 154, 156–158, 173–182, 191–193, 200, 205–207, 225
Child labor, 12, 42, 57, 85, 103, 136, 143, 148–151, 158

301